Optimal Decisions in
Markets and Planned Economies

Optimal Decisions in Markets and Planned Economies

EDITED BY

Richard E. Quandt and Dušan Tříska

Routledge
Taylor & Francis Group

LONDON AND NEW YORK

First published 1985 by Westview Press

Published 2019 by Routledge
52 Vanderbilt Avenue, New York, NY 10017
2 Park Square, Milton Park, Abingdon, Oxon OX14 4RN

Routledge is an imprint of the Taylor & Francis Group, an informa business

Library of Congress Cataloging-in-Publication Data
Optimal decisions in markets and planned economies / edited by
    Richard E. Quandt and Dušan Tříska.
        p. cm.
    1. Production (Economic theory). 2. Industrial organization
(Economic theory). 3. Microeconomics. 4. Comparative economics.
5. Marxian economics. I. Quandt, Richard E. II. Tříska,
Dušan.
HB241.F54 1990
338.5—dc20   89-38411
                                                                  CIP

ISBN 13: 978-0-367-28197-7 (hbk)
ISBN 13: 978-0-367-29743-5 (pbk)

Contents

PART 3
OPTIMIZATION IN MARKETS

PART 4
COLLECTIVE CHOICE AND POWER SHARING

PART 5
DEMAND, EXPECTATIONS AND DISEQUILIBRIUM

Contents

PART 6
STRATEGIES AND GENERAL EQUILIBRIUM

Preface

The papers in the present volume represent a subset of those presented at *Micromodels 1989*, an International Conference on Microeconomic Analysis, which took place at Liblice Castle, Czechoslovakia, from March 20 to 24, 1989. The conference's goal was declared to be to "... contribute to the formation of microeconomic concepts that describe common features of the behavior of agents in economies of various types." Apart from this general objective, participants were left free to choose the problems to be investigated and the methods to be employed in their analyses.

While socialist and capitalist modes of organizing economic activity are sometimes held up as polar opposites, the thrust of many of the papers in this volume is that there are numerous subtle gradations and that near the boundaries of the two systems they blend into each other by imperceptible degrees; if not in terms of concrete institutions, at least in terms of the analytical categories that economists employ. A consequence of this view is that many contributions in this volume—while they may emphasize primarily one of the two frameworks—could, *mutatis mutandis*, be applied to the other. Many of the fundamental categories that the papers in this volume deal with transcend particular forms of economic organization. These include the basic methodology of optimizing an objective function subject to constraints, as well as particular ideas such as bargaining power, subsidy and bailout seeking, the valuation of information, power and profit-sharing, social decision criteria, inventory behavior, market imperfections and many others.

Part 1 contains two papers that study explicitly the comparative aspects of planned and market economies. The papers in Part 2 represent attempts to understand better the motivations of enterprise managers in a socialist economy. Part 3 tackles a variety of issues in the context of market economies; some of these, such as the question of supervision of an agent by a principal, have obvious relevance for planned economies as well. Part 4 deals explicitly with expectations of demand, adjustment mechanisms and disequilibrium and has broad relevance for both types of economies.

Part 5 is devoted to questions of collective choice and the distribution of power. Finally, Part 6 contains various approaches to questions of general equilibrium.

We regret that we could not include in this volume more papers on this subject. On the one hand, we had to be mindful of a space constraint. On the other hand, we were conscious of the need to present in this volume a balance of ideas and approaches to the issues of planning and markets in capitalism and socialism. These two considerations compelled us to omit a number of valuable contributions in preparing this volume. We are very grateful to all who offered papers for this volume and wish to express our belief that *everybody* made an essential contribution.

Richard E. Quandt
Dušan Tříska

Acknowledgements

The Conference was held at the invitation of the Czechoslovak Academy of Sciences and its Institute of Economics. In addition to these, financial support was received from Princeton University, the National Science Foundation and from the Alfred P. Sloan Foundation. We are grateful to all of the above for their support.

We owe an enormous debt to the local Organizing Committee which consisted of Józef Zieleniec (Chairman), Vladimír Benáček (Secretary), Jiří Hlaváček, Miroslav Hrnčíř, Dimitrij Loula, Dušan Tříska and Alena Zemplinerová. Their tireless efforts have made the Conference a great success.

In preparing this volume for publication, we have received very great editorial help from Sudir Shah, Demosthenes Tambakis and Katharine S. Carter. The latter has also earned our gratitude by typesetting the manuscript with great accuracy and devotion. Without their help, preparation of the volume would have been a much more difficult task. The manuscript was typeset in TeX in Computer Modern font.

R.E.Q.
D.T.

Contributors

Contributors to the volume:

István Ábel
University of Economics, Budapest, Hungary

John P. Bonin
Wesleyan University, Middletown, CT, USA

Rose-Anne Dana
CEPREMAP, Paris, France

Krisztina Demeter
University of Economics, Budapest, Hungary

Gérard Duménil
CEPREMAP, Paris, France

Wolfgang Eichhorn
University of Karlsruhe, Karlsruhe, Federal Republic of Germany

Monique Florenzano
CEPREMAP, Paris, France

Helmut Funke
University of Karlsruhe, Karlsruhe, Federal Republic of Germany

Wulf Gaertner
University of Osnabrück, Osnabrück, Federal Republic of Germany

Esther Gal-Or
University of Pittsburgh, Pittsburgh, PA, USA

Stephen M. Goldfeld
Princeton University, Princeton, NJ, USA

Christian Gourieroux
CEPREMAP, Paris, France

Louise Grenier
University of British Columbia, Vancouver, BC, Canada

Jiří Hlaváček
Institute of Economics, Prague, Czechoslovakia

Manfred J. Holler
University of Aarhus, Aarhus, Denmark

Viggo Høst
University of Aarhus, Aarhus, Denmark

Barry W. Ickes
Pennsylvania State University, University Park, PA, USA

Vesa Kanniainen
University of Helsinki and Research Institute
of the Finnish Economy, Helsinki, Finland

Nicholas M. Kiefer
Cornell University, Ithaca, NY, USA

Cuong Le Van
CEPREMAP, Paris, France

Dominique Lévy
CEPREMAP, Paris, France

Valeri Marakulin
Institute of Mathematics, Novosibirsk, USSR

Irina Peaucelle
CEPREMAP, Paris, France

Małgorzata Pilarska
Systems Research Institute, Warsaw, Poland

Richard E. Quandt
Princeton University, Princeton, NJ, USA

Larry Samuelson
Pennsylvania State University, University Park, PA, USA

Frans Spinnewyn
Catholic University of Leuven and CORE, Belgium

Jacek Stefanski
Systems Research Institute, Warsaw, Poland

Jan Svejnar
University of Pittsburgh, Pittsburgh, PA, USA

Dušan Tříska
Institute of Economics, Prague, Czechoslovakia

Valeri A. Vasiliev
Institute of Mathematics, Novosibirsk, USSR

Claus Weddepohl
University of Amsterdam, Amsterdam, Netherlands

Bengt-Arne Wickström
Johannes Kepler University, Linz, Austria

Józef Zieleniec
Institute of Economics, Prague, Czechoslovakia

Other participants:

Zoltán Bara, Vladimir Benáček, Helena Blahoutová, Walter Bossert, Aleš Bulíř, Satya R. Chakravarty, Attila Chikán, Marek Dabrowski, Oldřich Dědek, Edwin Deutsch, Vladimír Dlouhý, Gotthard Forbrig, Susanne Fuchs-Seliger, John P. Gould, Bingxing Gu, Richard F. Hartl, Christian Hjorth-Andersen, Monika Hollmannová, Milan Horniaček, Miroslav Hrnčíř, Vratislav Izák, Jiří Jonáš, Stefan Kawalec, Jan Klacek, Jana Klacková, Václav Klaus, Jan Kodera, Josef Kotrba, Antonín Kotulan, Dimitrij Loula, Miroslav Maňas, Alexander Mehlmann, Michal Mejstřík, Jan Mládek, Wieslaw Otta, Vesna Pasetta, Josef Pöschl, Vladimír Rudlovčák, Victor G. Sokolov, Alexander I. Sotskov, Lenka Šťastná, Andrzej Straszak, Otakar Turek, Ilia Petrov Tzvetanov, Jaroslav Vanek, Milan Vlach, Yifang Wang, Grazina Wisniewska, Alena Zemplinerová.

PART ONE

Comparative Economic Systems

1

Microeconomic Categories in Different Economic Systems: The Firm

Józef Zieleniec

The aim of this paper is to call attention to the fact that in the study of centrally planned economies important microeconomic categories and models are often used in an inadequate manner. The source of this inadequacy is an interesting and important problem for analysis; its clarification could help to develop the methodological points of departure for microeconomics as such and enhance its set of instruments.

The study of the behavior of economic agents in a centrally planned economy of the Eastern European type has characteristic features that allow us to decide quite easily whether an author lives within or outside such an economy. The writings of Western authors usually employ a standard apparatus and standard model categories, which have been derived from categories used in the study of market economies. In these models we encounter such notions as the firm, prices, profits or equilibrium; they are used in the study of centrally planned economies in a manner which is analogous to that used in standard models. But the substantial differences in the content of these terms between traditional liberal economies and a centrally planned economy are almost never mentioned. Hence the relevant consequences for the construction of models are not formulated. Such authors—usually because they have never experienced the reality of a centrally planned economy—often are not aware of the fact that statements

purporting to describe the reality of a centrally planned economy on the
basis of their models are wrong. Since the economic profession is divided
into Western and Eastern sectors and discussions often take place in each of
them separately, they do not even seem to influence each other and no feed-
back seems to develop that might cause the models of a centrally planned
economy to evolve further.

The freqent inadequacy of models constructed in countries where experience with a centrally planned economy does exist is caused by different
reasons. Economists in centrally planned economies are usually aware of
the difference between the phenomena in a market–oriented and centrally
planned economy that happen to have the same name. The majority of
economists in Eastern Europe are very well aware of the difference between
the concepts of the enterprise, profits, money or equilibrium in a centrally
planned economy and these same categories in a market economy; it was on
the basis of the usefulness of these concepts in the latter type of economy
that the main microeconomic categories and models were developed. But
a lack of tradition and experience in the use of standard models, as well as
inadequate theoretical erudition have often led to endeavors that tend to
stay within the framework of textbook outlines rather than risk a departure from a central economic paradigm. The discrepancy between results
yielded by models and reality, which will of necessity exist in such an approach, is then interpreted as an immanent quality of economic theory and
a necessary consequence of its axiomatic structure and basic assumptions
that cannot be changed.

The reaction to the inadequacy of the above cited procedures used to
describe the behavioral aspects of the functioning of a centrally planned
economy often goes to the opposite extreme, which we encounter frequently
in socialist countries: instead of standard models used within the framework of traditional approaches, new theories are created, on an almost *ad
hoc* basis for every aspect of the functioning of a centrally planned economy. The common trait of such approaches is the fact that they are created
without sufficient linkage to the pool of existing economic theory.[1] Thus
problems seem to be solved merely by renaming them. The majority of

---

[1] In this paper I shall not deal with those schools of microeconomics which in the
centrally planned economies form (or until recently formed) the basis for the education
of economists and which form the so-called political economy of socialism. The fact that
it is completely devoid of analytical instruments causes the approach to be entirely tele-
ological; hence it has no instruments of its own for anything but normative statements.

these theories are then developed further only by their authors, which is an outcome of the fact that such approaches exist separately from the main-stream of microeconomics. The only exception to this rule that I know is Kornai's (1971) approach; many economists use the terminology he has introduced, even if frequently a different model context is used.

We shall now try to demonstrate the possibility of resolving the contra-diction between opposite approaches when describing microeconomic prob-lems in centrally planned economies—i.e., the contradiction between a de-scription which uses the readily available categories and models that were created in a different system context, without trying to reinterpret them, and an approach which is based on the creation of radically new theories, which have intentionally eliminated the links with the mainstream of eco-nomic thinking and frequently changed their subject matter and method so profoundly that it is difficult to include them in economics.

When we attempt to resolve this contradiction and seek model ap-proaches to describe the microeconomic problems of a centrally planned economy, we can assume that the reality of these economies is related to the reality of market economies in such a manner that microeconomic cat-egories and models, which would adequately describe their behavior, will be a *generalization* of classical microeconomic categories and models. From this point of view we can analyze various microeconomic categories. Below we concentrate on discussing the category of the firm as an economic agent and some problems connected with this.

The notion of the firm obviously centers on the existence of the en-trepreneur, who manages the firm in his own interest. The firm must solve optimization problems: what level of inputs and outputs should be cho-sen so as to achieve a maximum for the objective function, which is most frequently profit. The limitations that the firm faces are derived from the market in which it functions and from the technology which it uses. When discussing the adequacy of such an approach, it is traditionally pointed out that problems exist which are the outcome of the structure of owner-ship. While we can assume a direct interest in profits on the part of the owner, this is not a matter of course when the manager is a hired person. It is also pointed out that within the firm a hierarchical structure exists. Various people carry out production proper, procurement and sales, while others determine objectives. It is also stressed that the transformation of these objectives into various activities is not a straightforward process. The problem of conflicting interests within a firm is often cited as an important factor in the firm's behavior, etc. The problems of the division of property and of decision-making is usually solved on the basis of the assumption that managers have other than profit preferences and by seeking an analytical relationship between these preferences and the decision variables of the firm. This is typical of Baumol's (1959) criterion of maximizing sales revenue and Williamson's (1964) expense preferences.

All these problems are of course very well known in a sharply focused form in a centrally planned economy. Here property and decision-making are separated in an absolute manner, because throughout the economy there is no agent who is the owner of capital. Property rights—i.e., the holding, disposition and use of property, which is the prerogative of entrepreneurship—are distributed among many places in the state apparatus. The basis of the functioning of the economy is similar to that of the so-called vertical management, which has a number of hierarchical levels. Each of these managerial levels deals to some extent with decisions concerning production, i.e., what will be produced and by what means. In spite of possible similarities, this type of command economy is not identical to an organization in which a single will is implemented with the aid of a hierarchical system. This is so because the market exists—even if imperfectly—where supply encounters demand and where the producer must sell his product. The whole economy is thus regulated by both the market and the organizational principle.

Under the conditions of a centrally planned economy, it is entirely impossible to find a person—the entrepreneur—to whom we could assign the interests of the firm; economic subjectivity is blurred and spread out throughout the whole hierarchical structure of the economy. The more we try to localize this subjectivity in a centrally planned economy, i.e., find the person whose decision personifies the behavior of the enterprise, the smaller the share of decision-making becomes concerning inputs and outputs of the enterprise which belongs to it. This huge diffusion of property rights is the cause of the fact that a description of the firm's behavior will run into methodological problems. Most authors attempt to analyze the behavior of a socialist enterprise in such a way that they assign decision-making in it to its director (manager), who defines its objective function. This is entirely in the spirit of traditional neoclassical analysis. But the problem is that we can introduce the assumption—which will be just as adequate—that decisions concerning the output of such a firm and the inputs which it uses

are made by some higher management preference. In addition, we can also
assume a coalition between these levels, etc.

The organizational pattern of a socialist economy is arbitrary and the
fact that some hierarchical units are called enterprises is essentially acci-
dental.[2]

In spite of the fact that various empirical analyses indicate how complicated the diffusion of decision-making is concerning a firm in a centrally
planned economy (Mlčoch, 1989), model analyses on this subject are limited
by a traditional approach and by the model instruments that are available.
Thus, if we wish to describe the behavior of a firm in a centrally planned
economy, we should be aware of the fact that in a model we must assume
the existence of *several* agents, with various objective functions, who make
decisions in the firm regarding its inputs and outputs and who have specific
individual preferences which are the outcome of their status in the economy.
In the upper layers of the hierarchy, decisions are made regarding the fate of
the firm in a longer time frame and at a higher degree of aggregation of its
production tasks; at lower levels, decisions concern shorter time frames and
specific commodities typical of the particular market. Decisions made by
higher hierarchical levels define the scope of decision-making at lower levels.
The manner in which each of these hierarchical entrepreneurs maximizes
his objective function depends not only on the chosen combination of inputs
and outputs, but also on the scope he has been given for his decision-making
by the higher level of the hierarchy; thus conflicts of interest may occur.
Their origin is in the different property rights which these entrepreneurs
have in relation to the firm. This conflict is the basis of the games which
are played along the vertical scale among entrepreneurs who have various
positions in the hierarchy. The firm will not only tend towards equilibrium
in relation to the market, but it will also acquire its internal equilibrium
when individual decision-making agents-entrepreneurs are mutually in a
Pareto-optimal state; this is determined by a set of decision-making areas
of individual decision-making agents in the hierarchy and their production
situations.

---

[2] For instance, the reorganization carried out last year in Czechoslovakia has led to
the renaming of so-called associations, which in fact were intermediate managerial bodies
between the central authority and the enterprise; they are now themselves enterprises and
their former subordinated units continue to be their components. Nothing has changed
in their economic behavior.

Of course, in the real economy a different language is used. Instead of decision-making areas we have plan tasks; the enterprise does not seek a combination of inputs and outputs, but fulfills the plans and all the hierarchical levels above it do the same. On the vertical scale, it is not a Pareto equilibrium which is being sought between various levels of the hierarchy, but rather a bargain about the plan to be carried out. Thus, by using the language of microeconomic analysis, we can express and finally describe in a model manner a key component of a centrally planned economy—the producer. But actually creating a model assumes the formulation of a hypothesis about the objective functions of individual decision-making agents-entrepreneurs in the vertical hierarchy. Some of these problems are dealt with by Hlaváček (1986).

The suggested analytical approach, which is clearly called for in the case of a hierarchical and market pattern found in a centrally planned economy, is of broader methodological significance: it can lead to a generalization of the notion of the firm. As already mentioned at the beginning, problems connected with a formulation of the decision-making criterion are traditional in the neoclassical theory of the firm and their origins are similar to those found in a centrally planned economy—the property structure, the organizational patterns, the conflicts, etc.

In a similar vein, it would be possible to analyze other categories and model approaches concerning microeconomics. A centrally planned economy has many features that are known from a market economy, but there they are not so important, while in a centrally planned economy they attain dominance; a description of the economy without taking them into account is meaningless. When we study the real economy as the outcome of the influence of two regulating principles—the market and the organizational principles—then the origin of these differences rests precisely in the much greater importance of the organizational type of regulation in centrally planned economies. But at the same time, that is the reason why attempts to reinterpret classical microeconomic categories in the conditions of a centrally planned economy represent a generalization, and deserve the attention not only of specialists in the study of socialist economies. These countries represent a sort of laboratory, unique for economists, not too different from a high-energy laboratory used by physicists, where phenomena which are manifest under normal conditions as tiny deviations, achieve large magnitudes; it is then easier to study the laws of their development.

References

Baumol, W. J. (1959) *Business Behavior, Value and Growth*, London: Macmillan.

Hlaváček, J. (1986) "Homo Se Assecurans," *Politická ekonomie* 34, 633-639.

Kornai, J. (1971) *Anti-Equilibrium. On Economic Systems Theory and the Tasks of Research*, Amsterdam: North Holland.

Mlčoch, L. (1989) *Chování čs. podnikové sféry* (The Behavior of the Czechoslovak Enterprise Sphere), Prague: EÚ ČSAV.

Williamson, O. E. (1964) *The Economics of Discretionary Behavior: Managerial Objectives in a Theory of the Firm*, Englewood Cliffs, NJ: Prentice Hall.

2

The Theory of the Firm Under Capitalism and Socialism ·

Barry W. Ickes

1. Introduction

Firms (or enterprises) are the pre-eminent form of economic organization in both the East and West. Economic theory has recently begun to
peer inside the firm, trying to explain why activities are organized within
firms—in essence, an exploration of Coase's (1937) query. This analysis
has, however, focused the question in the context of market economies.
The concern has been with the advantages of firms over market transactions *within* the context of a conventional market system. This literature
has led to much analysis of what determines the boundaries of the firm,
and, in particular, on the factors that encourage or discourage integration,
merger, and contract (Williamson, 1985; Alchian, 1984; Hart, 1988). The
corresponding question—What are the forces that lead to firms, or enterprises, in socialist economies?—is rarely asked.

This question is of some interest, however, especially in the context of
economic reform in the socialist world. Since economic reform programs often involve a devolution of authority to the enterprise, one is led naturally
to ask about the role of such reformed enterprises within the socialist economy. In particular, one would like to identify the advantages of the firm as

* Thanks to Keith Crocker, Ed Coulson, Richard Quandt, Larry Samuelson and the
participants at *Micromodels 89* for comments on a previous draft of this paper.

an organizational mode in the socialist context. This is an important pre-requisite to an analysis of the benefits of reforming the management system of a planned economy. This paper attempts to contribute to this problem by focusing on the nature of the firm under capitalism and socialism.

2. Characterization of the Firm

We begin with a characterization of what is meant by a firm. It is important to obtain a clear notion of what a firm is so that we can undertake a comparative analysis of its operation. Since Coase (1937) a large literature has developed focusing on the relative advantages of markets versus firms in coordinating economic activity. Firms are sometimes thought of as those types of transactions that are not organized via markets. This will not do, however, for a comparative theory, since under socialism there is another alternative to the enterprise: that of complete centralization via command.

The economies generated by specialization and the division of labor imply that in advanced economies most production takes place via the co-operation of many agents who combine to pool their physical and human assets. These coalitions may form for a single specific purpose, or they may persist over time. In the former case we will refer to them as transient coalitions. Market exchange is of this type. The types of coalitions that we are interested in in this paper, firms and enterprises, are persistent coalitions. Indeed, one of the defining elements of a firm is its persistent structure of relationships. A key problem for a theory of economic organization is to explain why some coalitions persist. We will argue that persistence is a means of economizing on bargaining costs.

Focusing on the persistence of coalitions draws attention to the repeated aspect of the relationships that constitute firms. Many complex transactions occur that involve detailed contracts, yet are not commonly thought of as firms; perhaps the best example of this would be procurement contracts between the military and defense contractors. Although these arrangements have many aspects that are also important in firms (e.g., principal-agent contracts, relationship-specific investments, pooled assets, etc.), there is a central difference. The relationships that constitute firms do not have *ex ante* designated terminal points. Firms (enteprises) are collections of agents who expect to work together on projects beyond the current one, and in fact expect that the organization will survive their (individual) departure.

The (implicit) contractual elements in firms do not have fixed periods for which the agreements bind.

This distinction is useful because it is not system specific. Transient coalitions are prevalent in Soviet-type economies (STE's) as well as capitalist ones. To make this notion of a firm operational, however, we must exclude coalitions of the whole. It makes no sense to treat the entire economy as a giant firm in the same sense in which we usually use this term. This also allows us to eliminate from consideration as a firm coalitions such as factories that do not operate on their own account (as in War Communism). Another critical element of the notion of a firm is that its success is judged by its performance as a unit.[1]

To make matters a bit more concrete, we define a coalition as a set of agents $x = (x_1, \ldots, x_n)$, an assignment of agents to tasks $a = (a_1, \ldots, a_n)$, a sharing rule $r = (r_1, \ldots, r_n)$ that assigns to each agent his/her payoff. The coalition S therefore consists of the triple (x, a, r). Notice that we do not include in x the customers of the coalition. To do so would vitiate the notion of persistence as the defining characteristic of the firm, since customers change frequently.[2] The total payoff to the coalition depends on the state of the environment, e. Let $V(S_i|e)$ be the value of the coalition S_i given environment e, *exclusive of bargaining costs*. For a given e, assume that there exists some set of coalitions $\hat{S}_i$ $(i = 1, \ldots, m)$, that yield maximal payoffs to their members (in the sense that they cannot obtain a higher payoff in any other viable coalition) given the environment e. This is what Ichiishi calls a "social coalitional equilibrium."

Such an equilibrium should exist under reasonable assumptions for any arbitrary e (Ichiishi, 1983; Theorem 5.7.1). If there are no bargaining costs, there is no reason to expect that the set of maximal coalitions will fail to form. Moreover, this configuration should resemble the solution to a design problem by a central planner for the same economy, subject to incentive constraints, and given full information about agents' characteristics. Under

---

[1] Historically, the emergence of the firm is associated with the invention of double-entry bookkeeping and the balance sheet. These innovations were critical in inducing the separation of the business and the family as economic units. It is precisely the development of the ability to view the performance of a business in its own right that led to the development of the firm. See Rosenberg and Birdzell (1986).

[2] Alternatively, we could partition x, a, and r into two subsets, the customers and everybody else. Elements of r for customers would be the prices paid. Persistence would then be defined with respect to the membership of the non-customer subset of x.

such conditions, organizations would be designed for a specific environment and would persist only as long as the environment did not change.

Bargaining costs change all this. Bargaining costs can be thought of in terms of the delay required to achieve agreement on the nature of the coalition. They arise for a variety of reasons (Milgrom and Roberts, 1987). One source emphasized in the transaction cost literature focuses on the role of specialized assets, both human and physical (Williamson, 1985; Klein, Crawford and Alchian, 1978). More generally, bargaining costs may be thought of in terms of private information about preferences and/or productivities. Without private information, the assignment problem (of agents to tasks) is basically one of calculation. With private information, however, agents must be induced to reveal their abilities, and the assignment problem becomes a revelation game. Hence solving the assignment problem will be a complex task that may involve serious negotiation and costly delay.

Now suppose the e changes. Let $\hat{S}_i$ be a member of the set of maximal coalitions given e. With the new environment e', there may now exist some other coalition $\hat{S}_j$, or set of coalitions, such that for the members of coalition S_i,

$$V(\hat{S}_j|e') > V(S_i|e')$$

where $\hat{S}_j$ is the maximal coalition given e'.[3] As e changes, the fact that S_i is no longer a maximal coalition implies that a surplus exists to be shared if a new coalition can be formed. If this surplus exceeds the bargaining costs associated with forming new coalitions, then we would expect to observe a change. Otherwise the coalition will persist even if there exists a positive surplus.

Since bargaining costs impede the formation of new coalitions, it follows that the greater these costs, the larger uncaptured surpluses will grow before they are captured. Attempts to capture these surpluses provide the impetus for the organizational changes—mergers, vertical integration, economic reforms—that periodically take place in various economic systems. The nature and frequency of these attempts, as well as who it is that initiates them, will, however, differ across economic systems. One goal of a comparative theory of the firm is to study how the different methods of

---

[3] When e changes, the new set of maximal coalitions most likely partition the agents into different groups. Hence the statement in the text is a bit loose. The key point is that when e changes, the set of coalitions in the core will almost surely change, so we would expect to see a different set of coalitions in the absence of bargaining costs.

capturing these surpluses affect their average magnitude (which is, in a sense, a measure of organization inefficiency) at a point in time as well as over time.

All of the variables that we subsume under e change continually, not at discrete junctures. Hence organizations are frequently faced with changes in e. Of course, the degree to which this represents a significant change for the firm in question will vary. And it implies that some coalitions will regard a change in e as a large change while others will deem it a minor one. This becomes an important point once we turn to the questions of how firms are formed and how they change.

3. Formation of Firms

In order to study how firms adapt to changes in e we must first discuss how they form. We have noted that bargaining costs inherent in coalition formation explain why coalitions persist. When firms initially form, these costs must be borne. How this occurs differs under capitalism and socialism, and this contrast is crucial to the comparative study of the firm.

Under capitalism, coalition formation occurs through the voluntary agreement of the members. Notice that the members really have two problems to solve. The first concerns bargaining over the elements of S. As we have seen, these costs grow with the complexity of the tasks involved. The second problem is the construction of a mechanism to cope with changes in e. Given the up-front costs that must be borne to form the coalition, it is in the interest of the membership to design a system that prevents the coalition from breaking up "too quickly."

Once we recognize these twin problems, the nature of the capitalist firm becomes clearer. Suppose that a single agent, the entrepreneur, takes on the burden of forming a coalition (there may be many agents competing to be the entrepreneur),[4] bearing the bargaining costs personally. This agent chooses a set x from among the potential members, and assigns tasks a to them along with a sharing rule r, within the limits imposed by the individual and group rationality constraints. In effect, the entrepreneur offers members of x fixed compensation rules and tasks, bargaining with

---

[4] We focus on the entrepreneur to emphasize the problem of forming coalitions. In modern corporations the organizational function is delegated to a management hired by the shareholders. We ignore the important incentive problems that stem from this principal-agent relationship.

each individually. Agreement will occur only if the reward exceeds what is available elsewhere. By offering contracts to agents individually, the entrepreneur breaks the free rider problem inherent in a coalition attempting to choose x, a, and r among themselves, since in the latter case each agent, or a subset of agents, has an incentive to try to hold the group hostage. If the entrepreneur can arrange a coalition at lower cost than the individual members can, the surplus can be shared.

In effect, the members of the coalition are offered the triple (x, a, r) in order to avoid the bargaining problem entailed in their choosing it themselves. While each agent would like to choose his/her payoff, the value of the coalition shrinks if each agent tries to hold it hostage. By converting the problem into $n - 1$ two-person bargaining games, the entrepreneur may lower the cost of gaining agreement, and hence share a larger total value.[5]

The entrepreneur also helps solve the second problem. By delegating authority to the entrepreneur to adjust the coalition—within limits—as e changes, the members avoid costly renegotiation. By delegating authority to the entrepreneur, the members allow for partial adjustments of the coalition that do not entail opening up all of the agreements on which the firm rests. This allows the coalition to persist, saving on bargaining costs, and allows it flexibility in the face of changes in e. Such flexibility would play an important role, for example, in the face of fluctuations in the demand for the firm's product.[6]

Of course, this role would be unnecessary if the parties could agree to (x, a, r) contingent on *every possible future state* of e. The inability to write a complete contract makes a once-and-for-all agreement costly relative to the entrepreneurial scheme. Hence arises the notion of the firm as a set of incomplete contracts (Grossman and Hart, 1986). But Grossman and Hart focus on the residual decision rights of the entrepreneur over the *assets* of the firm that are not already contracted for. Here the decision rights of the

---

[5] Milgrom and Roberts (1987, p.18) argue similarly that "If the cost of negotiating short-term contracts were always zero then ... organizing economic activity through market exchange would always be perfectly efficient. On the other hand, when the costs of negotiating periodic exchange agreements are sufficiently high ... there are associated savings to be realized by placing the activity under centralized control, so that potentially costly disputes can be settled quickly by central authority." Their focus, however, is only on market economies, and their concern is with the actions agents take to influence the decisions of higher authorities.

[6] Compare for example the difficulty in adjusting employment of the Yugoslav worker-managed firm to that of a U.S. firm when demand changes.

entrepreneur pertain to the authority to adjust the coalition in the face of new information.[7] Notice that even if the firm owned no physical assets, there would still be an advantage to this type of organization, owing to the conservation of resources expended on bargaining costs.

This formulation provides a simple explanation of "why capital hires labor" (Putterman, 1985). The input of the entrepreneur is distinctly up-front; that is to say, the entrepreneur organizes the coalition. Once formed, the agents no longer need him, except to deal with the possibility of future changes in e. For this reason the organizer will not bear the bargaining costs in exchange for a $1/n$ share in the firm, since the other members would have every incentive to renege on the agreement, once the coalition was formed. Combining ownership (i.e., control over assets) with the entrepreneurial role, on the other hand, serves as a device to make the agreements self-enforcing, since the other agents cannot expropriate the entrepreneur without losing access to the firm's assets.

But even if the entrepreneur's role is combined with ownership, what prevents the rest of the coalition from leaving the firm *en masse*, renting capital elsewhere, and sharing the rent owed to the entrepreneur? This would, of course, entail additional bargaining over how the interest costs would effect r, but it might nonetheless be optimal if e never changes. But if e changes, the coalition is once again faced with bargaining over x, a and r, plus the additional complication of the capital charges. This is important because any changes in the size of the coalition effects the interest burden the members have assumed.

But why can't the members simply *hire* the entrepreneur to perform the organization function? This is a critical question, because in modern corporations shareholders hire managers to perform this function. The question is why a particular subset of x, the shareholders, can while another subset, the workers, cannot. Suppose then that labor owns the firm and hires the entrepreneur. What prevents a subset of the coalition from trying to reopen negotiations over r? What is to prevent a subset of x from trying to hold the rest of the coalition hostage? This becomes an important

---

[7] Though in some sense these are not *residual* decision rights in that the entrepreneur has authority within limits to adjust the coalition. It is the delegation of the authority to make marginal decisions that makes the entrepreneur valuable. As we shall see, there is an important reason why this particular member of the coalition should also own (retain "residual decision rights" in the Grossman-Hart terminology) the assets of the firm, but it derives from the prior function of dealing with the bargaining problem.

consideration anytime *e* changes and the entrepreneur has adjusted **x** and
a. Clearly the coalition cannot *ex ante* insure against this by delegating
authority over **r** to the entrepreneur. For this, in effect, confers ownership
to the entrepreneur. This continuous threat of re-opening the bargaining
over **r** anytime *e* changes dissipates the value of the assets labor has purchased.[8]

The shareholders, on the other hand, cannot individually or as a group
hold the coalition hostage. They can, of course, sell their shares, or if they
act collectively, replace management. But they do not have an instrument—
aside from the management they hire—available to alter **r**. Indeed it is by
hiring the manager to mediate with the workers that the shareholders are
able to benefit from the reduction in bargaining costs. This suggests that
the value of the firm can be thought of as the capitalized value of these
saved resources.

4. The Enterprise Under Socialism

So far we have focused on the formation of firms under capitalism. The
picture is quite different under socialism. In this case coalitions are formed
by imposition from above, rather than through voluntary association of
the agents.[9] This is a necessary consequence of the state's control over
the means of production; indeed, this is often taken to be the essence of
socialism. For our purposes the important point is that the internal organization of the enterprise under socialism is not a response to the bargaining
problem inherent in coalition formation.[10]

A consequence of the imposition from above is that the boundaries of
coalitions (enterprises) under socialism are determined by the planners'
(leadership's) problem of achieving effective coordination of the various elements within the economy without using markets. The nature of this
problem ("the coordination problem") is heavily influenced by the costs of

---

[8] Mailath and Postlewaite (1988) study this question, focusing on private information
about reservation wages. This clearly is a component of the costs of negotiating over **r**.

[9] This is why the cooperative movement has received so much attention. This is the
aspect of *perestroika* that seems the greatest departure from the conventional STE.

[10] This does not mean that bargaining problems are not important under socialism.
Bargaining is an essential aspect of the relations between units in a hierarchy. The
point in the text is that under socialism there is no bargaining problem concerning the
formation of the enterprise. For an analysis of bargaining problems under socialism, see
Tříska in this volume.

communicating information, which limit the degree to which decisions can be centralized.[11] Because of these "informational constraints" complete integration of the socialist economy is infeasible and enterprises play a central role.

When coalitions are *imposed*, bargaining costs are irrelevant. Higher authorities choose **x**, **a**, and **r**. The coalition must still satisfy individual rationality constraints, but if external opportunities are limited, these constraints bind at lower resource cost to the authorities. The *imposition* of the coalition obviates the need of members to bargain in order to reach agreement. Although these costs are avoided, the authorities must bear a *design* cost—that of putting together the organization (a cost also borne by the entrepreneur). Viewed in isolation (that is, in terms of a single coalition) this is just a portion of the costs associated with coalition formation. It is important to note, however, that the authorities must bear this cost with respect to each of the coalitions they choose to form. Hence the authorities must consider the aggregate design cost associated with coalition formation.

It is the need to economize on design costs that explains the persistence of coalitions in socialist economies.[12] The planners must compare the efficiency gains from re-forming coalitions with the costs associated with designing new ones. These costs are likely to be high, since changes in *e* most likely alter the effectiveness of many coalitions. But redesigning many coalitions simultaneously is more costly than doing so one coalition at a time. Notice that when coalition *j* chooses to change its structure, it may impose costs on other coalitions $i \neq j$, since the opportunities available to members in those coalitions have changed. A chain reaction may occur throughout the economy. The members of coalition *j*, however, do not bear the costs imposed on the other coalitions. But planners must consider these costs, since they bear the design costs. Hence their proclivity for redesigning coalitions will be constrained. Two propositions follow:

---

[11] One is tempted to include the constraints imposed by the need to induce agents truthfully to reveal private information, but it is difficult to make the case that this consideration played a crucial role in setting the boundaries of the enterprise. However, one might argue that reforms of STE's have been heavily influenced by the need to satisfy these constraints.

[12] One notes that if the planners in socialist economies "plan from the achieved level," then there will be a strong persistence in economic activity. This may lead to slower changes in *e*, and hence a lesser need to reform coalitions (compared to capitalist economies) even in the absence of design costs.

Proposition 1. *Organizational changes—re-forming coalitions—occur less frequently in socialist economies than in capitalist economies.*

Proposition 2. *Organizational changes are more likely to occur in bunches in socialism and piecemeal in capitalism.*

These two propositions both stem from the idea that under socialism coalitions are imposed and changes in coalitions are the result of imposed decisions from above. Hence planners will be concerned with the aggregate costs and benefits of organizational change rather than just the local (i.e., coalition-specific) ones. Proposition 1 depends on the assumption that design costs are increasing in the number of organizations. Proposition 2 follows from the fact that with change imposed from above, it is likely that when e has changed sufficiently to warrant such a change for a given enterprise, the planners will deem it efficient to make widespread changes.

This contrast between the capitalist firm and socialist enterprise follows from the fact that under socialism there are fewer authorities (i.e., agents with design rights) than there are enterprises. This forces on the authorities a general equilibrium view of the design problem. The capitalist firm takes as given the external environment when a change in the coalition is contemplated. Since the authorities in socialism are responsible for many enterprises, they will necessarily be concerned with the implications of the change in e for each of the enterprises under their control. This does not mean that the authorities may not experiment with organizational innovations. What it does mean is that the concern of the authorities is with the general equilibrium consequences, which is clearly a much more difficult problem. Hence we would expect the authorities to be less willing to open it up frequently.

An important corollary of the preceding argument is that the complexity of the general design problem tends to induce a homogeneous solution to changes in e. An easy way to simplify the design problem is to search for uniform solutions across enterprises. This greatly reduces the number of potential solutions. Under capitalism coalitions solve their own design problems; hence heterogeneity of structure is more likely. There are two important points. The first is that the particular situations of various enterprises might call for different institutional responses. The second is that many potential design changes may prove inefficient in practice. Hence, if homogeneous solutions are implemented, there is a risk that widespread mistakes may be introduced.

We have emphasized that under capitalism the residual design authority is the entrepreneur. Management of the firm is associated with (hired by) this agent. Notice that under socialism management is also appointed by the agent in charge of design (i.e., the state). However, there is an important difference. The management of the capitalist enterprise serves to economize on bargaining costs. The director of the socialist enterprise serves to economize on coordination costs (those costs associated with organizing the interaction of enterprises without markets). Hence the management of a socialist enterprise is heavily constrained in its ability to alter the structure of the enterprise since, unlike its capitalist counterpart, design rights are not delegated. Nonetheless, the director's compensation is tied to performance of the unit. This has important consequences.

To see the importance of this distinction, notice that the major decision problem of the socialist manager is to cope with the uncertainties generated by the supply system. Given the complexity of the coordination problem, responsibility is delegated to the managers. That is, *the purpose of the socialist manager is not to cope with changes in e, but rather to cope with the uncertainty contained in any particular e.*[13] Yet it is precisely the managers who have the best information on potential improvements in organization appropriate to changes in *e*. The entrepreneur has every incentive to initiate such changes, as the residual gains are his. For the socialist enterprise, however, the gains are external to the firm, and are likely to complicate the director's situation. This follows since changes in the organization of an enterprise alter the supply problems faced by a manager without alleviating his/her responsibility over them.

Indeed, one would expect directors to act as filters of information relating to potential surpluses achievable through coalition changes. This should be true, to some extent, under both capitalism and socialism, since changes in coalitions may jeopardize the position of managers. Capitalist firms tend to mitigate the filtering problem by (partially) compensating managers with stock options. The market for corporate control comes into play when stock options are insufficient inducements. These instruments are not available under socialism. More generally, the problem is that the gains from changing a coalition are less likely to remain within the socialist

---

[13] Ericson (1983) shows how the supply system can generate great uncertainties in supplies even in an economy with no aggregate shocks, which can be taken as no changes in e.

enterprise.[14] This is partly due to the greater external opportunities open to members of coalitions under capitalism, which necessitates higher compensation to keep agents within the firm. This is another way of pointing out the beneficial effects of competitive pressures on the performance of firms.

The situation of the socialist enterprise is much like that of a division in a large corporation. Note, however, that the division of a capitalist firm faces transfer prices for a small portion of its transactions, while the socialist enterprise faces, in effect, only transfer prices. Hence fewer gains will be internalized, and a smaller number of potential improvements will be transmitted to higher authorities. This also makes it much more difficult for the socialist manager efficiently to organize the internal operations of the enterprise.

It is important to recognize, however, that managers of socialist enterprises will be less likely to generate potential improvements, interest aside. This owes to the lack of external information possessed by the socialist manager relative to his capitalist counterpart. If prices do not reveal relative scarcities, then it is difficult for a manager to know what types of improvements will be socially beneficial. Notice that the capitalist manager need not concern himself with social benefits—it is coalition benefits that are relevant. Coalition changes under socialism must face a tougher standard due to the above-mentioned problem of a smaller number of authorities. And managers are not likely to possess sufficient information (even if they had the interest) to learn of such changes. This suggests why, given the price system that operates under socialism, design rights are not delegated to managers. Without information about opportunity costs it is not at all clear that such control could, or would, be used efficiently.

5. Conclusion

The purpose of this paper was to present a framework for the comparative study of the firm. By focusing on the nature of the firm under the two systems, we derived several hypotheses about the nature and pace of organizational change. We have seen that such changes occur more frequently and in a piecemeal fashion under capitalism. Socialist enterprises evolve in

---

[14] The *Shchekino* experiment provides an excellent example. Managers who participated in the experiment were told that they would be able to keep some of the gains due to labor saving, but these gains were quickly ratcheted away (Rutland, 1984).

a more punctuated (abrupt) fashion. This means that the potential surpluses (which may be thought of as inefficiencies, if we ignore bargaining
costs) tend to grow larger under socialism before changes take place. It
also implies that the resulting changes tend to be more dramatic.

These differences in economic organization may have important consequences for economic performance. If designing institutional improvements
is problematic, then searching for homogeneous solutions may result in
wide-scale errors. The piecemeal nature of change under capitalism implies that only previously successful innovations are likely to be copied. If
organizational change is a trial-and-error process, then the imposition of
comprehensive solutions may be costly.

The approach taken here also suggested that care should be taken in
discussions of decentralizing STE's. In particular, it makes a big difference
whether increased managerial autonomy involves greater delegation of design rights, a reform that only makes sense if combined with a change in
the way prices are formed. If not, then the devolution of authority implies
greater responsibility for managers, without more control over the nature
of the firm. This most likely induces managers to take actions that insulate
themselves from the vagaries of the system; actions that often conflict with
the purposes of reform (Ickes, 1988).

References

Alchian, A. (1984) "Specificity, Specialization, and Coalitions," *Journal of
Institutional and Theoretical Economics*, 140, 34-49.

Coase, R. (1937) "The Nature of the Firm," *Economica*, 4, 386-405.

Ericson, R. E. (1983) "A Difficulty with the 'Command' Allocation Mechanism," *Journal of Economic Theory*, 31, 1-26.

Grossman, S. and Hart, O. (1986) "The Costs and Benefits of Ownership:
A Theory of Vertical and Lateral Integration," *Journal of Political
Economy*, 94, 691-719.

Hart, O. (1988) "Incomplete Contracts and the Theory of the Firm," *Journal of Law, Economics, and Organization*, 4, 199-239.

Ichiishi, T. (1983) *Game Theory for Economic Analysis*, New York: Academic Press.

Ickes, B. W. (1988) "On the Difficulties of Reforming a Soviet-type Economy," Working Paper 3-88-5, The Pennsylvania State University.

Klein, B., Crawford, R., and Alchian, A. (1978) "Vertical Integration, Appropriable Rents, and the Competitive Contracting Process," *Journal of Law and Economics*, **21**, 297-326.

Mailath, G. and Postlewaite, A. (1988) "Workers Versus Firms: Bargaining over a Firm's Value," CARESS Working Paper 88-11, University of Pennsylvania.

Milgrom, P. and Roberts, J. (1987) "Bargaining and Influence Costs and the Organization of Economic Activity," Research Paper 934, Graduate School of Business, Stanford University.

Putterman, L. (1985) "On Some Recent Explanations of Why Capital Hires Labor," *Economic Inquiry*, **22**, 171-187.

Rosenberg, N. and Birdzell, L. (1986) *How the West Grew Rich*, Basic Books.

Rutland, P. (1984) "The Shchekino Method and the Struggle to Raise Labour Productivity in Soviet Industry," *Soviet Studies*, **36**, 345-365.

Williamson, O. (1985) *The Economic Institutions of Capitalism*, New York: The Free Press.

PART TWO

Optimization in Planning

3

Bargaining and Search in Imperfect Markets: A Centrally Planned Economy

Dušan Tříska

1. Introduction

No real-world market is perfect, just as no economy in reality is perfectly competitive. Two distinct consequences of market imperfections have been observed. First, price signals do not intermediate to the economic agents complete information about the scarcity of the goods and services demanded. This lack of knowledge motivates the agents towards a more or less extensive *search* for the missing information.

Secondly, the definition of an economic agent itself becomes somewhat ambiguous. In particular, a firm can no longer be represented as a single-objective decision-making unit exercising its complete set of property rights. A genuine firm must rather be viewed as a coalition of at least two conflicting sub-microeconomic units seeking to attain their self-interest through the process of *bargaining*.

Both search and bargaining can be analyzed with the traditional tools of microeconomics. The fundamental notions of the analysis will be a valuation of information, search costs and bargaining costs. As a result of these "additional" costs, a concept of a loss in efficiency can be established and discussed.

Elsewhere (Tříska, 1988) we have discussed the problem of optimal search costs of a socialist consumer facing short supplies in some markets.

In what follows, we shall confine ourselves to the analysis of decision-making in a socialist firm. We shall attempt to introduce the essentials of our approach to bargaining between a central planning authority and socialist enterprises.

2. Property Rights Distribution and a Socialist Firm

Once the concept of socialist ownership was established, a peculiar discrepancy between the distributions of power and information emerged. Formally, the power was given to representatives of the state, while the information needed for realistic decision-making has, naturally, remained in the hands of the enterprises' managers. These two types of agents, here referred to as *the planners* and *the producers*, have to confront in reality their formal and informal powers, in order to arrive at a mutually acceptable demand for and supply of the enterprise's product.

A stubborn conflict between the interests of the planner and the producer can be observed, as each of the two seeks to attain a maximal share of the gains provided by production.

The questions of what the gains are and how they are being divided into the planner's and the producer's shares constitute the focus of this paper.

3. Plan and Action

Our term *plan* will represent two types of planning targets observable in reality. First, there are the targets that specify in physical units "required" amounts of inputs and outputs. Secondly, there are the targets established as certain aggregate indicators of efficiency, i.e., the minimal level of profit.

Our term *action* seeks to suggest that it need not be the producer's genuine intention to meet any of the above planning targets. By an action we shall describe what amounts of inputs and outputs will be actually consumed and produced. Later we shall show to what extent these actual amounts correspond to established planning targets.

For the sake of brevity and conciseness we shall restrict ourselves to only one input x and one output y. The above distinction between plan and action can be then expressed by strict differentiation between two types of variables:

(i) $\mathcal{X}, \mathcal{Y}$, representing planning targets, or planning amounts of input and output, respectively,

(ii) X, Y, representing actual amounts consumed and produced.

Given this, our initial fundamental thesis will assert that it is within the *producer's* power to affect not only what his action $\vec{Y} = (X, Y)$ will be but also what his planning targets $\vec{y} = (\mathcal{X}, \mathcal{Y})$ will amount to. (Further steps of the analysis incorporate the producer's ability to affect also the planning targets of the efficiency kind.)

4. The Planning Constraint

Given the two types of choice variables, planning and actual, we must ask what constraints on their values can be observed. As to the actual variables X and Y, we shall fully rely on the tradition of a well-defined, well-behaved production function $f(X)$ and a production-possibilities set F situated "below" $f(X)$.

Unfortunately, no like tradition is at hand for constraining the planning variables $\mathcal{X}$ and $\mathcal{Y}$. Here we extend the discussion in Hlaváček and Tříska (1987) where the notion of the so-called planning constraint was introduced, apparently in the spirit of Baumol (1959) and Portes (1969).

The planning constraint is denoted by $g(\mathcal{X})$ in Figure 1 and has the following meaning:[1] By $g(\mathcal{X})$ the planner indicates the minimal amount of the planned output, should the planned input be at the level $\mathcal{X}$. The function $g(\mathcal{X})$ thus indicates the lower frontier of the planner's tolerance. He, as a planner, will not tolerate planning targets $(\mathcal{X}, \mathcal{Y})$ "worse than" $g(\mathcal{X})$. Put differently, he will only accept plans "better than" $g(\mathcal{X})$, i.e., the plans from a plan-feasible set $\mathcal{P}$, defined as

$$\mathcal{P} = \{\vec{y} = (\mathcal{X}, \mathcal{Y}); \mathcal{Y} \geq g(\mathcal{X})\}.$$

The graph of $g(\mathcal{X})$ can therefore be interpreted as the planner's indifference curve. Indeed, it is true by definition that the points on the lower frontier of $\mathcal{P}$ yield the same level of planner's satisfaction. Hence it is no coincidence in Figure 1 that $g(\mathcal{X})$ is drawn as an increasing and convex function. Its shape reflects our hypothesis that the basic interests of the planner rest upon maximizing profit or some profit-type indicator.

---

[1] The interpretation should be compared to that of Hlaváček (1990) in this volume.

Figure 1: The Maximization Problem in x,y-Space

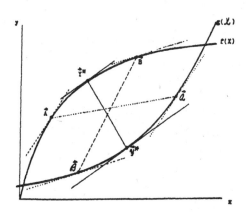

5. Tautness of Planning

The planning constraint $g(\mathcal{X})$ can, therefore, be interpreted as our second type of planning target. It should be stressed that this target establishes the planned, as opposed to the actual level, of efficiency. By establishing $g(\mathcal{X})$, the *planner* makes it explicit what plans $(\mathcal{X}, \mathcal{Y})$ he will or will not regard as feasible, *i.e.*, efficient enough.

It has become commonplace in recent literature to discuss how "hard" or "soft" constraints on economics agents, namely firms, may be—see, for example, Kornai (1986), Leibenstein (1976). In terms of this discussion, $g(\mathcal{X})$ must be conceived of as "hard" in the following sense: it is relatively easy for the planner to prevent plans $(\mathcal{X}, \mathcal{Y})$ that would contradict his preferences. It is indeed much easier than his consequent insistence that the once-established plans be fulfilled in reality by the producer. The same constraint $g(\mathcal{X})$ is, therefore, "soft" with respect to the producer's actions (X, Y). It is within the producer's power to decide whether and by how much he will fulfill or overfulfill the plan.

The concept of constraint hardness thus appears to us as altogether meaningless; should a constraint be soft, it would be no constraint whatsoever.

Unlike this, a great role can be ascribed to constraint tautness. In the tradition of Hunter (1961), Ickes (1986), Keren (1972), we shall also speak of the tautness of plans. Intuitively speaking, the "nearer" the function $g(\mathcal{X})$ is to the production function $f(X)$, the tauter the planning constraint is.

Later we shall show in what sense it is in the producer's interest to affect the level of his plan's tautness. At this stage, however, we shall assume that the relative position of $g(\mathcal{X})$ and $f(X)$ is given and held fixed.

6. The Bonus

Given the constraints $\vec{\mathcal{Y}} \in \mathcal{P}$ and $\vec{Y} \in F$, we may now ask what concept will accurately represent the producer's satisfaction. To begin with, we assume that the only interest of the producer is to maximize a *bonus* offered to him by the planner on the conditions that $\vec{\mathcal{Y}}$ has been fulfilled. Put formally, the bonus function or the incentive scheme in our basic model is

$$\Psi = \Psi(\mathcal{X} - X, Y - \mathcal{Y}) = \Psi(\Delta x, \Delta y),$$

where $\Delta x = \mathcal{X} - X$ and $\Delta y = Y - \mathcal{Y}$, and the function Ψ is assumed to be increasing and concave in both Δx and Δy. In other words, it is assumed that the producer's bonus is established so as to increase according to how much he overfulfills the plan in both the input and output; we expect that the returns to overfulfillment will be decreasing.[2]

Decision making by the producer can then be represented by the following maximization problem:

$$\max \Psi(\Delta x, \Delta y)$$
$$\text{subject to } \mathcal{Y} \geq g(\mathcal{X})$$
$$Y \leq f(X) \tag{1}$$
$$\vec{\mathcal{Y}}, \vec{Y} \geq 0$$

7. Optimal Plans and Optimal Action

Let us emphasize that by solving (1), the producer chooses an optimal plan-action combination $(\vec{\mathcal{Y}}^*, \vec{Y}^*)$ that would yield a maximal bonus.

Generally speaking, the solution $(\vec{\mathcal{Y}}^*, \vec{Y}^*)$ need not exist, and even when it does, it is still rather laborious and tedious to produce the first order

---

[2] See inequalities ($A3$) and ($A4$) of the Appendix. In terms of Goldfeld and Quandt's paper in this volume, Ψ is a generalized two-sided loss (penalty) function.

(necessary) conditions with adequate accuracy. In the Appendix we offer a concise outline of the relatively complex mathematical analysis. Here we shall only attempt to summarize its three major results.

Our first outcome seems to be fully in harmony with our intuition: geometrically speaking (see Figure 1), the optimal plan $\vec{\mathcal{Y}}^* = (\mathcal{X}^*, \mathcal{Y}^*)$, if it exists, lies on the graph of $g(\mathcal{X})$, while the optimal action $\vec{Y}^* = (X^*, Y^*)$ is on the graph of $f(X)$. Put differently, $\mathcal{Y}^* = g(\mathcal{X}^*)$ and $Y^* = f(X^*)$.

The second result of our analysis may be a little less obvious: the necessary condition for the solution of (1) is

$$\frac{dg(\mathcal{X}^*)}{d\mathcal{X}} = \frac{df(X^*)}{dX}. \tag{2}$$

Geometrically speaking, the condition asserts that the straight lines tangent to $g(\mathcal{X})$ and $f(X)$ at the optimal points $\vec{\mathcal{Y}}^*$ and $\vec{Y}^*$ are parallel. Indeed, an infinite number of plan-action pairs fit this condition. (See, for example, the pairs $(\vec{A}, \vec{A})$ and $(\vec{B}, \vec{B})$ in Figure 1.)

The third result of our analysis is that from among the pairs satisfying the necessary condition (2), the producer will choose that one for which

$$\frac{dg(\mathcal{X}^*)}{d\mathcal{X}} = \frac{df(X^*)}{dX} = \frac{\dfrac{\partial \Psi(\Delta x^*, \Delta y^*)}{\partial \Delta x}}{\dfrac{\partial \Psi(\Delta x^*, \Delta y^*)}{\partial \Delta y}}, \tag{3}$$

where the optimal differences Δx^* and Δy^* are given as $\Delta x^* = \mathcal{X}^* - X^*$, $\Delta y^* = Y^* - \mathcal{Y}^*$.

In Figure 2 we demonstrate the representation of (1) in the space of the differences Δx, Δy. The properties of the curve E are discussed in depth in the Appendix. There we also show that E contains all points to which there correspond plan-action pairs satisfying (2). From among them the producer chooses the pair to which the above equality (3) applies. It should also be clear from Figure 2 that the "nearer" to the origin 0 the line E lies, the tauter is the planning constraint.

8. Shadow Prices

If the bonus $\Psi(\Delta x, \Delta y)$ is accepted to represent the producer's preferences, it should be understandable that the ratio of its partial derivatives represents the producer's marginal rate of substitution, or *MRS*.

Analogously, given the interpretation of the planning constraint $g(\mathcal{X})$ as the planner's indifference curve, its derivative must represent his marginal

Figure 2: The Maximization Problem in $\Delta x, \Delta y$–Space

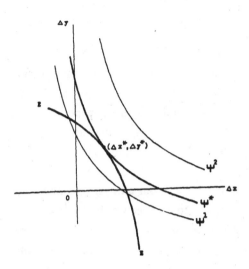

rate of substitution, or *mrs*. (Note that while *MRS* is a function of both the planning and actual variables, *mrs* depends solely on the planning ones.)

Using the ordinary notation for the marginal product *MP*, our major finding (3) can be rewritten as

$$mrs^* = MP^* = MRS^*.$$

Apparently, mrs^* and MRS^* can be interpreted as the equilibrium shadow prices, emerging as a result of the planner-producer interaction and assuring that they reach agreement.

Three types of prices have thus been established: (a) the official prices, (b) the shadow prices implicitly contained in the planning constraint (see Drewnowski, 1961), (c) the shadow prices put forth by the incentive scheme. In a socialist system all three price systems depend to a degree on the central planning authority. If inconsistencies can be observed among the three systems, serious complications can arise for economic agents. However, there is a sharp difference between the responses of consumers and producers to these inconsistencies. The consumer faces the official prices and his only option is to search for the missing information (Tříska, 1988). The producer, who shares the property with the planner, may accommodate through some type of dialogue, bargaining with the aim of establishing

equilibrium. Of course, if it exists, it applies to the two bargaining parties
only. Whether one of them may represent the consumer's interests is, of
course, questionable.

9. Bargaining Costs

Let us now relax the assumption that it is not within the producer's
power to affect the level of the plan's tautness. In other words, our further
analytical step will suggest that it is in the producer's interest and ability
to affect the position of the planning constraint $g(\mathcal{X})$. Such a producer
is capable of launching certain bargaining efforts, or the infamous "battle
over the plan."

On admitting these efforts to our analysis, we must investigate all their
economic consequences. In this paper we shall introduce two types of consequences occurring simultaneously. The first type covers all direct costs
caused by bargaining. The second type consists of changes in the enterprise's production capacity.

Figure 3: Consequences of Bargaining in x,y–Space

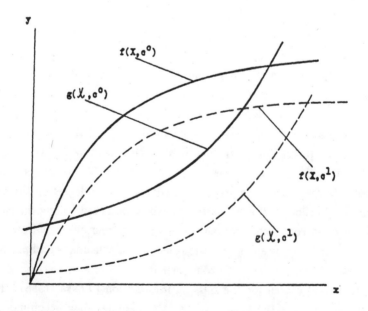

Figure 4: Consequences of Bargaining in $\Delta x, \Delta y$-Space

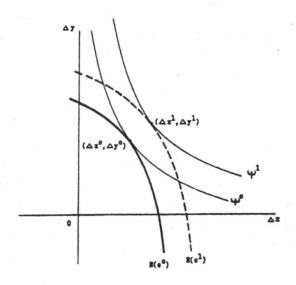

The second consequence of bargaining can best be described geometrically. In Figure 3 we have depicted that simultaneously with the shift in $g(\mathcal{X})$, a corresponding shift of $f(X)$ occurs. In words, the more involved in bargaining a socialist manager (the producer) becomes, the less his effort can be devoted to his "proper" managing and organizing production. The bigger the costs c will be, the deeper inside the original set F the newly created function $f(X, c)$ lies.[3]

The shift in the relative position of $g(\mathcal{X}, c)$ and $f(X, c)$ can be represented in the space of the differences $\Delta x, \Delta y$ as a shift of the curve $E(c)$ in Figure 4.

It is also possible to interpret $E(c)$ as an isocost curve in the following sense: To each $(\Delta x, \Delta y) \in E(c)$ correspond equal minimal bargaining costs, provided that $(\Delta x, \Delta y)$ is feasible.

The decision problem of the producer can then be formulated as follows:

$$\max\{\Psi(\Delta x, \Delta y) - c\}$$
$$\text{subject to } (\Delta x, \Delta y) \in E(c) \tag{4}$$

---

[3] Managerial labor of two types have been introduced in Goldfeld and Quandt (1988): the ordinary one and the specialized (whining) one. In our paper it is, in fact, suggested that the quantities of the two types of labor are negatively correlated.

However simple (4) may appear, its solution is a rather complicated matter, which is doubtless beyond the scope and purpose of this paper. Yet, it is apparent that (4) will also produce equilibrium shadow prices distinct from those set officially. Still more important is that the solution of (4) may lie inside the original production possibilities set F. Inefficiency of this optimum is, therefore, beyond any reasonable doubt. (Methodological consequences of this result should be contrasted with the discussion in de Alessi (1983).)

10. Conclusions

We have attempted to analyze the behavior of an enterprise facing a specific type of non-market regulation. Our model has assumed that the objective of the enterprise's manager (the producer) is the maximization of the so-called bonus or, what comes to almost the same thing, the difference between the regulatory (planning) target and the producer's actual performance. Further, the producer has been assumed to be capable of affecting not only his actual inputs and outputs, but—to a degree—also the planning targets. Officially, the latter fall under the sovereign authority of the planner; informally, as observed in reality, the targets become a subject of producer-planner bargaining.

Its impact on the "efficiency" of the existing prices has been presented in some depth (see also the Appendix). By contrast, we could only briefly sketch what consequences the bargaining process can have on the producer's production capacity.

Appendix

It may be useful to summarize our fundamental assumptions on the planning constraint $g(\mathcal{X})$, the production function $f(X)$ and the incentive scheme $\Psi(\mathcal{X} - X, \mathcal{Y} - \mathcal{Y}) = \Psi(\Delta x, \Delta y)$:

$$\frac{dg(\mathcal{X})}{d\mathcal{X}} > 0, \qquad \frac{d^2 g(\mathcal{X})}{d\mathcal{X}^2} > 0 \qquad\qquad (A1)$$

$$\frac{df(X)}{dX} > 0, \qquad \frac{d^2 f(X)}{dX^2} < 0 \qquad\qquad (A2)$$

$$\frac{\partial \Psi(\Delta x, \Delta y)}{\partial \Delta x} > 0, \qquad \frac{\partial \Psi(\Delta x, \Delta y)}{\partial \Delta y} > 0 \qquad\qquad (A3)$$

$$\frac{\partial^2 \Psi(\Delta x, \Delta y)}{\partial \Delta x^2} < 0, \qquad \frac{\partial^2 \Psi(\Delta x, \Delta y)}{\partial \Delta y^2} < 0. \qquad (A4)$$

Given (A1)–(A4), we can write our first proposition concerning the decision-making problem (1) and its solution as follows:

Proposition 1. *Let the pair* $\vec{y}^*$, $\vec{Y}^*$ *solve (1). Then* $\mathcal{Y}^* = g(\mathcal{X}^*)$ *and* $Y^* = f(X^*)$.

Proof. Assume the contrary. Then we can easily derive a contradiction with (A3) and (A4). ∎

Consequently, we can confine the investigation to the points in the graph of $g(\mathcal{X})$, denoted by $G(g)$, and the graph of $f(X)$, denoted by $F(f)$.

In order that economically sensible results be obtainable, the analysis must be carried out in the space of differences $\Delta x, \Delta y$. The transformation can be effected as follows. Consider a given point $\vec{Y}^0$ in $F(f)$. To every plan $\mathcal{Y} \in G(g)$ there corresponds exactly one combination of differences $\mathcal{X} - X^0, Y^0 - \mathcal{Y}$. Since $\vec{Y}^0$ is fixed, the set of all such differences is K^0, where

$$K^0 = \left\{ \Delta x, \Delta y; \Delta y = Y^0 - g(X^0 + \Delta x), X^0 + \Delta x \geqq 0 \right\}.$$

It is apparent, due to (A1), that the function $\Delta y = Y^0 - g(X^0 + \Delta x)$ is well defined, strictly decreasing and strictly concave.

In general, as the point $Y = f(X)$ moves along $F(f)$, a system of curves $K(\Delta x, \Delta y; X, Y) = 0$ will be produced. These curves may, of course, intersect: more than one plan-action pair may correspond to a particular combination of $\Delta x, \Delta y$.

This very unpleasant ambiguity will be overcome here in the following way. It will be shown that an envelope to the system of curves exists.

Proposition 2. *Exactly one plan-action pair corresponds to a given point in the envelope.*

Proof. Assume the contrary, and let two different actions $\vec{Y}'$ and $\vec{Y}''$ correspond to the point of the envelope. By the definition of the system of curves, we may write

$$\frac{\partial g(X' + \Delta x)}{\partial \Delta x} = \frac{\partial g(X'' + \Delta x)}{\partial \Delta x}$$

which, of course, contradicts our assumption (A1). ∎

Proposition 3. *If a solution to (1) exists, it will necessarily lie in the envelope.*

Proof. Suppose that the optimum $(\Delta x^*, \Delta y^*)$ does not lie in the envelope but below it. Due to (A3) and (A4), the preferences are strictly convex. Hence there can always be found a neighborhood of $(\Delta x^*, \Delta y^*)$ such that it will contain only feasible combinations of $\Delta x, \Delta y$, at least some of which will yield a higher bonus than that associated with $(\Delta x^*, \Delta y^*)$. This contradicts that $(\Delta x^*, \Delta y^*)$ is an optimum. ∎

Mathematically speaking, the system $K(\Delta x, \Delta y; X, Y) = 0$ constitutes a so-called one-parameter system of curves, with X being the only parameter, as $Y = f(X)$. Mathematical theory introduces the notion of a discrimination curve to describe such a system and defines it as a solution to the equations

$$K(\Delta x, \Delta y; X) = 0$$
$$\frac{dK(\Delta x, \Delta y; X)}{dX} = 0. \tag{A5}$$

Substituting for K in (A5) we easily obtain

$$\frac{df(X)}{dX} = \frac{dg(\mathcal{X})}{d\mathcal{X}}. \tag{A6}$$

Recall that property (A6) applies to all elements of the discrimination curve and that it is the same property that was denoted as (2) in Section 7, or as $MP = mrs$ in Section 8. We now state

Proposition 4. *The discrimination curve is the envelope to the system of curves K.*

Proof. It will suffice to show that all points of the curves in the system are regular, i.e., that the first derivatives of these curves with respect to Δy are everywhere nonzero. But these derivatives are all equal to -1. ∎

Already Proposition 3 suggested that there exists a one-to-one function $X(\Delta x)$, which ascribes to each combination in the envelope exactly one pair $(\vec{\mathcal{Y}}, \vec{Y})$, where $\vec{\mathcal{Y}} \in G(g)$ and $\vec{Y} \in F(f)$. Implicitly, the function $X(\Delta x)$ is given by (A6). Due to (A1) and (A2), we know not only that the explicit function exists, but also that it is continuous and differentiable. By differentiating (A6) with respect to Δx and writing $X(\Delta x)$ for X and $X + \Delta x$ for $\mathcal{X}$, we obtain

$$\frac{dX(\Delta x)}{d\Delta x} = \left[\frac{\dfrac{d^2 g(\mathcal{X})}{d\mathcal{X}^2}}{\left(\dfrac{d^2 f(X)}{dX^2} - \dfrac{d^2 g(\mathcal{X})}{d\mathcal{X}^2}\right)} \right] \left(\frac{dX(\Delta x)}{d\Delta x} + 1 \right).$$

This last formula leads to our concluding propositions, both extremely important for the existence and uniqueness of the solution to (1). We thus have

Proposition 5. $X(\Delta x)$ *is strictly decreasing.*

Proposition 6. *The envelope to the system of curves* $K(\Delta x, \Delta y, X) =$ 0 *is strictly decreasing and concave.*

Proposition 6, in fact, states that the curves $K(\Delta x, \Delta y, X) = 0$ are of the type depicted in Figures 2 and 4 as E. Proofs of the last two propositions consist of tedious differentiation and application of the properties (A1)–(A4) and are, therefore, omitted.

Referring to Propositions 1–6, we can now reformulate problem (1) as

$$\max \Psi(\Delta x, \Delta y)$$
$$\text{subject to } \Delta y = f\big(X(\Delta x)\big) - g\big(X(\Delta x) - \Delta x\big). \tag{A7}$$

Simple application of the Kuhn-Tucker procedure to (A7), given the above-discussed properties of $X(\Delta x)$, easily yields the central result (3) of our paper, or

$$mrs^* = MP^* = MRS^*$$

which introduced into our analysis the concept of shadow equilibrium prices. (For a detailed analysis see Tříska, Havelka and Hollmannová (1988).)

References

Baumol, W. J. (1959) *Business Behavior, Value and Growth*, New York: Harcourt Brace and World.

de Alessi, L. (1983) "Property Rights, Transaction Costs and X-Efficiency," *American Economic Review* **73**, 64-81.

Drewnowski, J. (1961) "The Economic Theory of Socialism: A Suggestion for Reconsideration," *Journal of Political Economy* **69**, 341-354.

Goldfeld, S. M. and Quandt, R. E. (1988) "Budget Constraints, Bailouts and the Firm under Central Planning," *Journal of Comparative Economics* **12**, 502-520.

———— (1990) "Output Targets, Input Rationing and Inventories," this volume.

Hlaváček, J. (1990) "Producers' Criteria in a Centrally Planned Economy," this volume.

Hlaváček, J. and Tříska, D. (1987) "The Planning Authority and its Marginal Rate of Substitution," *Ekonomicko-matematický obzor* **23**, 38-54.

Hunter, H. (1961) "Optimal Tautness in Development Planning," *Economics of Development and Cultural Change* **8**, 561-572.

Ickes, B. (1986) "On the Economics of Taut Planning," *Journal of Comparative Economics* **10**, 388-399.

Keren, M. (1972) "On the Tautness of Plans," *Review of Economic Studies* **39**, 469-486.

Kornai, J. (1986) "On the Soft Budget Constraint," *Kyklos* **39**, 3-30.

Leibenstein, H. (1976) *Beyond Economic Man*, Cambridge: Harvard University Press.

Portes, R. (1969) "The Enterprise under Central Planning," *Review of Economic Studies* **36**, 197-212.

Tříska, D. (1988) "Consumer under Supply Constraint: Homo Sectans," *Ekonomicko-matematický obzor* **24**, 303-319.

Tříska, D., Havelka, P., and Hollmannová, M. (1988) "Optimálni úroveň napjatosti plánu," ("Optimal Tautness of Planning"), Working Paper, Institute of Economics, Prague.

4

Producers' Criteria in a Centrally Planned Economy

Jiří Hlaváček

1. Introduction

This paper discusses the following questions:

1. What is the prevailing economic motivation of the producers in a centrally planned economy (CPE) and why?
2. Is it possible to change the producers' objective function by partial measures affecting the mechanism of central control, e.g., by reforms that go as far as to abolish direct command rules and to supersede them by the principle of economic self-financing?

Section 2 outlines a model of the typical producer in a CPE and presents an answer to the first set of questions. The second question is addressed in Sections 3 and 4 where we also discuss some of the problems that arise from implementing reforms of the traditional economic mechanisms of centrally planned economies.

2. Self-securing Behavior by Producers

The models that describe the behavior of producers usually assume that they prefer outputs located on the production possibility curve, i.e., on the boundary of the set of production possibilities. The fact that the producer's real position is below the technological boundary of the production set is explained by the large number of decision makers in the firm (Simon, 1957), the cost of search (Stigler, 1961), transaction costs (Williamson, 1975), the effort involved in realizing the output (Hunter, 1961; Keren, 1972), the irrelevance of the utility maximization principle for the agent's decision-making (Simon, 1957; Leibenstein, 1976), or stochastic factors (Stiglitz, 1975).

The view expressed in this paper is that the reasons that lead the producer in a CPE to choose a point below the production possibility curve are peculiar to CPEs. In the first place, it is characteristic of the local economic environment that only those decision makers who operate below their production possibility curves are likely to survive. In order to discuss this problem in more detail, we introduce a model of the producer *Homo se assecurans*. By this name we denote a producer who "secures himself" (or hedges) and thus survives, thanks to the existence of a maximal possible "reserve cushion," which is the difference between his production possibilities and actually realized outputs.

A specific characteristic of production in any centrally planned economy is the existence of two objective functions on a (unique) production set. Apart from his own production function, the behavior of the producer also depends on another agent, who is his principal. This agent will be referred to as the "planning center."

The planning center exercises its influence over the producer in the first instance by the plan. The plan can be regarded as a reduction of the production set either "from below"—thus setting the lower limit of tolerated inefficiency—or "from the right hand side"—thus expressing the limited quantity of available resources. Therefore, we assume the existence of a set of feasible vectors of inputs, and with each vector $\vec{x}$ from this set, a vector of outputs can be associated as $\vec{y} = \vec{g}(\vec{x})$, with the property that the planning center is just willing to accept the combination $(\vec{x}, \vec{y})$ as representing a useful expenditure of resources $\vec{x}$.

In order to avoid formal complications, from now on we shall deal only with a producer of a unique and homogeneous output y. That will allow us to switch from a vector plan-feasible function $\vec{g}(\vec{x})$ to a scalar plan-feasible function $g(\vec{x})$. In addition, in the figures we shall limit ourselves to a single input x.

The plan-feasible function $g(\vec{x})$ represents the lower bound of acceptable production efficiency by the planning center. In that sense, the schedule $g(\vec{x})$ can be conceived of as an indifference curve (or isoquant) representing the planning center's objective function. This schedule connects those hypothetical production situations $(y, \vec{x})$ of the producer that bring the center the same (minimally acceptable) level of satisfaction.

The center experiences diminishing marginal utility from the production of a given producer and, hence, the isoquants of the center's objective function are convex, which is equivalent to saying that the plan-feasible function $g(\vec{x})$ is convex. In this case, which we call the standard case, the planning center requires that, as the scale of production increases, production become more efficient with each additional unit of output.

The convexity of the $g(\vec{x})$ function becomes an even more realistic assumption if, at the same time, the planning center takes into account the increasing relative scarcity of the given resources. In that case, the producer is expected to compensate for the growing marginal loss of the resource, as evaluated by the center, when he increases the scale of production.

Note that we did not have to consider the producer's production function while formulating the planning constraint $y \geqq g(\vec{x})$. The planning center can, therefore, disregard the diminishing marginal returns of the producer and is free to evaluate the producer's production situation exclusively according to the center's own subjectively felt need. This depends to a large extent on the nature of market disequilibrium; e.g., in the case of excess demand, the planning center has to stand up to a critique from the public or the political authorities, which undoubtedly has some influence on the shape or position of both objective functions and the plan-feasible function $g(\vec{x})$. Thus, the planning center fulfills two functions which, in a competitive economy, are exercised by the market. In the first place, it plays the role of a "speaker" for the buyers, providing the producers with information about marketing possibilities. In the second place, it is the body of control, overseeing inefficiency, so that it does not exceed certain limits.

The producer himself—as opposed to the planning center—has to respect the production function constraints. His production set is given by

$$Y = \{(y, \vec{x}); g(\vec{x}) \leqq y \leqq f(\vec{x})\},$$

where the function $f(\vec{x})$ indicates the maximal volume of output that the producer is able to obtain from given resources $\vec{x}$.

We shall assume that the production function is given exogenously for each producer. Concretely, it is the upper bound of the production set that is determined not only technologically but also (in a given economic environment) economically. It can be interpreted as a maximal volume of output that the given decision maker (producer) is capable of achieving by his own activity, if the available input is $\vec{x}$.

At the same time, we shall assume that the plan-feasible function is also exogenously given for the producer. We can now define the concept of this function more precisely. It is the (minimal) volume of production about which the producer assumes *ex ante* at the moment of decision making that it is *ex post* sanctioned by the planning center as an efficient use of inputs $\vec{x}$. In fact, it is not an *ex ante* proclaimed plan (even though it may be changed during or after the planning period), but an *ex ante* idea of the producer about an *ex post* attitude of the center. It is a type of rational expectation of the producer.

The producer's production set Y represents the set of all his decision-making alternatives. If the set Y is neither empty nor a single-element set, the producer selects from it by using his own objective function.

What is the "natural" objective function of the producer in the situation discussed? We cannot answer this question before learning what the impact of the producer's actual decision will be on the position of his future production set (future plan) in the next planning period.

All this is closely connected with the so-called indexed method of planning that has prevailed in all socialist economies. The planning center has no precise information about the production possibilites of the producers under its command, while at the same time it is subject to social and political pressures to increase the efficiency of production in the economic system. The fact that the planning center does not know the production possibilities of individual producers leads to a uniform specification of the required efficiency growth, so that the actually achieved efficiency is increased by a certain (usually egalitarian) percentage.

The producer who chooses an output on the upper frontier of his production set would most probably not survive two planning periods: he would be incapable of fulfilling the more demanding requirements of the center for the second period. The producer's aversion to allocating resources in the region close to the upper boundary of the production set is multiplied by the degree of uncertainty in his relationship with other producers and, in particular, with his suppliers.

If the planning center is unwilling to accept the routine explanation for the failure to fulfill the plan that there was a shortfall of input supplies, the producer is liable to challenge or prosecution. All such shortfalls are, therefore, more easily coped with by drawing on one's own reserves. It is evident that a higher probability of economic survival in the given economic environment can be expected by those producers (managers) whose output is significantly below their production function.

Underlying this are sensible economic incentives. It is sensible to prefer a more comfortable situation or, in other words, to minimize the effort needed for the achievement of a certain goal. It is the main objective of any manager of an enterprise to ensure its economic survival. More efficient production by an enterprise (firm) is, at the same time, more management-skill intensive, which is another reason why the manager prefers the less demanding production situation with as low an efficiency as the center permits. Thus, when we look at this problem both from the outside (from the point of view of the producer's capacity for economic survival) and from the inside (the producer's tendency to choose an easier path to the goal), it follows that the producer in the planning environment has a strong motivation to maximize his production reserve, i.e., the difference between his maximal production capacity and the planning center's minimally sanctioned level of output.

The producer's optimization problem can then be expressed as follows:

$$\max r(\vec{x}, y) = f(\vec{x}) - y$$
$$\text{subject to} \quad g(\vec{x}) \leqq y \leqq f(\vec{x}) \tag{1}$$

where $\vec{x}$ is the vector of inputs in physical units, y is the amount of output in physical units, $f(\vec{x})$ is the production function, $g(\vec{x})$ is the plan-feasible function and $r(\vec{x}, y) = f(\vec{x}) - y$ is the production reserve.

We label this model of the producer's allocative decision making as a model of *Homo se assecurans*, i.e., a "man securing himself." While prices so far have been absent from the model, they may become a parameter of the plan-feasible function $g(\vec{x})$, and usually do so in reality. We can allow for that if, in place of the planning constraint $g(\vec{x})$, a floor for producers' profits is introduced instead (see Sections 3 and 4). In that case, we deal with producers' decision making based on an economic criterion. Analogously to the profit maximizing producer, the producer *Homo se assecurans* maximizes his distance from input-output combinations that run a sizeable risk that he will exit from the scene. In a competitive, market-type, economy the "zone of peril" is represented by the set of input-output combinations that have low profitability. One the other hand, in a socialist economy of the traditional (planned) type, this zone is represented by a set of taut plans, i.e., the plan prescribed by the center can easily threaten the economic position of the managers because they cannot fulfill the target. We have to add that the tautness of the plan is greater, if the firm's profitability in the previous period was greater. Given the different nature of "zones of peril" in these two economic environments, the producers behave in distinctly different ways, even though they have to be judged as economically rational in both cases, as implied by our assumptions.

In Hlaváček and Tříska (1987) we derive the dependence of the solution of (1) on the properties of the plan-feasible function $g(\vec{x})$, i.e., the dependence of the producer's optimum on the properties of the planning center's preferences. It has been shown there that

(1) the optimal production point $(y, \vec{x})$ is located on the lower bound of the production set, i.e., $y = g(\vec{x})$;

(2) if the function $g(x)$ is differentiable, the optimum is reached for a vector $\vec{x}^*$ such that

$$\frac{\partial f(\vec{x}^*)}{\partial x_i} = \frac{\partial g(\vec{x}^*)}{\partial x_i}.$$

The first condition for the optimum implies that the producer *Homo se assecurans* will not overfulfill the plan—or more precisely, has no a *priori* intention of overfulfilling it. The second condition can be interpreted as a requirement for the marginal product to equal the planning center's marginal rate of substitution.

Figure 1 illustrates the location of the optimum for the producer of our type in the case of scalar input and output. As can be seen, the optimum is located at point $(g(x^*), x^*)$, such that at x^* the slopes of the tangents of both functions $f(x)$ and $g(x)$ are identical. The optimal production point (y^*, x^*) is defined by a tangent point of isoquants, each belonging to one of the interacting agents. It is clear that this is a Pareto-optimal situation for both agents.

If the relationship between the producer and the planning center, i.e., their bargaining power, is changed, then another planning center's isoquant is substituted for $g(x)$, thus shifting the optimum along the set P, which represents the set of all potential production points and is a quasi-contract curve. An input-output combination outside the set P can be changed in a direction that is advantageous for both agents.

Figure 1: The Optimum of Producer *Homo Se Assecurans*

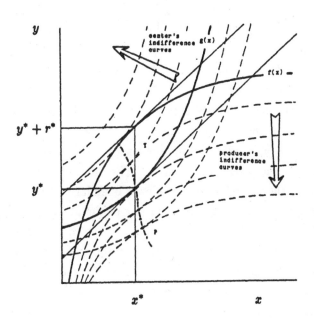

If the planning center sets a more demanding target, its increasing tautness calls forth a shift in the allocation of the producer along the set P. The
figure suggests that the planning center has at its disposal a regulatory tool:
if there is a need to increase the amount of output, the planning center will
call for a more demanding planning target. As we shall explain later, the
result is not so straightforward, since the producer's reaction can be quite
unexpected. In some cases, he might decide to increase the level of output,
while in others he might decide to reduce output or even fail to exhibit any
output sensitivity to the degree of tautness of the plan. All these cases will
be analyzed by using a model representing a partially reformed economic
mechanism with central control.

3. A Partially Reformed Economy with Central Control

We now consider the following model of economic management: the
planning center conditions the economic survival of the producers on their
ability to self-finance their operations while the prices of inputs $\tilde{w}$ and the
price of the output p are subject to the control of the center.

This model is a particular case of the model discussed above. Assume now that the plan-feasible function $g(x)$ has the explicit linear form

$$g(\vec{x}) = \left(\frac{1}{p}\right) \vec{w} \cdot \vec{x}.$$

As far as the objective function is concerned, the previous assumption remains unchanged: the producer again maximizes the reserve between his production capacity and the level of production actually carried out.

The reduction of the planning constraints to the sole requirement of profitability in economic self-financing does not, as we shall see, by itself cause a change in the producer's motives. The only difference from the previous model is the special form of the lower boundary of the production set. Nevertheless, this does not set aside any of the previous reasons for the inefficient behavior of the producer. On the contrary, this alteration can lead in reality, at least temporarily, to a strengthening of the tendency to secure oneself with the aid of a reserve. If the principle of self-financing entrepreneurship—intended to be the essence of reform in Czechoslovakia and other countries—were effective, the lower boundary of the production set would have to be definitely firmer than prior to such reform, when the firm had available a number of loopholes through which it could introduce slack into the plan a *posteriori*. The risk of arriving at an empty production set after an alteration of relative prices can be a serious threat, especially when the abolition of a large number of direct commands would also cause the disappearance of many certainties that producers had enjoyed before.

It is questionable whether the planning center, having given up direct commands, still retains some control over the level of output. During the early stages of reform, the faultless functioning of market forces cannot be assumed. If the factor markets do not work properly, then it is quite clear that the planning center would have to intervene in order to increase or decrease the output levels of certain commodities. The question is this: will the planning center be able to control the producers without reverting to the former method of direct commands?

In order to answer this question, we must analyze the supply function of the producer—at our abstract level of reasoning. We shall inquire into the dependence of the optimal level of output y (analyzed from the producer's point of view) on the output's price, given that the prices of inputs are kept fixed. The optimal level of output is given by the solution of the following problem:

$$\max r(\vec{x}, y) = f(\vec{x}) - y$$

$$\text{subject to} \quad f(\vec{x}) \geq y \geq \left(\frac{1}{p}\right) \vec{w} \cdot \vec{x}. \tag{2}$$

Suppose that the production function $f(\vec{x})$ is strictly concave and differentiable and that the production set is compact and has a non-empty interior. Then our problem has a unique solution $(\vec{x}^*, y^*)$, where

$$\frac{w_i}{p} = \frac{\partial f(\vec{x}^*)}{\partial x_i}, \quad y^* = \left(\frac{1}{p}\right) \vec{w} \cdot \vec{x}^*. \tag{3}$$

Consider, for the sake of simplicity, a producer with one homogeneous (scalar) input. The function $f(x)$ is strictly concave; hence, $f'(x)$ is decreasing, which means that it can be inverted. Define $\Phi(p) = f'^{-1}(w/p)$. Then, for a fixed input price w, we obtain

$$y^*(p) = \left(\frac{w}{p}\right) \Phi(p),$$

$$\frac{dy^*(p)}{dp} = \left(\frac{w}{p}\right) \left[\Phi'(p) - \frac{\Phi(p)}{p}\right].$$

The sign of the derivative $dy^*(p)/dp$ depends on the sign of $\Phi'(p) - \Phi(p)/p$. None of the possibilities can be excluded, even if the production function is strictly concave. For example, for a logarithmic production function, $y = k\log(x)$ for $x > 1$, we have $\Phi(p) = k(p/w)$. For $p \geq \tilde{p} = w/k$, which is a necessary condition for a non-empty production set Y, we obtain $\Phi'(p) = \Phi(p)/p$, and the physical volume of output $y^*(p)$ is completely insensitive to the change in the output price (see Figure 2). One the other hand, consider the production function $y = k\sqrt{x}$. Then $\Phi(p) = p^2/(4w^2)$, $\Phi'(p) = p/(2w^2) > \Phi(p)/p$. The producer now increases the volume of output whenever the price of output rises (for $p > \tilde{p} = 2w/k$). Finally, in the third example of a strictly concave production function $y = \tilde{y} - k/x$ for $x > k/\tilde{y}$, we obtain $\Phi(p) = \sqrt{pk/w}$, $\Phi'(p) = (1/2p)\sqrt{kp/w} < \Phi(p)$ (for $p > \tilde{p} = kw/\tilde{y}^2$). In this case the producer reacts to an increase in the price of output in a paradoxical way, i.e., by decreasing the supply.

It would not be useful to discuss in detail when each of these three cases becomes effective. What is essential is that the planning center, which notoriously lacks reliable information about the individual producer's production function, has no grounds to assume that the supply function is increasing or decreasing. The planning center's situation can be compared to a driver, who sits at a steering wheel, but does not know whether a left

Figure 2: The Producer *Homo Se Assecurans* with Constant Supply

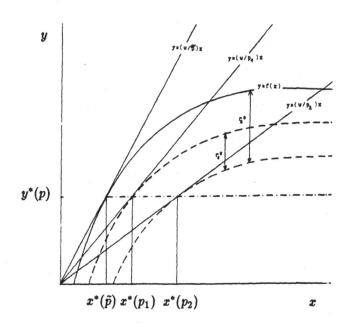

turn of the wheel will steer the car to the right or the left, or result in no change of direction at all. In order to avoid a crash there may be no other alternative but to raise a guide-rail along the desired path. The planning center is forced to set new supplementary constraints on the producer's production set, that is to say, to return to direct command rule.

4. Contractual Prices in a Centrally Planned Economy

As the previous section implies, the simple installation of the principle of budgetary self-financing cannot lead to a substantial change in the functioning of the economy. The empirical evidence points in the same direction: for example, in Hungary, from the late 1960s on, direct targeting by the central plan was markedly restrained without any serious subsequent change in behavior in the production sphere. The producer's objective to have as slack a plan as possible was more or less altered by switching to the objective of receiving a higher selling price.

A tool often mentioned as a possible countervailing device to the former inflationary behavior of producers is the so-called contractual price. The idea is that the buyer is motivated to obtain the lowest possible price and, thus, he represents a reliable source of countervailing forces to the inflationary behavior of suppliers. It is assumed that in the process the buyer can exercise greater bargaining power than the center.

Such reasoning appears to be sound and seems to be capable of limiting the producer's principal motivation to reduce his efficiency as a supplier. The contractual price in period t does not depend on the efficiency level of the producer; higher efficiency in period $t-1$ can be shown to have no direct influence on the substantial limit to be put on the production set in period t. If the economy is subject to the self-regulating mechanism of demand and supply, it seems to be true that the counter-efficient behavior of the producer loses its rationale.

Even in this case the situation is not so clear-cut and the optimism in expecting profit-oriented behavior here is not a matter of course. In what follows we shall prove that the paternalism of the center alone leads by itself to the reserve maximizing behavior of producers.

There is no guarantee that the economic reform will automatically generate a market-clearing mechanism such that the conditions for the existence of an equilibrium contractual price for both the supplier and the buyer will always be satisfied. This is the case if the buyer is simultaneously a producer (not a final consumer). The production sets of both producers (supplier and buyer) depends on the price of the commodity traded. The increase in price extends the supplier's production set; this happens at the expense of the buyer's production set, which contracts. A decrease in price acts in reverse. It is clear that there exists a low price $\tilde{p}$ that represents the supplier's break-even point. All prices that allow one to find at least one allocation with nonnegative profit fall into the interval $(\tilde{p}, +\infty)$. Analogously, there exists a high price $\tilde{\tilde{p}}$, where for any $p > \tilde{\tilde{p}}$ the buyer cannot cover his costs. The set of all prices that are compatible with economic viability falls into the interval $(0, \tilde{\tilde{p}})$.

In imperfect markets we cannot rule out $\tilde{\tilde{p}} < \tilde{p}$, which means that there does not exist a price allowing viability for both producers: $(\tilde{p}, +\infty) \cap (0, \tilde{\tilde{p}}) = \emptyset$. That is just the moment for the center to intervene. It can, for example, introduce a multiple price regime or another form of subsidy. The exit or entry of firms, as it naturally occurs in competitive economies, will not take place here, since the center is motivated by the guarantee of viability for both agents. Given the fact that paternalistic behavior by the center has been an inherent feature of the economic system in all socialist societies, there are no grounds for presuming that the near future will be any different.

There is still another alternative—perhaps one that is even more relevant than the factual non-existence of an equilibrium contractual price. It is the alternative of collusion among producers, who only pretend to the center that such equilibrium prices do not exist. The center has only very limited means to figure out this subterfuge, because it does not know the production sets of either producer. The net payoff from collusion is the subsidy that the paternalistic center has been lured into granting. The success of the "trick" depends on successfully concealing the correct information about the production set from the center. On the other hand, the transition to a more efficient allocation gives the center direct information about the producer's production possibilities. It thus seems that the paternalistic behavior of the center alone provides a *raison d'être* for the counter-efficient strategy of producers.

References

Hlaváček, J. (1986) "Homo se assecurans," *Politicka ekonomie* **34**, 633-639.

———— (1987) "A Model of Dialogue between the Planning Centre and the Producer," *Proceedings of* 4th *Mezhdunarodnyj Microsymposium '87*, Prague, Institute of Economics, VP 282.

Hlaváček, J. and Tříska, D. (1987) "Planning Authority and Its Marginal Rate of Substitution: Theorem Homo Se Assecurans," *Ekonomicko-matematicky obzor* **23**, 38-53.

Hunter, H. (1961) "Optimal Tautness in Development Planning," *Economic Development and Cultural Change* **9**, 561-572.

Keren, M. (1972) "On the Tautness of Plans," *Review of Economic Studies* **39**, 388-399.

Leibenstein, H. (1976) *Beyond Economic Man*, Cambridge: Harvard University Press.

Simon, H. (1957) *A Model of Man*, New York: Wiley.

Stigler, G. J. (1961) "The Economics of Information," *Journal of Political Economy* **69**, 213-225.

Stiglitz, J. (1975) "Incentives, Risk and Information: Notes Towards a Theory of Hierarchy," *Bell Journal of Economics* **6**, 552-579.

Williamson, O. (1975) *Markets and Hierarchies: Analysis and Antitrust Implications*, New York: The Free Press.

5

The Enterprise and the Economic Center: Control and Cooperation

Jacek Stefanski and _Małgorzata Pilarska_

1. Introduction

An important role in an economy is played by the system of relations between the government or economic center and the enterprises. These relations can vary from full control in centrally planned economies to total independence of enterprises at the other, rather theoretical extreme. In a highly centralized economy, the center controls both the inputs and outputs of a firm, and the center's main task is to design a production plan (Burkov and Shchepkin, 1984). In practice, such a plan prescribes a large number of targets which are intended to guide the behavior of the enterprise. However, as reality suggests, centralized systems of this type do not appear to be very efficient. One of the main reasons for this is that a firm often does not behave according to the planners' wishes because the employees have their own interests. On the other hand, the efficiency of labor-managed enterprises is also not remarkable; for instance, they frequently do not adapt properly to changes in their environment (Madzar, 1987; Meade, 1972). There is a growing recognition in East European countries of these general difficulties and, hence, an interest in other decision structures involving enterprises and the economic center.

In this paper we develop simple game theory models, which concentrate on center-enterprise relations in several decision structures. The inconsistency of the center's and the enterprises' goals is taken into account. We discuss three different hierarchical structures where the center can control the capital to which a firm has access. The structures differ in the decision sequence and information available to the parties. A coalition structure in which a governmental agency (representing the center) is a shareholder of a firm is also discussed. In the latter case, the decisions made in an enterprise result from a bargaining process between shareholders.

The following decision variables will be distinguished in the model: labor L, capital K, production q, price p and an average wage w. The whole decision vector is denoted by v, i.e., $v = (L, K, w, q, p)$. It is assumed that the maximal available L and K are limited: $0 \leq L \leq \overline{L}$, $0 \leq K \leq \overline{K}$, while w must be within an admissible range: $\underline{w} \leq w \leq \overline{w}$. Production q cannot be greater than the level determined by the production function f: $0 \leq q \leq f(L, K)$. The firm operates in a market described by an inverse demand function P, i.e., $P(q)$ is the maximal price for which the quantity q can be sold. Thus, $0 \leq p \leq P(q)$. The above inequalities give us a set V of admissible decision vectors v.

The goal functions of the center and the firm are denoted by $G_C(v)$ and $G_F(v)$, respectively. We assume for simplicity that decision makers have complete knowledge about the system.

2. Control Structures

The key factors which determine a decision structure are a decision sequence (i.e., what decisions are made by each party and when), and possibly additional strategic abilities (e.g., to make announcements about strategies to be applied in the future).

Administrative Control

By administrative control we mean a highly centralized structure in which the center makes decisions about all the variables in the vector v. It does this in such a way as to maximize its goal function G_C:

$$v^* = \arg\max_{v \in V} G_C(v). \tag{1}$$

The set V of admissible decisions in such a centralized system follows, at least theoretically, from the general balance made at higher than the enterprises' level (in reality there exist problems with associating inputs with outputs; see Goldfeld and Quandt (1990)).

Since G_C need not be connected with the firm's revenue or profit, it can happen that the price is lower than its upper bound (i.e., $p < P(q)$). It can also happen that $q < f(K, L)$. In theory, an appropriate incentive system can be designed that allows the latter case to be avoided (Burkov and Shchepkin, 1984; Hlaváček, 1990). However, in practice this does not solve the problem of poor efficiency in administrative control.

Hierarchical Structures

Let us consider a situation in which the center determines a value of capital K, while the enterprise takes the other decisions which, for convenience, will be denoted by v_F: $v_F = (L, w, q, p)$. In such a situation various information structures are possible. We shall discuss three of them.

Decision Sequence A. The decision process consists of two steps: (1) The center determines $K \in [0, \overline{K}]$; (2) the firm decides about $v_F \in V_F$, where V_F is the set of admissible decision vectors v_F. A strategy for the firm will be denoted by $\tilde{v}_F$, i.e., $\tilde{v}_F : [0, \overline{K}] \to V_F$.

The optimal strategy for the firm is its optimal reaction to a given K:

$$\tilde{v}_F^R(K) = \arg\max_{v_F \in V_F} G_F(K, v_F). \tag{2}$$

Since it is assumed that the center knows G_F, it is in a position to foresee $\tilde{v}_F^R$ and can take it into account when calculating the optimal value of capital:

$$K^* = \arg\max_{K \in [0, \overline{K}]} G_C(K, \tilde{v}_F^R(K)). \tag{3}$$

Of course, the optimal decision of the enterprise is

$$v_F^* = \tilde{v}_F^R(K^*). \tag{4}$$

From a formal point of view, decision sequence A describes a Stackelberg game with simple information structure (Basar and Oldser, 1982). In this game the center is the leader and the firm the follower.

Decision Sequence B. Let us now consider a similar situation but with a reversed sequence of decisions. As before, the decision sequence consists of two steps: (1) The firm makes a decision about $v_F \in V_F$, (2) the center decides about $K \in [0, \overline{K}]$.

The center's strategy will be denoted by $\tilde{K}$, i.e., $\tilde{K} : V_F \to [0, \overline{K}]$, and its optimal strategy can be determined as

$$\tilde{K}^R(v_F) = \arg\max_{K \in [0, \overline{K}]} G_C(K, v_F). \tag{5}$$

Then the firm's optimal decision should take into account the optimal re-action of the center:

$$v_F^* = \arg\max_{v_F \in V_F} G_F(\tilde{K}^R(v_F), v_F). \tag{6}$$

The optimal decision of the center is computed as a function of v_F^*:

$$K^* = \tilde{K}^R(v_F^*) \tag{7}$$

The above decision structure can occur when the firm first informs the center about its plans concerning v_F, and then the center decides about K. Since the center's reaction according to (5) is foreseeable, it seems natural that the firm takes it into account when considering the choise of v_F in (6).

Decision Sequence C. In this decision structure, the center may an-nounce its strategy. After that, the firm makes its decisions, and then the center decides about K according to the previously declared strategy. In this case the decision sequence consists of three steps: (1) The center an-nounces its strategy $\tilde{K} \in \mathcal{K}$; (2) the firm decides about $v_F \in V_F$; (3) the center makes its decision about $K = \tilde{K}(v_F)$, where $\mathcal{K}$ is a class of admissible strategies for the center.

Similarly to Case A, the center is the leader. However, the information structure of the game is different from that of game A, because now the leader is more powerful—the leader's strategy can be announced in advance and used to influence the follower's behavior. This information structure is often called "reversed" since the leader acts after the follower, although $\tilde{K}$ is announced first.

The strategy of the firm $\hat{v}_F : \mathcal{K} \to v_F$ is now defined differently from $\tilde{v}_F$, because the information available to the firm is not the same as in the structure A. Knowing the announced $\tilde{K}$, the enterprise determines its optimal strategy as a function of $\tilde{K}$:

$$\hat{v}_F^R(\tilde{K}) = \arg\max_{v_F \in V_F} G_F(\tilde{K}(v_F), v_F). \tag{8}$$

The problem faced by the center consists of designing an optimal strategy to be announced:

$$\tilde{K}^* = \arg\max_{\tilde{K} \in \mathcal{K}} G_C(\tilde{K}(v_F), v_F), \tag{9}$$

where

$$v_F = \hat{v}^R(\tilde{K}).$$

Thus the optimal decisions of the parties will be the following:

$$v_F^* = \hat{v}_F^R(\tilde{K}^*),$$
$$K^* = \tilde{K}^*(v_F^*). \tag{10}$$

Coalition Structure

This structure differs considerably from the previously outlined hierarchical structures. Now the center becomes a shareholder of the firm, and in this way, using its ownership rights, influences the firm's policy. G_F and G_C denote, as previously, subjective goals. However, in the present case both parties are shareholders of the enterprise at the same time and, therefore, they are both interested in maximizing the dividends that they receive. The share of the profit of the firm paid as dividend is $\beta\pi(v)$, where $\beta \in [0,1]$, and dividends are paid in proportion to the invested capitals of the two partners, i.e., K_C and K_F.

Decisions about the vector v are now made jointly by both parties. Depending on whether the capitals K_C and K_F are also the subjects of negotiation, we can distinguish two cases: Case A, when K_C and K_F are subject to negotiation, and Case B, when the capital shares K_C and K_F are not subject to negotiation. We shall, in turn, outline these cases.

Case A. Let us denote the maximal capital a partner considers possible to invest in the firm under consideration by $\overline{K}_C$ and $\overline{K}_F$ respectively. The part of the capital not invested in the firm, i.e., $\overline{K}_i - K_i$, $i \in \{C, F\}$, can be invested in alternative undertakings and yields a profit rate λ, $\lambda \in [0,1]$. Then the partners' goals consist of both the primary goals G_C and G_F, and the goals bound up with the profits yielded by invested capitals. We shall approximate the combined objectives as a linear combination

$$\hat{G}_i(K_C, K_F, v_F) = \alpha_{i1} G_i(K_C + K_F, v_F)$$
$$+ \alpha_{i2}\left[\frac{K_i}{K_C + K_F}\beta\pi(K_C + K_F, v_F) + \lambda(\overline{K}_i - K_i)\right]$$
$$i \in \{C, F\} \tag{11}$$

where $K_i \in [0, \overline{K}_i]$, $v_i \in V_F$, $\beta \in [0,1]$, $\alpha_{i1}, \alpha_{i2} \geq 0$. If we denote the set of admissible decisions by $\overline{D} = [0, \overline{K}_C] \times [0, \overline{K}_F] \times V_F$, the set of feasible outcomes will be the following:

$$\hat{S} = \{(g_C, g_F) : g_C = \hat{G}_C(K_C, K_F, v_F), \ g_F = \hat{G}_F(K_C, K_F, v_F),$$
$$(K_C, K_F, v_F) \in \overline{D}\}. \tag{12}$$

The partners C and F face the problem of choosing a pair $(g_C, g_F) \in \hat{S}$ (together with the associated decisions (K_C, K_F, v_F)). Since now the enterprise is a coalition of two partners, it seems natural that the above-mentioned choice is made by them jointly, and results from a bargaining process. In other words, we have a bargaining game $(\hat{S}, (g_C^0, g_F^0))$, where $\hat{S}$ is a feasible set (12) and (g_C^0, g_F^0) is the so-called status quo (or disagreement) point. There are various solutions to bargaining games (Roth, 1979). In general, denoting a chosen solution concept by Ψ, we have

$$(g_C^*, g_F^*) = \Psi(\hat{S}, (g_C^0, g_F^0)) \tag{13}$$

which also determines the negotiated decisions (K_C^*, K_F^*, v_F^*). For instance, if the popular Nash concept (Nash, 1950) is applied, we would have

$$(K_C^*, K_F^*, v_F^*) =$$
$$\arg\max_{(K_C, K_F, v_F) \in \overline{D}} \left\{ [G_C(K_C, K_F, v_F) - g_C^0][G_F(K_C, K_F, v_F) - g_F^0] \right\}. \tag{14}$$

The disagreement point employed in (13) is determined by the case in which each partner is forced to act independently, as the only owner of the firm:

$$\begin{aligned} g_C^0 &= \max_{(K_C, v_F) \in D_C} \hat{G}_C(K_C, 0, v_F) \\ g_F^0 &= \max_{(K_F, v_F) \in D_F} \hat{G}_F(0, K_F, v_F) \end{aligned} \tag{15}$$

where $D_C = [0, \overline{K}_C] \times V_F$, $D_F = [0, \overline{K}_F] \times V_F$. Note that the status quo (15) depends heavily on financial constraints $\overline{K}_C$ and $\overline{K}_F$.

We would like to point out one more aspect. The bargaining solution (K_C^*, K_F^*, v_F^*) yields an outcome (g_C^*, g_F^*) which is Pareto optimal in $\hat{S}$. Since the triple (K_C^*, K_F^*, v_F^*) is chosen jointly in order to yield a group-rational solution, then a lowering of K_i^*, for instance, could be compensated by a suitable change of v_F^*. In other words, the final negotiated capitals K_C^* and K_F^* do not reflect merely the "financial power" of the partners. This is bound up with the complementarity of concessions about K_i and the components of the vector v_F during negotiations.

Case B. Case A referred to situations in which new investment was needed, and then the partners negotiated their capital contributions. Let us now consider a situation in which there is no such need and, hence, the parties have fixed numbers of shares, denoted by M_C and M_F. As previously, they are interested in maximizing their dividends as well as in maximizing their primary goals G_C and G_F. Joining these two objectives in a linear combination, we obtain the parties' goals functions

$$G_i^s(v) = \alpha_{i1}G_i(v) + \alpha_{i2}\frac{M_i}{M}\beta\pi(v), \qquad (16)$$

where $\beta \in [0,1]$ and $M = M_C + M_F$. The set of feasible outcomes is

$$S = \left\{(g_C, g_F) : g_C = G_C^s(v), \ g_F = G_F^s(v), \ v \in V\right\}.$$

As previously, the partners are faced with a bargaining problem. As a status quo we now take the point $(g_C^0, g_F^0) = (0,0)$. To solve the bargaining problem, a non-symmetric Nash solution (Roth, 1979) can be used:

$$(g_C^*, g_F^*) = \arg\max_{(g_C, g_F) \in S} (g_C - g_C^0)^{\nu_C}(g_F - g_F^0)^{\nu_F} \qquad (17)$$

where the coefficients

$$\nu_C = \frac{M_C}{M}, \qquad \nu_F = \frac{M_F}{M} \qquad (18)$$

reflect the non-symmetry between parties, which follows from the different numbers of shares they own.

The following aspect seems worth mentioning. In the above considerations we have distinguished two parties: the center C and the firm F. As a matter of fact, F represents here the managers as well as the employees of the firm. Their primary goals are, however, different. Employees are interested in maximizing their incomes, while managers want to increase profits, sales, their own prestige, etc. In other words, there is a conflict of interests between these two groups, and thus the firm's goal function should result from a compromise achieved in the labor-management game (Stefanski, 1985; Spinnewyn and Svejnar, 1989).

3. Illustrative Models

In order to illustrate some of the problems that arise when we consider the above-outlined decision structures, we shall consider a very simple model. Let us assume that the inverse demand function is linear, $P(q) = d_0 - d_1 q$, $d_0 > 0$, $d_1 \geq 0$, the production function is of the Cobb-Douglass type, $f(L, K) = b_0 L^{b_1} K^{b_2}$, $b_0, b_1, b_2 > 0$, and profit is computed as revenue minus the costs of capital and labor, $\pi(v) = pq - rK - wL$. Recall that v is the decision vector $v = (L, K, w, q, p)$.

Consider two types of enterprise: a managerial firm which maximizes profits

$$G_F^1(v) = \pi(v), \tag{19}$$

and a labor-managed firm which maximizes the average income of workers

$$G_F^2(v) = \frac{\beta\pi(v)}{L} + w, \tag{20}$$

where β, $\beta \in [0,1]$, determines the part of profit paid as bonuses to employees. Concerning the center, we assume that it wants to maximize an expression which reflects production efficiency in some manner; e.g.,

$$G_C(v) = \frac{q}{(L + a_L)(K + a_K)}, \tag{21}$$

where $a_K, a_L > 0$.

Note that

$$\arg\max_{q\in[0,f(L,K)]} G_F^1(v) = \arg\max_{q\in[0,f(L,K)]} G_F^2(v)$$
$$= \arg\max_{q\in[0,f(L,K)]} G_C(v) = f(L,K),$$

which means that for each party it is optimal to use the whole production capacity. We can then put $q = f(L,K)$. In a similar way we obtain $p = P(q)$. Note also that $\arg\max_{w\in[\underline{w},\overline{w}]} G_F^1(v) = \underline{w}$, $\arg\max_{w\in[\underline{w},\overline{w}]} G_F^2(v) = \overline{w}$. Thus, instead of v, we need consider only two of its components, namely L and K.

Let us consider the center and a managerial firm and take the value of capital which each of them prefers. This is illustrated in Figure 1 which shows a family of parametric curves, with K as a parameter, for different values of L. It appears that for smaller values of L (curve 1), the center prefers a higher value of K than the firm—see points **A** and **B**. However, for larger L the preferences are reversed—see points **C** and **D** on curve 4. Note also that for certain values of L the parametric curves intersect; e.g., curve 2 at point **E** which means that the same pair of outcomes can be yielded by two different pairs of decisions.

Hierarchical structures A and B described in Section 2 are similar, but there is one important difference—the roles of the partners are reversed. The following question can arise: is it always the case that it is better for a party to be a leader than a follower? It appears that this is not always true. Figure 2 illustrates the case when it is more advantageous for the firm to be a follower (at point **A**) than the leader (point **B**). On the other hand,

Figure 1: Parametric Curves for Different *L*'s

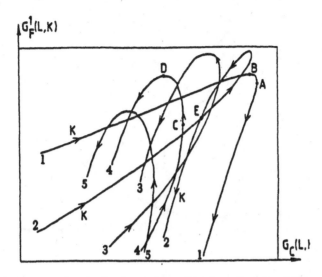

the center prefers to be the leader (point **A** rather than the follower (point **B**). In other words, in this particular case the preferences of both parties coincide—they both prefer the solution at point **A**, that is structure of type **A**.

However, in general there are four possibilities: (1) Both parties want to be the leader; (2) *C* wants to be the leader and *F* the follower; (3) the

Figure 2: The Case when Followership Is Preferable

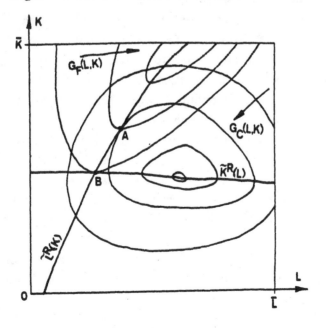

Figure 3: Inducible Regions $\Phi(\mathcal{K}_1)$ and $\Phi(\mathcal{K}_2)$

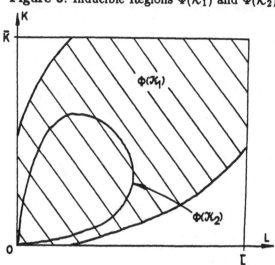

reverse, in that C wants to be the follower and F the leader; (4) both want to be followers. In the second case both parties prefer decision structure A, and in the third case they both prefer structure B. In cases (1) and (4), however, their preferences are different.

The above-mentioned question is worth considering because in a situation in which C and F do not for the same structure, an additional game can be played in the economic system. This game involves who will be the leader and who the follower.

Decision structure C described in Section 2 gives much more freedom to the leader but, at the same time, his optimization problem becomes more difficult. The difficulty follows from the fact that he must now choose his strategy in the form of a function. In order to facilitate the process of determining the leader's optimal strategy, the concept of an inducible region can be used (Chang and Luh, 1984).

The power that the leader has in structure C depends heavily on the class $\mathcal{K}$ of his admissible strategies. In real life, however, there always exist some limitations concerning the strategies that can be applied, and hence it is interesting to look at the ways in which $\mathcal{K}$ influences the final solution of the game. This can best be illustrated by using the concept of an inducible region Φ.

The idea of applying Φ is the following: instead of looking for the optimal leader's strategy in a strategy space, we delineate in decision space a region of inducible solutions, and then use this region to find optimal decisions. After that it is relatively easy to find an appropriate strategy which generates these decisions.

For example, the definition of an inducible region as a function of the class $\mathcal{K}$ is the following in our case:

$$\Phi(\mathcal{K}) = \{(L, K) \in D \mid \exists \tilde{K} \in \mathcal{K} : L = \hat{L}^R(\tilde{K}), K = \tilde{K}(L)\} \qquad (22)$$

where D is the set of admissible decision pairs (L, K), and $\hat{L}^R$ describes the firm's best reaction to the announced strategy of the center computed according to (8).

Assume for a moment that there are no constraints on the form of the strategy $\tilde{K}$ that the leader can announce. Denote such a class by $\mathcal{K}_1$, i.e., $\mathcal{K}_1$ consists of all functions $[0, \overline{L}] \rightarrow [0, \overline{K}]$. Denote the pair of decisions best for the leader by (L^C, K^C):

$$(L^C, K^C) = \arg\max_{(L,K) \in D} G_C(L, K). \qquad (23)$$

Now the best thing the leader can do is to announce the following strategy:

$$\tilde{K}(L) = \begin{cases} K^C, & \text{if } L = L^C; \\ h(L), & \text{if } L \neq L^C. \end{cases} \qquad (24)$$

where h is a strategy which penalizes the firm most:

$$h(L) = \arg\min_{K \in [0, \overline{K}]} G_F(L, K). \qquad (25)$$

The firm can, however, always secure itself the value

$$\overline{g}_F = \max_L G_F(L, h(L)). \qquad (26)$$

This means that the leader can induce decisions only from the following set:

$$\Phi(\mathcal{K}_1) = \{(L, K) \in D \mid G_F(L, K) > \overline{g}_F\}. \qquad (27)$$

In this case the inducible region is the largest possible. Note that the strategy (24) need not be continuous. In practice, it is doubtful whether such a strategy could be employed.

Consider now a class of the leader's strategies which are very simple in form, namely linear:

$$\tilde{K}(L) = \mu L, \qquad (28)$$

where $\mu = tg(m)$, $m \in [0^\circ, M]$, $M < 90^\circ$. Denote such a class of strategies by $\mathcal{K}_2$. After computing $\Phi(\mathcal{K}_2)$, it appears that in this case the inducible region is a curve in the (L, K) plane.

The forms of $\Phi(\mathcal{K}_2)$ as well as of $\Phi(\mathcal{K}_1)$ are shown in Figure 3. It appears that only in the case when $(L^C, K^C) \in \Phi(\mathcal{K}_2)$ would the leader not be disappointed because of the narrowing of his class of admissible strategies. On the other hand, if $(L^C, K^C) \in \Phi(\mathcal{K}_1)$, then it depends on particular values of the parameters of the model whether the firm would prefer class $\mathcal{K}_1$ or $\mathcal{K}_2$.

We shall briefly mention only one more aspect. Consider the credibility of the leader's announcements in decision structure C. Note that the sequence of decisions in this case is such that the leader implements his strategy after the follower's action. Then there is a question of whether the leader will be tempted to apply a strategy that is different from the one previously declared. In general, we can distinguish two cases (Luh, Zheng and Ho, 1984)—whether the leader has the above-mentioned temptation when

(1) the follower behaves rationally, i.e., according to $\hat{v}_F^R$ given by (8);
(2) the follower for some reason deviates from $\hat{v}_F^R(\tilde{K})$.

We can say that a leader's strategy is *fully* credible if he does not want to deviate from his declared strategy in either case. It appears that to satisfy the second case, this strategy must be equivalent to (5), which is a very restrictive condition. As to the first case: if $(L^C, K^C) \in \Phi(\mathcal{K})$ or $K^* = \tilde{K}^R(L^*)$, then the leader will stick to his strategy, otherwise the answer depends on the shape of $\Phi(\mathcal{K})$ in relation to the isoquants of G_C. For the class $\mathcal{K}_2$ of linear strategies, for instance, the center would be tempted to make a decision which does not coincide with the declared $\tilde{K}$.

4. Concluding Remarks

We discussed a group of models focusing on the relations between a firm and the center (a governmental agency). The study of these relations was indirectly motivated by the weakness of administrative control in centrally planned economies. We have concentrated on strategic aspects and emphasized the conflict of interests between the firm and the center. The consequences of this conflict manifest themselves in different ways, depending on the particular decision structure through which the two parties are associated.

Only some of the problems that can be studied with the help of the proposed models are mentioned, and many worthy of analysis are not. For instance, the problem of the credibility of strategies declared by the center has one more aspect of great practical importance. Assume that the center-firm game is repeated many times, which would bring the model closer to reality. In such a situation, if the center bluffs, i.e., does not make decisions according to the previously declared strategy (having in mind short-run benefits), then it destroys its reputation for the future, which might be harmful to both parties.

On the other hand, fully credible and at the same time optimal strategies very seldom exist. What should the center do in such cases? In general, one can imagine two approaches: one which consists of finding some kind of compromise between credibility and optimality, and second, one which consists of emphasizing optimality at the sacrifice of credibility, or vice-versa.

References

Basar, V. T. and Oldser, G. J. (1982) *Dynamic Coperative Game Theory*, London: Academic Press.

Burkov V. N. and Shchepkin, A. N. (1984) "The Theory of Organizational Management and Business Games in the USSR," *Large Scale Systems*, **7**, 207-219.

Chang, T. S. and Luh, P. B. (1984) "Derivation of Necessary and Sufficient Conditions for Single-stage Stackelberg Games Via the Inducible Region Concept," *IEEE Transactions on Automatic Control*, **AC-29**, 63-66.

Goldfeld, S. M. and Quandt, R. E. (1990) "Output Targets, Input Rationing and Inventories," this volume.

Hlaváček, J. (1990) "Producer's Citeria in a Centrally Planned Economy," this volume.

Luh, P. B., Zheng, Y. P. and Ho, Y. C. (1984) "Credibility in Stackelberg Games," *Systems and Control Letters*, **5**, 165-168.

Madzar, L (1987) "Self-management System and the Mixed Economy," *Ekonomiski Pregled*, 215-230.

Meade, J. E. (1972) "The Theory of Labour-Managed Firms and of Profit-Sharing," *Economic Journal*, 402-428.

Nash, J. (1950) "The Bargaining Problem," *Econometrica*, **18**, 155-162.

Roth, A. E. (1979) *Axiomatic Models of Bargaining*, Springer-Verlag.

Stefanski, J. (1985) "A Game Theory Model of Labor-Management Conflict and Compromise," in *Economic Psychology*, edited by H. Brandstaetter and E. Kirchler, Linz: Trauner Verlag.

Spinnewyn, F. and Svejnar, J. (1990) "On the Dynamics of a Participatory Firm: A Model of Employer-Worker Bargaining," this volume.

6

Output Targets, Input Rationing
and Inventories ·

Stephen M. Goldfeld and *Richard E. Quandt*

1. Introduction

The enterprise or firm in a socialist planned economy may frequently
find itself constrained in two ways: on the one hand, it is obligated to produce an output level that is as close as possible to a target level Q^* and, on
the other hand, it may find that it cannot obtain all the inputs it desires for
production. Since inputs are not necessarily rationed at all times, the firm
may wish to purchase inputs earlier than would be necessary in the absence
of rationing, if at the earlier time they are available with no restrictions.
Kornai (1979, 1980, 1985) has argued that such anticipatory purchases ex-
acerbate conditions of shortage, since even in periods in which the supply of
inputs would otherwise be plentiful, firms will make anticipatory purchases
and eliminate the potential surplus of the input commodity in question.

It is particularly relevant to examine what happens to this mechanism
if the quality of inputs is variable. It is variously noted (Kornai, 1980, p.
37; 1982, p. 29) that chronic shortage leads to a deterioration of output
quality, since the shortage causes potential buyers to accept any goods.
Substandard input quality may act as if it were another form of rationing,
which may then further intensify anticipatory purchases. Hence, the logic

---

* We are indebted to the National Science Foundation and the National Council for
East European and Soviet Research for support.

of central planning suggests the existence of a self-reinforcing mechanism that exacerbates shortages.

In Section 2 we outline a model to analyze these questions and in Section 3 we perform some numerical experiments. Section 4 deals with some extensions of the analysis. Section 5 contains brief conclusions.

2. A Theoretical Model

The actions of the manager in our model take place on two discrete dates, namely, at time 0 and time 1. Production occurs at time 1 instantaneously with whatever inputs are at hand. The central planning authority gives the manager a target output level Q^* and the enterprise has a strictly concave production function $Q = f(y)$ with a single input y; his target level of inputs is y^*, given by $Q^* = f(y^*)$. He is penalized for producing an output level less than Q^* and we assume that the penalty is quadratic in the deviation from Q^*.[1] With the exception of one case in Section 4, the manager has no incentive to produce more than Q^* in our setup, which will lead to a one-sided loss function. The manager can order the input y on any of the two dates. There is no limitation on the amount that he can receive on date 0 and the amount of the input received on that date is y_0. However, there is a carrying charge or inventory cost of c_1 per unit of input obtained at time 0. He may also order an amount y_1 on date 1; however, rationing may be in effect on that date and the amount he receives is a random variable.

The Basic Case

We assume that the amount of the input that he receives on date 1 is a random variable x, with pdf $h(x)$, and is uninfluenced by his desire for a quantity y_1. It is convenient to assume that $h(x)$ has support $(0, \infty)$. The total input that will be available is

$$y^* = y_0 + y_1 \quad \text{if} \quad y_1 \leqq x$$
$$y_0 + x \quad \text{if} \quad y_1 > x.$$

It follows immediately that the expected cost function is

---

[1] On managerial incentives, see Davis and Charemza (1989).

$$E(C) = c_1 y_0 + \int_0^{y^* - y_0} c_2 \left[f(x + y_0) - Q^* \right]^2 h(x) dx, \qquad (1)$$

where the first term is the inventory cost and the second term is the penalty for missing the target. The objective of the manager is to minimize (1) with respect to y_0.[2] It should be noted that neither the revenues received from the sale of output, nor the cost of the inputs appears in the objective function. We are implicitly assuming that input and output prices are set administratively and that any discrepancy between revenues and costs is eliminated by taxes or subsidies.[3] The first order condition is

$$\frac{dE(C)}{dy_0} = \int_0^{y^* - y_0} 2c_2 \left[f(x + y_0) - Q^* \right] f'(x + y_0) h(x) dx$$
$$- c_2 \left[f(y^*) - Q^* \right]^2 h(y^* - y_0) + c_1 = 0, \qquad (2)$$

where the second term is obviously zero; the second order condition is

$$\frac{d^2 E(C)}{dy_0^2} =$$
$$2c_2 \int_0^{y^* - y_0} \left[f'(x + y_0)^2 + \left(f(x + y_0) - Q^* \right) f''(x + y_0) \right] h(x) dx. \qquad (3)$$

Proposition 1. *The second order condition for a minimum is always satisfied.*

Proof. By the definitions of y^* and Q^*, $f(x + y_0) \leqq Q^*$. The result then follows from the concavity of the production function. ∎

Clearly, optimization of $E(C)$ is subject to the constraint $y_0 \geqq 0$ and, if the unconstrained solution of (2) yields a negative y_0, then the constrained, economically meaningful solution is $y_0 = 0$. (Since $E(C)$ is strictly convex, we need not search for another interior solution.)

---

[2] This is the only variable he needs to choose, since Q^* and, hence, y^* are given and he would never order an amount y_1 greater than $y^* - y_0$.

[3] This, in itself, creates a novel incentive structure with which we shall not deal here. See Goldfeld and Quandt (1988).

The Case of Defective Inputs

We now consider a model that is similar to the basic case in all respects except the realistic modification that only a fraction ϵ of inputs ordered is of standard (good) quality, so that a fraction $1 - \epsilon$ is defective and, thus, unusable.[4] For simplicity, we assume that the same value of ϵ applies to both y_0 and y_1; this is tantamount to assuming that at time 0, the manager has to decide on y_0 on the basis of the knowledge he has about ϵ and in the belief that this knowledge is also applicable to y_1.

At time 0 the manager acquires y_0 units of the input of which ϵy_0 units are usable. He will then need $y^* - \epsilon y_0$ good units at time 1 and, hence, he has to order $(y^* - \epsilon y_0)/\epsilon$ units to be assured of an adequate supply of good ones. In fact, he receives an amount which is the min $(x, (y^* - \epsilon y_0)/\epsilon)$. It follows that the expected cost function is

$$E(C|\epsilon) = c_1 \epsilon y_0 + \int_0^{y^*/\epsilon - y_0} c_2 \left[f\left(\epsilon(x + y_0) \right) - Q^* \right]^2 h(x) dx. \qquad (4)$$

If ϵ is itself a random variable on $(0, 1)$ with pdf $g(\epsilon)$, the expected cost function to be minimized is

$$E(C) = \int_0^1 E(C|\epsilon) g(\epsilon) d\epsilon. \qquad (5)$$

The mechanism we envisage here is therefore the following. The manager knows that ϵ is a random variable with pdf $g(\epsilon)$, but he also knows that ϵ is not resampled every time he orders; rather, it is characteristic of the supplier of inputs he uses. Thus, whatever ϵ is drawn when he receives y_0, it is the same ϵ that characterizes the order at time 1.[5]

A somewhat simpler version of (5) is obtained if we assume that ϵ can attain only two values: 1.0, in which case all units of inputs are good, and $\epsilon_0 < 1$, where these two outcomes occur with probabilities p and $1 - p$, respectively. The expected cost then is

$$E(C) = pE(C|1) + (1 - p) E(C|\epsilon_0). \qquad (6)$$

---

[4] We assume that any defective inputs can be disposed of without cost so that they do not need to be inventoried.

[5] This assumption is relaxed in Section 4.

As before, there is no guarantee that the optimal solution to y_0 is positive. Also, the comparative statics results of interest are difficult to derive and we investigate these questions in more detail in Section 3.

An Example

For the rest of this section we consider a simplified example in order to illustrate the solution and to analyze the comparative statics of the model. In this example we assume that the production function is $f(y) = y$ and that $h(x) = \beta e^{-\beta x}$, the exponential density.[6] At first we assume that there are no defective inputs. We equate the first derivative of $E(C)$ to zero, which yields

$$y^* - y_0 + \frac{1}{\beta}\left[e^{-\beta(y^*-y_0)} - 1\right] = \frac{c_1}{2c_2}. \tag{7}$$

The left-hand side is zero at $y_0 = y^*$, is arbitrarily large when y_0 tends to $-\infty$ and has negative slope for all $y_0 < y^*$; the right-hand side is a constant. Hence, a unique solution exists. Moreover, this solution will be positive, if at $y_0 = 0$, the left-hand side exceeds the right. That will be the case if and only if $y^* + (\exp(-\beta y^*) - 1)/\beta > c_1/2c_2$.

The interpretation of this condition is straightforward. A positive optimal y_0 is likely to exist, if the inventory cost is small relative to the penalty of underproducing. Since this is likely to be the case in a centrally planned economy, it is plausible that the expectation of rationing actually induces anticipatory input purchases. The condition is likely to fail when β is very small. (It is easy to verify that the limit of the left-hand side of the condition as $\beta \to 0$ is zero.) The reason for this is that as $\beta \to 0$ the probability that rationing will occur itself goes to zero and, hence, positive anticipatory purchases make no sense.

Assume now that the condition for a unique positive solution holds. Then we have the following comparative statics results: $\partial y_0/\partial y^* = 1$, $\partial y_0/\partial \beta > 0$, $\partial y_0/\partial c_1 < 0$, $\partial y_0/\partial c_2 > 0$. To see these results we take the total differential of the first order condition, obtaining

---

[6] This form of rationing is chosen for computational convenience and is not intended to be realistic.

$$\left[1 - e^{-\beta(y^* - y_0)}\right] dy^* - \left[1 - e^{-\beta(y^* - y_0)}\right] dy_0 + \tag{8}$$

$$\left[-\frac{1}{\beta^2}\left(e^{-\beta(y^* - y_0)} - 1\right) + \frac{1}{\beta}e^{-\beta(y^* - y_0)}(y_0 - y^*)\right] d\beta = \frac{1}{2c_2} dc_1 - \frac{c_1}{2c_2^2} dc_2.$$

The results for $\partial y_0 / \partial y^*$, $\partial y_0 / \partial c_1$, $\partial y_0 / \partial c_2$ follow trivially and are obviously sensible. To get the result for $\partial y_0 / \partial \beta$ note that the coefficient of $d\beta$ in (8) is positive, if $e^{\beta(y^* - y_0)} > 1 + \beta(y^* - y_0)$, which it obviously is from the Taylor series expansion of $e^{\beta(y^* - y_0)}$. A large value of β implies that large input allocations are improbable; hence, all the results are clearly reasonable.

The same example can be analyzed in the case of defective inputs. In particular, if we restrict attention to the two-point distribution used in (6), the relevant first order condition, analogous to (7), is given by

$$p \left[(y^* - y_0) + \frac{1}{\beta}\left(e^{-\beta(y^* - y_0)} - 1\right)\right] + \tag{9}$$

$$(1-p)\left[\epsilon_0^2 \left(\frac{y^*}{\epsilon_0} - y_0 + \frac{1}{\beta}\left(e^{-\beta(y^*/\epsilon_0 - y_0)} - 1\right)\right)\right] = \frac{c_1}{2c_2}\left[p + (1 - p)\epsilon_0\right].$$

As in the case of (7), there is a set of restrictions on the parameters (including p and ϵ_0) which assures that (9) yields a unique positive solution for y_0. Some further restrictions will assure that the optimal y_0 is less than y^*. In this range, total differentiation of (9) yields the following comparative statics results: $\partial y_0 / \partial y^* > 1$, $\partial y_0 / \partial \beta > 0$, $\partial y_0 / \partial c_1 < 0$ and $\partial y_0 / \partial c_2 > 0$. With the exception of the first of these the results are identical to those in the no-defective case. More general comparative statics results are difficult to obtain analytically, even in this simple example. Consequently, in the next section, when we consider a more realistic example, we shall analyze the behavior of the optimal y_0 by numerical methods.

3. The Defective-Input Case Explored Further

In the present section we shall compute the optimal y_0 level for the defective-input model with expected cost function (6) under various assumptions.[7] The production function is taken to be

$$Q = y^\alpha \tag{10}$$

---

[7] Numerical optimization employed the GRADX algorithm of the GQOPT package.

Table 1. Base Case Parameter Values

$$c_1 = 1.0$$
$$c_2 = 0.1$$
$$Q^* = 100.0$$
$$\epsilon_0 = 0.7$$
$$p = 0.9$$
$$\alpha = 0.8$$
$$\mu = 200.0$$
$$\sigma^2 = 50.0$$

and the distribution of x is truncated normal, so that

$$h(x) = \frac{1}{\sqrt{2\pi}\sigma} \exp\left\{-(x-\mu)^2/2\sigma^2\right\} / \operatorname{Prob}\{x \geq 0\}. \tag{11}$$

The parameters that can be varied are c_1, c_2, Q^*, ϵ_0, p, α, μ and σ^2. We vary the parameters one at a time, holding all others at their "base case" values, which are given in Table 1. It should be noted that μ and σ^2 refer to the parameters of the normal density, which gets truncated; the mean and variance of the truncated density are 219.95 and 45.85, respectively. At the base case values the optimal $y_0 = 55.2$. The total expected cost is 106.467.

Table 2 displays the optimal y_0 levels for sundry variations of the parameters; these are kept at their base values, except the parameter named at the top of each column, which varies in equal increments as we move down that column from the lowest to the highest value shown in parentheses. For this reason one particular row in each column reproduces the base case; this occurs in row six of each column, except column 3, where it occurs in the last row.

The comparative statics behavior of y_0 is qualitatively as expected. An increase in Q^* increases the anticipatory buying of y_0. In fact, for $Q^* = 75, 80$, no y_0 is necessary. For higher values of Q^* the quantity of good inputs needed rises absolutely and in percentage terms (for $\alpha = 0.8$, $y^* = 316.23$ when $Q^* = 100$, and $y^* = 397.17$ when $Q^* = 120$, resulting in a

74   *Goldfeld and Quandt*

Table 2. Effect on y_0 of Parameter Variations

Q^* (75.0–120.0)	ϵ_0 (0.45–0.90)	p (0.45–0.90)	α (0.75–0.84)	c_1 (0.75–1.20)	μ (150.0–240.0)	σ^2 (25.0–70.0)
0	57.64	94.20	128.64	74.91	104.93	50.16
0	57.59	88.81	112.10	70.74	95.07	51.00
2.51	57.22	83.71	94.47	66.70	85.15	51.77
19.96	56.66	78.91	78.99	62.78	75.20	52.69
37.58	56.00	74.37	66.27	58.96	65.22	53.84
55.24	55.24	70.10	55.24	55.24	55.24	55.24
73.28	54.37	66.06	44.81	51.59	45.24	56.86
92.25	53.40	62.25	34.36	48.02	35.24	58.66
111.82	52.36	58.65	23.66	44.52	25.25	60.59
130.26	51.25	55.24	12.86	41.09	15.25	62.56

near doubling of inputs bought early as a percentage of the good inputs needed). The increase in ϵ_0 and in p both increase the expected fraction of good inputs, and the effect of increasing either results in a decline in the quantity of y_0.

The joint effect on y_0 of variations in p and ϵ_0 can perhaps best be seen by computing for each p and ϵ_0 combination the expected fraction m of good inputs $(m = p + (1 - p)\epsilon_0)$ and the standard deviation of the fraction of good inputs $s = (1 - \epsilon_0)[p(1 - p)]^{1/2}$ and computing a response surface by regressing y_0 on m and s. This yields the regression equation

$$y_0 = 361.159 - 310.614m - 57.076s$$
$$(103.364)\ (-92.450)\ (-14.080)$$

where t values are in parentheses and $R^2 = 0.9987$. An increase in both the mean and the standard deviation significantly reduces y_0.

The effect of increasing α is to diminish y_0. Clearly, the larger α is, the smaller is the y^* needed to produce Q^* and, hence, the smaller y_0 will be. As α increases, not only does y_0 decrease, but it also decreases as a fraction of y^* (from $0.27 = 128.64/464.16$ to $0.053 = 12.86/240.41$). An increase in c_1 relative to c_2 makes carrying inventories more expensive and reduces y_0. The (arc) elasticity of y_0 with respect to c_1 is increasing as y_0

falls, namely from 0.89 to 1.96. Finally, as μ increases or as σ^2 declines, y_0 falls. This is to be expected, since both changes have the effect of reducing the probability that the manager will be rationed at all. Here again, we can employ the response surface methodology. We regress y_0 on the true mean and variance of the truncated normal, which are implied by μ and σ^2. Denoting these by μ_t and σ_t^2, respectively, we have

$$y_0 = 241.020 - 0.995\mu_t + 0.729\sigma_t^2$$
$$(153.191) \; (-140.618) \; (46.466)$$

with an $R^2 = 0.9991$, which clearly tells the same story.

While these examples are only illustrative, it is noteworthy that the effects are quite pronounced and that very substantial anticipatory buying occurs, if either the probability of rationing is high or the expected number of defective inputs is high. The qualitative results are not contingent on the assumption of truncated normality, because similar results are obtained if the Weibull distribution is employed.

4. Extensions

We consider three modifications of the models discussed earlier.

Production Uncertainty

It is plausible to argue that the outcome of the production process is not known with certainty by the manager (Goldfeld and Quandt (1988)). The production function is then written as

$$Q = f(y)e^u, \tag{12}$$

where u is a random variable and where, in the first instance, it is reasonable to assume that $u \sim N(0, \omega^2)$. Denoting the normal density by $n(0, \omega^2)$, we then replace (4) by

$$E(C|\epsilon, u) = c_1 \epsilon y_0 + \int_0^{y^*/\epsilon - y_0} c_2 \left[f(\epsilon(x + y_0))e^u - Q^* \right]^2 h(x) \, dx, \tag{13}$$

and $E(C|\epsilon)$ becomes

$$E(C|\epsilon) = c_1\epsilon y_0 + \int_{-\infty}^{\infty}\int_0^{y^*/\epsilon-y_0} c_2\Big[f\big(\epsilon(x+y_0)\big)e^u$$

$$- Q^*\Big]^2 h(x)n(0,\omega^2)dxdu \qquad (14)$$

$$= c_1\epsilon y_0 + \int_0^{y^*/\epsilon-y_0} c_2\Big[f\big(\epsilon(x+y_0)\big)e^{2\omega^2} + Q^{*2}$$

$$- 2f\big(\epsilon(x+y_0)\big)Q^*e^{\omega^2/2}\Big]h(x)dx.$$

In order to choose plausible values for ω^2 we assume that $f(\ )e^u$ differs from $f(\ )$ 95 percent of the time by no more than 5 (or 10) percent. This leads to ω^2 values of 0.00065 and 0.0026, respectively. We repeat only the experiment in which Q^* varies, with the remaining parameters set to base case values. The values of y_0 are in Table 3.

Two interesting features emerge. The first one is that the sensitivity of y_0 to modest production uncertainty is slight in absolute terms; thus, for example, a production uncertainty that changes output by no more than 10 percent 95 percent of the time alters the base case y_0 from 55.24 to 54.96, i.e., less than 1/2 percent. The second feature is that the direction of the effect is not uniform: at relatively low levels of Q^*, production uncertainty

Table 3. Effect on y_0 of Q^* Variations

Q^*	$\omega^2 = 0$	$\omega^2 = 0.00065$	$\omega^2 = 0.0026$
75.0	0	0	0
80.0	0	0	0
85.0	2.51	2.34	1.81
90.0	19.96	19.80	19.30
95.0	37.58	37.45	37.05
100.0	55.24	55.17	54.96
105.0	73.28	73.30	73.34
110.0	92.25	92.35	92.66
115.0	111.82	111.98	112.44
120.0	130.26	130.41	130.87

reduces the optimal y_0, while at higher levels of Q^*, it increases y_0.

We suggest the following intuition for this phenomenon. At low Q^* levels the probability that the enterprise will be rationed is small, and over- or underproduction is not very costly (since stochastic deviation from $f(\epsilon(x + y_0))$ is multiplicative). Hence, it makes sense to save on inventory costs by reducing y_0, particularly because stochastic overproduction can (partially) compensate for input rationing. However, at high Q^* values, rationing is likelier and the penalty for underproduction increases, which suggests that y_0 ought to increase.

Independent Distributions of Defective Inputs

In the previous sections it was assumed that, once ϵ is drawn, it applies equally to time 0 and time 1. While this is not necessarily a bad assumption (the enterprise may deal repeatedly with the same supplier of inputs, who may not effect significant changes over the short run in his own production processes), it is clearly only one of several possible scenarios. A polar opposite to this assumption of perfect correlation between the defective rates on the two dates is complete independence.[8]

To implement this assumption we assume specifically that at time 0 the fraction of "good" inputs is 1.0 or ϵ_0 with probability p_0 and $1 - p_0$, respectively, and that at time 1 the corresponding magnitudes are ϵ_1 and p_1. A slight generalization of (6) yields for expected cost

$$
\begin{aligned}
E(C) = {} & p_0 p_1 \int_0^{y^*-y_0} c_2 \left[f(y_0 + x) - Q^* \right]^2 h(x) dx \\
& + p_0(1 - p_1) \int_0^{(y^*-y_0)/\epsilon_1} c_2 \left[f(y_0 + \epsilon_1 x) - Q^* \right]^2 h(x) dx \\
& + (1 - p_0)p_1 \int_0^{y^*-\epsilon_0 y_0} c_2 \left[f(\epsilon_0 y_0 + x) - Q^* \right]^2 h(x) dx \\
& + (1 - p_0)(1 - p_1) \int_0^{(y^*-\epsilon_0 y_0)/\epsilon_1} c_2 \left[f(\epsilon_0 y_0 + \epsilon_1 x) - Q^* \right]^2 h(x) dx \\
& + c_1 y_0 \left(p_0 + (1 - p_0)\epsilon_0 \right).
\end{aligned} \tag{15}
$$

We report only two experiments in which we minimize (15) for various Q^*

---

[8] An interesting possibility among "intermediate" scenarios is that the manager employs some prior density for ϵ at time 0 and employs for time 1 the posterior density based on the realization at time 0.

levels (see Table 4). In the first, $\epsilon_1 = 0.7$, $p_1 = 0.9$; the same values as we use for ϵ_0, p_0, respectively. This is the case in which uncertainty concerning defective inputs is heightened and, as one might expect, y_0 increases throughout as compared with Table 2. In the other case, $p_1 = 1.0$ and this case corresponds to no uncertainty about defective inputs at time 1. The obvious consequence, which can be seen from Tables 2 and 4, is that y_0 diminishes.

Manipulable Rationing

An alternative form of rationing takes place when the amount of the input received is influenced by the amount ordered by the firm. The simplest and most plausible way this can occur is if the manager receives xy_1, when y_1 is ordered at time 1 and x is a random variable distributed over the $(0,1)$ interval. In this case the penalty function must be symmetric, i.e., overproduction must also be penalized; otherwise the manager would have no incentive to order a finite amount. The expected cost function is

$$E(C) = \int_0^1 c_2[f(y_0 + xy_1) - Q^*]^2 h(x)dx + c_1 y_0. \tag{16}$$

The first order conditions for a minimum are

$$\frac{\partial E(C)}{\partial y_0} = 2c_2 \int_0^1 [f - Q^*] f' h(x)dx + c_1 = 0 \tag{17}$$

and

$$\frac{\partial E(C)}{\partial y_1} = 2c_2 \int_0^1 [f - Q^*] f' x h(x)dx = 0, \tag{18}$$

where f and f' have $y_0 + xy_1$ as their argument. Taking the total differential of (17) and (18) and solving for $\partial y_0/\partial c_1$ and $\partial y_0/\partial c_2$, we obtain

$$\frac{\partial y_0}{\partial c_1} = \frac{-\partial^2 E(C)/\partial y_1^2}{D} \tag{19}$$

$$\frac{\partial y_0}{\partial c_2} = \left\{ -2\int_0^1 [f - Q^*]f'h(x)dx\,(\partial^2 E(C)/\partial y_1^2) + 2\int_0^1 [f - Q^*]f'xh(x)dx\,(\partial^2 E(C)/\partial y_0 \partial y_1) \right\}\Big/ D, \tag{20}$$

Table 4. Effect on y_0 of ϵ_1, p_1

Q^*	$\epsilon_0 = 0.7 \quad \epsilon_1 = 0.7$ $p_0 = 0.9 \quad p_1 = 0.9$	$\epsilon_0 = 0.7 \quad \epsilon_1 = -$ $p_0 = 0.9 \quad p_1 = 1.0$
75.0	0	0
80.0	0	0
85.0	4.35	0
90.0	21.69	14.93
95.0	39.20	32.45
100.0	56.76	50.05
105.0	74.73	68.07
110.0	93.63	87.10
115.0	113.29	107.09
120.0	132.35	126.27

where D is the determinant of the Hessian matrix. If the second order conditions hold, then $\partial y_0 / \partial c_1 < 0$. Further, the second integral in the numerator of (20) is zero by (18) and the first integral is $-c_1/2c_2$ by (17). Hence, $\partial y_0 / \partial c_2 > 0$. None of the other comparative statics derivatives is given unambiguously and we again resort to a simplified example.

It is easy to show that on the same simplifying assumption as before, that the production function is linear and, on the further assumption that $h(x)$ is uniform; $E(C)$ is given by

$$E(C) = c_2(y_0 - Q^*)^2 + c_2 y_1 (y_0 - Q^*) + c_2 y_1^2/3 + c_1 y_0. \qquad (21)$$

The manager now has to decide on both y_0 and y_1. Setting the first partial derivatives of $E(C)$ equal to zero, we get

$$\begin{aligned} y_0 &= Q^* - 2c_1/c_2, \\ y_1 &= 3c_1/c_2. \end{aligned} \qquad (22)$$

This provides the solution if and only if $Q^* \geq 2c_1/c_2$; otherwise the optimal solution is obtained by setting $y_0 = 0$ and minimizing (21) with respect to y_1 alone, which yields $y_1 = 3Q^*/2$.[9] The qualitative result from (22) is

---

[9] It is obvious that the second order conditions hold.

that the optimal y_0 declines as c_1, the inventory cost, increases relative to c_2. The total expected input use, $y_0 + E(x)y_1$, equals $Q^* - c_1/2c_2$, while the total amount ordered, $y_0 + y_1$, equals $Q^* + c_1/c_2$, which exceeds y^*, the amount required to produce the target output level.

In the case of defective inputs we replace y_0 and y_1 in (21) by ϵy_0 and ϵy_1, respectively, and assume that ϵ is uniformly distributed on $(0,1)$. Equation (21) can then be shown to be

$$E(C) = c_2 \left[\frac{y_0^2}{3} + Q^{*2} - y_0 Q^* + \frac{y_0 y_1}{3} - \frac{y_1 Q^*}{2} + \frac{y_1^2}{9} \right] + \frac{c_1 y_0}{2}.$$

If we set the partial derivatives equal to zero, then $y_0 = 3Q^*/2 - 3c_1/c_2$, $y_1 = 9c_1/2c_2$. This is the solution if $Q^* \geq 2c_1/c_2$. The expected input use is $y_0 + E(x)y_1 = (3/2)(Q^* - c_1/2c_2)$, which is 50 percent greater than in the case with no defective inputs. This increase is less than the doubling that might be suggested by the mean defective rate of .5. This attenuation obviously stems from the symmetric quadratic penalties embodied in the objective function, (16).

5. Conclusions

We formulated several related models in which an input is subject to rationing and may be defective. We have considered both manipulable and nonmanipulable rationing and treated in some detail variations in three sources of uncertainty: the uncertainty of the rationing process, the uncertainty of the production process itself, and that pertaining to the fraction of inputs which turn out to be defective. Since the enterprise is able to purchase the input at an earlier time, we concentrated on the quantity y_0 of early purchases which, however, incur a carrying cost. While some analytic results are available, much of the comparative statics analysis was based on numerical computations with illustrative functions. In all cases the behavior of y_0 appeared sensible.

Some interesting questions remain for future research and we mention only four areas:

(1) To the extent that both Q^* and the rationing of the input are set by the central planning authority, it may be plausible to argue that the density of the input ration x should be explicitly conditional on Q^*; thus, $h(x)$ would have to be replaced everywhere by $h(x|Q^*)$.

(2) The analysis may be extended to two or more inputs, which would allow an examination of the dependence of y_0 on the elasticity of substitution between inputs.

(3) As mentioned earlier, the manager may perform a Bayesian update and employ for the density of the fraction of defectives at time 1 the appropriate posterior density.

(4) Finally, the model is limited due to its two-period nature. It would be desirable to provide a full dynamic formulation in which inputs can be stored for more distant periods in the future.

We hope to shed light on these questions in future work.

References

Davis, C. and Charemza, W. (1989) "Introduction to Models of Disequilibrium and Shortage in Centrally Planned Economies," in *Models of Disequilibrium and Shortage in Centrally Planned Economies* (ed. by C. Davis and W. Charemza), London: Chapman and Hall.

Goldfeld, S. M. and Quandt, R. E. (1988) "Budget Constraints, Bailouts and the Firm Under Central Planning," *Journal of Comparative Economics* **12**, 502-520.

Kornai, J. (1979) "Resource-Constrained Versus Demand-Constrained," *Econometrica* **47**, 801-820.

―――― (1980) *The Economics of Shortage*, Amsterdam: North-Holland.

―――― (1982) *Growth, Shortage and Efficiency*, Oxford: Blackwell.

Quandt, R. E. (1986) "Enterprise Purchases and the Expectation of Rationing," *Economics Letters* **21**, 13-15.

7

Behavior of the Socialist Firm Under Indirect Control *

István Ábel and *John P. Bonin*

1. Introduction

The major problems of firm behavior in socialist planned economies are generally well known. There are several sources of inefficiency and this variety is reflected in the diverse approaches employed in the micro-models of this type of firm. Goldfeld and Quandt (1988, 1990), following Kornai (1980), focus on the so-called *soft budget constraint* phenomenon. They analyze a competitive firm with bailout-seeking activity and describe the mechanism of how central planning suggests the existence of a self-reinforcing mechanism that exacerbates shortages.

Ickes (1990) presents a framework for detecting the causes of low performance and slow adaptability in socialist firms as a consequence of differences in coalition formation in economic organization. The control of agents in oligopolistic situations is analyzed by Gal-Or (1990); the analysis sheds new light on another promising approach that could be used to model the behavior of firms under central planning.

In this paper we describe the socialist firm as a regulated monopoly, assuming that no central plan targets are imposed on quantity decisions but that the decisions are influenced by various taxes and subsidies.

* Ábel wishes to acknowledge the financial support of OTKA TS-1/4. Bonin is grateful to the International Research Exchange Board for a travel grant and to the American Philosophical Society and Wesleyan University for financial support.

2. The Hungarian Enterprise Under
Financial Regulation

In the current planning environment in Hungary, financial regulation has replaced administrative directives as an instrument for influencing enterprise behavior. Ábel and Székely (1988) use a modified profit function to describe the objective function of the Hungarian enterprise. Following this work, we define a modified profit function as

$$Z = (1-r)[p(q)q - C(q)] - tq - sp(q)q - vC(q) \qquad (1)$$

where Z is the modified profit, r is the rate of profit taxation, $p(q)$ is the inverse demand function or the pricing schedule set by the regulator, q is output, $C(q)$ is total cost, t is a tax (or subsidy) per unit of output, s is a tax (or subsidy) per unit of revenue, and v is a tax assessed as a percentage of cost.

In this general form, the modified profit function allows the regulator to specify four financial parameters (r, t, s and v) and, in addition, to set the price schedule. Consequently, the specification is well suited to our positive model of regulation in Hungary. An enterprise having Z as its objective function will choose output q according to the first order condition

$$\frac{dZ}{dq} = (1-r-s)[p(q) + qp'(q)] - (1-r+v)C'(q) - t = 0. \qquad (2)$$

If we define $E = -(dq/dp)/(q/p)$, the price elasticity of the regulator's price schedule, we obtain after rearrangement the following:

$$p(q) = \frac{C'(q)(1-r+v)+t}{(1-r-s)(1-1/E)}. \qquad (3)$$

As is clear from (3), if the regulator wishes to use all parameters, so that the marginal cost pricing solution is obtained, he must know $C'(q)$. Interestingly, however, if we set $t = 0$, (3) can be written as

$$\frac{p(q)}{C'(q)} = \frac{E(1-r+v)}{(E-1)(1-r-s)}. \qquad (4)$$

For an efficient outcome, the left-hand side of (4) must equal unity. Since $(1-r+v) > 0$ and $(1-r-s) > 0$, $E > 1$ for a well-defined solution, and from (4) $E < \infty$. Then, for an efficient outcome to be induced, the regulator must set $(1 - r + v) < (1 - r - s)$ because $E/(E - 1) > 1$. Consequently,

$-s > 0$ for efficiency. Therefore, the regulator must subsidize the enterprise to induce it to produce an efficient output level. This is similar to a result in Domar (1974), where he shows that it is necessary to subsidize a socialist firm in a monopoly situation to encourage an increase in output from the profit maximizing level.

3. Price Regulation and Cost Exaggeration

Consider the pricing policy of the regulator. In particular, Ábel and Székely (1988) assume that the price elasticity can be written as

$$E = \frac{p}{a - p}. \tag{5}$$

The parameter a indicates that there is a maximum above which the regulatory authorities will not allow the price to be set (in essence, the regulator would rather close down the enterprise than set a price higher than a). Also notice from (5) that $p > a/2$ for $E > 1$. In the range $a/2 < p < a$, the enterprise and the regulator can be considered to bargain over the price. The specification given in (5) indicates that the closer the firm tries to push price towards its upper limit, the more resistance it faces from the regulator. Institutionally speaking, the enterprise has to threaten to cause more significant shortages (output reductions) per unit of price increase the higher the price is. Consistent with Hungarian practice, price is set to cover average cost and to allow some positive profit so that we let

$$p = \frac{(1 + A)C(q)}{q} \tag{6}$$

where A is the mark-up rate. Now we assume that the firm reports its unit cost to the regulator and that price is set on this basis. Since the regulator has no direct information about the enterprise's unit cost, cost may be misreported. Therefore, let (6) be rewritten as

$$p = (1 + A)(c + x) \tag{7}$$

where c is the true unit cost unknown to the regulator and x is a factor of exaggeration (misreporting of the true cost). Using the definition of E and integrating (5), we obtain

$$q = \frac{a - p}{b} \tag{8}$$

where $1/b$ is the constant of integration.

Consider (1) with $t = 0$ and also let $v = 0$ because the regulator cannot observe cost by assumption. Also notice that the profit tax r is assessed on the cost information reported, while actual profit to the firm is different if $x \neq 0$. Notice that if profit were observable to the regulator, he would discern cost directly because he knows the revenue. In case of misreported unit cost, the modified profit of the firm will be different from (1) and will exceed it by xq. In this special case (assuming $t = 0$, $v = 0$) the modified profit is of the following form:

$$Z = (1 - r)[p(q)q - (c + x)q] - sp(q)q + xq. \tag{1'}$$

Rearrangement of (1') with the aid of (7) and (8) yields

$$\begin{aligned} Z =&(1 + A)(c + x)\left[\frac{a - (1 + A)(c + x)}{b}\right](1 - s) \\ &- rA(c + x)\left[\frac{a - (1 + A)(c + x)}{b}\right] \\ &- c\left[\frac{a - (1 + A)(c + x)}{b}\right]. \end{aligned} \tag{9}$$

The first term in (9) is revenue adjusted by a tax or subsidy if $s \neq 0$. The second term is the profit tax assessed on revenue minus reported cost. The third term is total actual cost. Therefore, Z is the actual profit to be maximized by the firm. We consider the maximization of (9) with respect to x to determine the optimal factor of exaggeration. The first order condition for a maximum can be written as

$$\begin{aligned} \left[\frac{a - (1 + A)(c + x)}{b}\right]&[(1 + A)(1 - s) - rA] \\ &- [(1 + A)(1 - s)(c + x) - rA(c + x) - c]\left(\frac{1 + A}{b}\right) = 0. \end{aligned} \tag{10}$$

After algebraic manipulation we obtain

$$x^* = \frac{a}{2(1 + A)} - c + \frac{c}{2(1 - r - s)A + 2(1 - s)}. \tag{11}$$

Now substitute (11) into (7) to obtain

$$p^* = \frac{a}{2} + \frac{c(1 + A)}{2(1 - r - s)A + 2(1 - s)} > \frac{a}{2}. \tag{12}$$

The inequality follows from $(1-r-s) > 0$. The solution here is different from the one found in Ábel and Székely (1988), because our formulation of the modified profit function in (9) is different from their formulation. Consequently, the optimal exaggeration factor leads to a price for which $E > 1$. Notice also that p^* increases with c, the true cost, and with A, the mark-up factor. Price also increases as the rate of the profit tax increases but it decreases as the subsidy increases (under the assumption that $s < 0$) in absolute value.

In principle, the last three are testable hypotheses. To relate our model of the Hungarian enterprise to the regulation literature, we propose a stylized representation of regulation in Hungary. The enterprise knows its operating cost parameter, c, but the regulatory authorities do not. The authorities use a cost mark-up pricing rule based on the "report" from the enterprise concerning operating cost. An alternative interpretation is that the enterprise requests a price increase based on reported cost increases. Consequently, the enterprise maximizes its profit by reporting a unit cost $m = c + x$ where x is the factor of cost exaggeration. The regulator sets the price according to the mark-up formula $p = (1 + A)m$ and demand is determined by the parameters of the price schedule given in equation (5). However, the regulator also sets two financial parameters, namely a profit tax rate r and a subsidy s per unit of sales revenue. Thus, the regulatory instruments are the three parameters A, r, and s and the firm determines its optimal factor of exaggeration by maximizing its modified profit function knowing the pricing rule and the quantity required at each price. In our interpretation, the profit tax is applied to estimated profit, not actual profit. Since the regulator observes only the output of the enterprise (actual deliveries), but not the operating costs, accounting profits for the purpose of taxation are assumed to be sales revenues minus reported operating costs. As a benchmark, we begin with a situation in which $r = s = 0$. If we change the assumptions concerning the economic environment and assume that the regulator can tax actual profit (perhaps because price is set initially depending on the cost report but profit and therefore cost can be observed later on), the solutions given above apply if we set $r = 0$. Intuitively, the profit tax is neutral as we would expect it to be for a profit maximizing firm earning rents. Then $p^* = (a + c)/2$ and consumer surplus is $S(p^*)$. Since $S'(p) = -q(p) < 0$ and p^* decreases as the absolute value of s increases when $s < 0$, the authorities can increase gross consumer surplus by subsidizing the enterprise. The cost of a subsidy $spq(p)$ must be subtracted from the change in gross consumer surplus to obtain the change in net consumer surplus so that, on the margin, granting a subsidy to the enterprise improves welfare if

$$q(p)(1 - sp) > 0 \iff s < \frac{1}{p}. \tag{13}$$

Starting with $p^* = (a + c)/2$ as the benchmark, (13) indicates that subsidizing an enterprise increases net consumer surplus so long as $s < 2/(a+c)$. As an example, suppose that the maximum price $a = 40$ and the true cost $c = 20$. Then $p^* = 30$ when $r = s = 0$ and $1/p^* = 0.033$. Clearly, a small *ad valorem* subsidy will increase net consumer welfare. When no profit tax is levied, net consumer surplus is given by

$$N(p) = S(p) + spq(p), \tag{14}$$

which takes into account the possibility that $s < 0$.

To maximize net consumer surplus, the first order condition is

$$\left[S'(p) + s\big[q(p) + pq'(p)\big] \right] \frac{dp}{ds} + pq(p) = 0. \tag{15}$$

Using $S'(p) = -q(p)$ and the definition of E, we have

$$\frac{dp}{ds} = \frac{p}{(1 - s) + sE}. \tag{16}$$

From p^* with $r = 0$ we can compute

$$\frac{dp}{ds} = \frac{a(1 - s) + c}{2(1 - s)^2 + 2(1 - s)sE}. \tag{17}$$

In our specification of the regulatory environment, an increase in the profit tax rate increases the price and therefore decreases consumer surplus. Of course, the profit tax may be imposed for distributional reasons, so that we would need to characterize social welfare in a more complex way for a general theory. Suffice it to say here that the regulated price will increase with the profit tax rate as the enterprise compensates for its loss in profit by increasing its factor of cost exaggeration (see (11)). Furthermore, as we noted, an increase in the mark-up rate or in the true cost c will also increase the price. It is interesting to contrast these last two changes with the changes in the profit tax rate and changes in the subsidy rate. In the latter two cases, price increases as r and s increase (since an increase in s,

Table 1. Response to Changes in Parameters

	Parameters			
Decision Variable	r	s	A	c
x^*	+	+	−	−
p^*	+	+	+	+

$s < 0$, is a decrease in the subsidy to the firm) because of an increase in the factor of cost exaggeration. However, both the mark-up rate and the true cost have both a direct and an indirect influence on price. An increase in the mark-up rate A decreases the factor of cost exaggeration as can be observed from (11). More importantly perhaps, a similar situation holds for an increase in true cost. Rearranging (11), we have

$$x^* = \frac{a}{2(1+A)} - \left[\frac{2(1-r-s)A+1-2s}{2(1-r-s)A+2(1-s)}\right]c. \qquad (18)$$

Since the term in brackets is positive, an increase in c decreases the factor of cost exaggeration. However, the cost report of the enterprise m includes c directly and the direct effect of an increase in true cost through the enterprise's cost report is sufficient to outweigh the decrease in the factor of cost exaggeration and lead to an increase in price.

4. Conclusion

The present simple model characterizes some important behavioral properties of the socialist firm under central planning. Table 1 summarizes the comparative statics results and allows a quick survey of the effects of changes in cost and regulatory parameters. The increase in the profit tax rate r increases cost exaggeration and price, and consequently decreases consumer surplus. At the same time, an increase in subsidy (a decrease in $s < 0$) has the opposite effect. An increase in the mark-up rate A or the true cost c decreases the factor of cost exaggeration but leads to an increase in price.

References

Ábel, I. and Bonin, J. P. (1989) "Regulatory Policy with Limited Information: An Application to Hungary," Working Paper No. 1989/3, University of Economics, Budapest.

Ábel, I. and Székely, I. (1988) "Price Regulation and Inventory Behavior of Companies under Central Planning," in *The Economics of Inventory Management*, ed. by A. Chikán and M. C. Lovell; Amsterdam: Elsevier North-Holland.

Domar, Evsey D. (1974) "On the Optimal Compensation of a Socialist Manager," *Quarterly Journal of Economics*, **88**, 1-18.

Gal-Or, E. (1990) "Does Increased Efficiency Require Tighter Control?", this volume.

Goldfeld, S. M. and Quandt, R. E. (1988) "Budget Constraints, Bailouts and the Firm under Central Planning," *Journal of Comparative Economics*, **12**, 502-520.

———— (1990) "Output Targets, Input Rationing and Inventories," this volume.

Ickes, B. W. (1990) "The Theory of the Firm under Capitalism and Socialism," this volume.

Kornai, J. (1980) *The Economics of Shortage*, Amsterdam: North-Holland.

8

On the Dynamics of a Participatory Firm: A Model of Employer-Worker Bargaining ·

Frans Spinnewyn and *Jan Svejnar*

1. Introduction

In this paper we present a cooperative and a noncooperative dynamic model, thereby extending the cooperative static models of management-worker bargaining examined by McDonald and Solow (1981) and Svejnar (1982,1986). The basic issue examined in these models is how an enterprise allocates rescources (i.e., sets employment) and divides surplus when workers have some influence in the decision-making process. The problem naturally arises in western unionized firms, but it is also especially relevant for Yugoslavian labor-managed firms and for the emerging participatory firms in Hungary and Poland. In the latter two countries, economic reforms have recently given workers considerable decision-making power and the question naturally arises how this will affect enterprise performance.

In their static models, McDonald and Solow and Svejnar focus on the determinants of (a) the trade union-management contract curve; and (b) a unique solution on the contract curve. They examine the set of possible solutions lying between the threat point of workers (the reservation or competitive wage W_c) and the threat point of the management (the zero profit isoprofit curve $\Pi = 0$), as diagrammed in Figure 1, with wages de-

* Svejnar's research was supported by NSF Grant No. SES 8821957 and by IREX. None of them is responsible for the views expressed.

noted by W and employment by L. These threat points, as well as the size of the union (worker collective) $\bar{L}$, are taken as exogenously given in the models, which depict cooperative game solutions that arise in the context of expected utility maximization by workers and profit maximization by the management. McDonald and Solow apply the Nash and Kalai-Smorodinsky bargaining solutions, while Svejnar proposes a power-related non-symmetric Nash solution.

The main findings in the static framework are that the contract curve may not only lie to the right of the marginal revenue product curve of labor R_L, with $(R_L < W)$, but may also be forward sloping; that bargaining power determines the location of the solution on the contract curve; and that the size of the union $\bar{L}$ may restrict the set of admissible solutions. The idea that the solution, which is efficient from the standpoint of the two parties, may lie to the right of the R_L curve (e.g., on the ACC', ADD' or AEE' contract curves in Figure 1) has generated considerable debate. In particular, the question arises as to how a union can enforce the ("excessive") employment aspect of the contract and prevent the management from reneging *ex post* and unilaterally reducing employment (and,

Figure 1: Marginal Product and Isoprofit Curves

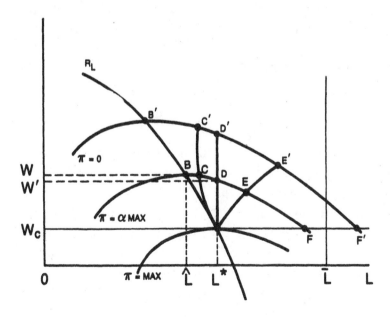

hence, increasing its profit) to the point where $W = R_L$. This question of managerial commitment has remained open and an influential ("monopoly unionism") school of thought argues that the inability of the union to control employment will result in an outcome on the R_L curve.

The two main shortcomings of the static models are that they treat the threat points and the size of the union as exogenous and that they do not have a consistent framework for the behavioral underpinnings of the bargaining outcome.

In this paper we address these problems. By using a dynamic framework with optimal strategies for both parties, and making the threat points as well as the size of the union endogenous, we first derive a dynamic cooperative solution and then employ a continuous version of the Rubinstein (1982) model to obtain a non-cooperative bargaining solution. The non-cooperative solution generates and, thus, justifies the expected payoff of the union, which we use as the lower bound in deriving the cooperative solution. Within a non-cooperative framework the contract gives workers a payoff that they cannot improve upon by launching a strike. Since our focus is on the determination of $\bar{L}$, we simplify the issue of determining employment L, given $\bar{L}$.

2. Assumptions and Preliminaries

We consider an economy where each firm produces a non-storable good and is faced with stochastic demand D. The production functions are characterized by constant returns to scale; hence, for a given capital stock, the production function may be expressed as

$$D = L,$$

where L is labor input. Demand is distributed according to a distribution function $G(D)$, the product price p is fixed and the firm also faces some fixed cost Z (e.g., for renting the capital).

The union or workers' collective $\bar{L}$ is made up of "trained" workers, where training is firm specific and costs k per worker. The firm employs workers from the pool $\bar{L}$. In low-demand states ($D < \bar{L}$) the firm employs D workers and unemployment occurs, while in high-demand states ($D > \bar{L}$) the firm employs all $\bar{L}$ workers and there is unsatisfied demand. Once $\bar{L}$ is set, the level of employment is completely determined by product demand.[1]

Ignoring for a moment training costs, we denote one-period profits by

$$\Pi(D,\bar{L}) = \begin{cases} (p-W)D - Z, & \text{if } D < \bar{L}; \\ (p-W)\bar{L} - Z, & \text{if } D \geq \bar{L}. \end{cases} \tag{1}$$

When employed, each worker receives a wage W and supplies effort worth e. When laid off, each worker receives unemployment benefits (or generates home production) worth b. Workers cannot save money, and are assumed to be randomly selected for work, when $D < \bar{L}$. The one-period expected wage is given by

$$U(D,\bar{L}) = \frac{D}{\bar{L}}(W-e) + (1 - \frac{D}{\bar{L}})b. \tag{2}$$

After taking expectations of equations (1) and (2), we obtain the expressions for expected income going to management (firm) and each worker, respectively, as

$$\bar{\Pi}(\bar{L}) = (p-W)\left[\bar{L} - \theta(\bar{L})\right] - Z, \tag{3}$$

and

$$\bar{U}(\bar{L}) = (W - e - b)\left[1 - \theta(\bar{L})/\bar{L}\right] + b, \tag{4}$$

where D_ℓ is the lower bound on D and $\theta(\bar{L}) = \int_{D_\ell}^{\bar{L}}[(\bar{L} - D)/\bar{L}]g(D)\,dD$ is the unemployment rate of the trained (unionized) workers. Noting that

$$\theta(\bar{L}) < G(\bar{L})\bar{L} \leqq \bar{L}, \tag{5}$$

we can establish that the expected income going to management (each worker) increases (diminishes) with a rise in $\bar{L}$:

$$\bar{\Pi}' = (p-W)\left[1 - G(\bar{L})\right] > 0, \tag{6}$$

$$\bar{U}' = (W - e - b)\left[\theta(\bar{L})/\bar{L} - G(\bar{L})\right]/\bar{L} < 0. \tag{7}$$

---

[1] Note that the stochastic demand and non-storable nature of the product make the determination of L, given $\bar{L}$, trivial. One could extend the analysis of this paper by assuming that output can be stored at a cost. This would introduce the question of accumulation of inventories and their relationship to employment L and layoffs.

Equations (6) and (7) highlight the basic problem. Firms prefer to have large pools of trained workers in order to minimize unsatisfied demand, but trained workers like to have small pools, which reduce the probability of income losses due to layoffs.[2]

3. The Cooperative Solution

In order to derive a solution we need to impose more structure on the problem. We introduce unemployment into the model by considering workers with infinite life spans and firms facing a mortality (bankruptcy) rate m.[3] Within the cooperative framework the solution will be Pareto-efficient from the two parties' standpoint and will divide the surplus between them in some unique way (e.g., symmetric or non-symmetric Nash). Suppose the solution gives the (trained) workers lifetime utility ϕ_u^e.[4] Our goal here is to characterize the optimal contract that will provide ϕ_u^e.

Each firm faces probability m that it will go bankrupt, in which case its workers become unemployed and expect lifetime utility ϕ_u^u. We assume that managers are risk neutral and that fixed costs Z include a risk premium should capital become worthless through bankruptcy. In view of the constant probability m of bankruptcy, the lifetime of each firm is exponentially distributed, and the cooperative solution can be characterized as the outcome of the following managerial optimization problem:

$$\phi_\Pi(\phi_u^e) = \max_{W,L} \frac{-Z + (p - W)\left[\bar{L} - \theta(\bar{L})\right]}{r + m} - k \max(\bar{L} - L^*, 0),$$

subject to

$$\frac{(W - e - b)\left[1 - \theta(\bar{L})/\bar{L}\right] + b + m\phi_u^u}{r + m} \geq \phi_u^e, \qquad (8)$$

---

[2] Note that in this paper we do not model the process by which workers are selected into the union (worker collective)—i.e., the "trained" pool. This insider-outsider problem is an interesting one and is addressed elsewhere (see Spinnewyn and Svejnar (1986)).

[3] Note that unemployment exists, but is not very well motivated in the static models. Our approach to introducing unemployment into the dynamic framework is one of several alternatives. Another way would be to model the retirement of existing workers and the admission of new ones. However, as will become clear later, this approach leads to a non-stationary problem in our framework.

[4] The level of ϕ_u^e is determined in the non-cooperative model of Section 4.

where ϕ_Π is the lifetime income of the management (firm), r is the interest (discount) rate and L^* is the initial pool of trained workers. The solution to problem (8) depends on whether $\bar{L}$ is greater or less than L^*. Hence, we consider the two cases separately.

For $\bar{L} \geq L^*$,

$$\partial\Psi/\partial\bar{L} = -k + \frac{1}{r+m}\left\{(p - W)\bar{G}(\bar{L}) + \frac{\lambda}{\bar{L}}(W - e - b)\bar{G}(\bar{L}) \right. \\ \left. - [\bar{U}(\bar{L}) - b]\right\} = 0, \tag{9}$$

where Ψ is the Lagrangian function, λ is the Lagrange multiplier and $\bar{G}(\bar{L}) = 1 - G(\bar{L})$ is the probability of full capacity demand. Moreover,

$$\partial\Psi/\partial W = \frac{1}{r+m}\left\{-[\bar{L} - \theta(\bar{L})] + \lambda[1 - \theta(\bar{L})/\bar{L}]\right\} = 0, \tag{10}$$

so that $\partial\phi_\Pi/\partial\phi_u^e = \lambda = \bar{L}$. From equations (8), (9) and (10) it follows that

$$k(r + m) + [r\phi_u^e - b + m(\phi_u^e - \phi_u^u)] = (p - e - b)\bar{G}(\bar{L}). \tag{11}$$

The left-hand side of equation (11) gives the marginal cost of increasing capacity, which is composed of three things:

(i) the training cost k times the interest and insurance cost against bankruptcy;

(ii) the rent (excess income) going to each employed worker $(\phi_u^e - b/r)$ times the interest cost;

(iii) the cost of laying off a worker $(\phi_u^e - \phi_u^u)$ when the firm goes bankrupt.

The right-hand side gives the net return from increased sales $(p - e - b)$ times the probability of full capacity demand.

From equation (11) it is easy to establish that $\bar{L}$ is a decreasing function of ϕ_u^e:

$$\frac{d\bar{L}}{d\phi_u^e} = -\frac{r + m}{(p - e - b)g(\bar{L})} < 0. \tag{12}$$

Equation (12) states that the two parties will train fewer workers (reduce the size of the union), if each worker receives a higher expected lifetime utility ϕ_u^e. Since W increases with ϕ_u^e, in terms of Figure 1, this result implies that higher wages will result in lower (jointly determined) values of $\bar{L}$.

As it turns out, this result provides an important modification of the static findings based on an exogenously given $\bar{L}$. It demonstrates that, in an expected utility maximization framework, bargaining effectively makes the size of the union (the relevant pool of workers) a joint decision of the existing (trained or unionized) workers and the management.

For $\bar{L} < L^*$ it can be shown that

$$W = \left[(r+m)\phi_u^e - b - m\phi_u^u\right]/\left[1 - \theta(L^*)/L^*\right] + e + b, \tag{13}$$

and that

$$\phi_\Pi(\phi_u^e) = \frac{1}{r+m}\Big\{ -Z + (p - e - b)\left[L^* - \theta(L^*)\right] \\ -\left[(r+m)\phi_u^e - b - m\phi_u^u\right]L^*\Big\}. \tag{14}$$

As these results indicate, for a given pool of initially trained workers L^*, there exists a critical value ϕ^* such that, for $\phi_u^e \leqq \phi^*$, $\phi_\Pi(\phi_u^e)$ is the solution to problem (8) and $\partial\phi_\Pi/\partial\phi_u^e = -\bar{L}$, where $\bar{L}$ solves (11).[5] For $\phi_u^e > \phi^*$, ϕ_Π is linear in ϕ_u^e and $\partial\phi_\Pi/\partial\phi_u^e = -L^*$. (We assume that $\phi_\Pi(\phi_u^e) > 0$ for $\phi_u^e \geqq \phi^* > 0$.)

The Contract Curve and Labor's Marginal Product

For $\bar{L} > L^*$ the marginal profit (with respect to $\bar{L}$) per unit of time is given by

$$\frac{\partial}{\partial \bar{L}}\Big\{(p - W)\left[\bar{L} - \theta(\bar{L})\right] - Z - k(r+m)(\bar{L} - L^*)\Big\} \\ = (p - W)\left[1 - G(\bar{L})\right] - k(r+m). \tag{15}$$

Setting equation (15) equal to zero, we have an expression for the marginal product curve of labor

$$(p - W)\bar{G}(\bar{L}) = k(r+m), \tag{15'}$$

which can also be interpreted as the equality between expected profit from increasing the pool of trained workers and the cost of training.

---

[5] Note that ϕ_Π is convex in ϕ_u^e.

In particular let $W^m(\bar{L})$ be the wage that makes the marginal profit equal to zero (i.e., traces the marginal product curve of labor). As seen in Figure 2, this curve is denoted as $W^m(\bar{L})$. Note that the highest wage, which makes equation (15) equal to zero, is $W = p - k(r + m)$ at $\bar{L} = D_\ell$. The lowest wage is given by the reservation wage $W_c = e + b$, which corresponds to $\bar{L}_c$ in Figure 2.

The contract curve is obtained by noting that

$$\phi_u^e = \left\{ (W - e - b)[1 - \theta(\bar{L})/\bar{L}] + b + m\phi_u^u \right\}/(r + m);$$

substitution into equation (11) yields

$$k(r + m) + (W - e - b)[1 - \theta(\bar{L})/\bar{L}] = (p - e - b)\bar{G}(\bar{L}). \qquad (11')$$

Equation (11') takes into account the expected surplus lost by trained (union) workers due to unemployment. Note that in equation (15) this cost is ignored because profit-maximizing (wage-taking) management would rather consider marginal profit $(p - W)$ than total marginal surplus $(p - e - b)$ in its optimization.

Figure 2: The Locus of Zero Marginal Profit

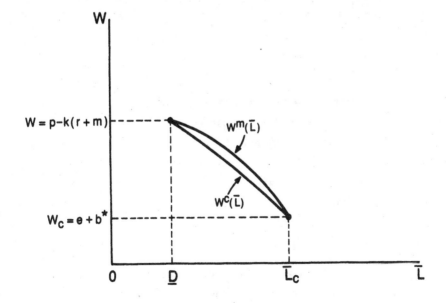

Let $W^c(\bar{L})$ be the contract curve satisfying equation (11′). If we rewrite this equation as

$$k(r+m) = (p-W)\bar{G}(\bar{L}) + (W-e-b)[\bar{G}(\bar{L}) - 1 + \theta(\bar{L})/\bar{L}]$$
$$= (p-W)\bar{G}(\bar{L}) + (W-e-b)[\theta(\bar{L})/\bar{L} - G(\bar{L})]$$
$$\leqq (p-W)\bar{G}(\bar{L}),$$

and compare it to equation (15), then clearly for $e+b \leqq W \leqq p-k(r+m)$ the contract curve $W^c(\bar{L})$ lies to the left of the marginal product curve of labor $W^m(\bar{L})$ (see Figure 2). Moreover, the comparison also demonstrates that the two curves coincide at the endpoints $W = e+b$ and $W = p-k(r+m)$.

The wage-taking (profit-maximizing) manager operating on $W^m(\bar{L})$ will train more workers than the "cooperating" manager operating on the contract curve $W^c(\bar{L})$, because the former ignores the income losses of trained workers due to unemployment. In the cooperative $[W^c(\bar{L})]$ framework, fewer workers will be trained (the union and firm pursue more restrictive admission policies), but the unemployment rate of the trained (union) workers will be lower.

As this discussion indicates, the dynamic framework, cast in terms of W and $\bar{L}$, complements in an important way the main findings of static models that treated $\bar{L}$ as given. The contract curve bends backward (rather than forward) and it lies to the left rather than to the right of the marginal revenue product curve of labor. The union workers (insiders) push the management toward more restrictive employment policies rather than toward featherbedding.

4. Non-cooperative Equilibrium

In order to characterize non-cooperative equilibrium, we must first outline the options available to the two parties. Consider an economy where all firms offer workers equal lifetime utility, because the training cost, price and the demand distribution are identical for equally productive workers. In this situation, individual rationality ensures that, in the presence of a powerless union, an equilibrium will satisfy

$$\phi_u^u = \frac{b - s + \alpha\bar{\phi}_u^e}{r + \alpha} = \frac{b}{r},$$

where s is the cost of search, α is the probability of leaving unemployment and becoming part of the trained/unionized pool, b/r is the lifetime utility of workers who do not search and $\tilde{\phi}_u^e$ is the lifetime utility solution if the union has no power.

Now suppose that the union can launch a strike, which would take a certain amount of time to be settled, and that during the strike workers would receive strike benefits which, together with the value of leisure, would be worth b^s. We will show that in this case ϕ_u^e can exceed $\tilde{\phi}_u^e$.

An important assumption here is that a strike, once launched, is difficult to stop immediately. This is empirically plausible and may reflect some asymmetric information between the union leaders and the rank and file (see, e.g., Ashenfelter and Johnson (1969)), a time lag in transmitting information within the union or simply a cooling-off period needed to bring the parties back to the bargaining table. Technically, this assumption is needed because it introduces a form of commitment, which makes the threat of a strike credible.

When the strike starts, there is probability α_c that the parties will agree to meet at the bargaining table and probability κ $(1 - \kappa)$ that the union (management) will make an offer.[6] If the union does make an offer, it will propose $\phi_u^{\max}(\tau)$ for itself, leaving $\phi_\Pi^{\min}(\tau) = \phi_\Pi[\phi_u^{\max}(\tau)]$ for the firm. Similarly, if the firm makes an offer, it will propose $\phi_\Pi^{\max}(\tau)$ for itself and, hence, $\phi_u^{\min}(\tau) = \phi_\Pi^{-1}[\phi_\Pi^{\min}(\tau)]$ for the union.

Let $\phi_\Pi^s(\tau)$ and $\phi_u^s(\tau)$ be the respective payoffs for the firm and the union, if they refuse the other party's offer and continue the disagreement. We model the resolution of the disagreement as a continuous version of the Rubinstein (1982) model with alternating offers. In this context the party that makes the offer leading to an agreement has an advantage ("wins") because the opponent is willing to accept an offer equal to the expected payoff of continuing disagreement.

As in contestable markets, the firm, realizing the implications of all possible moves, will make offers such that a strike does not occur. Nevertheless, each party's probability of winning the strike (i.e., κ and $1 - \kappa$), as well as the parameter capturing the delay in undertaking negotiations α_c, will help determine the sharing of surplus between the firm and the workers even in the absence of a strike.

Formally, the strike will end after the first meeting at time τ, leaving the maximum advantage to the proposing party, if

---

[6] There is, of course, also probability m that the firm will go under, but this is a random event not caused by the strike.

$$\phi_u^{\max}(\tau) \geqq \phi_u^{\min}(\tau) = \phi_u^{s}(\tau), \tag{16}$$

and

$$\phi_\Pi^{\max}(\tau) \geqq \phi_\Pi^{\min}(\tau) = \phi_\Pi^{s}(\tau). \tag{17}$$

The constant probability α_c that the parties agree to meet for negotiations implies that the time to the first round of negotiations is exponentially distributed. It follows that

$$\phi_u^{s}(t) = \int_t^{\infty} e^{[-(r+m+\alpha_c)(\tau-t)]}\Big\{ b^s + \alpha_c\big[\kappa\phi_u^{\max}(\tau) + (1-\kappa)\phi_u^{s}(\tau)\big]$$
$$+ m\phi_u^{u}\Big\}d\tau, \tag{18}$$

$$\phi_\Pi^{s}(t) = \int_t^{\infty} e^{[-(r+m+\alpha_c)(\tau-t)]}\Big\{ -Z + \alpha_c\big[\kappa\phi_\Pi^{s}(\tau)$$
$$+ (1-\kappa)\phi_\pi^{\max}(\tau)\big]\Big\}d\tau, \tag{19}$$

and, denoting time derivatives by a dot, we also note that

$$\dot\phi_u^{s}(t) = (r+m+\alpha_c\kappa)\phi_u^{s}(t) - [b^s + m\phi_u^{u} + \alpha_c\kappa\phi_u^{\max}(t)], \tag{20}$$

$$\dot\phi_\Pi^{s}(t) = [r+m+\alpha_c(1-\kappa)]\phi_\Pi^{s}(t) - [-Z + \alpha_c(1-\kappa)\phi_\Pi^{\max}(t)]. \tag{21}$$

From equations (18)–(21) it follows that, for all τ,

$$\phi_u^{\min}(\tau) = \phi_u^{s}(\tau) =$$
$$\int_\tau^{\infty} e^{[-(r+m+\alpha_c\kappa)(x-\tau)]}\big[b^s + m\phi_u^{u} + \alpha_c\kappa\,\phi_u^{\max}(x)\big]dx \tag{22}$$
$$= \frac{b^s + m\phi_u^{u}}{r+m+\alpha_c\kappa} + \int_t^{\infty} e^{[-(r+m+\alpha_c\kappa)(x-\tau)]}\alpha_c\kappa\phi_u^{\max}(x)dx,$$

and

$$\phi_\Pi^{\min}(\tau) = \phi_\Pi^{s}(\tau) = \int_\tau^{\infty} e^{[-(r+m+\alpha_c(1-\kappa))(x-\tau)]}\alpha_c(1-\kappa)\phi_\Pi^{\max}(x)\,dx$$
$$+ \frac{-Z}{r+m+\alpha_c(1-\kappa)}. \tag{23}$$

In a stationary environment $\phi_u^s(\tau)$ and $\phi_\Pi^s(\tau)$ are constant, so that

$$\phi_u^{\min} = \frac{1}{r+m+\alpha_c\kappa}(b^s + m\phi_u^u + \alpha_c\kappa\phi_u^{\max}), \qquad (24)$$

and

$$\phi_\Pi^{\min} = \frac{1}{r+m+\alpha_c(1-\kappa)}[-Z + \alpha_c(1-\kappa)\phi_\Pi^{\max}]. \qquad (25)$$

We next examine the conditions under which $\phi_u^e = \phi_u^{\min} > \tilde{\phi}_u^e$ is an equilibrium—i.e., when making an offer ϕ_u^e equal to $\phi_u^{\min}$ is an optimal and sustainable strategy of the firm. First, note that if $\phi_u^e = \phi_u^{\min}$, the workers cannot increase their expected payoff by launching a strike, so that ϕ_u^e is sustainable. Secondly, if $\phi_u^{\max} \geq \phi_u^{\min}$ and ϕ_u^e is the initial situation, then the optimal pool of trained workers $\bar{L}$ for $\phi_u^{\max}$ is smaller than for ϕ_u^e. This implies that if a strike were to be launched and won by the workers, the pool would remain unchanged at $\bar{L}$ and $\phi_\Pi(\phi_u^{\max})$ would be the linear function given by equation (14).

Moreover, since $\bar{L}$ remains the same whether the union or the firm wins in the dispute, and since workers are assumed to be risk neutral, it follows that

$$\begin{aligned}
\phi_\Pi^{\max} + \bar{L}\phi_u^{\min} &= \phi_\Pi^{\min} + \bar{L}\phi_u^{\max} \\
&= [b - Z + (p-e-b)(\bar{L} - \theta(\bar{L}))]/(r+m) \qquad (26) \\
&= S,
\end{aligned}$$

and that $\bar{L}$ is given by equation (11). Upon rearranging equation (26), we see that

$$\phi_\Pi^{\max} - \phi_\Pi^{\min} = \bar{L}(\phi_u^{\max} - \phi_u^{\min}), \qquad (27)$$

and equations (24)–(27) lead to

$$\phi_u^{\min} = \frac{b^s + m\phi_u^u}{r+m} + \frac{\alpha_c\kappa}{\alpha_c+r+m}\frac{1}{\bar{L}}\left[S - \frac{\bar{L}(b^s + m\phi_u^u) - Z}{r+m}\right] \qquad (28)$$

$$\phi_\Pi^{\min} = \frac{-Z}{r+m} + \frac{\alpha_c(1-\kappa)}{\alpha_c+r+m}\left[S - \frac{\bar{L}(b^s + m\phi_u^u) - Z}{r+m}\right], \qquad (29)$$

and

$$\phi_\Pi^{\max} - \phi_\Pi^{\min} = \frac{r+m}{\alpha_c + r + m}\left[S - \frac{\bar{L}(b^s + m\phi_u^u) - Z}{r+m}\right]. \tag{30}$$

Note that if an agreement is infinitely delayed ($\alpha_c = 0$), either because the parties never get together or one of them always refuses the other's offer, then the payoff for the union is

$$\frac{b^s + m\phi_u^u}{r+m},$$

while that for the firm is

$$\frac{-Z}{r+m}.$$

These two payoffs are natural threat points and an agreement can be reached only if

$$S - \frac{b^s + m\phi_u^u}{r+m}\bar{L} + \frac{Z}{r+m} \geq 0. \tag{31}$$

In that case $\phi_\Pi^{\max} \geq \phi_\Pi^{\min}$ and $\phi_u^{\max} - \phi_u^{\min} \geq 0$.

Equations (27)–(31) make it clear that the party which "loses" the strike obtains its threat-point payoff plus a share in the difference between the surplus in a strike-free outcome and the sum of the threat points. The share increases with the probabilities that the party would win in the future, if it forced disagreement (κ or $1 - \kappa$), and that the parties would sit down to bargain (α_c). The party that wins obtains its threat point plus the remainder. For example, if the firm (management) wins, then equations (27)–(29) indicate that the union would receive a share $\alpha_c\kappa/(\alpha_c + r + m)$, while the firm would obtain a share equal to $[\alpha_c(1-\kappa)+r+m]/(\alpha_c+r+m)$. Finally, note that when α_c tends to infinity, $\phi_\Pi^{\max} - \phi_\Pi^{\min}$ tends to zero in equation (29).

Market Equilibrium

On the basis of these results, it is possible to characterize an equilibrium in the market. The firms will post offers such that $\phi_u^e = \phi_u^{\min}$, where

$$\phi_u^{\min} = \frac{b^s + m\phi_u^u}{r+m} + \frac{\alpha_c\kappa}{\alpha_c + r + m}\frac{1}{L}\Big\{b + (p - e - b)[\bar{L} - \theta(\bar{L})] \tag{32}$$
$$- \bar{L}(b^s + m\phi_u^u)\Big\},$$

$$\phi_u^u = \frac{b-s}{r+\alpha} + \frac{\alpha}{r+\alpha}\phi_u^{\min}, \tag{33}$$

and

$$(r+m)k + r\phi_u^e - b + m(\phi_u^e - \phi_u^u) = (p-e-b)[1-G(\bar{L})]. \tag{34}$$

Conditions (32)–(34) yield a solution for $\phi_u^{\min}$ and $\bar{L}$, which in turn determines S and ϕ_u^u. The firm's profit is then given by

$$\phi_\Pi^{\max} = -\frac{Z}{r+m} + \frac{\alpha_c(1-\kappa)+r+m}{\alpha_c+r+m}\Big\{b+(p-e-b)[\bar{L}-\theta(\bar{L})] \tag{35}$$
$$-\bar{L}(b'+m\phi_u^u)\Big\}.$$

Since the ϕ_u^e offer cannot be contested, it will therefore be accepted by the workers.

5. Discussion of the Results

The dynamic analysis carried out in this paper provides a framework for addressing several issues that were not adequately tackled in previous static models.

First, our dynamic model allows the threat points of the parties to be naturally defined as the payoffs obtained during an infinitely long strike.

Secondly, the ability of the workers (union) to strike or otherwise impede production is shown to be an important tool for extracting a share of surplus. The optimal policy of the firm (management) is to offer workers a lifetime utility ϕ_u^e, which takes into account workers' power to impede production and, consequently, exceeds the equilibrium lifetime utility with no power $\tilde{\phi}_u^e$. The solution to the dynamic bargaining problem, hence, reflects the nature of the strike and can be expressed in terms of each party's probability of winning the strike (κ and $1-\kappa$) and the speed with which the parties can get together and reach an agreement (α_c). The model shows that, in an economy with unemployment, a trade union can increase the expected utility of a union member above that of an unemployed person.

Finally, we show how the static wage-employment W-L determination is complemented by the wage-union size W-$\bar{L}$ tradeoff. Once the size of the union (pool of trained workers) $\bar{L}$ is determined endogenously, it becomes clear that, in terms of $\bar{L}$, the contract curve lies to the left of the marginal revenue product curve. Moreover, our dynamic analysis opens up the possibilities of examining the impact of various factors on the size of the union (trained labor force) $\bar{L}$. For example, it follows from equation (32) that increasing the value of strike benefits b^s raises $\phi_u^{\min}$ and, hence, decreases the optimal size of the union (trained workers) $\bar{L}$.

In future research it will be interesting to examine models with (i) a more complex determination of employment (ii) risk aversion of workers, (iii) heterogeneity of firms and (iv) the admission of new workers when workers have finite life spans.

References

Ashenfelter, O. C. and Johnson, G. G. (1969) "Bargaining Theory, Trade Unions and Industrial Strike Activity," *American Economic Review* **59**, 35-49.

McDonald, I. M. and Solow, R. M. (1981) "Wage Bargaining and Employment," *American Economic Review* **71**, 968-980.

Rubinstein, A. (1982) "Perfect Equilibrium in a Bargaining Model," *Econometrica* **50**, 97-110.

Spinnewyn, F. and Svejnar, J. (1986) "Optimal Membership, Employment and Income Distribution in Unionized, Participatory and Labor-Managed Firms," Cornell Univ., Working Paper #362.

Svejnar, J. (1982) "On the Theory of a Participatory Firm," *J. of Economic Theory* **27**, 313-330.

———, (1986) "Bargaining Power, Fear of Disagreement and Wage Settlements: Theory and Evidence from U.S. Industry," *Econometrica* **54**, 1055-1078.

PART THREE

Optimization in Markets

9

Does Increased Efficiency Require Tighter Control?

Esther Gal-Or

1. Introduction

Our objective is to demonstrate that, in oligopolistic markets, the firms that are inherently more efficient devote greater resources to control agents who perform services on their behalf. This increased control is obtained by devoting more resources to audit the unit cost of the agent, or by undertaking the activities performed by the agent through vertical integration. Regardless of the way we interpret increased control, we demonstrate that the firm facing the lower unit cost of production is the one which devotes greater resources to such activity.

In the model that we develop, the agents may be other firms that provide components of the product or inputs required in production. They may be retailers providing resources to promote the sale of the product, or they may be managers in charge of supervising the production process. In order to allow for various interpretations of the type of services provided by the agents, we refer to the agents' services as being provided in an "external stage" of production, which when combined with the "internal stage" yields the final output. The unit cost of providing the services at the external stage is stochastically determined. While an agent can perfectly observe the realization of its unit cost, the firm knows only the prior distribution function governing it. Unless the firm reallocates resources to monitor the unit cost of its agent, it has to rely on the agent's report about its cost in determining the terms of trade with him. The terms of trade are determined by contracts prior to any productive activity. In the contract each firm selects three variables: the quantity of output that it requires its agent to produce, the reward of the agent, and the decision whether to audit the report of the agent. All three variables are determined contingent upon the report of the agent about his or her unit cost.

We model the behavior of duopolistic firms as consisting of two subforms. In the first, contracts are signed, and in the second, production takes place contingent upon contracts signed by both firms in the first subform of the game. We demonstrate that the monitoring decision of each firm is characterized by a single cutoff point, above which reports about unit costs are audited. Specifically, if the agent reports that its unit cost is less than the selected cutoff point, the report is not audited. Otherwise, the firm allocates the resources required in order to determine the true realization of its agent's unit cost. The optimality of this form of monitoring policy has been established previously in the literature in the context of a single principal (see, for instance, Baron and Besanko (1984), Dye (1986), and Kanodia (1985)).

Compared with a world of complete information, where the firm can always observe the unit cost of the agent, we demonstrate that the absence of monitoring in the lower tail of the distribution of the agents' unit costs can be interpreted as leading to an indirect increase in the unit variable cost of production. The longer the tail of the distribution over which reports are not audited, the more significant this indirect increase of unit variable cost. The reason why the absence of monitoring can be interpreted as having such an implicit effect on the unit variable cost is that the firm is trying to eliminate any incentives for its agent to lie about the agent's private information. This is possible only if the agent is required to produce lower quantities of output, as if the firm were facing higher unit variable cost than it really does. This indirect effect implies, in particular, that the firm that is less likely to audit its agent is the one that produces lower quantities of output, since its combined "direct and indirect unit variable cost" is higher.

We derive the reaction functions that determine the monitoring policies of both firms. Each reaction function is downward sloping, implying that when one firm raises the cutoff point above which it audits the report of its agent, the rival responds by reducing its own cutoff point. Hence, the response to reduced auditing by one firm is increased auditing by the other.

The reason why the monitoring reaction functions are downward sloping is the indirect effect of incomplete information on the unit variable cost of each firm. As was pointed out earlier, the longer is the lower tail over which reports are not audited, the more significant is the indirect increase of unit variable cost. This implies that when a firm reduces its auditing activity, it incurs higher unit variable cost and has less incentive to produce. The rival can take advantage of such reduced incentives to produce by devoting more resources to auditing, in order to facilitate increased production.

The monitoring reaction function of the firm shifts inwards the more efficient the firm is. This implies that for any level of auditing activity of the rival, the more efficient firms have stronger incentives to audit, as reflected by lower cutoff points above which auditing takes place. Therefore, at the equilibrium, more efficient firms devote more resources to monitoring their agents. Since the efficient firm covers a larger share of the market, its loss from the absence of monitoring, as reflected by higher unit variable cost, is more significant than that of the inefficient firm.

2. The Model

Two firms produce a homogeneous product, the production of which is completed in two stages. The first stage of production is performed by the firm itself and the second stage is performed by an agent who provides services to the firm. We refer to the first stage as the internal stage of production, and to the second as the external stage of production. Each firm contracts with an independent agent for the provision of the services required at the external stage. The agent representing the firm may be a retailer who devotes resources to promote the sale of the product of the firm. It may be another firm that produces a component required for the production of the product, or it may be a manager in charge of supervising the production process of the firm. Regardless of the way we interpret the type of services provided at the external stage, we assume that the agent is more efficient in providing these services. Specifically, it is never worthwhile for the firm to perform by itself the activities required at the external stage of production. We assume that the agent of each firm can be selected from a very large population of potential agents.

The aggregate demand facing the product is of the form

$$p = a - bQ \qquad a, b > 0 \tag{1}$$

where p is the price and Q is the aggregate output level produced by both firms. The unit cost of completing the internal stage of production is a constant for a given firm. It is denoted by c_i for firm i, where $c_1 < c_2$. Hence firm 1 is inherently more efficient in producing the product than firm 2.

The unit cost of completing the external stage of production is denoted by v_i for the agent representing firm i. This unit cost is stochastically determined, independently of the unit cost of the agent of the other firm. The density function $g(\ )$ and the cumulative distribution function $G(\ )$ describe the common marginal distribution of either v_1 or v_2. Hence, the efficiency of the agents in providing the services at the external stage is governed by an identical distribution function. We assume that the density is defined over the support $V \equiv [v_0 - u_0, v_0 + u_0]$, where

$$E(v_i) = v_0 \qquad \mathrm{Var}(v_i) = \sigma^2 \quad \text{for} \quad i = 1, 2$$
$$Cov(v_1, v_2) = 0 \tag{2}$$

We assume that the agent of the firm can observe its unit cost perfectly but that the firm knows only the prior distribution of this cost. However, the firm may decide to audit the unit cost of its agent. Specifically, by spending an amount of K dollars, the firm can observe perfectly the unit cost of its agent.[1]

The trade between the firm and its agent is determined by a contract prior to any production activity. In the contract, the firm selects three decision variables: the quantity of output that it requires its agent to produce at the external stage of production, the reward of the agent for the services he or she performs, and the circumstances under which the firm decides to audit the unit cost of its agent. Given our assumption that final production is completed in two stages, the quantity of output that the firm requires its agent to produce at the external stage has to coincide with the quantity produced by the firm itself at the internal stage of production. We denote the three decision variables of firm i by q_i, J_i, and m_i, respectively. Each of those variables can be selected contingent upon the report of the agent about his or her unit cost of production. We denote this report of

---

[1] This simple monitoring technology of the firm can be replaced by a more realistic assumption relating the accuracy of the audit to the amount of resources devoted to the monitoring activity. Under such an alternative formulation, firms endogenously decide how much to spend on monitoring.

agent i by $\hat{v}_i$, where $\hat{v}_i \in V$. The contract between the firm and its agent is determined, therefore, by the following three functions: $q_i(\hat{v}_i)$, $J_i(\hat{v}_i)$, and $m_i(\hat{v}_i)$, where $q_i : V \to \Re_+$, $J_i : V \to \Re_+$, and $m_i : V \to \{0, 1\}$. If $m_i = 0$, the firm decides not to audit the unit cost of the agent, and if $m_i = 1$, the firm allocates the required resources in order to audit its agent.

We formulate the game between the two firms as consisting of two sub-forms. In the first subform, each firm signs a contract with its agent to perform the external services required for the production of the product. The contracts become common knowledge at the end of the first subform. At the beginning of the second subform, each firm communicates with its agent about the state of its unit cost. Production, rewarding, and auditing are subsequently determined, contingent upon the report and the contracts selected by both firms at the first subform of the game.

3. Formulation of the Problem

On the basis of the contracts selected in the first subform, the agent of firm i selects its report $\hat{v}_i$ about cost in order to maximize the agent's profit given by

$$R_i \equiv \pi_R^i(\hat{v}_i; v_i) = J_i(\hat{v}_i) - v_i q_i(\hat{v}_i). \tag{3}$$

Define by $W_i(v_i) \equiv \pi_R^i(v_i; v_i)$, the profits of agent i at the equilibrium with truthful revelation. Then, over regions where the report is not audited, the following differential equation determines the profits of the agent:

$$\frac{\partial W_i}{\partial v_i} = -q_i(v_i) \quad \text{if} \quad m_i(v_i) = 0. \tag{4}$$

Over regions where the report of the agent is audited, the firm can observe the realization of v_i and reward the agent with the lowest possible amount consistent with the nonnegativity constraint on profits. In this case, the gross payoff of the agent is $J_i(v_i) = v_i q_i(v_i)$, and the net payoff is zero, namely

$$W_i(v_i) = 0 \quad \text{if} \quad m_i(v_i) = 1 \tag{5}$$

The only way constraints (3)–(5) can coexist is if the monitoring decision of the firm is determined in terms of a single cutoff point v_i^*. Any report about a realized value of unit cost in excess of v_i^* is audited, and any report about a realized value of unit cost that is smaller than v_i^* is not.

We can now state the constrained maximization problem facing firm i as an optimal control problem. The problem reduces to the choice of the cutoff point v_i^* and two functions specifying the quantity produced by the agent, $q_i(v_i)$, and its equilibrium profits, $W_i(v_i)$ over the region where auditing does not take place $(v_i \leq v_i^*)$. Those three decision variables are selected in order to maximize the expected profits of the firm, subject to constraints imposed by the characteristics of contracts which induce truthful revelation, and subject to limited liability on the part of the agent. In the statement of the problem, we suppress the argument v_i in the functions $q_i( )$ and $W_i( )$.

Optimal Contracting

In light of the above, the optimal contracting problem is specified as follows: Maximize with respect to v_i^*, q_i, W_i the function

$$
\begin{aligned}
R_i = &\int_{v_0-u_0}^{v_i^*} [(a - bEq_j - c_i - v_i)q_i - w_i]g(v_i)\,dv_i \\
&+ \int_{v_i^*}^{v_0+u_0} \frac{(a - bEq_j - c_i - v_i)^2}{4b} g(v_i)\,dv_i - K(1 - G(v_i^*))
\end{aligned}
\tag{6}
$$

subject to

$$
W_i' = -q_i, \tag{7}
$$

$$
W_i \geq 0. \tag{8}
$$

4. Derivation of the Equilibria

The problem stated in the previous section is an optimal control problem with $q_i( )$ the control variable and $W_i( )$ the state variable, the evolution of which is governed by the differential equation (7).

Define the following "revised unit cost" $\hat{c}_i$ as

$$
\hat{c}_i = c_i + \int_{v_0-u_0}^{v_i^*} G(t)\,dt. \tag{9}
$$

Then the solution for the quantities of output can be derived to be

$$
bq_i(v_i) = \begin{cases}
\dfrac{2a - 3c_i - \hat{c}_i + 2\hat{c}_j + v_0}{6} - 0.5\left(v_i + \dfrac{G(v_i)}{g(v_i)}\right) & v_i \leq v_i^* \\[3mm]
\dfrac{2a - 3c_i - \hat{c}_i + 2\hat{c}_j + v_0}{6} - 0.5v_i & v_i > v_i^*
\end{cases}
\tag{10}
$$

for $i,j = 1,2$; $i \neq j$. Notice that the quantity imposed upon the agent is discontinuous at the cutoff point v_i^*. At this point, the quantity of output jumps upwards by an amount $G(v_i^*)/2v_i^*$. In order to induce the agent truthfully to reveal his or her private information over the region in which the report of the agent is not audited, it is necessary to restrict output compared with a world in which information is complete. This restriction of output generates the discontinuity of $q_i(\ )$ at v_i^*.[2]

From (1) we can compute the expected output produced by each firm as follows:

$$bEq_i = \frac{a + \hat{c}_j - 2\hat{c}_i - v_0}{3} \qquad i,j = 1,2; \; i \neq j. \qquad (11)$$

If each firm could observe the costs of its agent, then the quantity produced would be given by an expression similar to (11), with the only change being that the c_i's replace the $\hat{c}_i$'s. Hence, the lack of observability of the agent's unit cost over the lower tail of the distribution $[v_0 - u_0, v_i^*]$ can be interpreted as causing an indirect increase in the unit variable cost of the firm, equal to the amount

$$0 \leq \hat{c}_i - c_i = \int_{v_0 - u_0}^{v_i^*} G(t)\, dt \leq u_0. \qquad (12)$$

The upper bound of inequality (12) is obtained if $v_i^* = v_0 + u_0$, and the lower bound is obtained when $v_i^* = v_0 - u_0$.

Differentiation of $R_i(\ )$ with respect to v_i^* yields[3] the monitoring reaction function of each firm as follows:

$$\frac{\partial R_i}{\partial v_i^*} \equiv T_i(v_i^*, v_j^*) = -G(v_i^*)\left[q_i(v_i^*) + \frac{1}{4bg(v_i^*)}\right] + Kg(v_i^*) \qquad (13)$$

In order to determine the shape of the "auditing reaction functions" of firms, it is necessary to determine the sign of $\partial T_i / \partial v_j^*$. From (13),

$$\frac{\partial T_i}{\partial v_j^*} = -\frac{1}{3b}G(v_j^*)G(v_i^*) < 0,$$

---

[2] For truthful revelation, it is necessary that $q_i(\ )$ is nonincreasing, which holds if $2 \geq Gg'/g^2$.

[3] At an interior equilibrium $T_i(v_i^*, v_j^*) = 0$, where $\partial T_i/\partial v_i^* < 0$. For uniqueness of the equilibrium and for the stability of the reaction functions, we also require that $(\partial T_i/\partial v_i^*)(\partial T_j/\partial v_j^*) - (\partial T_i/\partial v_j^*)(\partial T_j/\partial v_i^*) > 0$.

Figure 1: Reaction Functions Determining Monitoring

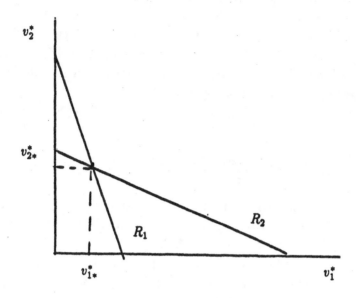

which implies that the reaction functions are downward sloping. Specifically, each firm responds to reduced auditing on the part of its rival by increasing its own monitoring activity. This result is quite reasonable, since reduced auditing implies an indirect increase in the firm's auditing cost and reduced production. At the Cournot equilibrium each firm responds to reduced production of its rival by increasing its own production. In the context of the monitoring activity, this increase of output is facilitated if the firm spends more resources in order to monitor its agent.

Another observation that follows from (13) is that the reaction function of the inherently more efficient firm (firm 1) lies closer to the origin than the reaction function of the inherently less efficient firm. Explicitly, for any level of monitoring activity of the rival, the more efficient firm has greater incentives to audit its agent. This observation follows for every v and w since $T_1(v, w) < T_2(v, w)$.[4]

In Figure 1, we describe the reaction functions of the firms which determine their monitoring policies. The symbol R_i designates the reaction

---

[4] At the equilibrium, $T_2(v_2^*, w) = 0$, where w is the cutoff point selected by the rival. From (13), $T_1(v_2^*, w) < 0$, which implies by the concavity of R_i that $T_1(v_1^*, w) = 0$ for $v_1^* < v_2^*$.

function of firm i, and v_i^* designates the equilibrium cutoff points. It is clear that $v_1^* < v_2^*$, namely the inherently more efficient firm is more likely to audit the report of its agent.

The reason why the more efficient firm monitors its agent more closely than the inefficient one is related to the indirect effect of monitoring on the unit variable cost of production. As explained earlier, that absence of monitoring has an implicit effect of raising the unit variable cost of the firm by an amount $\hat{c}_i - c_i$. This increase of unit cost is more significant the less resources the firm allocates to monitoring. Since the efficient firm covers a larger share of the market, such an increase of its unit variable cost reduces its expected profits to a larger extent than the reduction in profits of the inefficient firm. As a result, the efficient firm is more careful about auditing its agent compared with the inefficient firm.

5. Concluding Remarks

We have demonstrated that oligopolistic firms are more likely to devote resources to monitoring their agents if they are inherently more efficient. The absence of monitoring imposes an implicit increase of the unit variable cost of the firm. The more efficient firm that covers a larger share of the market loses more significantly from such an implicit increase of variable costs. As a result, it is more willing to devote resources in order to eliminate its uncertainty about the technology facing its agent.

References

Baron, D. and Besanko, D. (1984) "Regulation, Asymmetric Information, and Auditing," *Rand Journal of Economics*, **15**, 447-470.

Baron, D. and Myerson, R. (1982) "Regulating a Monopolist with Unknown Costs," *Econometrica*, **50**, 911-930.

Bonanno, G. and Vickers, J. (1988) "Vertical Separation," *The Journal of Industrial Economics*, **36**, 257-265.

Dye, R. (1986) "Optimal Monitoring Policies in Agencies," *Rand Journal of Economics*, **17**, 339-350.

Fershtman, H. and Judd, K. (1987) "Equilibrium Incentives in Oligopoly," *American Economic Review*, **77**, 339-350.

Gal-Or, E. (1987) "Duopolistic Vertical Restraints," Working Paper No. 650, University of Pittsburgh.

———— (1988) "Incentives to Monitor in Duopolistic Agency Models," Working Paper No. 672, University of Pittsburgh.

Grossman, S. and Hart, O. (1986) "The Costs and Benefits of Ownership: A Theory of Vertical and Lateral Integration," *Journal of Political Economy*, **94**, 691-719.

Harris, M. and Raviv, A. (1979) "Optimal Incentive Contracts with Imperfect Information," *Journal of Economic Theory*, **20**, 231-259.

Holmstrom, B. (1982) "Moral Hazard in Teams," *Bell Journal of Economics*, **13**, 324-340.

Kanodia, C. (1985) "Stochastic Monitoring and Moral Hazard," *Journal of Accounting Research*, **23**, 175-193.

Rey, P. and Stiglitz, J. (1986) "The Role of Exclusive Territories in Producers' Competition," Working Paper, Princeton University.

Riordan, M. and Sappington, D. (1987) "Information, Incentives, and Organizational Modes," *Quarterly Journal of Economics*, **102** ,243-263.

10

Optimal Auctions and Market Structure ·

Larry Samuelson

1. Introduction

Recent developments in economics make available two approaches to the study of economic exchange. Microeconomics initially concentrated on modeling trading processes as markets. Within this framework, attention was devoted to examining how behavior was affected by market structure. When considering the theory of the firm, for example, particular attention was given to the differences between perfect and imperfect competition. Key findings include that a firm will set its price equal to marginal cost if and only if it is perfectly competitive, and that the outcome will be efficient if and only if the market is perfectly competitive.

More recently, microeconomists have broadened their scope of inquiry to examine the mechanism design problem. Here, the means by which trading potentially occurs are not restricted to perfectly or imperfectly competitive markets. Instead, interest also turns to alternative procedures that might be created to transfer goods from sellers to buyers. One such mechanism is an auction, and a host of possible auction designs have been considered. A central result in auction theory is that in an isolated auction, a seller maximizes expected revenue by conducting an auction subject to a

* Financial support from the National Science Foundation and Hewlett Foundation is gratefully acknowledged.

reservation price which is higher than the seller's valuation. This yields an inefficient outcome, much like a monopoly.

The purpose of this paper is to establish some links between the market and mechanism design approaches to the study of trading processes. We compare the analysis of firm behavior under perfect and imperfect competition contributed by the market approach and the analysis of optimal auctions contributed by the mechanism design literature. We show that existing results on optimal reservation prices are the auction equivalent of monopoly pricing and establish additional reservation price results which are the equivalent of competitive pricing. The result is an enhanced understanding of the similarities and contrasts of the two approaches.

To accomplish this we must first devote some attention to the theory of auctions. Consider an auction involving risk-neutral buyers with privately known valuations independently drawn from identical distributions. Suppose that buyers' payments can depend only on their bids. The optimal auctions literature has established that the seller then maximizes expected revenue by holding any of an English, Dutch, sealed-bid first price or sealed-bid second price auction and by setting a reservation price below which the good will not be sold. The optimal reservations price is independent of the number of buyers and is higher than the seller's valuation.[1]

The auction literature has generally examined isolated auctions with a fixed number of buyers. In practice, buyers may have alternatives to attending a particular auction. The rules of the auction, including the reservation price, may then affect the number of buyers who attend. This introduces new incentives into the seller's choice of reservation price and in general will alter the optimal level of the latter.

Sections 2 and 3 examine the optimal reservation price in an auction which is part of such a larger market structure. We construct a "market" with a large number of buyers and sellers. Sellers first announce reservation prices; buyers then choose which auctions to attend; and auctions are held. A buyer's alternative to a given auction is to attend a different auction, and a seller's reservation price may affect the number of attending buyers.[2]

---

[1] Auction theory is developed in Milgrom and Weber (1982), Myerson (1981), Riley and Samuelson (1981) and McAfee and McMillan (1987b).

[2] Peters (1986a, 1986b) and Wolinsky (1986) provide alternative models involving auctions and market structures in which reservation prices do not play a role in buyers' choices of which auction to attend.

Let $\tilde{z}$ be the optimal reservation price in an auction with an exogenously fixed number of buyers. It is immediately apparent that sellers in the market just described will have an incentive to reduce their reservation prices below $\tilde{z}$, if doing so attracts additional buyers, since a marginal reduction from $\tilde{z}$ has no effect on expected revenue for a given number of buyers, but increases the number of buyers. The main result of Sections 2 and 3 is that if and only if the seller is insignificant in the market (in a sense to be precisely defined, but which essentially stipulates that no single seller can affect buyers' equilibrium expected payoffs), then the seller will set a reservation price equal to the seller's valuation.[3]

The seller's reservation-price-setting behavior in an isolated auction suggests an analogy between a monopoly and an auction seller. A monopoly sets a price which does two things: it induces an inefficient outcome, since some buyers whose valuations exceed the monopoly's valuation (cost) do not purchase the good; and it increases the monopoly's revenue by forcing those buyers who do purchase to do so at a higher price. Similarly, the auction seller's reservation price has two effects: it induces inefficiency in the form of the possibility that the good is not sold even though buyers exist whose valuation exceeds the seller's (though the buyers' valuations do not exceed the reservations price); and again it increases the seller's expected revenue by inducing buyers with higher valuations to increase their bids.

This analogy can be carried one step further: The result that an auction seller will set a reservation price equal to the seller's valuation if and only if the seller is insignificant is analogous to the result that a firm sets price equal to marginal cost if and only if the firm is insignificant (perfectly competitive). Thus, we have completely parallel results from the theories of firm behavior and auctions.

The alternatives to attending an auction may not always be attendance at an alternative auction. Section 4 constructs a more general model by letting potential buyers be characterized by a cost of attendance, where this

---

[3] Engelbrecht-Wiggans (1987a) provides two examples in which sellers will set reservation prices of 0 (the seller's valuation is 0 in each case) in order to attract buyers. Our analysis differs from his in considering general (rather than uniform) distributions; in allowing sellers to have non-zero valuations (and, hence, ensuring that equality of reservation price and value is an interior and not corner solution); and in constructing a model of the market that allows the connection between optimal reservation prices and the insignificance of individual sellers to be examined. McAfee and McMillan (1987a) state a result which matches that of our general model in Section 4.

cost includes direct costs incurred to attend as well as the opportunity costs of neglecting available alternatives (including possibly alternative auctions). A seller is insignificant in this case if and only if the supply of buyers is perfectly elastic. We again find that the optimal reservation price equals the seller's valuation if and only if the seller is insignificant.

2. The Model

Consider a market consisting of a number of identical sellers, each of whom owns a single indivisible commodity valued by a seller at $\phi \geq 0$, and a number of buyers. The market operates as follows. First, each seller announces a reservation price. Each buyer then chooses which seller's auction to attend, possibly employing a mixed strategy. Upon executing these strategies and arriving at a particular seller's auction, each buyer has a valuation drawn independently from the density f (with cumulative distribution F) on the interval $[0, 1]$. Sealed-bid first price auctions are then held by each seller subject to the seller's announced reservation price.[4]

Suppose, initially, that we have finite numbers B and S of buyers and sellers; these are denoted by b_j, $j = 1, 2, \ldots, B$ and by s_i, $i = 1, 2, \ldots, S$. A market outcome consists of a specification of a reservation price for each seller and a specification of the probability with which a buyer visits a seller. We let $z(s_i)$ denote seller s_i's reservation price. We assume that buyers pursue identical search strategies and let $p(s_i)$ denote the probability that a given buyer attends seller s_i's auction.[5] We then calculate two additional probabilities: Define $Q(x)$ to be the probability that the maximum valuation among the buyers that visit seller s_i is less than or equal to x; and define $P(x)$ to be the probability that the maximum valuation

---

[4] Intuitively, we can think of valuations being drawn after arrival at a seller because buyers must inspect the good in question. Technically, this formulation has the advantage that buyers are identical during the search stage of the game. Wolinsky (1986) employs a similar convention.

[5] When choosing which auctions to attend, buyers are identical because they have not yet taken their independent draws from the buyer valuation distribution. We assume that buyers choose symmetric search strategies, so that the probability that a buyer attends the auction of seller s_i, given by $p(s_i)$, does not vary across buyers, even though it may be that $p(s_i) \neq p(s_j)$. This assumption yields symmetric equilibria.

among a buyer's rivals is less than or equal to x. Then[6]

$$Q(x) = \left[1 + p(s_i)\big(F(x) - 1\big)\right]^B, \tag{1}$$

$$P(x) = \left[1 + p(s_i)\big(F(x) - 1\big)\right]^{B-1}. \tag{2}$$

We would like to examine this market when buyers and sellers are sufficiently numerous to be individually insignificant. To do this we examine the limit of the market as B and S become arbitrarily large, while the relative magnitudes of B and S are preserved. To guide this construction, first note that if B is increased and the product $p(s_i)B \equiv k$ is held constant (to capture the intuition that the relative magnitudes of buyers and sellers and, hence, the expected number of buyers to arrive at a seller's auction remains unchanged), then the limiting values of $Q(x)$ and $P(x)$ are

$$Q(x) = e^{k(F(x)-1)}, \tag{3}$$

$$P(x) = e^{k(F(x)-1)}. \tag{4}$$

Intuitively, we can think of k as the limiting counterpart of the buyer/seller ratio for sellers whose auctions are attended with probability $p(s_i)$ in the initial finite model.

This suggests the following limiting economy. First, let buyers and sellers be indexed by real numbers in the intervals $[0, B]$ and $[0, S]$, respectively, with B and S being the measures of buyers and sellers. Second, we will simplify the analysis by confining attention to symmetric equilibria in which the identical sellers set identical reservation prices and buyers adopt identical search strategies. Let z^* be the equilibrium reservation price and let $k(z^*) = B/S$ be the resulting buyer/seller ratio of each seller.[7]

An equilibrium for this market is now easily defined. The basic requirement is that z^* be such that no seller can achieve a higher payoff by

---

[6] To derive these expressions, note that $1 - p(s_i) + p(s_i)F(x)$ is the probability that a particular buyer either chooses another auction, which gives a probability of $1 - p(s_i)$, or chooses this auction but has a valuation lower than x, which gives a probability of $p(s_i)F(x)$. Then $Q(x)$ and $P(x)$ are the probabilities that this occurs for all B buyers and all $B - 1$ rival buyers. See Wolinsky (1986) for a similar derivation.

[7] We have $k(z^*) = B/S$ because the presumption of identical equilibrium reservation prices and search strategies gives $p(s_i) = 1/S$ and $k = p(s_i)B = B/S$. Samuelson (1987) provides a more rigorous development of the model that allows asymmetric equilibria, though the analysis is still confined to symmetric equilibria.

unilaterally changing strategies to some reservation price z''. Such a reservation price would attract a buyer/seller ratio of $k(z'')$. To investigate the latter, let $H(z, k(z))$ be the expected payoff (calculated before the reservation price is drawn) to a buyer who attends an auction with reservation price z and buyer/seller ratio $k(z)$. Recalling that z^* is the equilibrium price, we find that a reservation price of z'' will attract a buyer/seller ratio of $k(z'')$, such that

$$H(z^*, k(z^*)) = H(z'', k(z'')). \tag{5}$$

Condition (5) indicates that in response to the appearance of reservation price z'', buyers adjust search strategies in order to equate the expected payoff at the seller in question with the *prevailing* expected payoff in the market. The appearance of the prevailing expected payoff in (5) reflects the fact that individual agents are insignificant in the market. Because the seller who switches to reservation price z'' is of measure zero, sufficient buyers can switch to or from this seller in order to achieve a buyer/seller ratio of $k(z'')$ without affecting buyer/seller ratios and, hence, buyers' expected payoffs at other sellers.

Now let $K(z, k(z))$ be the expected payoff to a seller who sets reservation price z and attracts a buyer/seller ratio of $k(z)$. The remaining condition for an equilibrium is then

$$K(z^*, k(z^*)) \geq K(z'', k(z'')) \tag{6}$$

for all $z'' \neq z^*$. Condition (6) requires that the seller earn at least as high a payoff from an equilibrium offer as from a non-equilibrium offer.

We can make these conditions less abstract by computing buyer and seller auction payoffs. Consider the buyer. The optimal bid for a buyer who has drawn valuation b is well known (see Wolinsky, 1986) to be

$$b - \left[e^{k(F(b)-1)}\right]^{-1} \int_z^b e^{k(F(x)-1)} \, dx. \tag{7}$$

Expression (7) reveals that the buyer submits a bid that falls short of the buyer's valuation, with the discrepancy chosen to balance the benefit of paying a lower price, if the auction is won, against the cost of possibly not winning the auction. The expected payoff to the buyer (before the buyer's valuation is drawn) at a seller with reservation price z and buyer/seller ratio k is then

$$\int_z^1 \left(bP(b) - P(b)\left(b - [e^{k(F(b)-1)}]^{-1} \int_z^b e^{k(F(x)-1)}\, dx \right) \right) f(b) db \qquad (8)$$
$$\equiv H(z,k),$$

where $\int_z^1 bP(b)f(b)db$ gives the expected benefit from winning the auction ($P(b)$ is the probability that a buyer of valuation b wins the auction) and the remainder of (8) gives the buyer's expected payment. Substituting for $P(b)$ from (4), we obtain

$$H(z,k) = \int_z^1 \left(be^{k(F(b)-1)} - e^{k(F(b)-1)} \right.$$
$$\left. \left(b - [e^{k(F(b)-1)}]^{-1} \int_z^b e^{k(F(x)-1)}\, dx \right) \right) f(b) db \qquad (9)$$
$$= \int_z^1 \left(\int_z^b e^{k(F(x)-1)} dx \right) f(b) db.$$

Next, the seller's expected payoff from an auction with reservation price z, valuation ϕ and buyer/seller ratio k, or $K(z,k)$, is given by

$$\int_z^1 \left(b - [e^{k(F(b)-1)}]^{-1} \int_z^b e^{k(F(x)-1)}\, dx \right) dQ(b) + \phi\left[1 - \int_z^1 dQ(b) \right]. \qquad (10)$$

Here, $dQ(b)$ is a density describing the likely valuation of the winning buyer. The first term in (10) then gives the seller's expected payoff from selling the good, while the second term gives the expected payoff arising from the possibility that the seller retains the good and receives the valuation ϕ. To simplify (10) we obtain, from (3),

$$dQ(b) = e^{k(F(b)-1)} k f(b) db.$$

Expression (10) is then

$$K(z,k) = k\int_z^1 \left(b - [e^{k(F(b)-1)}]^{-1} \int_z^b e^{k(F(x)-1)}\, dx \right) e^{k(F(b)-1)} f(b) db$$
$$+ \phi\left[1 - \int_z^1 ke^{k(F(b)-1)} f(b) db \right] \qquad (11)$$
$$= 1 - ze^{k(F(z)-1)} - \int_z^1 e^{k(F(b)-1)} db - kH(z,k) + \phi e^{k(F(z)-1)},$$

where the last equality is achieved via integration by parts.

3. Equilibrium

We can now consider the issue of the optimal level of z. We must find a z^* that maximizes the seller's payoff, given that a function $k(z)$ allocates a buyer/seller ratio of $k(z^*) = B/S$ to reservation price z^* and a ratio $k(z)$ that satisfies (5) to other values of z. The fact that z^* maximizes the seller's payoff ensures that if z^* is interior, or $z^* > 0$, then z^* must satisfy

$$\Gamma(z^*) \equiv \frac{\partial K(z^*, k(z^*))}{\partial z} + \frac{\partial K(z^*, k(z^*))}{\partial k} \frac{\partial k(z^*)}{\partial z} = 0, \qquad (12)$$

where condition (5) ensures that $k(z)$ satisfies

$$\frac{\partial H(z^*, k(z^*))}{\partial z} + \frac{\partial H(z^*, k(z^*))}{\partial k} \frac{\partial k(z^*)}{\partial z} = 0. \qquad (13)$$

¿From (11) we can calculate the derivative in (12) to be

$$\Gamma(z) = (\phi - z)e^{k(F(z)-1)}kf(z) - k\left[\frac{\partial H(z,k)}{\partial z} + \frac{\partial H(z,k)}{\partial k} \frac{\partial k}{\partial z}\right]$$

$$+ \left((\phi - z)e^{k(F(z)-1)}(F(z) - 1) - \int_z^1 e^{k(F(b)-1)}\right. \qquad (14)$$

$$\left.(F(b) - 1)db - H(z,k)\right)\frac{\partial k}{\partial z}.$$

Condition (13) ensures that the bracketed term in (14) equals zero. We now consider a reservation price set equal to the seller's valuation. Setting $z = \phi$ and using (9), we obtain

$$\Gamma(\phi) = \left(\int_\phi^1 e^{k(F(b)-1)}(1 - F(b))db - \int_\phi^1 \int_\phi^b e^{k(F(x)-1)}dx\, f(b)db\right)\frac{\partial k}{\partial z}.$$

Integration of the second term by parts yields

$$\Gamma(\phi) = \left(\int_\phi^1 e^{k(F(b)-1)}db - \int_\phi^b e^{k(F(x)-1)}dx\, F(b)\bigg|_\phi^1\right)\frac{\partial k}{\partial z} = 0. \qquad (15)$$

The first order condition is thus satisfied at $z = \phi$, and the optimal reservation price duplicates the seller's valuation.[8]

To gain some insight into this result, consider a market with a finite number of buyers and sellers, so that if a seller i raises i's reservation price, then the switching of buyers to other sellers from seller i increases the number of buyers attending other sellers' auctions sufficiently that the buyers' payoffs at these other auctions decrease. Then (13) is replaced by

$$\frac{\partial H(z,k)}{\partial z} + \frac{\partial H(z,k)}{\partial k}\frac{\partial k}{\partial z} > 0, \tag{16}$$

and we have $\Gamma(\phi) > 0$. In this case the optimal reservation price will be set higher than the valuation. Intuitively, the seller i finds it more profitable to increase the reservation price in this case than in the case where (13) holds, because doing so now increases the number of buyers at alternative sellers enough to decrease the buyers' payoffs at these alternative sellers. This makes buyers less willing to abandon seller i and yields a payoff to seller i of increasing the reservation price that is higher than the payoff which appears when (13) holds. The seller then optimally sets a reservation price higher than the seller's valuation. As the number of buyers and sellers grows, the optimal reservation price will approach the seller's valuation.

An example illustrates this point. Let the buyer/seller ratio, B/S, be 5/2. Let seller reservation prices be 0 and let buyers' valuations be uniformly distributed over the unit interval. If the number of buyers attending a given seller's auction is fixed, then the optimal reservation price is .5. If there are two sellers and buyers search according to our model, the optimal reservation price can be calculated to be approximately .26. In the infinite counterpart of this model the optimal reservation price is 0.

To gain an alternative perspective, notice that the buyer's expected payoff appears in the expression for the seller's expected payoff given by (11). The key step in establishing the optimality of a reservation price equal to the seller's valuation was the realization that variations in the reservation price cannot affect the equilibrium buyer's expected payoff. Our results thus reveal that the seller can profitably raise the reservation price above the seller's valuation if and only if doing so allows the seller to transfer gains-from-trade from the buyer to the seller. Such a transfer is in turn

---

[8] Direct calculation of the first derivative, from (14), shows that the first derivative has the sign of $z - \phi$, verifying that second order conditions hold at $z = \phi$.

possible if and only if the actions of the seller can affect buyers' equilibrium payoffs at other sellers. In the absence of such an effect the option of attending an alternative auction fixes buyers' payoffs and prevents the seller from appropriating gains-from-trade from buyers. The seller then cannot achieve an increased payoff by raising the reservation price above the seller's valuation.

4. Generalization

This section examines an alternative, more general model. Consider a single seller. Let buyers who might potentially attend this seller's auction be characterized by a cost of attending. This includes direct costs of attending the auction as sell as the opportunity costs of foregone alternatives. We can then define a function $\theta : \Re_+ \rightarrow \Re_+$, denoted $\theta(c)$, which identifies the number of buyers with attendance costs at most c. Intuitively, this is a supply-of-buyers curve. A reservation price of z now induces $k(z)$ buyers to attend (modulo potential integer problems), where $k(z)$ satisfies

$$\theta\Big(H\big(z, k(z)\big)\Big) = k(z). \tag{16}$$

This equilibrium condition requires that the number of buyers attending the auction adjust, so that the expected payoff of attending equals the marginal buyer's cost of attending.

In this model a seller can affect buyers' equilibrium payoffs if and only if the supply of buyers curve is not perfectly elastic, so that the derivative $\partial\theta/\partial c$ is positive and various values of $H(z, k(z))$ are potential solutions to (16). We can then characterize a seller as insignificant if and only if the supply of buyers *is* perfectly elastic.[9] The observation with which the previous section closed, namely that a seller can profitably raise the reservation price above the seller's valuation if and only if doing so affects buyers' equilibrium payoffs at other sellers, is easily seen to hold if the phrase "at other sellers" is replaced with "from alternative activities," with the analysis of (13) - (15) continuing to hold. Notice in particular that the effect of our simultaneous auctions market was to induce a perfectly elastic supply of buyers facing each seller.

---

[9] If the supply of buyers is perfectly elastic, then there is an unlimited supply of buyers at some cost, say c', so that $\theta(c)$ is a vertical line at c'. In equilibrium we then must have $H(z, k(z)) = c'$ for (16) to hold. Engelbrecht-Wiggans (1987b) constructs a model with an effectively perfectly elastic supply of buyers.

We thus again find that the seller will set a reservation price equal to the seller's valuation if and only if the seller is insignificant. While this is a familiar result, we have now achieved a significant generalization. Insignificance can now be characterized as a perfectly elastic supply of buyers and the equivalence of competitive behavior, and insignificance holds regardless of the nature of the market generating the supply of buyers.

5. Discussion

An intuitive interpretation can be given to these results that provides our desired link between market and mechanism design approaches. Consider a seller conducting an auction with an exogenously specified number of buyers. The optimal reservation price is higher than the seller's valuation. This causes the trading process to be inefficient, in that cases will arise in which the seller retains the good even though a bidder exists whose valuation exceeds the seller's. However, the seller exploits the reservation price and the competition among the bidders to increase expected revenue by inducing higher bids from those bidders with valuations which exceed the reservation price. This is analogous to the practice of a conventional monopoly, which sets a price that is inefficiently high but increases the monopoly's profit level.

Now embed this auction in a market in which reservation prices attract buyers. Suppose that seller i is insignificant in the sense that an adjustment in seller i's reservation price does not, through its effect on the buyers' search or auction attendance strategies, affect the buyers' payoffs from other sellers or alternative activities (though it may affect the number of buyers who attend seller i's auction and, hence, seller i's payoff). Then the optimal reservation price will be the seller's valuation, ϕ. If sellers are not insignificant, so that the buyers' strategy adjustments which follow a variation in the reservation price of a single seller do affect buyers' expected payoffs at other sellers or alternative activities, then the optimal reservation price exceeds ϕ.

This reinforces the analogy between reservation price setting and monopoly behavior. A reservation price of ϕ is analogous to a competitive price in that it yields an efficient outcome. An auction seller who does not compete for buyers achieves an increased payoff by the inefficient action of raising the reservation price above the competitive level. When the auction seller is embedded in a market-like process in such a way that the seller is competitive (cannot affect buyers payoffs), the seller is deprived of market power, which causes him to set the efficient price. If the seller is not insignificant (can affect payoffs), then market power is wielded in the form of a price higher than the competitive price.

This analogy can be pushed one step further. The sellers in this market set reservation prices which are privately optimal. Interest then turns to the conditions under which the incentives created by the market are such that this quest of private optimality yields a socially optimal outcome. The socially optimal reservation price is ϕ, since then and only then do no cases arise in which a good remains unsold in spite of the presence of a buyer matched with a seller with the former's valuation exceeding the latter's. We then have the familiar result that decentralized private optimization yields a socially efficient outcome if and only if agents are competitive.

References

Engelbrecht-Wiggans, R. (1987a) "On Optimal Reservation Prices in Auctions," *Management Science*, to appear.

———— (1987b) "Optimal Auctions: The Efficiency of Oral Auctions without Reserve for Risk Neutral Bidders with Private Values and Costly Information," Working Paper 1316, Univ. of Illinois.

McAffee, R. P. and McMillan, J. (1987a) "Auctions with Entry," *Economics Letters* **23**, 343-347.

———— (1987b) "Auctions and Bidding," *Journal of Economic Literature* **25**, 699-738.

Milgrom, P. R. and Weber, R. J. (1982) "A Theory of Auctions and Competitive Bidding," *Econometrica* **50**, 1089-1122.

Myerson, R. B. (1981) "Optimal Auction Design," *Mathematics of Operations Research* **6**, 58-73.

Peters, M. (1986a) "Ex Ante Price Offers in Matching Games: Non Steady States," Working Paper 8611, Univ. of Toronto.

———— (1986b) "Ex Ante Pricing and Bargaining," Mimeo, Univ. of Toronto.

Riley, J. and Samuelson, W. (1981) "Optimal Auctions," *American Economic Review* **71**, 381-392.

Samuelson, L. (1987) "Optimal Reservations Prices for Competitive Auctions," Working Paper, Penn. State Univ.

Wolinsky, A. (1986) "Dynamic Markets with Competitive Bidding," Research Report 157, Hebrew Univ. of Jerusalem.

11

Increasing Returns
and Selling Expenses

Claus Weddepohl

1. Introduction

Increasing returns are not consistent with price-taking behavior; that is, at a given price, there is no maximum of profits (unless this maximum happens to be zero). Therefore, no supply function exists, and an equilibrium in a single market cannot result from equality of supply and demand.

Similarly, in a general equilibrium model with increasing returns in some sectors, a Walrasian equilibrium does not exist, so that other types of equilibrium have to be defined. At least two approaches are possible:

(i) Define a system of prices that does not result from price-taking behavior in the increasing-returns sector, but apply a pricing rule that ensures Pareto-efficient equilibrium allocations. This approach has resulted in different pricing rules, particularly marginal and mean-cost pricing. Cornet (1988) gives an overview of the literature on general equilibrium and increasing returns.

(ii) Assume that firms are profit maximizers and study the equilibria that may occur under noncooperative behavior. In this paper we follow the second approach, using a partial equilibrium model. Clearly, we can at best expect some kind of Nash equilibrium and the solutions will generally not be Pareto-efficient.

If, under increasing returns, production is profitable at some level, it is then more profitable at any higher level and profit-maximizing supply is infinite. Firms will want to produce and sell as much as possible and excess supply will always remain. The sales of each firm depend on how the consumers distribute their demand among firms. In Weddepohl (1978) it was assumed that this distribution was given by fixed market shares. In practice we observe that firms not only spend money on technologically necessary inputs, but also on activities, like advertising and related things, frequently summarized by the term marketing, which are believed to promote sales and to increase the firm's market share. It seems obvious that how much a firm's selling expenses effect sales depends on the relative efforts of the firm rather than on the absolute amount spent. It is not implausible to assume that selling expenses of a single firm show decreasing returns

A production function describes the inputs necessary for the production of a commodity, and the increasing returns stem from either fixed cost or economies to scale in production. The costs of producing and selling are complementary.

In the present paper we explore the following idea: If production shows increasing returns, but selling expenses show decreasing returns, then the behavior of selling expenses becomes dominant, so that the combination of the two leads, at least locally, to a convex total cost function. As a result, the most profitable production exists at given price and given selling expenses of other firms.

In Section 2 we present a model with a finite number of firms and define equilibrium in this model. In order to find out if the model can describe behavior that is "competitive," we study a model with a continuum of firms in Section 3. Section 4 contains our conclusions.

2. A Model with a Finite Number of Firms

There is a finite set $I = \{1, 2, \ldots, n\}$ of firms that produce a homogeneous commodity. Let y_i be the production and sales of firm i and let $y = (y_1, y_2, \ldots, y_n)$. All firms have the same concave cost function $f(y_i)$, where the following assumption can be made:

Assumption. $f(y_i) \geqq 0$, f is twice differentiable, $f'(y_i) > 0$ and $f''(y_i) < 0$.

The implication is that mean costs are above marginal costs: $f(y_i)/y_i > f'(y_i)$. There is a decreasing demand function $D(p)$ with demand $x = D(p)$ at price p. Consumers always buy at the lowest price, which implies that all firms have to sell at the same price. Consumers have to decide from which firm they will buy. Their decision, with respect to the supplier, depends on the selling expenses of the firms. Let s_i be the selling expenses of firm i, with $s = (s_1, s_2, \ldots, s_n)$ and $\hat{s}_i = (s_1, s_2, \ldots, s_{i-1}, s_{i+1}, \ldots, s_n)$; then

$$S = \sum_I s_i, \qquad \hat{S}_i = \sum_{j \neq i} s_j.$$

It is assumed that each firm's market share $\alpha_i = y_i/x$ equals the fraction of its selling expenses to total selling expenses; that is,

$$\alpha_i = s_i/S = s_i/(s_i + \hat{S}_i), \tag{1}$$

with $\sum \alpha_i = 1$.

Here α_i is an increasing and concave function in s_i, since $\partial \alpha_i/\partial s_i > 0$ and $\partial^2 \alpha_i/\partial s_i^2 < 0$. For given total demand x, firm i's sales are $y_i = \alpha_i x$. We can obtain the selling expenses necessary to sell y_i by inverting (1):

$$s_i = \frac{y_i \hat{S}_i}{x - y_i} = \frac{\alpha_i \hat{S}_i}{1 - \alpha_i}, \tag{2}$$

which clearly is increasing and convex in y_i or α_i. Now profit equals

$$\pi_i(y_i; \ p, x, \hat{S}_i) = py_i - f(y_i) - s_i, \tag{3}$$

or equivalently,

$$\pi_i(\alpha_i; \ p, x, \hat{S}_i) = p\alpha_i x - f(\alpha_i x) - s_i. \tag{4}$$

Assumption A. First, we assume that the price p is given.

Definition 2.1. *For given p and $x = D(p)$, an equilibrium consists of s^* and y^*, such that each firm's profit is*
(I) nonnegative, and
(II) maximum for given value of $\hat{S}_i$.

Clearly, this is a Nash equilibrium in a noncooperative game with payoff functions (3) or (4) and with strategies y_i or α_i, s_i being defined by (2).

If a nonnegative profit is not attainable, then the firm will be inactive; that is, $y_i = 0 = s_i$. For a local maximum it is required that

$$\partial \pi_i / \partial \alpha_i = (p - f'(\alpha_i x))x - \frac{\hat{S}_i}{(1 - \alpha_i)^2} = 0. \tag{5}$$

For (5) to give a maximum it is also required that the second-order condition holds:

$$-f''(\alpha_i x)x^2 - \frac{2\hat{S}_i}{(1 - \alpha_i)^3} < 0. \tag{6}$$

Now (5) gives an optimal α_i as well as optimal s_i and y_i; as in the standard model, minimization of the cost function gives supply of firm i.

We only consider *symmetric equilibrium*, with $m \leq n$ the number of active firms. Then $\alpha_i = 1/m$, $y_i = x/m$, and $s_i = S/m$, $\hat{S}_i = (m - 1)s_i$; hence, (5) becomes

$$p - f'(x/m) - \frac{(m - 1)s_i}{x(1 - 1/m)^2} = 0, \tag{7}$$

which gives

$$s_i = \frac{(m - 1)x}{m^2}(p - f'(x/m)). \tag{8}$$

Since π must be nonnegative,

$$\pi(p, m) \equiv px/m - f(x/m) - \frac{(m - 1)x}{m^2}(p - f'(x/m)) \geq 0. \tag{9}$$

Differentiating with respect to m,

$$\partial \pi / \partial m = (p - f'(x/m))[-2x/m^3] - f''(x/m)[(m - 1)x^2/m^4], \tag{10}$$

and substituting the second-order condition (6) in (10), we obtain

$$\partial \pi / \partial m < (p - f'(x/m))[-2x/m^3]$$
$$+ (p - f'(x/m))\frac{2m}{x(m - 1)}\frac{(m - 1)x^2}{m^4} = 0. \tag{11}$$

If (6) holds, then $\pi(p, m)$ is *decreasing* in m and (9) can be rewritten as:

$$(1/m)\left[(px - f'(x/m))x/m - \{f(x/m) - f'(x/m)x/m\}\right] \geq 0,$$

which gives

$$m \leqq \frac{p - f'(x/m)}{f(x/m)/(x/m) - f'(x'/m)}. \tag{12}$$

Note that at $m = 1$, (8) gives $s = 0$ and (12) reduces to $p - f(x)/x \geqq 0$. With $\hat{S} = 0$, (4) is just the optimum condition for a monopolist. Since $\pi(p, m)$ is decreasing in m, two cases can be distinguished:

(i) $\pi(p, m) \geqq 0$ for all $m \leqq n$; that is, (12) holds for all $m \leqq n$;

(ii) $\pi(p, m) \geqq 0$ for some integer M, if $m \leqq M$ and $\pi(p, m) < 0$, for $m > M$.

In the first case, all firms will be active. In the second case, at most M fims can make a nonnegative profit; hence, exactly M firms are active in an equilibrium with price p (and demand $x = D(p)$). If there are less than M active firms in the second case, Condition II of Definition 2.1 is not satisfied for nonactive firms. It will be profitable for a new firm to become active, since it will then get a positive profit at $x/(m+1)$ and the profit of the other firms will then decrease by (11). Entry stops as soon as $m = M$, for then no profit can be made by an entrant.

Assumption B. Suppose that the price is not given, but that each firm has to set a price.

If the price is not given, another condition is to be added in order to define an equilibrium: It should not be profitable for any firm to set a lower price. Since it was assumed that consumers always buy at the lowest price, a firm having a lower price than other firms will absorb all demand, whatever the selling expenses. Hence, a price cut initiated by one firm must be followed by all. On the other hand, if a firm sets a higher price, the firm will lose all demand and there is no reason for the others to follow. Hence, no firm will ever set a higher price.

This leads to the following definition:

Definition 2.2. An equilibrium *consists of* p^*, s^* *and* y^*, *such that* Conditions (I) and (II) of Definition 2.1 hold, and

(III) for all $p \leqq p^*$:

$$p^* D(p^*)/m - f(D(p^*)/m) - s_i^* \geqq p D(p)/m - f(D(p)/m) - s_i^*. \tag{13}$$

Condition (III) implies, for $x^* = D(p^*)$, that

$$x^* + [p^* - f'(x^*/m)] (dx/dp) \geq 0,$$

or equivalently,

$$dx^*/dp \geq \frac{-x^*}{p^* - f'(x^*/m)}, \tag{14}$$

which clearly means that the price cannot be higher than the price the firm would set, if it were a monopolist with demand function $D(p)/m$.

Any pair (p, m) determines an equilibrium, if (14) holds and if m is the largest integer to satisfy (12). Consequently, there may exist different equilibria: the higher the price, the larger the set of active firms m is, but the price must always satisfy (14). There may be room only for a number of active firms smaller than n.

Example. $x = A - Bp$, $A > 0$, $B > 0$; $f(y_i) = a + by_i$.
For a given price (12) becomes

$$m \leq h(p) = \frac{\sqrt{(p - b)(A - Bp)}}{\sqrt{a}}. \tag{a}$$

For every p there is a largest integer that satisfies (a) and that gives an equilibrium, if $h(p) \geq 1$. In Figure 1 the function $h(p)$ and the set of equilibrium pairs (p, m) are depicted, with $A = 20$, $B = 1$, $a = 1$ and $b = 1$.

If the price is free, then Condition III of Definition 2.2 gives

$$p \leq (A/B + b)/2, \tag{b}$$

and now equilibria are determined by all p and m, which satisfy (a) and (b). The function $h(p)$ attains its maximum at $(A/B + b)/2$. In Figure 1 only the points to the left of $(A/B + b)/2 = 10.5$ represent equilibria (with $n > 9$); hence, there is room for at most 9 firms.

3. A Model with a Continuum of Firms

The model of the previous section is typical of monopolistic competition. The number of firms is finite and the selling expenses, s_i, of an individual firm affect total selling expenses, S_i. With free prices an individual firm can influence the price (compare (13)).

Figure 1: The Function $h(p)$.

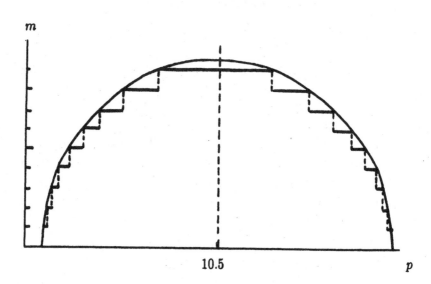

We now try to generalize the model in such a way that it gets a more competitive character, which requires firms to become "insignificant." In general, this can be achieved in two ways: by letting the number of firms increase, or by taking a measureable set of firms.

The second method is applied below. We again study a market for a homogeneous commodity. The commodity can be produced by a set of firms, $I = [0, 1]$. Firms are denoted by $t \in I$; here I is an atomless measure space, with a σ-algebra generated by Borel sets and with measure μ (see Hildenbrand, 1974). For $A \subset I$, the measure is $\mu(A)$, with $\mu(I) = 1$; hence, $\mu(A)$ is the fraction of firms that are in A. The set $\{t\}$, which contains a single firm, is negligible; that is, $\mu\{t\} = 0$.

There is a demand function $x = D(p)$. Production is an *integrable* function, $y : I \to \Re$, where $y(t)$ is the production of $t \in I$. Total production is

$$Y = \int_I y(t)dt$$

and, since the measure of I equals 1, Y can be interpreted as *mean* production of the set of firms I. Then $A \subset I$ produces

$$Y(A) = \int_A y(t)dt.$$

All firms have the same concave cost function, $f(y)$, which shows decreasing mean and marginal costs (increasing returns to scale). As before, we now assume the following:

Assumption A. $f(y(t)) \geqq 0$, f is twice differentiable and $f'(y(t)) > 0$ and $f''(y(t)) < 0$.

Let the function $s : I \to \Re$ give the *selling expenses* of each firm. The selling expenses of $A \subset I$ are

$$S(A) = \int_A s(t)dt \qquad (15)$$

and the *mean selling expenses* (with respect to I) are

$$S = S(I).$$

We define *relative selling expenses* by the function $\sigma : I \to \Re$, with

$$\sigma(t) = s(t)/S; \qquad (16)$$

now, obviously,

$$\int_I \sigma(t)dt = 1. \qquad (17)$$

We do not assume that the market share is identical to relative selling expenses, as in Section 2, because in that case the share $\alpha(t)$, and also the sales $y(t)$ of firm t, would be, at given S, a linear function of $s(t)$ (since $\mu\{t\} = 0$). It should, however, be a *concave* function of $s(t)$, in order to ensure that the total cost function becomes a convex function for sufficiently high sales.

Let $\varphi : \Re \to \Re$ be a function, on which we assume the following:

Assumption B. (i) φ is an increasing and strictly concave function: $\varphi'(z) > 0$, $\varphi''(z) < 0$ with $\varphi(0) = 0$ and $\varphi(1) = 1$;

(ii) the function $z\varphi'(z)/\varphi(z)$ is increasing.

Part (ii) of Assumption B means

$$\varphi'(z)/\varphi(z) + z\varphi''(z)/\varphi(z) - z[\varphi'(z)/\varphi(z)]^2 \geqq 0$$

and, since by Part (i) of Assumption B, $\varphi'(z)/\varphi(z) > 0$, Part (ii) is equivalent to

$$[1 - z\varphi'/\varphi + z\varphi''/\varphi'] \geqq 0. \tag{18}$$

The condition $\varphi(1) = 1$ is just a normalization rule, as can be seen in (19) and (20) below. Part (ii) of Assumption B requires that the last term of (18), which is negative, be small enough, taking into account that the second term satisfies $z\varphi'(z)/\varphi(z) < 1$. It holds, e.g., for $\varphi(z) = z^c$, for $0 < c < 1$.

We define *weighted relative* selling expenses by

$$\gamma(t) = \varphi(\sigma(t)), \ \Gamma(\sigma) = \int_I \gamma(t)dt. \tag{19}$$

Then the "market share," the intensity of demand of firm t, is

$$\alpha(t) = \gamma(t)/\Gamma(\sigma), \tag{20}$$

which means that, if mean demand equals x, then $\alpha(t)x$ will be the demand directed toward firm t. Clearly,

$$\int_I \alpha(t)\,dt = 1,$$

and we have $\alpha(t) = 0$, if $\sigma(t) = 0$ and $S \neq 0$.

If $s(t) = s$ for all $t \in I$, then

$$\sigma(t) = 1 \text{ for all } t,$$
$$\gamma(t) = \varphi(1) = \Gamma(\sigma) = 1,$$
$$\alpha(t) = 1 \text{ for all } t,$$
$$S = s;$$

hence, if all firms have the same selling expenses, then their share equals 1.

If $s(t) = s$ for all $t \in A$, with $\mu(A) = a < 1$, and $s(t) = 0$ for $t \notin A$, then

$$\sigma(t) = 1/a > 1,$$
$$\gamma(t) = \varphi(1/a), \ \Gamma(\sigma) = a\varphi(1/a) > 1,$$
$$\alpha(t) = 1/a > 1,$$
$$S = s/a;$$

hence, if a fraction a of firms have the same selling expenses, then their share will be $1/a$.

Let

$$g(z) = \varphi^{-1}(z). \tag{21}$$

By Part (i) of Assumption B, g is strictly convex; therefore, $g'(z) > 0$ and $g''(z) > 0$.

If demand equals x, given $\sigma(v)$ for $v \neq t$, then the demand directed toward firm t equals $y(t) = \alpha(t)x$, with

$$\alpha(t) = \frac{\varphi(\sigma(t))}{\Gamma(\sigma)}. \tag{22}$$

Using (21), we know that the (relative) selling expenses necessary to sell a share $\alpha(t)$ can be expressed as a function of $\alpha(t)$, mean selling expenses S and mean relative selling expenses $\Gamma(\sigma)$:

$$\sigma(t) = g(\alpha(t)\,\Gamma(\sigma));$$

clearly, the selling expenses necessary for selling $\alpha(t)x$ are

$$s(t) = S\sigma(t) = Sg(\alpha(t)\,\Gamma(\sigma)) = Sg(y(t)\,\Gamma(\sigma)/x) \tag{23}$$

and, given $\Gamma(\sigma)$, these selling expenses are increasing and strictly convex in $\alpha(t)$ or $y(t)$.

Definition 3.1. *A solution is* p^0, x^0, $s^0 : I \to \Re$, $\alpha^0 : I \to \Re$, $y^0 : I \to \Re$, *such that:*
(i) $x^0 = D(p^0)$;
(ii) $\alpha^0(t) = \varphi(\sigma^0(t))/\Gamma(\sigma^0)$, $S^0 = \int s^0(t)\,dt$, $\sigma^0(t) = s^0(t)/S^0$;
(iii) $y^0(t) = \alpha^0(t)x^0$.

If the *convexity* of g dominates the *concavity* of f for sufficiently high values of $\alpha(t)$ (or $y(t)$), then the total cost function

$$c(\alpha(t)x,\ S,\ \Gamma(\sigma)) = f(\alpha(t)x) + Sg(\alpha(t)\Gamma(\sigma)) \tag{24}$$

becomes locally convex for sufficiently large $\alpha(t)$ and S. In other words, it will be increasing and have a positive second derivative w.r.t. $\alpha(t)$, for

$\alpha(t)$ larger than some minimum, and show the "normal" behavior which is frequently assumed for cost functions in terms of output: c' first decreasing, then increasing. Then the marginal cost function also goes through the minimum of the mean cost function and both mean and marginal costs are first decreasing and then increasing.

In order to ensure that the required convexity holds we assume the following:

Assumption C. If

(i) $p \geq f(x)/x$,

(ii) $S \geq \varphi'(1)(p - f'(x))x$,

then for $\alpha \geq 1$ and $\Gamma \geq \varphi(\alpha)/\alpha$: $x^2 f''(\alpha x) + \Gamma^2 Sg''(\alpha\Gamma) > 0$.

It seems reasonable to assume that g will dominate for large S. Assumption C requires that this is true for the particular value of S, given in Part (ii), and this value is related to the cost function f.

The cost function (24) gives total cost of firm t, as long as S and $\Gamma(\sigma)$ remain constant, which means that other firms stick to s, while firm t adjusts $s(t)$; the values of $s(t)$, $\sigma(t)$ and $\gamma(t)$ do not affect the integrals (that equal S, 1 and $\Gamma(\sigma)$, respectively), since the measure of a firm is zero. Profits of firm t are

$$\pi(\alpha(t);\ p, x, S, \Gamma(\sigma)) = p\alpha(t)x - f(\alpha(t)x) - Sg(\alpha(t)\Gamma(\sigma)). \qquad (25)$$

A local maximum in the increasing part of the total cost function is obtained at $\alpha(t)$, such that (compare (5)):

$$px - xf'(\alpha(t)x) - \Gamma(\sigma)Sg'(\alpha(t)\Gamma(\sigma)) = 0, \qquad (26)$$

from which follow a share $\alpha^*(t)$, selling expenses $Sg(\alpha^*(t)\Gamma(\sigma))$ and sales $\alpha^*(t)x = y^*(t)$.

For the solution $\alpha(t)$ to be a maximum, the second-order condition must hold (see (6)), such that:

$$x^2 f''(\alpha(t)x) + [\Gamma(\sigma)]^2 Sg''(\alpha(t)\Gamma(\sigma)) > 0. \qquad (27)$$

For the moment, we assume that this is true.

Clearly, profits must also be nonnegative. If indeed the total marginal costs are increasing—that is, (27) is true—then profit is nonnegative, if and only if mean costs are above marginal costs:

$$x f'\big(\alpha(t)x\big) + \Gamma(\sigma)\, Sg'\big(\alpha(t)\Gamma(\sigma)\big) \leqq \frac{f\big(\alpha(t)x\big) + Sg'\big(\alpha(t)\Gamma(\sigma)\big)}{\alpha(t)x}. \quad (28)$$

Assume $S > 0$ and $\alpha^*(t)$ is the solution to (26). Then three possibilities exist:

1) The profit function attains a single global maximum at $\alpha^*(t)$ with positive profit:

$$\pi\big(\alpha^*(t);\ p, x, S, \Gamma(\sigma)\big) > 0.$$

2) The profit function attains a single local maximum at $\alpha^*(t)$ with zero profit:

$$\pi\big(\alpha^*(t);\ p, x, S, \Gamma(\sigma)\big) = 0;$$

hence, making selling expenses $Sg\big(\alpha^*(t)\Gamma(\sigma)\big)$ and sales $\alpha^*(t)x$ is equivalent to being inactive with $s(t) = 0$ and $\alpha(t) = 0$.

3) The profit function attains a single local maximum at $\alpha^*(t)$ with negative profit:

$$\pi\big(\alpha^*(t);\ p, x, S, \Gamma(\sigma)\big) < 0;$$

hence, it is optimal to be inactive with $s(t) = 0$ and $\alpha(t) = 0$.

An *equilibrium* is a solution where each firm chooses $\alpha(t)$, so that it is optimal given the value of mean selling expenses S and $\sigma : I \rightarrow \Re$; that is, the optimal choices generate the optimal choices. Thus, it is a *Nash equilibrium*.

Definition 3.2. *A solution,* p^*, x^*, $s^* : I \rightarrow \Re$, $\alpha^* : I \rightarrow \Re$, $y^* : I \rightarrow \Re$, *is an equilibrium, given* p^*, *if for all* $t \in I$:

(i) $\alpha^*(t) = \arg\max\Big\{ p^*\,\alpha(t)x^* - f\big(\alpha(t)x^*\big) - S^*g\big(\alpha(t)\Gamma(\sigma^*)\big)\Big\}$;

(ii) $\pi\big(\alpha^*(t);\ p^*,\ x^*,\ S^*,\ \Gamma(\sigma^*)\big) \geqq 0$.

Given $s : I \rightarrow \Re$, S and $\Gamma(\sigma)$ are identical for all firms. Since their cost functions are the same, they maximize the same profit function $\pi\big(\alpha;\ p, x, S, \Gamma(\sigma)\big)$. If π has just a single positive maximum in α, then only *symmetric* equilibria can occur, where all active firms have the same share.

Proposition 3.1. *Two kinds of symmetric equilibrium can exist, with* $S^* > 0$:

(i) *for all $t \in I$, $s^*(t) = s^* = S^*$, $\alpha^*(t) = \sigma^*(t) = 1$,*

$$\pi\big(1;\ p, x, S^*, \Gamma(1)\big) \geqq 0;$$

(ii) *there exists $A \subset I$, with $\mu(A) = a < 1$, such that*
    (a) *for all $t \in A$: $s^*(t) = s^*$, $\alpha^*(t) = \sigma^*(t) = 1/a$,*
    (b) *for $t \in I \setminus A$: $s^*(t) = \sigma^*(t) = \alpha^*(t) = 0$,*
    (c) *$S^* = as^*$ and $\pi(1/a);\ p, x, S^*, \Gamma(\sigma^*)) = 0$.*

Proof. Let $(p^*, x^*, s^* : I \to \Re$, $\alpha^* : I \to \Re$, $y^* : I \to \Re$ be an equilibrium, with $S^* > 0$. Note that S^* and $\sigma^* : I \to \Re$ are identical for all $t \in I$. If $\pi\big(\alpha^*(t);\ p^*, x^*, S^*,\ \Gamma(\sigma^*)\big) > 0$, all firms t must choose the same $\alpha^*(t) = \alpha^*$, and since $\int \alpha^*(t) dt = 1$, $\alpha^* = 1$. If, however, $\pi\big(\alpha^*(t);\ p^*, x^*, \Gamma(\sigma^*)\big) = 0$, then each firm must choose either $\alpha^*(t) = \alpha^*$ or $\alpha^*(t) = 0$, both of which give zero profit.

Since $\int \alpha^*(t) d(t) = 1 = \mu(A)\alpha^*$, we know that $\mu(A) = 1/\alpha^*$.

Remark. We have not proved existence of an equilibrium. If, for all S and $\Gamma(\sigma)$, the optimal choice $\alpha(t) = 0$, then it is not profitable for any firm to be active. However, we did not define the optimal choice of $\alpha(t)$ for $S = 0$. In order to be able to define equilibria with no selling costs, we should define optimal selling costs when other firms do not have them. This is not a straightforward matter, due to problems with continuity. Therefore, we will ignore the problem for the time being.

Let p be given and let us consider equilibria with arbitrary values of $\alpha \geqq 1$. If $A \subset I$ of firms is an active subset, with $\mu(A) = a < 1$, then $s(t) = s$ for $t \in A$ and $s(t) = 0$ for $t \notin A$.

We have $S = as$, $\alpha(t) = \sigma(t) = 1/a$ and $\gamma(t) = \varphi(1/a)$ for $t \in A$, $\Gamma(\sigma) = a\varphi(1/a)$; hence, $\alpha(t) = 1/a$ for $t \in A$ and $y(t) = x/a$. Note that

$$g'(\alpha\Gamma)\Gamma = g'\big(\varphi(\alpha)\big)\varphi(\alpha)/\alpha = \varphi(\alpha)/[\alpha\varphi'(\alpha)],$$

since $g'\big(\varphi(\alpha)\big) = 1/\varphi'(\alpha)$. Substitution of these values in (26) gives

$$S = s/\alpha = \frac{p - f'(\alpha x)x}{(1/\alpha)\varphi(\alpha)g'\big(\varphi(\alpha)\big)} = \frac{\big[p - f'(\alpha x)\big] x \varphi'(\alpha)}{\varphi(\alpha)/\alpha}. \qquad (29)$$

By the concavity of φ, we know that $\alpha\varphi'(\alpha)/\varphi(\alpha) < 1$; hence, the selling costs of each firm are a fraction of the return minus the cost of production evaluated at marginal costs (see (8)).

Note by Part (ii) of Assumption B that S is increasing in α. If $\alpha = 1$, then (29) reduces to

$$S = s = \left[p - f'(x)\right] x \varphi'(1). \tag{30}$$

The second derivative of the cost function, with $\alpha = \sigma = 1$, $\Gamma = 1$, is thus

$$f''(x)x^2 + g''(1)S,$$

while

$$g'(\alpha\Gamma) = g'(1) = 1/\varphi'(1).$$

Now S, given by (30), satisfies Condition (ii) of Assumption C, and so the second-order condition is satisfied and the obtained value of α is a local maximum.

Similarly, for $\alpha = \sigma = 1/a > 1$, $\Gamma = a\varphi(1/a)$, the second derivative of the cost function is

$$f''(ax)x^2 + g''\left(\varphi(1/a)\right)S;$$

by (29),

$$S = (p - f'(ax))x \left[a\varphi'(\alpha)/\varphi(\alpha)\right] > \left[(p - f'(x))x\right]\left[\varphi'(1)\right],$$

with the last inequality following from Part (ii) of Assumption B, because $f'(ax) < f'(x)$, for $\alpha > 1$.

Condition (ii) of Assumption C is satisfied and the obtained value of α is a local maximum.

Profit as a function of $\alpha = 1/a$ is defined by

$$\begin{aligned} \pi(p, x, \alpha) &= p\alpha x - f(\alpha x) - \alpha S \\ &= p\alpha x - f(\alpha x) - (p - f'(\alpha x))x\alpha^2 \varphi'/(\varphi/\alpha), \end{aligned} \tag{31}$$

and we know that the derivative, with respect to α and using the second-order condition (27), is

$$\partial\pi/\partial\alpha = x(p - f'(\alpha x))\left[1 - 2\alpha\varphi'/\varphi - \alpha^2\varphi''/\varphi\right.$$
$$\left. + \alpha^2(\varphi')^2/\varphi^2\right] + f''x^2\alpha^2\varphi'/\varphi$$
$$> (p - f')x\left[1 - 2\alpha\varphi'/\varphi - \alpha^2\varphi''/\varphi + \alpha^2(\varphi')^2/\varphi^2 + \alpha\varphi''/\varphi'\right]$$
$$= (p - f')x\left[1 - \alpha\varphi'/\varphi\right]\left[1 - \alpha\varphi'/\varphi + \alpha\varphi''/\varphi'\right] \geqq 0.$$

$$(32)$$

It is positive because, by convexity of φ, $\varphi'/(\varphi/\alpha) > 1$ and the last term is nonnegative by Part (ii) of Assumption B and (18). Therefore, profit as a function of α is *increasing* for $\alpha \geqq 1$.

Proposition 3.2. *A symmetric equilibrium at p exists, if and only if* $\pi(p, x, \alpha) \geqq 0$, *for some* $\alpha \geqq 1$.

Proof. If $\pi(p, x, 1) \geqq 0$, then there exists an equilibrium with all firms active and making a nonnegative profit, with S defined by (30).

If $\pi(p, x, 1) < 0$, then for some $\alpha > 1$, $\pi(p, x, \alpha) = 0$, since π is increasing. Then there is an equilibrium with active firms $A \subset I$ and $\mu(A) = 1/\alpha$, with s given by (29).

If $\pi(p, x, \alpha) < 0$ for all $\alpha \geqq 1$, no equilibrium can exist.

Thus, we find a symmetric equilibrium for each p (or $x = D(p)$) with zero profit, if $\pi(p, x, \alpha) = 0$ and has a solution $\alpha \geqq 1$, with $a = 1/\alpha$. If $\pi(p, x, 1) > 0$, we have found an equilibrium with all firms active: $a = 1$, $\alpha = 1$ and positive profits, S, following from (29).

So far, we have only considered equilibria with given prices. In the finite model of Section 2 we added Condition III in Definition 2.2, requiring that no firm can profitably decrease the price, given that it assumes that the decreased price will become the market price, with the same share.

This argument does not work in the present model, if we identify individual firms with points in I, having measure zero: What is the effect of the decrease of the price by a single firm on other firms? Will it mean that other firms lose all demand or at least a substantial fraction of demand? If a single firm absorbs all demand, its sales become infinite and it is not clear what this means.

All firms are identical; hence, if a decrease of the price is profitable, it is profitable for all firms. It is reasonable to assume that a coalition—that is, a subset of the firms with positive measure—will take the initiative with a price cut, and that all firms will then follow. In this case we get an upper bound of the price by adding the following condition: For all $p \leq p^*$, an equilibrium price must satisfy:

$$p^* \alpha^* D(p^*) - f(\alpha^* D(p^*)) - s^* \geq p \alpha^* D(p) - f(\alpha^* D(p)) - s^*,$$

which implies that

$$D(p^*) + \left[p^* - f'(\alpha^* D(p^*)) \right] dD(p^*)/dp \geq 0. \tag{33}$$

This means that the price cannot be higher than the price of a monopolist with demand function $\alpha^* D(p)$.

Example. Let us say that

$$f(y) = 2\sqrt{y},$$
$$\varphi(\sigma) = \sqrt{\sigma},$$
$$D(p) = A - Bp.$$

Then

$$g(\alpha(t)\Gamma(\sigma)) = S[\alpha(t)\Gamma(\sigma)]^2 = S[\alpha(t)]^2 [\Gamma(\sigma)]^2,$$
$$g' = \partial g/\partial \alpha = 2S[\alpha(t)] [\Gamma(\sigma)]^2,$$

and

$$f'(\alpha(t)x) = \partial g/\partial \alpha = \sqrt{x/\alpha(t)}.$$

The optimum value of $\alpha(t)$ follows from

$$px - \sqrt{x/\alpha(t)} - 2S[\Gamma(\sigma)]^2 \alpha(t) = 0.$$

In an equilibrium with $\alpha(t) = 1$, $y(t) = x$ and $s(t) = S$ for all t, we have $\sigma(t) = 1 = \sqrt{\sigma(t)}$ for all t and $\Gamma(\sigma) = 1$, implying

$$px - \sqrt{x} - 2S = 0.$$

Hence, if $px - f(x) = px - 2\sqrt{x}$ is nonnegative, then

$$s(t) = S = [px - \sqrt{x}]/2$$

is also nonnegative. Total profit must be nonnegative as well, and gives

$$Ax - Bx^2 - 2\sqrt{x} - s(t) = (Ax - Bx^2)/2 - 1.5\sqrt{x} \geq 0,$$

which is true in some interval (x_1, x_2), provided A is sufficiently high. For any x in this interval an equilibrium exists. The second-order condition holds, so that

$$f'' + g'' = -\sqrt{x}/2 + 2S = 2px - 1.5\sqrt{x} \geq 0.$$

For $p = 4 - x$ and $\alpha = 1$, the nonnegative profit condition

$$-0.5x^2 + 2x - 1.5\sqrt{x} = 0$$

holds in the interval $1 \leq x \leq 1.697$; that is, for $2.303 < p < 3$. (The region where return minus production costs is positive is $0.292 < x < 2.8$.)

By inserting the functions f, φ, g and D in (29), we obtain

$$s = \left[px/a - \sqrt{(x/a)}\right]/2.$$

Insertion of this into the profit function gives

$$0.5px/a - 1.5\sqrt{(x/a)} = 0 = 0.5(Ax - Bx^2)/a - 1.5\sqrt{(x/a)};$$

by solving this equality, we obtain

$$a = \frac{p^2 x^2}{9x} = \frac{p^2 x}{9} = \frac{p^2(A - Bp)}{9}.$$

For $x = 4 - p$, we find the following conditions:

(i) if $p = 3$, then $a = 1$, $\alpha(t) = 1$, $x = 1$, $y(t) = 1$, $\pi(t) = 0$, for all $t \in I$;

(ii) if $p = 2.35$, then $a = 1$, $\alpha(t) = 1$, $x = 1.65 = y(t)$, $\pi(t) = 0.012$, for all $t \in I$;

(iii) if $p = 2$, then $a = 8/9$, $\alpha(t) = 9/8$, $x = 2$, $y(t) = 18/8$, $\pi(t) = 0$, for all $t \in A$;

(iv) if $p = 1$, then $a = 1/3$, $\alpha(t) = 3$, $x = 3$, $y(t) = 9$, $\pi(t) = 0$, for all $t \in A$.

In Figure 2 we depict a as a function of p, with the solid line giving equilibrium pairs (p, a) at given prices. Profit is zero, except in the region where the curve is above 1 and $a = \alpha = 1$. Condition (33) holds for $p \leq 2.3946 \equiv \hat{p}$. In the region $p \leq \hat{p}$ note that the smaller the price, the smaller the set of active firms and the bigger each active firm's sales become.

Figure 2: *a* as a Function of *p*.

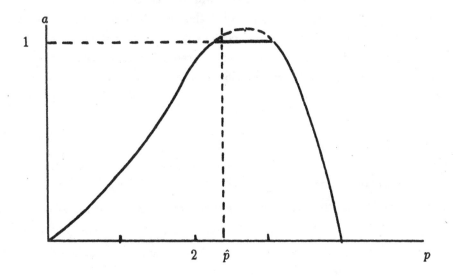

4. Conclusions

We have seen that in both versions of the model a continuum of equilibria will exist where the price is in an interval and each price in this interval corresponds to a number of active firms or a set of active firms. The higher the price, the more firms that can be active. In the finite model there exists a maximum price and a maximum number of firms. Obviously, the equilibria are not efficient: only a single firm without selling expenses can produce efficiently a certain amount of the commodity. The result is basically the same in a similar model with market shares given a *priori* and not resulting from selling expenses (see Weddepohl, 1978).

The theory cannot explain which of the many equilibria will obtain, as is usually the case with theories on equilibrium. In a real market of the type described in the model, the number of firms and the price must be the result of the history of the market. If the cost function or the demand changes at some moment in time, a new equilibrium must be established with a different number of firms and a different price, or a combination of the two. If the price adjustment is fast enough, the set of active firms will remain the same; if not, then inactive firms will enter or active firms will leave the market. A true dynamic model would be necessary to make this precise.

The model presented in this paper is rather restrictive, since it assumes identical cost functions and symmetry in the market share distribution. It should be generalized in order to allow for differences in cost functions and not necessarily identical shares for identical selling costs. Furthermore, the effect of selling costs on the market-share distribution should be stochastic rather than deterministic.

References

Cornet, B. (1988) "General Equilibrium Theory and Increasing Returns," *J. Economic Theory* **17**, 103-118.

Hildenbrand, W. (1974) *Core and Equilibria in a Large Economy*, Princeton: Princeton Univ. Press.

Weddepohl, C. (1978) "Increasing Returns and Fixed Market Shares," *International Economic Review* **19**, 405-414.

12

Product Variety:
The Performing Arts Market ·

Louise Grenier

1. Introduction

This paper is concerned with product differentiation. Product differentiation applies to a large number of economic activities, but the analysis here is done for a specific sector, the performing arts market. The need for a special study of product differentiation in this sector arises because performing arts companies do not maximize profit, as it is usually assumed in the product differentiation literature. Instead, a firm maximizing utility subject to a zero profit constraint is proposed, special attention being paid to the case where the firm maximizes quality only. Quality is especially interesting because it is not necessarily related to consumption. For example, a consumer can obtain utility from knowing that a certain good of certain quality is produced without actually having to consume it.

Product differentiation can be vertical or horizontal. Horizontal differentiation (diversity) captures the fact that, given two diverse products offered at the same price, some consumers prefer one and some the other. Vertical differentiation (quality) refers to the fact that, given two products of different quality available at the same price, all the consumers prefer the one with the highest quality.

---
* I am grateful to the DAAD and the SSHRC for financial support and to Margaret Slade for useful comments.

As already mentioned, quality is important for the firm and for the consumer, since their respective utility functions may depend on this variable. In this spirit, a study of vertical differentiation in the performing arts market has been done by Hansmann (1981). This approach is appropriate if one looks at a specific artistic production or if it is possible to consider an aggregate of diverse artistic productions with a proper measure of the overall quality. This is not enough, though, to analyze the fact that consumers also care about the difference between types of performing arts—ballet versus concerts, for example. For this reason, the present paper tries to combine vertical and horizontal differentiation.

Both aspects, diversity and quality, have been combined in a study by Neven and Thisse (1988), but only in a general spatial model of product differentiation. In spatial models, diversity arises because consumers differ. An alternative approach is used here; following Spence (1976), consumers are identical but diversity is by itself desirable. It is intuitive to think, in the case of performing arts, that a consumer wants to see different types of performances.

The aim of this paper is to investigate how the firms' behavior differs from the behavior of a social planner maximizing the total surplus. Section 2 introduces the notation, describes the agents' behavior and presents the basic assumptions of the model. Section 3 analyzes the impact of the ith firm on the total surplus. Section 4 looks at what happens when a firm maximizes quality and Section 5 offers some concluding remarks.

2. The Model

As previously mentioned, this paper deals with the performing arts market. Hence, the goods looked at are artistic productions. The quantity here is measured in terms of the number of performances, but it could also easily be done in terms of the size of the audience.

There are n potential firms indexed by $i = 1, \ldots, n$. To simplify the analysis, it is assumed that each firm produces only one type of good at one level of quality. Here x_i is the number of performances of type i (x_i is a nonnegative real number and $x = [x_1, \ldots, x_n]$), and q_i is the quality level at which the good i is produced (q_i is a positive real number, $q_i \in [\underline{q}, \bar{q}]$ with $\underline{q} < \bar{q}$, and $q = [q_1, \ldots, q_n]$).

We denote by $U(x, q)$ the gross benefit function in monetary terms of the representative consumer and assume that it is nondecreasing in each variable.

The consumer can only choose x, the number of performances of each type he/she wants to attend; the quality level q is decided by the producers and known by the consumer. The consumer chooses x to maximize his/her net surplus

$$U(x,q) - \sum_{i=1}^{n} p_i x_i,$$

where p_i is the price of a performance of type i (at quality i). For an interior solution, the first order conditions are

$$\frac{\partial U(x,q)}{\partial x_i} = p_i \qquad \text{for} \qquad i = 1, \ldots, n. \tag{1}$$

Turning to the firm, the net revenue function of each firm is

$$p_i x_i - c_i(x_i, q_i) \qquad \text{for} \qquad i = 1, \ldots, n,$$

where $c_i(x_i, q_i)$ is the the cost function of the ith firm. It is nondecreasing in the number of performances x_i and the quality level q_i.

It is assumed that each firm is a nonprofit organization facing a zero profit constraint:

$$p_i x_i - c_i(x_i, q_i) = 0 \qquad \text{for} \qquad i = 1, \ldots, n.$$

Given this constraint, different assumptions concerning the firms' behavior can be investigated. Assuming that the companies are concerned to some extent with the quality level of their performances and the size of their audience (the number of performances), we can then write their objective function as a utility function, nondecreasing in its arguments and depending on the quality and the number of performances, namely, $V(x_i, q_i)$.

Special cases of the above are companies maximizing quality, the size of the audience (the number of performances) or the revenue.

The firms' problem in the general case can be stated as

$$\max V(x_i, q_i)$$

with respect to x_i, q_i, subject to

$$p_i x_i - c_i(x_i, q_i) = 0, \qquad i = 1, \ldots, n,$$

and also implicitly subject to the consumers' behavior.

For each firm the Lagrangean is:

$$V(x_i, q_i) + \lambda[p_i x_i - c_i(x_i, q_i)];$$

or, by the consumer first order conditions given in (1):

$$V(x_i, q_i) + \lambda\left[\frac{\partial U(x, q)}{\partial x_i} x_i - c_i(x_i, q_i)\right].$$

For an interior solution, the first order conditions for each firm are

$$\frac{\partial V(x_i, q_i)}{\partial x_i} + \lambda\left\{\frac{\partial^2 U(x, q)}{\partial x_i^2} x_i + \frac{\partial U(x, q)}{\partial x_i} - \frac{\partial c_i(x_i, q_i)}{\partial x_i}\right\} = 0, \qquad (2)$$

$$\frac{\partial V(x_i, q_i)}{\partial q_i} + \lambda\left\{\frac{\partial^2 U(x, q)}{\partial x_i \partial q_i} x_i - \frac{\partial c_i(x_i, q_i)}{\partial q_i}\right\} = 0. \qquad (3)$$

The social planner's objective function—the total surplus—is the sum of the consumer and producer surplus in monetary terms:

$$T = U(x, q) - \sum_{i=1}^{n} c_i(x_i, q_i).$$

For first-best results, this function is maximized without constraints, which leads to the following first order conditions:

$$\frac{\partial U(x, q)}{\partial x_j} - \frac{\partial c_j(x_j, q_j)}{\partial x_j} = 0, \qquad \text{for} \qquad j = 1, \ldots, n, \qquad (4)$$

$$\frac{\partial U(x, q)}{\partial q_j} - \frac{\partial c_j(x_j, q_j)}{\partial q_j} = 0, \qquad \text{for} \qquad j = 1, \ldots, n, \qquad (5)$$

where the four partial derivatives may be denoted as MU_{x_i}, MC_{x_i}, MU_{q_i} and MC_{q_i}. At this stage it is desirable to compare the social planner's solution (first order conditions (4) and (5)) to the firms' solution (first order conditions (2) and (3)), but one needs to make further assumptions or to use other welfare measures to draw conclusions. For this reason the next section looks at the impact of the ith firm on the total surplus, and in Section 4, attention is limited to the case where a firm maximizes quality.

3. The Impact of the ith Firm on Total Surplus

The impact of the ith firm on the total surplus is given by

$$\Delta T_i = U(x,q) - U(x - x_i e_i, \; q - q_i e_i) - c_i(x_i, q_i),$$

where e_i is a vector of dimension n, composed of zeros, except in the ith position, where there is a one. In using this measure, apart from a zero profit constraint, we make no precise statement about the behavior of the firms. It is not possible with this measure to conclude whether the number of firms actually entering the market is optimal, or if the level of quality and quantity at which those firms produce is optimal. Nevertheless, it is useful to see that, given the behavior of other firms, consumers will always benefit from the entry of a new firm; and that entry of firms that would be beneficial for the consumer might not occur.

Result 1. *If the marginal benefit of the number of performances attended decreases at all levels of quality, then*
(i) *a firm may decide to enter if and only if it increases the consumer surplus; but*
(ii) *a firm may decide not to enter (possibly because of negative profit), even though it would be beneficial for the consumer.*

Proof. The ith firm enters if and only if profits are nonnegative:

$$p_i x_i - c_i(x_i, q_i) \geq 0;$$

or, by condition (1):

$$\frac{\partial U(x,q)}{\partial x_i} \geq \frac{c_i(x_i, q_i)}{x_i}.$$

If we assume marginal benefits decrease with respect to the number of peformances attended, it follows that

$$\begin{array}{c} \text{average utility of a unit} \\ \text{of good } i \text{ at quality } q_i \end{array} > \begin{array}{c} \text{marginal utility of a unit} \\ \text{of good } i \text{ at quality } q_i \end{array},$$

or

$$\frac{U(x,q) - U(x - x_i e_i, \; q - q_i e_i)}{x_i} > \frac{\partial U(x,q)}{\partial x_i}.$$

Combining both inequalities, one finds that

$$\frac{U(x,q) - U(x - x_i e_i, \; q - q_i e_i)}{x_i} > \frac{c_i(x_i, q_i)}{x_i}, \tag{6}$$

or, since x_i is a positive number,

$$\Delta T_i = U(x, q) - U(x - x_i e_i,\ q - q_i e_i) - c_i(x_i, q_i) > 0. \qquad (7)$$

This shows that a firm enters if and only if it increases the consumer surplus, as seen in part (i) of Result 1. To show part (ii) of this result, we start with the nonentry condition (negative profit) for the firm:

$$p_i x_i - c_i(x_i, q_i) < 0;$$

or, using condition (1):

$$\frac{\partial U(x, q)}{\partial x_i} < \frac{c_i(x_i, q_i)}{x_i}.$$

This inequality can still hold in the case where the consumer surplus is increased, because it is consistent with inequality (6), which is equivalent to an increase in the consumer surplus. Hence, there may exist some utility and cost functions, such that these inequalities occur:

$$\frac{\partial U(x, q)}{\partial x_i} < \frac{c_i(x_i, q_i)}{x_i} < \frac{U(x, q) - U(x - x_i e_i,\ q - q_i e_i)}{x_i}.$$

4. Optimality of the Quality-maximizing Firm

It was already mentioned that quality may provide utility to the consumer without being related to consumption. Since the consumer pays only for the quantity he/she consumes, the laissez-faire market might not capture the part of the benefit that comes from quality independently of consumption. Hence, one might think that the quality level provided then is not sufficient. But such reasoning does not necessarily hold if the firm cares about quality. A formal demonstration of this is provided here, through the polar case of a firm maximizing quality.

The firm's problem is the same as before, except that the objective function can now be written as

$$V(x_i, q_i) = q_i,$$

which implies

$$\frac{\partial V(x_i, q_i)}{\partial x_i} = 0 \quad \text{and} \quad \frac{\partial V(x_i, q_i)}{\partial q_i} = 1.$$

Hence, the first order conditions become

$$\lambda \left\{ \frac{\partial^2 U(x,q)}{\partial x_i^2} x_i + \frac{\partial U(x,q)}{\partial x_i} - \frac{\partial c_i(x_i,q_i)}{\partial x_i} \right\} = 0, \tag{8}$$

$$\lambda \left\{ \frac{\partial^2 U(x,q)}{\partial x_i q_i} - \frac{\partial c_i(x_i,q_i)}{\partial q_i} \right\} = -1. \tag{9}$$

We denote the sum of the first two terms in (8) by MR_{x_i}, the last term by MC_{x_i}, and the two terms in braces in (9) by MR_{q_i} and MC_{q_i}, respectively. These conditions tell us that the firm behaves like a monopolist with respect to quantity by producing up to a point where the marginal revenue of a unit equals its marginal cost. It is easy to see from equations (4) and (8) that, if $\partial^2 U(x,q)/\partial x_i^2 < 0$ (marginal utility decreasing with respect to quantity), then $MR_{x_i} < MU_{x_i}$ for a given (x,q) chosen by a firm maximizing quality. Consequently, $MC_{x_i} < MU_{x_i}$, since $MR_{x_i} = MC_{x_i}$ in the case of a firm maximizing quality. Starting at the firm's level, the social planner would like to increase the quality produced to reach the point where $MC_{x_i} = MU_{x_i}$, with the following result:

Result 2. *If $\partial^2 U(x,q)/\partial x_i^2 < 0$, then the firm underproduces x_i— that is, limits the number of performances—compared to what a social planner maximizing the total surplus would produce at the same level of quality.*

In the case where the social planner chooses the quality level (q_i) for a given number of performances, no conclusion can be drawn; both situations/break —too much and too little quality—are possible. From the firm's first order conditions it is known that production occurs at a point where the marginal revenue is inferior to its marginal cost. In this case it is possible that this level is such that $MR_{q_i} < MU_{q_i}$, $MR_{q_i} > MU_{q_i}$, or $MR_{q_i} = MU_{q_i}$; consequently, no conclusion as to whether the quality level produced by a firm maximizing quality is less than, greater than or equal to what a social planner would decide can be made.

5. Concluding Remarks

For the social planner the first-best solution is naturally the desired one. But a first-best solution requires a lot of information, information that is not necessarily available and/or is costly to gather. The idea of doing such an analysis is then to find some general guidelines, which a central agent with some intervening power could use to design policies. First, nothing can be said in general about the optimum production plan for all firms at the same time. Actually, if it is assumed that all goods are strongly complementary (i.e., the marginal revenue of the good i increases when the production of the good j increases) at any level of quality, then the private solution does not offer enough variety, as shown by Spence (1976). This is certainly a strong result, but the assumption it is based on (that goods are strongly complementary) does not appear too realistic in the case of performing arts productions.

Given that there is not enough information to compute every firm's optimal production plan, what is the best a central agent can do? Looking at the impact of the ith firm on the total surplus, we offer conclude:

(1) a central agent should not prevent any artistic production from occurring, since it has been shown that there cannot be too many; and

(2) a central agent probably ought to encourage the creation of new artistic productions, since it is possible that some productions which would increase the total surplus do not get produced.

But of course, the difficulty in the latter case is to encourage the right creations. To get more precise guidelines one needs to look at specific cases of firms' behavior. In the interesting case where the firm maximizes quality, an increase in the number of performances or in the size of the audience is desirable. But even in the case where consumers like quality independently of consumption, it is not possible to tell whether the firm over- or underproduces quality. For this reason, some basic investigations about performing arts companies' objective functions are important.

The present analysis is very limited. Important avenues remain to be explored. The first one is certainly to look at other special cases of the firms' behavior, such as maximizing audience size. A second one is to investigate corner solutions. Finally, a third avenue to explore is what happens when donations and subsidies are introduced into the revenue function of the firm.

References

Hansmann, H. (1981) "Nonprofit Enterprise in the Performing Arts," *Bell Journal of Economics* 12, 341-361.

Neven, D. and Thisse, J.-F. (1988) "On Quality and Variety Competition," Working Paper, INSEAD.

Spence, M. (1976) "Product Selection, Fixed Costs and Monopolistic Competition," *Review of Economic Studies* 43, 217-235.

13

Prices Before and After Vertical Mergers of Firms

Wolfgang Eichhorn and *Helmut Funke*

1. Introduction

It is well known that a commodity which is sold by a producer P to a sales firm S before it becomes available to consumers, may cost consumers more than in the case in which the two firms merge; in this connections see, e.g., Weintraub (1949), Niehans (1959), Eichhorn (1973), Funke (1977), Eichhorn and Funke (1977).

Is this an argument for the vertical concentration of firms? The answer to this question would be yes, if in any realistic model of markets before and after the vertical merger of firms the same result always emerged, namely that consumer prices decline.

In what follows, we present a model that consists of only one producer P and only one sales firm S. The firm P produces k goods and sells them to S. We point out here that we get very strong and invariant results concerning the prices before and after the merger of P and S. This is so without imposing any restrictive assumptions on the cost functions of P and S or on the sales function of S. To get the results, it is not necessary that these functions be known. All we need is the existence of certain maxima of the profit functions of P and S. We notice that this assumption is natural in a model that compares prices which are required to be optimal.

The results to be presented in this paper have been obtained with the aid of the so-called LeChâtelier-Samuelson principle in its global form, i.e., without any differentiability or continuity assumptions; see Eichhorn and Oettli (1972).

2. The Model

A producer P produces k goods and sells them to a sales firm S at prices $\mathbf{r} = (r_1, \ldots, r_k)$. Firm S sells the goods at prices $\mathbf{p} = (p_1, \ldots, p_k)$ to many price-taking consumers.

Let

$$\mathbf{f} = (f_1, \ldots, f_k)$$

be the sales function, i.e., the function that assigns to each price vector $\mathbf{p}$ the vector of the k quantities sold when $\mathbf{p}$ is required. Let C_P and C_S be the cost functions of firms P and S, respectively, and let

$$\mathbf{rf} = r_1 f_1 + \cdots + r_k f_k.$$

The profit functions, F_P and F_S, of firms P and S are given by

$$F_P(\mathbf{r}, \mathbf{p}) = \mathbf{rf}(\mathbf{p}) - C_P\big(\mathbf{f}(\mathbf{p})\big) \tag{1}$$

and

$$F_S(\mathbf{r}, \mathbf{p}) = (\mathbf{p} - \mathbf{r})\mathbf{f}(\mathbf{p}) - C_S\big(\mathbf{f}(\mathbf{p})\big), \tag{2}$$

respectively. The profit F for both firms is

$$\begin{aligned} F(\mathbf{p}) &= F_P(\mathbf{r}, \mathbf{p}) + F_S(\mathbf{r}, \mathbf{p}) \\ &= \mathbf{pf}(\mathbf{p}) - C_P\big(\mathbf{f}(\mathbf{p})\big) - C_S\big(\mathbf{f}(\mathbf{p})\big). \end{aligned} \tag{3}$$

We assume that

- There exists $\mathbf{p}^2$, such that

$$F(\mathbf{p}^2) \geq F(\mathbf{p}) \quad \text{for all } \mathbf{p}; \tag{4}$$

- For any price vector $\mathbf{r}$ required by the producer P, there exists exactly one $\mathbf{p} = \mathbf{p}(\mathbf{r})$ such that

$$F_S\big(\mathbf{r}, \mathbf{p}(\mathbf{r})\big) > F_S(\mathbf{r}, \mathbf{p}) \quad \text{for all } \mathbf{p} \neq \mathbf{p}(\mathbf{r}); \tag{5}$$

- There exists $\mathbf{r}^1$, such that

$$F_P\big(\mathbf{r}^1, \mathbf{p}(\mathbf{r}^1)\big) \geq F_P\big(\mathbf{r}, \mathbf{p}(\mathbf{r})\big) \quad \text{for all } \mathbf{r}; \tag{6}$$

- There exists r^2, such that

$$p^2 = p(r^2). \tag{7}$$

3. The Results

Special cases of inequalities (4), (5), (6) are

$$F(p^2) \geqq F(p^1), \tag{4'}$$

$$F_S(r^1, p^1) > F_S(r^1, p^2) \qquad (p(r^1) = p^1, p^1 \neq p^2), \tag{5'}$$

$$F_S(r^2, p^2) \geqq F_S(r^2, p^1), \tag{5''}$$

$$F_P(r^1, p^1) \geqq F_P(r^2, p^2). \tag{6'}$$

As can be learnt from Eichhorn and Oettli (1972), the mathematical core of the LeChâtelier-Samuelson principle is nothing but

- adding up the inequalities (4'), (5'), (5''), (6') and
- learning interesting things from the new (and sometimes surprising) inequalities that arise.

For instance, summing up (5') and (5'') yields, by (2),

$$(r^2 - r^1)(f(p^2) - f(p^1)) < 0 \qquad (p^2 \neq p^1) \tag{8}$$

and summing up (4'), (5') and (6') and considering (1), (2) and (3) we find that

$$(r^2 - r^1)f(p^2) < 0. \tag{9}$$

We point out here that inequalities (8) and (9) are valid no matter what the cost functions of firms P and S look like.

There is a lot of information that can be obtained from inequalities (8) and (9). For instance, inequality (9) tells us that the optimum price vector r^1 of the producer P is *greater* than the price vector r^2 in the following sense: The vector $f(p^2)$ of goods bought by the consumers, when the firms maximize their common profit, costs more with r^1 than with r^2. Note that $p(r^2) = p^2 =$ the profit maximizing vector. With this observation in mind, let us consider inequality (8). It reveals a tendency of the price vector p^2 to be, in a sense, *smaller* than the price vector p^1 which had to be paid by the consumers, if firm P required its optimum prices r^1 from firm S, and firm S required its optimum prices, namely $p(r^1) = p^1$, from the consumers.

If only one commodity is produced and sold, i.e., if $k = 1$, our assertions can be stated more precisely. Then we get from (9)

$$r^1 - r^2 > 0, \tag{10}$$

(since $f(p^2) \geqq 0$). Because of (10), we conclude from (8)

$$f(p^2) > f(p^1) \quad \text{for } p^1 \neq p^2. \tag{11}$$

This implies $p^1 \neq p^2$, if we assume, as usual, that the sales function f is a nonincreasing function of the price p.

References

Eichhorn, W. (1973) "Modelle der vertikalen Preisbildung," *Mathematical Systems in Economics* 6, Meisenheim/Glan.

Eichhorn, W. and Funke, H. (1977) "LeChâtelier-Samuelsonsches Prinzip und vertikale Unternehmenskonzentration," in *Quantitative Wirtschaftsforschung, Wilhelm Krelle zum 60. Geburtstag*, ed.by H. Albach, E. Helmstädter and R. Henn; Tübingen: J. C. B. Mohr (Paul Siebeck).

Eichhorn, W. and Oettli, W. (1972) "A General Formulation of the LeChâtelier Principle," *Econometrica* 40, 711-717.

Funke, H. (1977) "Modelle des Mehrproduktenoligopols," *Mathematical Systems in Economics* 37, Meisenheim: Verlag Anton Hain.

Niehans, J. (1959) "Monopolpreis, vertikale Integration und Mengenrabatt," *Schweizerische Zeitschrift für Volkswirtschaft und Statistik* 95, 328-334.

Weintraub, S. (1949) *Price Theory*, New York-Toronto-London: Pitman Publ. Co.

14

Optimal Production
and Inventory Policies:
The Incentive Effects of Taxation

Vesa Kanniainen

1. Introduction

The task of modelling the behavior of a firm is a highly challenging one. The fundamental question relates to why firms exist in the first place and why they have the organizational forms we observe.[1] Given that a firm is a highly complex organization, understanding its targets and objectives is the key to the explanation of its behavior.

To what extent should the firm acquire productive inputs, how large should its productive capacity be and how much ought the firm to produce for the market in order to behave optimally? How much inventory should it carry from one period to the next? And in what way should it aim to finance its activity? These are the key issues of the current paper, which also extends the analysis to the interaction between government policy and the firm. Obviously, a firm in a socialist economy faces these very same problems, as does a firm in a market economy.[2] The problems of modelling are similar enough but they are due to different reasons.

What is reasonable to assume about a firm's objectives? This has been

---

[1] See Ickes (1990) and Spinnewyn and Svejnar (1990) in this volume.

[2] Goldfeld and Quandt (1990), Ábel (1990).

a difficult problem in the case of modelling a socialist firm, because it is difficult to judge how risks are shared between management and the public sector. In the case of a private-ownership economy, this task is, at least at first sight, somewhat easier. Indeed, the model to be formulated in the current paper presumes that the nature of capital markets allows us to invoke the so-called separation theorem. This says that the investment plan can be decided upon regardless of the desired time pattern of the consumption plan.[3] Accordingly, we assume that the firm aims at maximizing its market value. To make sense, this presumes that the stock market can be assumed effectively to monitor corporate management. Though often adopted, this assumption is not completely harmless, given that ownership and control are separate activities. However, for the positive analysis of tax incentives, there is no need to become involved with the well-known agency problem which is based on informational asymmetries.

This paper is structured as follows. Section 2 summarizes the main lessons from the theory of optimal taxes, so as to provide a perspective for the analysis of the interaction between the production sector and the government. Section 3 formulates the optimal production and inventory policy of a monopolistic firm and a competitive firm. Section 4 introduces the government's tax policy and derives the allocational implications of tax incentives.

2. Optimal Taxation of Business Profits

Governments exercise control over firms in a variety of ways. Clearly, sharing of profits has been institutionalized in quite a different manner in socialist and market economies. However, it may not be wrong to point out that some common features exist. While bailouts signify the risk-sharing arrangements in the former, the corporate income tax performs a similar type of insurance function in the latter. That is to say, the government participates through loss offsets not only in profit sharing, but also in carrying its share of business risks. Obviously, this has an impact on security markets where risks are priced and allocated.

Some tax systems are better than others. The optimal tax problem can

---

[3] Drèze and Modigliani (1972) provide the conditions when the use of the separation theorem is justified.

be stated as follows.[4] Given that the government is facing some revenue requirement, what taxes should it levy in order to minimize the undesired allocational distortions in the private sector? In market economies, taxes are
normally collected on the basis of consumer goods, wage and capital income
and wealth. The international tax-reform wave of the 1980's is a symptom
of the fact that temporal distortions in the labor market, intertemporal
distortions in the supply of capital and distortions in production exceed
acceptable levels.

The problem of optimal taxation is obviously of the second-best type.
However, we know that if it were possible to define the so-called pure economic profit, the latter could and, hence, should be taxed away. Since it is
a lump sum transfer between the shareholders and the government, a tax
on pure profits would result in no welfare loss and should, therefore, be
utilized before one resorts to any distortive taxation.

In the model to be formulated below, we assume a particular form of
distortion. It is maintained that, due to informational problems, pure economic profits do not base directly and explicitly constitute the tax base.
Consequently, input taxation will be distortive. Fundamentally, this information problem arises because the cost of capital is actually an unobservable shadow price instead of being an observable market price.

3. A Model of Production and Inventory Policy

As a prerequisite for a positive analysis of tax incentives, let us first
formulate a model of a firm which is a monopolist in the product market,
but a price-taker in all other markets. The focus is on the long-run analysis
with no explicit demand uncertainty.

The following assumptions are made about the technology of production. Output Y is produced in strict proportions with a combination of
material inputs (U) and other productive inputs. The latter is denoted by
$f(L, K, S)$. L stands for labor and K for capital. The variable S stands
for the stock of inventories of productive inputs. Hence inventories are regarded as a capital asset. With no loss of generality, set $Y/U = Y/f(\ ) = 1$.
The function f exhibits nonincreasing returns to scale and it is strictly increasing and differentiable in L, K, and S. Since the first derivatives of f
are assumed to exist, the firm is assumed to have an option of economizing

---

[4] For an excellent survey of the theory of optimal taxation see Stern (1984).

on labor and capital services via adjustment of inventories when it faces changes in the costs of L or K. The value of S in the production process can be rationalized in terms of the reduced costs of organizing production.

The firm is assumed to be a price-taker in the markets for inputs. Let w stand for the wage rate, p_K for the price of capital goods and q for the price of material inputs. In the market for the output, the firm faces a downward sloping demand schedule $p = D(Y)$ with $dp/dY < 0$.

Suppose that life-cycle savers own equity claims to the firm's assets. Denote their opportunity cost by α. Because equity owners have to carry the main share of the firm's risks, α can be expected to exceed the riskless capital market rate, say i, to the extent that the firm's profits are correlated with the rest of the economy. This is the major implication of the celebrated capital asset pricing model. Hence, the market price of the firm's cash flow is represented as

$$V(0) = \int_0^\infty X(s) \exp\{-\alpha s\}\, ds, \tag{1}$$

where $X(s)$ stands for the dividend stream

$$X(s) = D(Y)Y - wL - p_K I - qJ - c(S). \tag{2}$$

Here I and J stand for capital and inventory investments, respectively. An assumption will be made in (2) that carrying inventories is subject to nondecreasing marginal costs, i.e., $c_S > 0$, $c_{SS} \geq 0$. Note that (1) is consistent with the portfolio equilibrium condition of the owners, i.e., $X(s) + dV(s)/dt = \alpha V(s)$. Let us now assume that the separation property holds and that there is no agency problem. Then the firm's optimal production and inventory policy can be derived from the maximization of (1) subject to given initial conditions on K and S—the state variables of the model—and subject to the equations of motion

$$\frac{dK}{dt} = I - \delta K, \qquad \frac{dS}{dt} = J - U. \tag{3}$$

The current-value Hamiltonian of our control problem is given by

$$H = D(Y)Y - wL - p_K I - qJ - c(S) + \mu_K(I - \delta K) + \mu_S(J - U), \tag{4}$$

where μ_K and μ_S denote the shadow prices (in current values) of capital and the stock of material inputs. Any candidate for the solution has to satisfy the following necessary conditions:

$$f_L(D'Y + D) - w - \mu_S f_L = 0 \tag{4a}$$

$$-p_K + \mu_K = 0 \tag{4b}$$

$$-q + \mu_S = 0 \tag{4c}$$

$$f_K(D'Y + D) - (\alpha + \delta)\mu_K - \mu_S f_K = -\frac{d\mu_K}{dt} \tag{4d}$$

$$f_S(D'Y + D) - (\alpha + f_S) - c_S = -\frac{d\mu_S}{dt}. \tag{4e}$$

Under mild conditions, these are also sufficient. Assuming stable prices and denoting by θ the price elasticity of demand, these equations can be rewritten as

$$p(1 - 1/\theta)f_L = w + q f_L \tag{5a}$$

$$p(1 - 1/\theta)f_K = p_K(\alpha + \delta) + q f_K \tag{5b}$$

$$p(1 - 1/\theta)f_S = c_S + q\alpha + q f_S \tag{5c}$$

Equations (5a) and (5b) describe the equality between the marginal revenue product and the marginal cost of labor and capital. The last term on the right hand side follows from the assumption concerning the technology. For example, a unit increase in capital services results, *ceteris paribus*, in an increase of output by f_K units, which increases the material costs by $q(dU/dK) = q f_K$. Equation (5c) suggests that the firm carries a positive amount of inventories even under stable prices when speculative behavior is ruled out. The right hand side gives the shadow price of inventory capital.

If the competitiveness of the industry, as measured by θ, increases, employment and the use of labor services become larger than in the monopolistic case given in (5b)–(5c). If there are constant returns to scale and if $c_{SS} = 0$, the inventory/production ratio stays constant when output expands. Note also, in this case, that the size of the firm is indeterminate. What happens to the inventory/production ratio at the level of the firm and at the level of the industry under decreasing returns? To get precise answers, one ought to parametrize both the technology and the cost function $c(S)$. However, it is clear that when aggregated over the whole industry, this ratio is lower in the competitive case than it is in the monopolistic case if $c(S)$ is concave.

4. Taxation of the Firm

Taxation adds another dimension of complexity to the model of the firm. The problem of the authorities is to determine both the corporation tax rate, say τ, the tax base and the tax rates on capital income, say τ_d for dividends, τ_g for capital gains and τ_i for interest.[5] There are several problems associated with determining the tax base. First, most tax systems deal differently with the cost of equity and cost of debt. Secondly, inflation adds to these problems, because it leads to incorrect pricing of the inputs. To judge the allocational implications, one has to know the incentive effect created by the taxation in terms of the relative prices given in (5a)–(5c). The model of this section goes beyond the earlier analysis of Kanniainen and Hernesniemi (forthcoming) in that long-term capital is included and the monopolistic firm is studied.

We make the assumption that only the cost of debt, iB, is deductible from the cost of financial capital, while the cost of equity is not directly deductible. This obviously creates an incentive for the firm to pay the profits out as dividends and instead raise capital by corporate borrowing.[6] Admittedly, many tax systems make attempts to reduce the overall effective tax rate on equity to the level of that on debt. But their effects may be limited to valuation effects.

However, there are reasons why the firm may not be able to extend its borrowing without restrictions. As an alternative to borrowing, it may resort to internal financing.[7] We, therefore, make the assumption that the firm adjusts its borrowing so as to keep its debt-to-asset ratio, $b = B/(p_K K + qS)$, constant. The portfolio equilibrium condition now reads as

$$(1 - \tau_d)X^\tau + (1 - \tau_g)dV/dt = (1 - \tau_i)iV.$$

Consequently, $(1-\tau_d)X^\tau/(1-\tau_g)$ replaces X and $\alpha^* = \left[(1-\tau_i)i+\pi\right]/(1-\tau_g)$ replaces α in (1). The quantity π stands for the risk premium. The

---

[5] Note that capital income is taxed twice, i.e., first at the level of the firm and secondly at the level of the owners.

[6] The incentive which was originally suggested by Modigliani and Miller (1963) does not exist if the progressive interest tax raises the before-tax rate of interest sufficiently, as shown by Miller (1977).

[7] The debt capacity may be limited for reasons related to moral hazard or adverse selection (Stiglitz and Weiss, 1981). Then debt and equity are complements. Moreover, as suggested by Myers (1984), management may prefer internal financing over external financing due to reasons of control.

corporation tax base, TB, is written as follows:

$$TB = D(Y)Y - wL - c(S) - iB - \delta^*(p_K^*, K) - q^*U - D. \qquad (6)$$

The tax depreciation δ^* has been written as a general function of historical prices p_K^* and the capital stock. Material inputs U are valued at current prices under LIFO only (i.e., $q^* = q$). Under FIFO, $q^*(t) = q(t - T)$ where $T = S/U$ is the average period of holding inventories. We introduce $D = D(L, K, I, J, S)$ as an undetermined deduction in order to study the tax base adjustments which are necessary to reduce or even eliminate the existing distortions. The tax-adjusted stream of dividends now read as $X^\tau = X + dB/dt - iB - \tau TB$ and the Hamiltonian is

$$H' = (1 - \tau_d)X^\tau/(1 - \tau_g) + \mu_K(I - \delta K) + \mu_S(J - U).$$

In order to study the first order conditions under taxation, we first solve for the shadow prices

$$\mu_K/\beta = (1 - b)p_K - \tau D_I \qquad (7a)$$

$$\mu_S/\beta = (1 - b)q - \tau D_J \qquad (7b)$$

where $\beta = (1 - \tau_d)/(1 - \tau_g)$. These can be substituted into the first order conditions with respect to L, K and S. We produce these in (8) and (9) for L and S. First define $\sigma = 1$ for FIFO and $\sigma = 0$ for LIFO, $\phi = (q^*/q)(1 + \sigma gT)$, and $g = qdq/dt$. Then

$$(1 - \tau)[(1 - 1/\theta)pf_L - w] = q(1 - \tau\phi)f_L - \tau(D_L + D_J f_L) \qquad (8)$$

$$\begin{aligned}(1 - \tau)[(1 - 1/\theta)pf_S - c_S - ibq - qf_S - \alpha^*q(1 - b) + qg] \\ = \tau[(1 - \phi)f_S + \alpha^*(1 - b)q - \alpha^* D_J - D_S - D_J f_S \qquad (9) \\ + \sigma q^*g - qg + dD_J/dt].\end{aligned}$$

The following can be proved in a straightforward manner. Let us first suppose that the tax base is adjusted for the true cost of long-term capital K. Then, if the purpose of the tax policy is to avoid direct allocational distortions in employment and inventory decisions of the firm, one should allow the following adjustment in the corporation tax base:

$$\begin{aligned}D_J = 0, \qquad dD_J/dt = 0, \\ D_L = qf_L(1 - \phi), \quad D_K = qf_K(1 - \phi), \qquad (10) \\ D_S = qf_K(1 - \phi) + \alpha^*q(1 - b) + \sigma gq^* - qg.\end{aligned}$$

This is one of the results in Kanniainen and Hernesniemi who also show that both the Canadian and the Nordic tax base adjustments are justified according to this result.[8]

The current model, however, has extended the analysis to the case where the adjustment of the tax base for the cost of long-term capital may be inappropriate due to, for example, historic cost depreciation. Suppose then that the corporation tax raises the pre-tax required return on capital, reducing the optimal K. As a result, while the conditions (10) continue to keep the right-hand sides of (8) and (9) equal to zero, employment and inventory stock cease to be maintained at their first-best levels. Due to the spillover effects, L and S tend to deviate from their socially optimal levels. When stating this result, one should not overlook the possibility that the pre-tax wage w is distorted in the first place due to the wage tax.

The final point of this analysis concerns the taxation of pure profits discussed in Section 2. Assume that the tax base (6) consists only of pure profits and is arrived at through the base adjustment of type (10) together with the true cost of capital, because then the right-hand sides of (8) and (9) equal zero, τ can be set as high as one with no allocational distortions.[9] Yet, to make the monopolist produce the competitive output, the intra-marginal tax should be associated with a marginal subsidy. The difficulty of measuring the market position of a firm is not, however, the real cause of the nonoptimality of $\tau = 1$ in practice. This is because, for a competitive firm, the tax base $TB = 0$ under constant returns to scale since no pure rents exist. The inherent problem is that of knowing what the true economic profits are. In this situation, the way in which the corporation tax should deal with the issue of risk taking is of major importance.

References

Ábel, I. (1990) "Behavior of the Socialist Firm under Indirect Control," this volume.

Drèze, J. H. and Modigliani, F. (1972) "Consumption Decisions Under Uncertainty," *Journal of Economic Theory* 5, 308-335.

---

[8] Note that the tax system may not be full neutral in the Johansson-Samuelson sense due to differentiated taxation of personal capital income (see Sinn , 1987, pp. 119-123).

[9] For a related analysis see Munk (1978)

Goldfeld, S. M. and Quandt, R. E. (1990) "Output Targets, Input Rationing and Inventories," this volume.

Ickes, B. W. (1990) "The Theory of the Firm Under Capitalism and Socialism," this volume.

Kanniainen, V. and Hernesniemi, H. (forthcoming) "The Cost of Holding Inventories, and the Demand for Labor and Capital Under Corporate Taxation," *Canadian Journal of Economics.*

Miller, M. H. (1977) "Debt and Taxes," *Journal of Finance* **32**, 261-275.

Modigliani, F. and Miller, M. H. (1963) "Corporate Income Taxes and the Cost of Capital: A Correction," *American Economic Review,* **53**, 433-443.

Munk, K. J. (1978) "Optimal Taxation and Pure Profit," *Scandinavian Journal of Economics* **80**, 1-19.

Myers, S. C. (1984) "Capital Structure Puzzle," *Journal of Finance* **39**, 575-592.

Sinn, H. W. (1987) *Capital Income Taxation and Resource Allocation,* Amsterdam: North-Holland.

Spinnewyn, F. and Svejnar, J. (1990) "On the Dynamics of a Participatory Firm: A Model of Employer-Worker Bargaining," this volume.

Stern, N. H. (1984) "Optimum Taxation and Tax Policy," *International Monetary Fund Staff Papers* **31**, 339-378.

Stiglitz, J. and Weiss, A. (1981) "Credit Rationing in Markets with Imperfect Information," *American Economic Review* **71**, 383-410.

PART FOUR

Collective Choice and Power Sharing

15

Positionalist Aggregation Functions and Distributive Justice

Wulf Gaertner

1. Introduction

In his book *A Theory of Justice* Rawls (1971) develops two principles of justice designed to define the fundamental terms of association among individuals in a society. According to the author, these principles are the object of a collective agreement or social contract in an initial situation of equality, the so-called "original position," a purely hypothetical situation where the individuals know the general facts about human society but do not have any particular information on their own personal circumstances. The first principle focuses on the basic liberties of citizenship and requires that these liberties be equal for all individuals in society, the second principle applies to the distribution of income and wealth and to the design of organizations.

The first half of the second principle can be referred to as the maximin criterion as applied to problems of equity and justice. Rawls himself called it the "difference principle." The higher expectations of the more advantaged members of society are just if and only if they are to the benefit of the least favoured. The two principles are the outcome of a unanimous collective decision. This choice can also be viewed from the standpoint of *one person* selected at random. "If anyone after due reflection prefers a conception of justice to another, then they all do, and a unanimous agreement can be reached"—see Rawls (1971, p. 139).

Harsanyi's (1955, 1978) utilitarian philosophy, which is based on the Bayesian concept of rationality, exists in two forms. In the first version, it is assumed that the personal preferences of each individual can be represented by a von Neumann-Morgenstern utility function and, moreover, the so-called moral preferences of a particular person j (j can be any individual in society) can be represented by an evaluation function which likewise has the properties of a von Neumann-Morgenstern utility function. Together with a third requirement of Pareto optimality these three assumptions imply the existence of a linear social welfare function which reflects the ethical evaluations of person j.

In Harsanyi's second version, "the equiprobability model for moral value judgments," an individual expresses a genuine moral value judgment if he/she does not know how the choice between two alternatives x and y, let's say, will affect him/her personally and, in particular, if he/she does not know what his/her own social situation will be under the two alternatives. More concretely, Harsanyi assumes that the individual would think that under either alternative he/she would have the same probability $1/n$ to hold anyone of the n possible social positions and, actually, to be put in the place of anyone of the n individuals in the society with probability $1/n$. It is important to emphasize that in both variants of Harsanyi's utilitarian setup, it is *one person* who evaluates alternative social states.

Gauthier (1978) holds that it is possible to evaluate being different persons in different circumstances and admits that comparisons of this sort will reveal wide agreement among those who make them. But then he adds that "each comparison has, necessarily, its own personal basis; each is made from the standpoint of a particular person, and since persons differ, not all comparisons will agree." Sen (1983, 1985) speaks of the possibility of "interpersonal variations of well-being rankings," which may be due to what he calls position-dependence.

We feel that Gauthier's as well as Sen's remarks are quite serious objections. The point they make should at least be viewed as a warning. In this paper, we shall therefore consider profiles of so-called "individual extended orderings." Instead of there being a single interpersonal evaluation embracing all the individuals in the different possible positions, we postulate that there be a list of interpersonal comparisons made by the different

Table 1. Profile of interpersonal evaluations

Individual 1:	(y,2)	(x,1)	(y,1)	(z,3)	(z,2)	(x,3)	(z,1)	(x,2)	(y,3)
Individual 2:	(x,1)	(y,2)	(z,2)	(y,1)	(z,3)	(x,2)	(x,3)	(y,3)	(z,1)
Individual 3:	(z,3)	(y,2)	(x,1)	(z,2)	(x,3)	(y,3)	(y,1)	(z,1)	(x,2)

members of society. We shall assume that the following statement is meaningful: According to individual i's interpersonal welfare judgment (any person i), person j in state x is at least as well off as person k in state y. Starting from a set of evaluations like this one, we shall consider the problem of aggregation. The process of amalgamating different individuals' interests or evaluations into some aggregate notion of social judgment is the typical approach of social choice theory. It is quite different from cooperative bargaining theory à la Nash, Kalai and Smorodinsky, and others, which will not be considered here.[1]

As an example, let us discuss a situation which comprises three individuals and three states, so that each individual has the task of evaluating and comparing nine positions of the form (x,i), (z,j), (y,k), ... to each other. In the above table we arrange more preferred positions to the left of less preferred positions.

In the given profile, individual 1, for example, considers person 2 under state y to hold the best position, himself/herself under state x to hold the second-best position, etc. Imagine a social choice rule which allows each of the three individuals to veto that social state under which he/she has to acquiesce in his/her worst possible position. Given the profile above, all three states will be vetoed.

Consider another rule which allows each individual to secure that alternative under which, according to his/her view, the minimal individual position is maximal (this rule clearly borrows from Rawls' difference principle). According to this procedure, neither x nor y nor z will be eliminated in the choice procedure.

Finally, consider a mechanism permitting each person to secure that social alternative which provides the person with his/her second-best posi-

---

[1] For an overview and discussion of several of these approaches, see, e.g., Kalai (1985) and Gaertner and Klemisch-Ahlert (1988).

tion. Again, all three states will "survive."

One problem with the three rules above is that profiles (such as ours) exist for which either all social states are eliminated or all states pass "the screening." A certainly much deeper problem is that all three procedures make use of only a small part of the total amount of information contained in a given profile.

For the case of extended orderings, Roberts (1980) derives an Arrow-type (1963) impossibility result. On the other hand, Suzumura (1983) proves the existence of two particular choice functions, both of which are two-stage choice rules using welfare information from both ethical and subjective preferences over social states. As both types of choice rules essentially apply the majority closure method, complete social indifference to all alternatives can be a frequent outcome, a feature that one may consider as somewhat undesirable.

In the following section an interpersonal positionalist rule will be discussed, based on the broad variant of the Borda method. Nonlinear transformations of this ranking rule are proposed in order to express equity considerations of a varying degree.

2. Positionalist Information and Nonlinear Ranking Rules

Let X be a finite set of feasible social states and let $N = \{1, 2, ..., n\}$ be a finite set of individuals with at least two elements. We define $\mathcal{R}$ as the set of all orderings on X. For every $R \in \mathcal{R}$, for any x, $y \in X$, $x R y$ means that from society's point of view, x is at least as good as y (strict preference P and indifference I being derived from R in the usual manner).

We introduce, as already indicated in Section 1, the concept of an individual extended ordering $\tilde{R}_i$ defined over the Cartesian product $X \times N$. For all x, $y \in X$ and all i, j, $k \in N$, $(x, j)\tilde{R}_i(y, k)$ means that from the standpoint of person i it is no worse to be individual j in state x than to be individual k in state y. One should note that this concept has a purely ordinal character and only permits interpersonal comparisons of welfare levels or individual positions as we shall say. $\{\tilde{R}_i\}$ stands for a list or profile of individual extended orderings and $\{\tilde{R}_i^a\}$, $\{\tilde{R}_i^b\}$, ... will denote different profiles. With $\tilde{R}_i$ being person i's extended ordering, let $T(X \times N)$ represent the set of all logically possible extended orderings from which each individual i can choose. We define the n-fold Cartesian product $\tilde{\mathcal{R}} = T(X \times N) \times ... \times T(X \times N)$ and call a mapping $f : \tilde{\mathcal{R}} \to \mathcal{R}$ a positionalist aggregation function (PAF).

A (positionalist) ranking rule assigns a real number (weight) to each individual position within a given profile. A ranking rule evaluates each social state according to the sum of real numbers (weights) assigned to the various individual positions pertaining to that state. For all $x \in X$ and all i, $k \in N$, let $\rho_i(x, k)$ be the weight attached to person k's situation under state x, according to individual i's extended ordering. The interpersonal ranking rule F is the rule such that for any profile $\{\tilde{R}_i\}$ and alternatives x, $y \in X$, $x F(\{\tilde{R}_i\}) y$, if and only if $\sum_i \sum_j \rho_i(x, j) \geqq \sum_i \sum_j \rho_i(y, j)$. Strict inequality in the latter relationship yields $x F(\{\tilde{R}_i\}) y \wedge$ not $y F(\{\tilde{R}_i\}) x$, which will be expressed by $x F^P(\{\tilde{R}_i\}) y$; equality leads to $x F(\{\tilde{R}_i\}) y \wedge y F(\{\tilde{R}_i\}) x$, which will be written as $x F^I(\{\tilde{R}_i\}) y$. We say that a positionalist aggregation function f is numerically representable, if and only if there exists an interpersonal ranking rule F such that $x R y \Longleftrightarrow x F(\{\tilde{R}_i\}) y$.

Unrestricted domain is a highly appealing condition. Within the framework of extended orderings this requirement may, however, collide with the Pareto principle. In order to avoid this clash, we shall restrict the domain of the PAF via Sen's (1970) identity axiom. In other words, we shall restrict the domain $\tilde{\mathcal{R}}$ of the PAF by the following requirement:

Identity Axiom. *A profile* $\{\tilde{R}_i\}$ *satisfies the identity axiom, if and only if* $\forall x$, $y \in X$, $\forall i \in N$:

$$[(x, i) \tilde{R}_i (y, i) \Longleftrightarrow \forall j \in N : (x, i) \tilde{R}_j (y, i)].$$

This axiom postulates that there be no discrepancy between person i's view about his/her own well-being in states x and y, let's say, and everybody else's view about i's well-being in states x and y. This restriction still permits quite a substantial variation in individual preferences, so that the aggregation problem by no means becomes trivial under the identity axiom. The set of admissible profiles under the identity axiom will be denoted by $\tilde{\mathcal{R}}^*$ with, of course, $\tilde{\mathcal{R}}^* \subset \tilde{\mathcal{R}}$.

We now discuss various conditions which one might perhaps like to see satisfied by any PAF. The first axiom, which bears the name of Suppes, is due to Hammond (1976). We consider permutations of the individuals in society. A permutation π is defined as any bijection between N and itself. For any $\{\tilde{R}_i\} \in \tilde{\mathcal{R}}^*$, we formulate the following relationship:

$$\forall \, x, \, y \in X, \, \forall i \in N : x \, s_i \, y \Longleftrightarrow$$
$$[\exists \, \pi \in \Pi, \, \forall j \in N : (x, j) \, \tilde{I}_i \, (y, \pi(j))],$$

where Π is the set of all permutations on N and $\tilde{I}_i$ denotes person i's indifference relationship, derived from $\tilde{R}_i$ in the ususal way. We can now state:

Suppes Indifference (S). $\forall x, \, y \in X : [\forall i \in N : x \, s_i \, y] \to x \, I \, y.$

This axiom says that any two states x and y are considered as socially indifferent whenever all persons agree that the individual positions of x and y are pairwise indifferent under permutations of individuals.

The following condition is well known from standard social choice theory but, of course, reformulated for our framework of extended orderings:

Strong Monotonicity (SM). *Let* $\{\tilde{R}_i^a\}$ *and* $\{\tilde{R}_i^b\}$ *be two profiles of extended orderings, such that for all* $j \in N, j \neq i, \tilde{R}_j^a = \tilde{R}_j^b$. *For individual* $i \in N$, *let there be* $x, \, y \in X$ *and* $k, \ell \in N$, *not necessarily distinct, such that*

$$(x, k) \, \tilde{I}_i^a \, (y, \ell) \wedge (x, k) \, \tilde{P}_i^b \, (y, \ell)$$

or

$$(y, \ell) \, \tilde{P}_i^a \, (x, k) \wedge (x, k) \, \tilde{R}_i^b \, (y, \ell),$$

while for all the remaining positions, $\tilde{R}_i^a$ *and* $\tilde{R}_i^b$ *coincide.*[2] *Then* $x \, R^a \, y$ *implies* $x \, P^b \, y$.

Strong Monotonicity makes the requirement that aggregation functions be positively responsive to small changes in individuals' preferences. An aggregation mechanism which satisfies SM avoids a large number of ties in the social ordering.

One can show that S and SM together imply the Strong Pareto Principle, which in terms of extended orderings can be defined as follows:

Strong Pareto Principle (SP). $\forall x, \, y \in X : [\forall i \in N : (x, i) \, \tilde{R}_i \, (y, i) \wedge$
$\exists j \in N : (x, j) \, \tilde{P}_j \, (y, j)] \to x \, P \, y.$

---

[2] $\tilde{P}_i$ denotes, of course, strict preference of person i.

Arrow's independence condition requires that, if one determines the social ordering among elements of a certain subset A of the set of alternatives, then changes of preference among the elements outside A have no influence whatsoever on the social ordering of the elements in A. Positionalist aggregation functions obviously do not fulfill this strong requirement. Let us, therefore, consider a weaker independence condition—though not formulated within an extended ordering framework, the basic idea can be found in Fine and Fine (1974).

For a given number of persons and a given number of alternatives, define X_S as the set of individual positions referring both to alternatives x and y and to any other alternative z, such that individual positions $(z, \cdot)$ are ranked:

(a) on a par with the highest position pertaining to x and y,

(b) on a par with the lowest position pertaining to x and y, and

(c) somewhere in between these extreme positions.

Furthermore, let X_T be the set that comprises all the other individual positions. We have $X_S \cup X_T = X_Q$, the latter being the set of all individual positions. We shall write $[\{\tilde{R}_i\}^S, \{\tilde{R}_i\}^T]$ for the configuration Q, which has

$$X_S \cup X_T = X_Q, (x \cdot)\tilde{R}_i^S(y, \cdot) \Longleftrightarrow (x, \cdot)\tilde{R}_i^Q(y, \cdot)$$

for $(x, \cdot), (y, \cdot) \in X_S$,

$$(v, \cdot)\tilde{R}_i^T(w, \cdot) \Longleftrightarrow (v, \cdot)\tilde{R}_i^Q(w, \cdot) \text{ for } (v, \cdot), (w, \cdot) \in X_T,$$

and $(x, \cdot)\tilde{P}_i^Q(v, \cdot)$ for any $(x, \cdot) \in X_S$ and any $(v, \cdot) \in X_T$. Thus, the configuration $[\{\tilde{R}_i\}^S, \{\tilde{R}_i\}^T]$ has all positions of X_S placed above all positions of X_T. The constellation $[\{\tilde{R}_i\}^T, \{\tilde{R}_i\}^S]$ is defined analogously.

We say that the interpersonal ranking rule F satisfies independence of lower extreme configurations, if $x F[\{\tilde{R}_i\}^S, \{\tilde{R}_i\}^T]y \Longleftrightarrow x F(\{\tilde{R}_i\}^S) y$, and that it satisfies independence of upper extreme configurations, if $x F[\{\tilde{R}_i\}^T, \{\tilde{R}_i\}^S]y \Longleftrightarrow x F(\{\tilde{R}_i\}^S) y$, where $x, y \in X$. Lower extreme configurations, for example, demand that, if a configuration of individual positions is joined to the bottom of another configuration, then the social ranking over the original configuration should undergo no changes. If F fulfills both lower and upper extreme configurations, we shall say it satisfies independence of extreme configurations (EC), which clearly is a weakening of Arrow's independence condition.

A requirement for standard social choice theory is often that of neutrality:

Neutrality (N). *If profile $\{\tilde{R}_i^b\}$ is obtained from profile $\{\tilde{R}_i^a\}$ by interchanging individual positions referring to x and y in each individual's extended ordering, then the social ordering generated for $\{\tilde{R}_i^a\}$ is exactly like the ordering for $\{\tilde{R}_i^b\}$, except that alternatives x and y have changed places.*

Here an interesting condition called stability (Gärdenfors, 1973) can be introduced. Two profiles, $\{\tilde{R}_i^a\}$ and $\{\tilde{R}_i^b\}$, are almost identical with respect to alternative x, if and only if there is at most one individual extended ordering $\tilde{R}_i$ and at most one position (z, k) such that $\tilde{R}_i^a$ is the same ordering as $\tilde{R}_i^b$ on the set of all individual positions, except for position (z, k), and $(z, k)\, \tilde{P}_i^a\,(x, \ell)$ and $(z, k)\, \tilde{I}_i^b\,(x, \ell)$ or $(x, \ell)\, \tilde{I}_i^a\,(z, k)$ and $(x, \ell)\, \tilde{P}_i^b\,(z, k)$ for some $k, \ell \in \{1, \ldots, n\}$. We can now formulate Gärdenfors's concept of stability, which says that "small" changes in individual preferences should generate "small" changes in the social preference relation.

Stability (ST). *A PAF is stable, if and only if not both $y\, P^a\, x$ and $x\, P^b\, y$ for any $y \neq z$ (where z is as in the above definition of almost identical profiles), whenever $\{\tilde{R}_i^a\}$ and $\{\tilde{R}_i^b\}$ are almost identical with respect to x.*

There are several ways to define the Borda ranking rule. We shall have to define this method within our framework of extended orderings. For fixed X and N, the cardinality of the set of all individual positions is given by $X \times N$. We set $\#(X \times N) = q$.

At this point, we only consider the case of linear preference orderings. With $r_i(x, k)$ having the same interpretation as $\rho_i(x, k)$ above, we let the value or weight of $r_i(x, k)$ be determined by the number of positions that are ranked below (x, k) by person i.[3] In addition, we define for any $S \subset X$, the numbering of positions belonging to subset S is based on the entire Cartesian product $X \times N$.

The latter requirement leads us to the broad version of the Borda rule

---

[3] This actually is Borda's (1781) own proposal. There are other suggestions as to the choice of the weights. These scores yield, however, the same social result as the original Borda numbers (see, e.g., Gärdenfors, 1973 and Young, 1974).

(on this see, e.g., Sen, 1977). The highest possible Borda score obviously is $q - 1$, the lowest possible score is 0. This ranking rule, which we shall denote as the linear broad Borda method, shows declining weights with diminishing desirability and a constant rank difference of unity for any two adjacent individual positions. The positionalist Borda method has, thus, become an interpersonal linear ranking rule F_L with the property that, for any $\{\tilde{R}_i\}$ and any $x, y \in X$,

$$x F_L(\{\tilde{R}_i\}) y \iff \sum_i \sum_j r_i(x, j) \geq \sum_i \sum_j r_i(y, j).$$

Various characterizations of the linear Borda rule exist in the literature: Gärdenfors (1973), Fine and Fine (1974), Young (1974), Nitzan and Rubinstein (1981), among others. Gärdenfors, for example, has shown that for at least three alternatives and at least three individuals, the only numerically representable PAF that satisfies neutrality, strong monotonicity and stability is the Borda function. The linear Borda rule fulfills various other properties, among them independence of extreme configurations and, of course, Suppes indifference, once the rule is generalized to the case of weak individual orderings.

Let us now consider nonlinear transformations of the original Borda weights $r_i(x, k)$. We define the class of transformed interpersonal ranking rules as, for any profile $\{\tilde{R}_i\}$ and any $x, y \in X$:

$$x F_T(\{\tilde{R}_i\}) y \iff \sum_i \sum_j \varphi(r_i(x, j)) \geq \sum_i \sum_j \varphi(r_i(y, j)),$$

where $\varphi(\cdot)$ is any strictly increasing nonlinear transformation of the positionalist values $r_i(x, j)$, $r_i(y, j)$, $i, j \in \{1, 2, \ldots, n\}$. Rules F_T, which make up this class, obviously evaluate any given social alternatives x and y according to the sums of transformed weights pertaining to x and y, where $\varphi'(\cdot)$ is strictly positive and $\varphi'(\cdot) \neq$ const.

We can now formulate the following result:

Proposition 2.1. *Under domain $\tilde{\mathcal{R}}^*$, elements F_T from the class of transformed interpersonal ranking rules satisfy Suppes indifference, strong monotonicity, neutrality and independence of extreme configurations, but not stability.*

Proof. It is easy to show that all rules F_T fulfill conditions S, SM (and, therefore, SP) and N. Since we have decided to base the numbering of positions on the entire Cartesian product $X \times N$, condition EC is satisfied naturally. That the elements F_T do not fulfill condition ST will be demonstrated with the help of particular preference profiles.

Consider the profiles in Table 2: the two individual positions in square brackets in $\tilde{R}_2^a$ denote indifferent positions.[4] It is immediately clear that the two given profiles are "almost identical with respect to alternative x," according to Gärdenfors's definition. From the set of strictly concave transformations, which clearly belongs to the class of transformed interpersonal ranking rules, we choose $\varphi(r(\cdot)) = [r(\cdot)]^{1/2}$. We obtain $y\,F_T^P(\{\tilde{R}_i^a\})\,x$ and $x\,F_T^P(\{\tilde{R}_i^b\})\,y$, so that stability is violated.

One can show that, given any strictly convex transformation, there also exists a pair of profiles such that condition ST is not fulfilled. Exactly the same is true if one uses, e.g., the logarithmic, reciprocal transformation $\varphi(r) = \exp\{a - b/r\}$, which has an "S-shape."

Obviously, the stability condition allows us to draw a line of demarcation between linear and nonlinear interpersonal ranking rules. We can, thus, formulate an impossibility result, which will be given without proof.

Proposition 2.2. *Not both* $y F_L^P(\{\tilde{R}_i^a\})\,x$ *and* $x F_L^P(\{\tilde{R}_i^b\})\,y$ *for the interpersonal ranking rule* F_L *or any positive linear transformation of* F_L, *whenever* $\{\tilde{R}_i^a\}$ *and* $\{\tilde{R}_i^b\}$ *are almost identical with respect to* x.

Table 2. Profiles $\{\tilde{R}_i^a\}$, $\{\tilde{R}_i^b\} \in \tilde{\mathcal{R}}^*$

$\tilde{R}_1^a$:	$(y,1)$	$(z,2)$	$(x,2)$	$(y,2)$	$(x,1)$	$(z,1)$	$(v,1)$	$(v,2)$
$\tilde{R}_2^a$:	$(z,2)$	$(y,1)$	$(x,1)$	$[(x,2)$	$(z,1)]$	$(v,1)$	$(y,2)$	$(v,2)$
$\tilde{R}_1^b$:	$(y,1)$	$(z,2)$	$(x,2)$	$(y,2)$	$(x,1)$	$(z,1)$	$(v,1)$	$(v,2)$
$\tilde{R}_2^b$:	$(z,2)$	$(y,1)$	$(x,1)$	$(x,2)$	$(z,1)$	$(v,1)$	$(y,2)$	$(v,2)$

---

[4] In the following rank assignment for indifferent positions, we assume that in individual i's extended ordering there are p positions, considered indifferent to each other; we calculate the mean value μ_p of what these positions would have been assigned, if they had been arranged in a strictly descending order; and we then assign the value of the transformation $\varphi(\cdot)$ at μ_p to each position in the tie.

If we had selected the class of narrow interpersonal ranking rules (see again Sen, 1977), we would have been able to apply the condition of independence of extreme configurations in order to distinguish between linear and nonlinear rules. Within our present concept of broad ranking rules this distinction could have been established as well by means of Hansson's (1973) property of strong positionalist independence. Also, Young's (1974) cancellation property and Fine and Fine's (1974) inversion condition would have been able to draw a line between linearity and nonlinearity. Consider, for example, Fine and Fine's requirement:

Inversion (IN). *For a given number of individuals and a given number of social alternatives, let all the individual extended orderings be reversed. Then the social ordering generated by PAF should also be reversed.*

Linear ranking rules clearly satisfy this property. Using a strictly concave or strictly convex transformation, one immediately sees that condition IN is no longer fulfilled.

After these rather technical statements we wish to come back to the main theme of this paper. Rawls' (1971) difference principle concentrates on the lowest individual positions. The lexicographic version of this rule, often called "the leximin principle," was successfully characterized by Deschamps and Gevers (1978) by means of a condition called "extreme equity axiom." Rawls has been widely attacked for his single-focus rule. Sen (1973) has argued that utilitarianism, on the other hand, "is much too hooked on the welfare *sum* to be concerned with the problem of distribution, and it is, in fact, capable of producing strongly antiegalitarian results." It is obvious that the equidistanced weighting scheme in the interpersonal linear ranking rule does not reflect much of an equity concept either. Through the linear decline of weights, adjacent positions in the upper part of an extended ordering are treated exactly the same way as neighbouring positions in the lower part.

Consider the two profiles in Table 3: one of the differences between them is that under $\{\tilde{R}_i^a\}$ the worst individual position occurs under alternative z, whereas under $\{\tilde{R}_i^b\}$ the worst position is tied to state x.

Table 3. Profiles $\{\tilde{R}_i^a\}, \{\tilde{R}_i^b\} \in \tilde{\mathcal{R}}^*$

$\tilde{R}_1^a$:	$(x,1)$	$(u,1)$	$(u,2)$	$(y,1)$	$(y,2)$	$(x,2)$	$(z,1)$	$(z,2)$
$\tilde{R}_2^a$:	$(x,1)$	$(u,2)$	$(y,2)$	$(u,1)$	$(y,1)$	$(x,2)$	$(z,1)$	$(z,2)$
$\tilde{R}_1^b$:	$(z,2)$	$(z,1)$	$(x,1)$	$(u,1)$	$(u,2)$	$(y,1)$	$(y,2)$	$(x,2)$
$\tilde{R}_2^b$:	$(z,1)$	$(z,2)$	$(x,1)$	$(u,2)$	$(y,2)$	$(u,1)$	$(y,1)$	$(x,2)$

For the present argument, we shall enlarge the two profiles by adding further alternatives. Let us suppose that a social decision is to be made between states x and y. We add five more states r, s, t, v and w with the respective individual positions and assume that in profile $\{\tilde{R}_i^a\}$ all these positions are ranked to the right of the positions of state z, while in profile $\{\tilde{R}_i^b\}$, these positions are ranked to the left of the individual positions pertaining to state z. We know that, according to the class of linear ranking rules, the social decision between x and y is the *same* in both situations. However, is there much of an equity problem in the first situation? States x and y apparently are rather advantageous in relation to most of the other available social states. Obviously, this cannot be said with respect to the second situation where individual 2 is very badly off indeed under state x.

In the following we wish to propose an equity criterion, which is in the spirit of Deschamps and Gevers' condition, but less extreme. For any $x, y \in X$ and any $j \in N$, consider positions (y,j) and (x,j), let's say, with $(y,j)\tilde{P}_i(x,j)$, according to person i's ordering. We say that for any $v \in X$ and any $h \in N$, the position (v,h) lies between (y,j) and (x,j), if

$$(y,j)\,\tilde{R}_i(v,h) \wedge (v,h)\,\tilde{P}_i(x,j)$$

or

$$(y,j)\,\tilde{P}_i(v,h) \wedge (v,h)\,\tilde{R}_i(x,j).$$

This fact will be denoted by $(v,h)\,B_i\,[(y,j),(x,j)]$. Also, as an auxiliary concept, we define for any $\{\tilde{R}_i\} \in \tilde{\mathcal{R}}^*, \forall\, x,y, \in X, \forall i \in N$:

$$x\gamma_i y \iff \Big\{ \exists\,\{j,k\} \subset N : (y,j)\,\tilde{P}_i\,(x,j), (x,j)\,\tilde{P}_i\,(x,k),$$
$$(x,k)\,\tilde{P}_i(y,k) \wedge \forall \ell \in N\backslash\{j,k\} :$$
$$(x,\ell)\,\tilde{I}_i\,(y,\ell) \wedge \text{ for any } v,z \in X \text{ and any}$$
$$g,h \in N : \#\{(v,g)\mid (v,g)\,B_i\,[(x,k),(y,k)]\}$$
$$\geqq \#\{(z,h)\mid (z,h)\,B_i\,[(y,j),(x,j)]\}\Big\}.$$

We now introduce the following equity axiom for interpersonal ranking rules:

Equity within Ranking Rules (EQ). $\forall x,y \in X$:

$$[\forall i \in N : x\,\gamma_i\,y] \to xF_T^P(\{\tilde{R}_i\})\,y.$$

Which class of interpersonal ranking rules satisfies axiom EQ? The following proposition provides an answer:

Proposition 2.3. *If and only if $\varphi(\cdot)$ is strictly concave and $\varphi'(\cdot) > 0$ everywhere, the resulting subclass of transformed interpersonal ranking rules satisfies axiom EQ.*

Proof. From the definition of relation γ_i, we find for any $x,y \in X$, any $i \in N$ and for all $\ell \in N\backslash\{j,k\}$ that $r_i(x,\ell) = r_i(y,\ell)$ and $\varphi(r_i(x,\ell)) = \varphi(r_i(y,\ell))$, thanks to our construction. Furthermore, due to the strict concavity of φ, we get for individuals $j,k \in N$:

$$\varphi(r_i(x,k)) - \varphi(r_i(y,k)) > \varphi(r_i(y,j)) - \varphi(r_i(x,j)) \to$$
$$\varphi(r_i(x,k)) + \varphi(r_i(x,j)) > \varphi(r_i(y,j)) + \varphi(r_i(y,k)).$$

Adding all transformed rank numbers connected with x and y, we obtain

$$\sum_h \varphi(r_i(x,h)) > \sum_h \varphi(r_i(y,h)).$$

If $\forall i \in N : x\,\gamma_i\,y$, then

$$\sum_i \sum_h \varphi(r_i(x,h)) > \sum_i \sum_h \varphi(r_i(y,h)) \iff xF_T^P(\{\tilde{R}_i\})\,y,$$

so that axiom EQ is satisfied.

From relation γ_i we know that $(x,k)\tilde{P}_i(y,k)$ and $(y,j)\tilde{P}_i(x,j)$. Due to the construction of an interpersonal ranking rule, it must be the case that $\varphi(r_i(x,k)) - \varphi(r_i(y,k)) > 0$ and $\varphi(r_i(y,j)) - \varphi(r_i(x,j)) > 0$, so that $\varphi'(\cdot) > 0$ everywhere. For the first difference we shall write $d_i(x,y;k)$, which is positive; the second difference will be multiplied by -1 and we write $d_i(x,y;j)$, which is, of course, negative. Now the summation of the d_i over all i can result in

$$\sum_i \sum_h \varphi(r_i(x,h)) \gtreqqless \sum_i \sum_h \varphi(r_i(y,h)).$$

Keeping in mind that in the definition of relation γ_i, we note that the number of positions (v,g) has to be at least as large as the number of positions (z,h), and that the aggregate result $x F_T^P(\{\tilde{R}_i\}) y$ can for the general case be secured only if φ is strictly concave.[5]

Elements F_T from the class of transformed interpersonal ranking rules with $\varphi(\cdot)$ strictly concave and $\varphi'(\cdot) > 0$ will, henceforth, be called equity-oriented interpersonal ranking rules, to be denoted by F_{EQT}. Since there is an infinite number of strictly concave functions, axiom EQ obviously produces some flexibility within the aggregation procedure. Differing degrees of concavity of the transformation function represent different degrees of equity-orientation. One can be very close to the distributive principle of Rawls or be quite far away from his single-focus rule.

The degree of desired equity for society can, thus, be varied continuously. The "proper" degree of equity should be decided upon by all members of society. Furthermore, it seems to us that this decision should be made in some abstract choice situation and not in a concrete case with which society may possibly be confronted.

The following result stems immediately from Proposition 2.1:

Proposition 2.1′. *Under domain $\tilde{\mathcal{R}}^*$, elements F_{EQT} from the class of transformed interpersonal ranking rules, satisfy Suppes indifference, strong monotonicity, neutrality and independence of extreme configurations, but not stability.*

It is clear from the construction of relation γ_i that positionalist aggre-

---

[5] Note that if $\#\{(v,g)\} = \#\{(z,h)\}$, then $x F_T^P(\{\tilde{R}_i\}) y$ could never hold, if φ were positive linear or were strictly convex.

gation functions, which are numerically representable by means of F_{EQT}, violate an axiom called separability or elimination. This condition says that the influence of indifferent or unconcerned individuals on the social ordering should be nil.

The general view in the social choice literature is that this axiom is very reasonable. Actually both utilitarianism and the Rawlsian leximin principle satisfy this property. As Fine and Fine (1974) write, this axiom "raises, however, the delicate question of whether the social decision may depend in some essential way upon a configuration as a unity."

This aspect may not be important in an election of a political candidate. In our view it is, however, highly relevant whenever distributive judgments have to be made. Here, the individual positions of all persons, one position against another, should be taken into consideration, no matter whether individuals express their strict preference or articulate instances of indifference in their extended orderings. Preference profiles have to be viewed *in their totality*.

References

Arrow, K. J. (1963) *Social Choice and Individual Values*, 2nd ed., John Wiley and Sons, New York.

de Borda, J. C. (1781) "Mémoire sur les élections au scrutin," *Histoire de l'Académie Royale des Sciences*, 657-665.

Deschamps, R. and Gevers, L. (1978) "Leximin and Utilitarian Rules: A Joint Characterization," *J. Economic Theory* **17**, 143-163.

Fine, B. and Fine, K. (1974) "Social Choice and Individual Rankings," Parts I and II, *Review of Economic Studies* **41**, 303-322 and 459-475.

Gaertner, W. and Klemisch-Ahlert, M. (1988) "Models of Bargaining and Distributive Justice," Working Paper, Univ. of Osnabrück.

Gärdenfors, P. (1973) "Positionalist Voting Functions," *Theory and Decision* **4**, 1-24.

Gauthier, D. (1978) "Social Choice and Distributive Justice," *Philosophia* **7**, 239-253.

Hammond, P. J. (1976) "Equity, Arrow's Conditions, and Rawls' Difference Principle," *Econometrica* **44**, 793-804.

Hansson, B. (1973) "The Independence Condition in the Theory of Social Choice," *Theory and Decision* 4, 25-49.

Harsanyi, J. C. (1955) "Cardinal Welfare, Individualistic Ethics, and Interpersonal Comparisons of Utility," *J. Political Economy* 63, 309-321.

———— (1978) "Bayesian Decision Theory and Utilitarian Ethics," Papers and Proceedings, *American Economic Review* 68, 223-228.

Kalai, E. (1985) "Solutions to the Bargaining Problem," in *Social Goals and Social Organization*, edited by L. Hurwicz, D. Schmeidler and H. Sonnenschein, Cambridge Univ. Press, Cambridge, U.K.

Nitzan, S. and Rubinstein, A. (1981) "A Further Characterization of Borda Ranking Method," *Public Choice* 36, 153-158.

Rawls, J. (1971) *A Theory of Justice*, Harvard Univ. Press, Cambridge, Mass., U.S.A.

Roberts, K. W. S. (1980) "Possibility Theorems with Interpersonally Comparable Welfare Levels," *Review of Economic Studies* 47, 409-420.

Sen, A. K. (1970) *Collective Choice and Social Welfare*, Holden-Day, San Francisco, Calif.

———— (1973) *On Economic Inequality*, Clarendon Press, Oxford.

———— (1977) "Social Choice Theory, A Re-examination," *Econometrica* 45, 53-89.

———— (1983) "Evaluator Relativity and Consequential Evaluation," *Philosophy and Public Affairs* 12, 113-132.

———— (1985) *Commodities and Capabilities*, North-Holland, Amsterdam.

Suppes, P. (1966) "Some Formal Models of Grading Principles," *Synthese* 6, 284-306.

Suzumura, K. (1983) "Resolving Conflicting Views of Justice in Social Choice," in *Social Choice and Welfare*, edited by P. K. Pattanaik and M. Salles, North-Holland, Amsterdam.

Young, H. P. (1974) "An Axiomatization of Borda's Rule," *J. Economic Theory* 9, 43-52.

16

Decentralization and Pressure-Group Activities

Bengt-Arne Wickström

1. Introduction

Political rent-seeking and lobbying activities play an important role in modern societies.[1] The greater the participation of political and bureaucratic organs in the economic life of a society, the greater the incentives are to engage in lobbying activities, since the potential rewards to a successful lobbyist depend directly on the size of the public cake. This problem has been analyzed by Wickström (1987), who shows within a simple noncooperative game that the number of active pressure groups in a society as well as the volume of their outlays on lobbying activities are an increasing function of the size of the public cake.

In this essay the distributional and efficiency properties of lobbying activities are studied within the framework of the same model. The focus will, thereby, fall on the number of potential pressure groups. This can be interpreted as the degree of centralization of the government authority. The more decentralized, either regionally or according to area of competence, the dividers of the public cake are, the fewer the pressure groups that naturally "belong" to any one authority.

---

[1] For a general discussion of these activities, see Buchanan et al. (1980) and Rowley et al. (1988).

2. The Model

The model is basically the same as in Wickström (1987).[2] It is assumed that there exists a number of potential pressure groups in the economy. Each group i is characterized by a strength parameter, n_i, such that $n_1 \geqq n_2 \geqq \ldots \geqq n_i \geqq n_{i+1} \geqq \ldots$. The size of the publicly provided rent (the "cake") is given by y. Each group i spends a certain amount of resources, x_i, in order to influence the government to give it a part of the cake.[3]

The fraction of the cake that a group receives, β_i, $\sum_i \beta_i = 1$, is proportional to the strength of the group and to the amount of resources the group expends on lobbying activities:

$$\frac{\beta_i}{\beta_j} = \frac{x_i n_i}{x_j n_j}. \tag{1}$$

This implies that

$$\beta_i = \frac{n_i x_i}{\sum_j n_j x_j}. \tag{2}$$

In other words, strength is an exogenously given characterization of the pressure group and is defined through (1) as the proportionality factor determining the marginal impact on the fraction of the cake received as a result of an increase in the lobbying effort.

The benefit to group i of the lobbying activity is

$$\pi_i = \beta_i y - x_i. \tag{3}$$

Each group will try to maximize this benefit. It is assumed that each one takes the activities of the other groups as a given datum in doing so; that is, they follow a Nash-Cournot strategy.

It is readily shown that this game has a unique equilibrium characterized by

---

[2] The main difference is that in the previous model it was assumed that the impact of rent seeking on the fraction of the cake that a pressure group receives is a concave function of the outlays on lobbying. This assumption accounts for the results on the change in the number of active pressure groups as the size of the cake changes, but would only have a marginal impact on the results of this essay. In the interests of simplicity, it is, therefore, dispensed with.

[3] The model could apply equally well to a market in monopolistic competition. The amount of advertising expenditure would determine here the market segments of the various sellers.

$$\beta_i(1 - \beta_i)y = x_i. \tag{4}$$

Combining (3) and (4), we get the equilibrium values of the net benefits of the game to any one group:

$$\pi_i = \beta_i^2 y. \tag{5}$$

Summation gives us the relative efficiency of the lobbying activities:

$$\frac{\sum_i \pi_i}{y} = \sum_i \beta_i^2. \tag{6}$$

This is the fraction of the cake that is not used up in the attempts to secure a portion thereof.

Taking the summation of (4) over all groups and dividing (4) by this sum, we obtain

$$\frac{\beta_i(1 - \beta_i)}{1 - \sum_j \beta_j^2} = \frac{x_i}{\sum_j x_j} = \frac{\beta_i/n_i}{\sum_j \beta_j/n_j}. \tag{7}$$

Division by β_i for $\beta_i > 0$ yields

$$\beta_i = 1 - \frac{N-1}{N}\nu_i, \tag{8}$$

where N is the number of pressure groups for which $\beta_i > 0$, the active groups, and ν_i is a normalized strength (or, rather, relative weakness) parameter:

$$\nu_i = \frac{1/n_i}{\frac{1}{N}\sum_{j=1}^{N} 1/n_j}. \tag{9}$$

We note that the condition for a pressure group to be active—that is, for $\beta_i > 0$—is

$$\nu_i < \frac{N}{N-1} = 1 - \frac{1}{N-1}. \tag{10}$$

We can now rewrite (6) as[4]

---

[4] The limit of the relative efficiency as N becomes infinite is zero here. To make the impact function concave (see footnote[2]) could change this result, if the marginal impact becomes infinite for small x. This is the case in Tullock (1980). His model is very similar to ours, but does not take into account in detail that the pressure groups can be of different strengths. Tullock introduces a "bias" into the game and analyzes some efficiency effects, but does not carry through the distributional analysis as the number of players changes.

$$\frac{\sum_i \pi_i}{y} = \frac{1}{N} + \frac{(N-1)^2}{N} V_N, \qquad (11)$$

where V_N is the variance of ν of the active pressure groups:

$$V_N := \frac{1}{N} \sum_i (1 - \nu_i)^2. \qquad (12)$$

3. Efficiency and the Number of Pressure Groups

Equation (11) immediately gives the result that the greater the relative efficiency, the greater is the variance V_N; that is, the more heterogeneous the pressure groups in the marginal impact of a given lobbying effort are, the greater the relative efficiency becomes. The relative efficiency also increases as the number of groups increases, if V_N is sufficiently large.

In general, a game with M groups is more efficient than a game with N groups, if and only if

$$M - N < N(M-1)^2 V_M - M(N-1)^2 V_N. \qquad (13)$$

If $M > N$ and the variances are the same and equal to V, then this reduces to

$$V > \frac{1}{NM - 1}. \qquad (14)$$

In other words, centralization leads to less waste per unit cake, if the strength of the pressure groups varies sufficiently.

If all active groups are of approximately equal strength, the game is more inefficient in general, but decentralization tends to increase the relative efficiency.

4. Distribution of Benefits and the Number of Pressure Groups

As in the previous section, we study two different games with N and M pressure groups, respectively. We assume that the potential number of pressure groups in the game with M active groups is larger than in the game with N active groups. Here M might be greater than or less than N, and K groups that take part in the game of size N will also take part in the game of size M. That is, M represents the centralized alternative and N

one of the decentralized possibilities, and $N - K$ groups in the decentralized
setting will not find it profitable to take part, if the game is centralized.

Analagously to definition (9), we define

$$\nu_i' = \frac{1/n_i}{\frac{1}{M}\sum_{j=1}^M 1/n_j} \tag{15}$$

for the groups in the centralized game. We also define the parameter

$$\eta_{N;} := \frac{\frac{1}{N}\sum_{i=1}^N 1/n_i}{\frac{1}{M}\sum_{i=1}^M 1/n_i}. \tag{16}$$

For any of the K groups that remain in the centralized version, we have
$\nu_i' = \eta_N \nu_i$. We also have the condition $\sum_{i=1}^M \nu_i' = M$, and the conditions
for a group to be active are

$$\begin{aligned} \nu_i' &< \frac{M}{M-1}, \\ \nu_i &< \frac{N}{N-1}. \end{aligned} \tag{17}$$

The assumption $K < N$ implies that there exists at least one group i, such

$$\nu_i < \frac{N}{N-1} \quad \text{and} \quad \eta_N \nu_i > \frac{M}{M-1}. \tag{18}$$

This implies that

$$\eta_N > \frac{M}{M-1} \frac{N-1}{N}. \tag{19}$$

If $K = N$, the interesting case is for $N < M$, and the fact that $\sum_{i=1}^N \nu_i = N$
gives us the same condition. We also immediately observe that (19) is
equivalent to the condition

$$\beta_{Ni} > \beta_{Mi} \quad \text{for} \quad i \in K. \tag{20}$$

All groups in the original game with N players will get a smaller portion of
the cake as the number of potential players increases and, as a consequence
of this, there is a change in the active players; that is, if at least one of
the new potential players enters the game, the old players will all get a
smaller portion of the cake, independently of whether and, if so, how many

of the old players leave the game. The change in the number of players is a consequence of the increase in the number of potential players. This, in turn, leads to (20).

In order to find the distributional characteristics of the game, we need to evaluate expressions like π_i/π_j for different-sized games. We assume that $n_i > n_j$, i.e., $\nu_i < \nu_j$. Straightforward calculations imply that the condition

$$1 < \frac{\beta_{Ni}}{\beta_{Nj}} < \frac{\beta_{Mi}}{\beta_{Mj}} \qquad \text{for} \qquad i, j \in K \qquad (21)$$

is equivalent to (19).

Since $\pi_i = \beta_i^2 y$, this also implies that

$$1 < \frac{\pi_{Ni}}{\pi_{Nj}} < \frac{\pi_{Mi}}{\pi_{Mj}} \qquad \text{for} \qquad i, j \in K. \qquad (22)$$

In other words, a weaker group always loses in relation to a stronger group as the number of potential players increases and, as a result, at least one new player enters the game. Again, the result is independent of whether old players leave the game or not.

Whether a certain group loses or wins absolutely depends, of course, on the changes in the size of the cake. If we denote by ϕ the quotient y_N/y_M, then it follows that $\pi_{Ni} > \pi_{Mi}$, if and only if $\phi\beta_{Ni}^2 > \beta_{Mi}^2$, or $\sqrt{\phi}\beta_{Ni} > \beta_{Mi}$. Simple calculations give us the final expression

$$\eta_N > \frac{N-1}{N} \frac{M}{M-1} \sqrt{\phi} + (1 - \sqrt{\phi}) \frac{M}{M-1} \frac{1}{\nu_i}. \qquad (23)$$

If ϕ is equal to one, then (23), of course, is always satisfied, since the fraction of the cake received by a player always decreases with an increasing number of potential players, which results in a change in the active players.

We further note that the weaker a player is and the bigger ϕ is (since $1/\nu_i < (N-1)/N$), the more likely it is that (23) will be satisfied.

Letting $\eta_N = 1$ and setting $\nu_i = 1$, we find that (23) is satisfied if $\phi > (N/M)^2$. That is, an "average" group will benefit from a smaller game, even if the cake is proportional to the square of the number of players. If all players are of equal strength, this means that all will benefit from decentralization, even when the cake is decreased as drastically as in this case. This, of course, quantifies the result on relative efficiency found in Section 3 for $V_M = V_N = 0$.

5. Concluding Remarks

We have found conclusive results on the distributional characteristics of a change in the number of potential players of a lobbying game. A smaller game always relatively benefits weaker groups. Even if the cake is reduced more than proportionally to the reduction in the number of active players, this can absolutely benefit weaker groups, as we have seen.

In a homogenous game a loss in the number of active players will also mean a gain in efficiency. But, on the other hand, if the strength of the players varies a lot, then a reduction in the number of active players will reduce efficiency.

Assuming that the size of the cake is proportional to the number of active players and that the average strength is independent of the number of players, $\eta_N = 1$, we find that any group below "average" strength will benefit absolutely from less players. Strong groups will benefit from a reduction only if all groups are of approximately equal strength; otherwise, they will lose from being in a smaller game.

In this essay we have loosely used the expressions "centralization" and "decentralization" to denote changes in the number of potential players in the game. It can happen, of course, that an increase in the number of potential players leads to fewer active participants in the game. This happens if a few newcomers increase the average strength of all potential players; that is, if $\eta_N > 1$. In the game there can be more groups who took part before the newcomers arrived and, thus, satisfied the condition $\nu_i < N/(N-1)$, but who do not satisfy the condition $\eta_n \nu_i < N/(N-1)$, than there are new groups satisfying the entry condition. This, then, reduces the number of active players.

In such a case "centralization" means fewer players and, hence, our results on efficiency would be reversed. This situation is more likely to occur the greater the variance V. This effect would, thus, make the case of higher efficiency as a result of centralization less likely.

As above, we denote by N the number of active players in the "decentralized" game and by M the number in the "centralized" one. The arguments above are collected in Table 1. We characterize the new players as weak, if $\eta_N < 1$, and as strong, if $\eta_N > 1$. If the new players are weak,

Table 1. Plausible Effects of Centralization

New Groups	V_N	N ? M	Efficiency	Distribution
Weak	small	<	−	−
	large	<	+	−
Strong	small	<	−	−
	large	>	−	−
Average strength	small	<	−	−
	large	<	+	−
		>	−	−

then the number of players can only increase. If, on the other hand, the new players are strong, the number can change in both directions. The number of players is more likely to decrease, if there are many weak players in the original game; that is, if V_N is large.

In the distribution column, the minus sign indicates a more uneven distribution of relative benefits among groups active in both games. The conclusion that can be cautiously drawn from the table is that, in most of the plausible cases, centralization has a negative effect on both the efficiency and the distribution characteristics of a lobbying game when used as a means for distributing public rent.

References

Buchanan, J. M., Tollison, R. D. and Tullock, G., Eds. (1980) *Toward a Theory of the Rent-seeking Society*, College Station: Texas A & M Univ. Press.

Rowley, C. K., Tollison, R. D. and Tullock, G., Eds. (1988) *The Political Economy of Rent-seeking*, Boston: Kluwer Academic Publishers.

Tullock, G. (1980) "Efficient Rent Seeking," in: Buchanan et al., 97-112.

Wickström, B.-A. (1987) "The Growth of Government and the Rise of Pressure Groups," in: R. Pethig and U. Schlieper, Eds., *Efficiency, Institutions and Economic Policy*, Heidelberg: Springer-Verlag, 39-57.

PART FIVE

Demand, Expectations
and Disequilibrium

17

The Form of Expected Demand in Hungary: A Mills-type Model[*]

Krisztina Demeter

1. Introduction

Production decisions of market participants depend on, among other things, expected demand. However, these expectations differ according to the different attitudes of economic agents.

This paper attempts to assess the main characteristics of demand expectations in Hungary. So far, this topic has been neglected in the Hungarian economic literature, although it can help considerably in describing and forecasting economic processes.

Our analysis is based on a Mills-type model. This model involves an unobservable expectational variable for demand; in order to estimate it, we need to find a proxy for it. Four theories of expectations have been used to create proxies: *naive* expectations, *adaptive* expectations of Nerlove, *implicit* of Mills and *rational* of Muth. The models were estimated by pooled cross-section data broken down into sectors.

On the basis of previous surveys, we apply two estimation methods in this study: simple OLS estimation and OLS estimation for transformed variables, where different dummies are used for different individuals (i.e., dummy variable models). The results obtained are not fully satisfactory.

---

[*] I am grateful to the scientific group lead by E. Zalai for financial support, and to I. Székely for his useful comments.

Although implicit and rational expectations provide good fit, all the model specification tests reject these theories. Moreover, tests of model selection do not pick a best model.

2. The Mills-type Model

Mills (1962) analyzes the production, sales and inventory decisions for a single homogenous commodity of a monopolistic firm in uncertain situations. He argues that the crucial decision variable is the *total supply* the firm can make available during the period. After determining the expected value of total revenue, he takes four different costs into consideration in order to get total supply. The model used in this paper (see Ábel and Székely, 1988) differs from the model of Mills (1957) in the fourth cost. While the latter model takes into account only the cost of changes in production, the former is a dynamic composite cost of logistics partially connected to the changes in production and partially to general cost considerations of changes in output inventories.

Without going into detail, we depict the Mills-type model as follows:

$$\Delta(Y + I_{-1}) = \alpha + \frac{\beta}{\beta + \epsilon}X^e - \frac{\beta}{\beta + \epsilon}(Y + I_{-1})_{-1} - \frac{\iota - \epsilon}{\beta + \epsilon}\Delta I_{-1} + u, \quad (1)$$

where Δ denotes the first difference operator, $Y + I_{-1}$ is supply, X stands for sales and ΔI_{-1} is the lagged value of output inventory investment. The parameters derive from the model itself. Mills' original model, for example, can be determined with the restriction of $\iota = 0$.

3. Theories for Creating Proxies for Expected Demand

Naive expectations. This is the simplest form for creating a proxy. In this case we get

$$X^e = \gamma X_{-1},$$

and the estimated equation is then

$$\Delta(Y + I_{-1}) = \alpha + \frac{\beta}{\beta + \epsilon}\gamma X_{-1} - \frac{\beta}{\beta + \epsilon}(Y + I_{-1})_{-1} \\ - \frac{\iota - \epsilon}{\beta + \epsilon}\Delta I_{-1} + u. \quad (2)$$

Adaptive expectations. To create a proxy in this form takes more operations. By this theory,

$$X^e = \sum_{j=1}^{\infty} \gamma^{j-1}(1-\gamma)X_{-j},$$

where $0 \leq \gamma < 1$ (see Mills, 1962). If we substitute this form for X^e in (1) and write the whole equation with one lagged period, multiplying by γ (see Harvey, 1981, p. 226), we can then extract this form from the substituted equation. Denoting $Y + I_{-1}$ by S, we obtain

$$\Delta S = (1-\gamma)\alpha + \gamma\Delta S_{-1} + \frac{\beta(1-\gamma)}{\beta+\epsilon}X_{-1} - \frac{\beta}{\beta+\epsilon}(S_{-1} - \gamma S_{-2})$$
$$- \frac{\iota-\epsilon}{\beta+\epsilon}(\Delta I_{-1} - \Delta I_{-2}) + u - \gamma u_{-1}.$$

If we rearrange this equation and take into account that $S - X = I$, we then get the estimated equation

$$\Delta S = (1-\gamma)\alpha - \frac{\beta\gamma}{\beta+\epsilon}\Delta S_{-1} - \frac{\beta(1-\gamma)}{\beta+\epsilon}I_{-1}$$
$$- \frac{\iota-\epsilon}{\beta+\epsilon}\Delta I_{-1} + \frac{\iota-\epsilon}{\beta+\epsilon}\gamma\Delta I_{-2} + v, \tag{3}$$

where $v = u - \gamma u_{-1}$.

Implicit expectations. This theory is as easy to use as the hypothesis about naive expectations, although the former is stochastic and implicit. The proxy takes the following form:

$$X^e = \gamma X + e, \tag{4}$$

where $E(X, e) = 0$. The estimated equation is then

$$\Delta(Y + I_{-1}) = \alpha + \frac{\beta}{\beta+\epsilon}\gamma X - \frac{\beta}{\beta+\epsilon}(Y + I_{-1})_{-1} - \frac{\iota-\epsilon}{\beta+\epsilon}\Delta I_{-1} + v. \tag{5}$$

The residual is $v = e + u$ and independent of all the regressors.

Rational expectations. This form is different from implicit expectations only in the properties of the residual. The proxy is formed the same way as (4), but e is independent of X^e ($E(X^e, e) = 0$) and not of X. Thus, we

have to use different estimation methods, although the systematic part is
the same.

4. Data

UNIDO Industrial Statistics provides annual time series on production
and inventories. According to the ISIC sectorial breakdown, 31 Hungarian
sectors were analysed with a time span of 11 years, from 1974 to 1984.[1]
The models use the following specifications: production, finished goods
inventories, sales (production *minus* change in finished goods inventories)
and supply (production *plus* finished goods inventories at the end of the
previous period).

5. Estimation Methods and Hypothesis Tests

As indicated above, two different estimation methods are applied: the
simple OLS estimation and the so-called "within estimation." The second
set of estimators (referred to as within estimators in the tables) belongs
to the dummy variable models (see Maddala, 1977, p. 322-326), where
individual effects are assumed to be present in the constant term; that is,
different dummies are used for different individuals. Time effects are not
assumed in this study, because two earlier papers (see Ábel and Székely,
1987; 1988), which use the same data base, indicate that time effects are
not significant.

The transformation used for the variables is:

$$\bar{x}_{it} = x_{it} - \bar{x}_{i\cdot},$$

where $\bar{x}_{i\cdot}$ is the mean for individuals. As the actual values of the estimated
coefficients of the dummies are of no special interest, only the usual F-tests
for the $H_0 : \alpha_1 = \alpha_2 = \ldots = \alpha_N$ are reported, where the α's are the
parameters of the dummies (see Maddala, 1977, p. 325).

Naive expectations. This can be estimated by the simple OLS method,
since the residual term is assumed to be normally distributed and independent from other regressors (see equation (2)). Two observations are lost by
omission in each sector, i.e., altogether 62.

---

[1] My thanks are due to I. Ábel for providing these data in a RATS-readable form.

Expectations are perfectly naive if $\gamma = 1$, otherwise they over- or underestimate real values of variables. A Wald test leads to a t-test for the sum of the coefficients of S_{-1} and X_{-1} against zero.

As mentioned earlier, we can examine the nested Mills' model with the restriction of $\iota = 0$. In this case the sum of S_{-1} and that of ΔI_{-1} is equal to minus one. Since we estimate the general model, this restriction can be checked with the usual F-test concerning linear restrictions. (Results of naive expectations can be seen in Table 1.)

Adaptive expectations. In this case we first have to find an instrumental variable for the lagged endogenous variable (ΔS_{-1}), so that it can be independent from the disturbance term. There are two possibilities: we risk inconsistent estimation with an almost perfect correlation between the instrument and the lagged supply change, or we use a weak but independent instrument. In this study the latter method is applied; that is, the regressors are S_{-1}, X_{-1} and ΔI_{-1}. The next step is to transform variables according to the MA(1) process in the residual (see Judge et al., 1980, p. 302).

After this transformation the conditions for consistent OLS estimation are completely fulfilled. Three observations are omitted at each individual (93 altogether).

The first task in hypothesis testing is to check whether γ is in the interval of $[0, 1)$. After an examination of boundary values, the two restricted forms—the static and naive expectations—can also be checked. Again, we use a Wald-type test (that is, the usual F-test) to examine the joint significance of ΔS_{-1} and ΔI_{-1}, when assuming static expectations, and to examine the joint significance of the constant and I_{-1} with the linear restriction of $\Delta I_{-1} = \Delta I_{-2}$ in the case of naive expectations.

The original Mills' model cannot be rejected if the $[-1, -1, 1]$ linear combination of the coefficients of $\Delta S_{-1}, I_{-1}$ and ΔI_{-1} is equal to one. The familiar F-test is used to check this hypothesis. (Results of adaptive expectations are in Table 1.)

Implicit expectations. Since this theory possesses the same characteristics as naive expectations (that is, the OLS estimation is consistent and the hypothesis tests are also the same), we do not have to go into detail about it. (Results of implicit expectations appear in Table 2.)

Rational expectations. In order to make X independent from the disturbance term in the model with rational expectations, we have to find an appropriate instrument for it. This can be estimated by regression, where the regressors X_{-1} represent the general processes of sales, and S involves the fluctuation of supply and demand. After determining the instrument, we again use the simple OLS estimation. The tests are not different from those used to check implicit expectations. (See Table 2.)

6. Model Specification Tests and Model Selection

The following model specification tests are considered:

1) RESET test as general diagnostics ($F_{(2,NT-k)}$, Ramsey (1969));
2) Moment test of normality ($\chi^2_{(2)}$, Jarque and Bera (1980));
3) White test for heteroscedasticity ($\chi^2_{(k(k+1)/2-1)}$, White (1980));
4) LM test for autocorrelation (t-ratio, Harvey (1981));
5) Berenblutt-Webb test for autocorrelation (D-W table, Berenblutt and Webb (1973)).

Remarks. Most of the tests are modified for degrees of freedom, according to the lost observations that originate from lags and differences. The RESET test is used in its original form; that is, the F-test of the second and third components of the estimated result variable is examined. Only the t-ratio of one lagged residual is checked in the LM tests.

Model selection. The adaptive and naive expectations are examined first, and since the latter is nested in the former, this analysis is performed in connection with adaptive expectations. Secondly, the models of implicit and rational expectations are compared by the Hausman test (1978). Depending on previous results, the better models—namely, adaptive and rational expectations—are compared pairwise in the end. Since they are non-nested models, JA tests of Cox are used to select the best model (see Fisher and McAleer, 1981).

7. Results and Consequences

Except for model selection, all the test results are reported in Tables 1 and 2. Estimation and hypothesis tests are performed by RATS version 1.20a. Below the values of the coefficients, t-tests are given in parentheses.

General remarks. The results for R^2 are very strange at first sight. While its value is almost one in the case of implicit or rational expectations, and is slightly higher for OLS than for within estimation, it is not more than 0.4 in the case of OLS for naive and adaptive expectations, and much worse for within estimation. The cause of these surprising results might be found in the adequacy (or inadequacy) of the models. Since the fit of the models of naive and adaptive expectations yields rather poor results with simple OLS estimation, the possibly unsuitable transformation of within

Table 1. Results for Naive and Adaptive Expectations

	Naive		Adaptive	
	OLS	Within	OLS	Within
Constant	−0.003	—	0.207	—
	(0.012)		(0.723)	
$S_{-1}/\Delta S_{-1}$†	−0.443	−0.318	0.904*	−0.365
	(1.915)	(0.616)	(7.052)	(1.183)
X_{-1}/I_{-1}†	0.531**	0.321	0.133	0.490
	(2.213)	(0.602)	(0.614)	(0.848)
ΔI_{-1}	2.077**	0.908	2.767*	0.808
	(2.529)	(1.150)	(2.920)	(0.814)
ΔI_{-2}	—	—	−2.524*	−1.203
			(2.711)	(1.155)
R^2	0.374	0.064	0.372	0.041
γ	1.199	1.010	0.912	1.488
RESET	0.047	0.018	0.460	0.793
Moment test	99.15*	99.80*	88.10*	122.3*
White test	7.032	5.553	10.78	18.88**
LM test	95.87*	3.101	83.23*	13.44*
Berenblutt-Webb test	1.268*	1.589	1.344*	1.877
$H_0 : \gamma = 1$	8.086*	0.125	0.331	0.469
$H_0 : \gamma = \emptyset$	—	—	25.40*	3.090**
$H_0 : \iota = \emptyset$	2.615	0.371	0.468	0.095
Individual effects test	—	4.384*	—	2.420*

* significant at 1% level   ** significant at 5% level

† The first refers to naive and the second to adaptive expectations.

estimation makes them completely uninterpretable.

It is also interesting to note that the higher the values of t-ratios are, the more stable the coefficients of the two estimations prove to be.

The moment test and the test of within individual effects does not differentiate the models, and they prove to be significant in every case. The first result is important from the point of view of the tests, which require normally distributed residuals. The second result is also interesting because of the values obtained. The individual effects are much higher for implicit and rational expectations than for the other models. Clearly, these effects contribute somehow to the results of R^2 and coefficients analyzed earlier.

Table 2. Results for Implicit and Rational Expectations

	Implicit		Rational	
	OLS	Within	OLS	Within
Constant	-0.408*	—	0.560*	—
	(6.086)		(155.1)	
X	0.921*	1.007*	1.096*	1.098*
	(59.28)	(137.6)	(1150)	(2239)
S_{-1}	-0.877*	-0.978*	-1.054*	-1.056*
	(54.64)	(133.7)	(1075)	(2184)
ΔI_{-1}	1.294*	0.133	0.082*	0.027*
	(6.317)	(1.559)	(7.479)	(5.107)
R^2	0.954	0.987	0.999	0.999
γ	1.050	1.029	1.040	1.039
RESET	15.58*	7.533*	4.945*	0.646
Moment test	102.5*	100.0*	102.4*	98.74*
White test	210.0*	170.0*	232.4*	234.7*
LM test	243.7*	246.7*	248.0*	248.0*
Berenblutt-Webb test	0.069*	0.580*	0.046*	0.354*
$H_0 : \gamma = 1$	24.10*	14.85*	434.0*	340.7*
$H_0 : \iota = \emptyset$	32.28*	1.695	153.6*	249.9*
Individual effects test	—	51.83*	—	36.80*

* significant at 1% level   ** significant at 5% level

The values of the t-ratios of the coefficients must affect the results of hypothesis tests. The higher the values of these ratios are, the higher the probability that the null hypotheses of the model specification tests will be rejected. For example, in the case of implicit and rational expectations, where the highest t values are obtained, only one restriction is not rejected ($\iota = 0$ for within estimation for implicit expectations) and one null hypothesis of model specification tests (RESET for within estimation for rational expectations) is not rejected.

Naive expectations. Although the RESET and White tests do not reject the null hypotheses, the results of the LM and Berenblutt-Webb tests indicate autocorrelation in residuals. Since the significance of coefficients is rather weak and the normality of residuals is rejected, we cannot, in fact, interpret other results (other hypothesis tests for simple OLS estimation, and all the results of within estimation).

Adaptive expectations. The results are similar to naive expectations, although the significance of coefficients is stronger. It is interesting that neither the nested model of static expectations ($\gamma = 1$) nor Mills' original model can be rejected.

Implicit expectations. Coefficients are strongly significant (except ΔI_{-1} for within estimation) and they remain stable across the two estimation methods. The value of γ is smaller than for naive expectations; however, the hypothesis of the lack of bias of expectations cannot be accepted. Mills' model is accepted for within estimation, but we have to take into account that the test involves the only non-significant coefficient of ΔI_{-1}. Despite good estimation results, the model specification tests indicate that something must be wrong with the dynamic specification of this model.

Rational expectations. The situation does not change too much when an instrument for sales is used. The coefficients become more significant, but the suspicion of poor specification remains. The restriction of Mills' original model is rejected in this model.

Model Selection

As indicated in the discussion of adaptive expectations, the nested model of naive expectations cannot be accepted.

The comparison of implicit and rational expectations by the Hausman test shows that the two models differ significantly; that is, the OLS estimation of implicit expectations cannot be consistent. The value of the test statistic is $\chi^2_{(4)} = 162.6$ for simple OLS estimations, and $\chi^2_{(3)} = 176.9$ for within estimations.

There is only one thing left: to compare the two best models pairwise. On the basis of the results of Cox-type tests (JA-tests), we find neither of these models is better. The values of the test statistics are $t = 7.082$ and $t = 46.59$ for the null hypothesis of adaptive expectations for simple OLS and within OLS estimations, respectively. The same values for the null hypothesis of rational expectations are $t = 23.1$ and $t = 5.015$.

Conclusions

On the basis of the results obtained, we cannot unambiguously choose one theory from those considered. The models of implicit and rational expectations give surprisingly good fits, but model specification tests fail to specify them in these models. Although the fit of the model of adaptive expectations is much poorer, the model selection tests do not reject it. The value of γ is always higher than one in all the models, which indicates that economic agents overestimate real values of demand irrespective of the way in which they form their expectations. (An exception to this is adaptive expectations.) The results are not obvious in regard to Mills' original model: two of the models accept it, but the other two do not.

References

Ábel, I. and Székely, I. (1987) "Cross-Country Comparison of Production and Inventory Decisions," Mimeograph, IIASA-ISIR Workshop, MKKE Budapest.

――――, (1988) "Price Regulation and Inventory Behavior of Companies under Central Planning," in *The Economics of Inventory Management*, edited by A. Chikán and M. C. Lovell, Amsterdam: Elsevier, 3-14.

Berenblutt, I. I. and Webb, G. I. (1973) "A New Test for Autocorrelated Errors in the Linear Regression Model," *J. of Royal Statistical Society* (Series B) **35**, 33-50.

Fisher, G. R. and McAleer, M. (1981) "Alternative Procedures and Associated Tests of Significance for Non-Nested Hypotheses," *J. of Econometrics* **16**, 103-119.

Harvey, A. C. (1981) *The Econometric Analysis of Time Series*, Oxford: Philip Allan.

Hausman, J. A. (1978) "Specification Tests in Econometrics," *Econometrica* **46**, 1251-1271.

Jarque, C. M. and Bera, A. K. (1980) "Efficient Tests for Normality, Homoscedasticity and Serial Independence of Regression Residuals," *Economic Letters* **6**, 255-259.

Judge, G. G., Griffith, W. E., Hill, R. C. and Lee, T. C. (1980) *The Theory and Practice of Econometrics*, New York: John Wiley.

Maddala, G. S. (1977) *Econometrics*, London: McGraw-Hill.

Mills, E. S. (1957) "The Theory of Inventory Decisions," *Econometrica* **25**, 222-238.

———, (1962) *Price, Output and Inventory Policy*, New York: John Wiley.

Muth, J. F. (1961) "Rational Expectations and the Theory of Price Movements," *Econometrica* **29**, 315-335.

Nerlove, M. (1983) "Expectations, Plans and Realizations in Theory and Practice," *Econometrica* **51**, 1251-1278.

Ramsey, J. B. (1969) "Tests for Specification Errors in Classical Linear Least Squares Regression Analysis," *J. of Royal Statistical Society* (Series B) **31**, 350-371.

White, H. (1980) "A Heteroscedasticity-Consistent Covariance Matrix Estimator and a Direct Test for Heteroscedasticity," *Econometrica* **48**, 301-318.

18

Expectations of Demand by Firms and Their Effect on Disequilibrium

Christian Gourieroux and *Irina Peaucelle*

1. Introduction

Production decisions of firms are generally based on expectations of the quantities demanded from them. Since these expectations will not, in general, coincide with realized demands, firms will produce too much or too little and this will imply some production inefficiency and some disequilibria. In this paper we are essentially concerned with these misadjustments and with the measure of the effects of prediction errors.

In Section 2 we describe a microeconomic model in which each firm has a production function with complementary factors. This firms maintains a production level equal to expected demand. There is no spillover effect between firms and between periods, so that the exchanged quantity relative to each firm is the minimum of real and expected demands. This microeconomic model may be used as a basis for determining aggregate quantities, such as the aggregate demand, the aggregate exchanged quantity, the proportion of firms in a given regime and the global measure of inefficiency. This aggregation is performed along the same lines as in Malinvaud (1982), Muellbauer (1978), Lambert (1984), Gourieroux and Laroque (1985). The aggregate measures depend, in particular, on the expectation errors through the expectation bias and the variance of the expectations.

In Section 3 we first examine the special case of rational predictions of demand. The absence of expectation bias and the usual orthogonality condition between the expectation and the expectation error allow a simple derivation of the various aggregate measures. It is then possible to analyze how these aggregates are modified when the price changes, when the heterogeneity of demand increases or when expectations are more precise.

In Section 4, the effect of expectation errors is studied more deeply by separating the effect of expectation bias from the effect of randomness of expectations. The computation of these effects is based on some interpretations of the elasticities in terms of some particular aggregates.

Finally, the introduction of a short-run dynamics on the price is discussed in Section 5.

2. The Model

We consider a continuum of firms indexed by ω. Each firm has a production function with K complementary factors, $k = 1, \ldots, K$. This production function is characterized by technical coefficients $A_k(\omega)$, $k = 1 \ldots, K$. A potential demand $D(\omega)$ is attached to each firm; this demand is partly unknown when production decisions are made. The firm ω expects a demand equal to $\hat{D}(\omega)$ and chooses the input levels adequately; these levels are

$$\hat{X}_k(\omega) = \hat{D}(\omega)/A_k(\omega), \qquad k = 1, \ldots, K.$$

When the exchanges between suppliers and demanders take place, the resulting exchanged quantities at the microlevel will be

$$Q(\omega) = \min\left(D(\omega), \hat{D}(\omega)\right). \tag{1}$$

Among the firms some overpredict demand and are constrained by real demand while others underpredict demand and the corresponding demand cannot be entirely satisfied. Then the two regimes are defined by whichever of the two inequalities $\hat{D}(\omega) > D(\omega)$ or $\hat{D}(\omega) < D(\omega)$ is satisfied.

When the distributions of the technical coefficients $A_k(\omega)$, $k = 1, \ldots, K$ and of the real and expected demands $D(\omega)$, $\hat{D}(\omega)$ are given, it is possible to compute the aggregate counterparts of all the previous quantities, simply by taking expectations. For example, the aggregate exchanged quantity is

$$\overline{Q} = E\{Q(\omega)\} = E\left\{\min\left(\hat{D}(\omega), D(\omega)\right)\right\}; \tag{2}$$

the proportions of firms in each regime are

$$\begin{aligned}
\pi &= \Pr\{\hat{D}(\omega) > D(\omega)\} \\
1 - \pi &= \Pr\{D(\omega) > \hat{D}(\omega)\}.
\end{aligned} \tag{3}$$

For the purpose of tractability, we will assume a particular form for the distribution of $(A_k(\omega), D(\omega), \hat{D}(\omega))$. In order to be compatible with the positiveness of these variables, we assume that they are jointly lognormally distributed. Therefore, it will be interesting to employ the logarithm of the different variables which are normally distributed. The logarithm will be denoted by lower-case letters; thus, $d(\omega) = \log D(\omega)$, $\hat{d}(\omega) = \log \hat{D}(\omega)$, etc.

3. Rational Expectation of Demand

The introduction of rational expectations in disequilibrium models has been discussed by Maddala (1984) at the macrolevel. In our case, the problem is examined at the microlevel and the results will have different interpretations.

The first point concerns the variable of which the rational expectation (RE) is taken. Indeed, we have to choose between the RE hypothesis about demand D or log-demand d. By analogy with the "tendency" surveys of firms in which the questions pertain to the percentage modification of demand, we shall opt for the second alternative. Moreover, this is the alternative that leads to simpler derivations.

Since $d(\omega)$ and $\hat{d}(\omega)$ are normally distributed, the RE hypothesis is characterized by the conditions of unbiasedness and the orthogonality between $\hat{d}(\omega)$ and $d(\omega) - \hat{d}(\omega)$. If η^2 is the variance of demand $d(\omega)$, σ^2 the mean square error (MSE), $\sigma^2 = V[d(\omega) - \hat{d}(\omega)]$ and m the average demand (i.e., the aggregate demand), then the distribution is

$$\begin{bmatrix} d \\ \hat{d} \end{bmatrix} \sim N \left\{ \begin{bmatrix} m \\ m \end{bmatrix}, \begin{bmatrix} \eta^2 & \eta^2 - \sigma^2 \\ \eta^2 - \sigma^2 & \eta^2 - \sigma^2 \end{bmatrix} \right\}.$$

Proportion of Demand-constrained Firms

Under the RE hypothesis, the probability of overpredicting equals the probability of underpredicting. Hence, $\pi = 1 - \pi = 0.5$. This is easily verified, since

$$\pi = \Pr\{\hat{D}(\omega) > D(\omega)\} = \Pr\{\hat{d}(\omega) > d(\omega)\} = \Pr\{\epsilon(\omega) > 0\},$$

where $\epsilon(\omega)$ is the prediction error. Thus, $\pi = 0.5$, since $\epsilon(\omega)$ has a centered normal distribution.

Modification of The Price

Usually the price p of the output is introduced through aggregate demand, i.e., through the function m, but it does not appear in the second-order moments. Therefore, if u (respectively, $\hat{u}$) denotes the centered log-demand (respectively, log-expected demand), we have

$$\overline{Q} = E\{\min[e^{u(\omega)}, e^{\hat{u}(\omega)}]\} = e^{m(p)}E\{\min[e^{u(\omega)}, e^{\hat{u}(\omega)}]\}.$$

We deduce directly that the price elasticity of the exchanged quantity equals the price elasticity of demand:

$$\frac{\partial \log \overline{Q}}{\partial \log p} = \frac{\partial \log m(p)}{\partial \log p} = \frac{\partial \log \overline{D}}{\partial \log p} = \frac{\partial \log \hat{D}}{\partial \log p}. \tag{4}$$

This equality is due to the unbiasedness assumption. On the average, a modification of the price has the same effect on D and $\hat{D}$, and also on the minimum of these quantities.

Calculation of the Exchanged Quantity

The exchanged quantity at the macro level is given by

$$\overline{Q} = e^{m(p)}E\{e^{\hat{u}(\omega)}\min[e^{u(\omega)-\hat{u}(\omega)}, 1]\} = e^{m(p)}E\{e^{\hat{u}(\omega)}\min[e^{\epsilon(\omega)}, 1]\}.$$

The error $\epsilon(\omega)$ and the prediction $\hat{u}(\omega)$ are uncorrelated or independent in our Gaussian case. Therefore, we obtain

$$\overline{Q} = e^{m(p)}E\{e^{\hat{u}(\omega)}\}E\{\min[e^{\epsilon(\omega)}, 1]\}$$

$$= e^{m(p)}e^{(\eta^2-\sigma^2)/2}\left[\Pr\{e^{\epsilon(\omega)} > 1\} + \int_{e^{\epsilon(\omega)}<1}\left(\frac{1}{\sigma\sqrt{2\pi}}\right)e^{\epsilon}e^{-\epsilon^2/2\sigma^2}\,d\epsilon\right]$$

$$= e^{m(p)+\eta^2/2-\sigma^2/2}[0.5 + \Phi(-\sigma)e^{\sigma^2/2}]$$

where Φ is the cdf of the standard normal distribution. Since $\overline{D} = e^{m(p)+\eta^2/2}$, we finally obtain the following expression:

$$\overline{Q} = \overline{D}e^{-\sigma^2/2}[0.5 + \Phi(-\sigma)e^{\sigma^2/2}]. \tag{5}$$

Figure 1: Excess Demand as a Function of σ

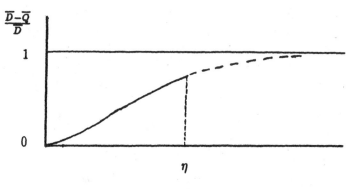

Precision σ

We note that the relative measure of excess demand is given by the ratio

$$\frac{\overline{D} - \overline{Q}}{\overline{D}} = -0.5e^{-\sigma^2/2} + \Phi(\sigma). \tag{6}$$

This excess demand depends only on the variance of the prediction error σ^2, but it is not linked to the price p or to the heterogeneity of demand η^2. In the limit case when $\sigma = 0$, no prediction error exists and this cause of disequilibrium disappears: we get $(\overline{D} - \overline{Q})/\overline{D} = 0$. When σ increases, the disequilibrium becomes increasingly important. The maximal disequilibrium is obtained when σ^2 equals the variance of the demand η^2.

4. Biased Predictions or Nonorthogonal Prediction Errors

As can be seen from the previous subsection, the rational expectations hypothesis is the conjunction of two hypotheses: those of unbiasedness and of orthogonality. We are alternately going to relax these conditions and examine how the previous results are modified.

Biased Predictions

The distribution of expected and real demands. We first consider the case of biased expectations, but with orthogonal prediction errors. The bias is denoted by B, so that the distribution of $(d, \hat{d})$ will be

$$\begin{bmatrix} d \\ \hat{d} \end{bmatrix} \sim N \left\{ \begin{bmatrix} m \\ m + B \end{bmatrix}, \begin{bmatrix} \eta^2 & \eta^2 - \sigma^2 \\ \eta^2 - \sigma^2 & \eta^2 - \sigma^2 \end{bmatrix} \right\}.$$

The proportion of demand constrained firms. This is given by

$$\Pr\{\hat{D} > D\} = \Pr\{\hat{d} > d\} = \Pr\{m + B + \hat{u} > m + u\},$$

where $\hat{u}$, u are the centered $\hat{d}$, d and, hence,

$$\pi = \Phi(B/\sigma). \tag{7}$$

As expected, this proportion is smaller or larger than 1/2, according to the sign of the bias; it is smaller (larger) if there is overprediction (underprediction). This proportion is a nondecreasing function of the bias and is also a monotonic function of the prediction error (nonincreasing for positive bias). It tends to 1/2 when σ tends to infinity.

The exchanged quantity. This is given by

$$E\{\min(\hat{D}, D)\} = E\{\min[e^{m+B\hat{u}}, e^{m+u}]\}$$
$$= E\{e^{m+\hat{u}}\min[e^B, e^\epsilon]\} = E\{e^{m+\hat{u}}\}E\{\min[e^B, e^\epsilon]\},$$
$$= e^{m+\eta^2/2-\sigma^2/2}\left[e^B\Pr\{\epsilon > B\} + E\{e^\epsilon\mathfrak{I}_{e^\epsilon<e^B}\}\right]$$

where $\mathfrak{I}_C$ is the indicator function, which has value 1 if condition C is true and value 0 if C is false. This aggregate quantity is the sum of two terms with simple interpretations. Indeed, the first term is

Figure 2: Proportion of Demand-constrained Firms
as a Function of σ

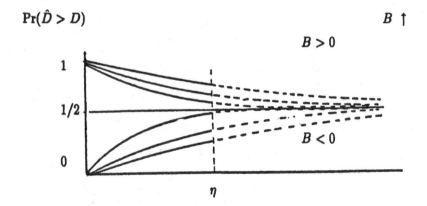

$$e^{m+\eta^2/2-\sigma^2/2}e^B \Pr\{\epsilon > B\} = E\{\hat{D}\Im_{\hat{D}<D}\} = E\{Q\Im_{\hat{D}<D}\}$$
$$= \overline{Q}E\left\{\frac{Q}{E\{Q\}}\Im_{\hat{D}<D}\right\} = \overline{Q}(1-P),$$

where P is the proportion of markets constrained by demand, this proportion being computed with weight proportional to the size Q of the firm. The second term is obviously equal to $\overline{Q}P$.

The analytic forms of these terms are easily obtained. We have

$$e^B \Pr\{\epsilon > B\} = e^B\left(1 - \Phi\left(\frac{B}{\sigma}\right)\right),$$

$$E\{e^\epsilon \Im_{e^\epsilon < e^B}\} = \left(\frac{1}{\sqrt{2\pi}}\right)\int_{-\infty}^{B/\sigma} e^{\sigma u}e^{-u^2/2}\,du = e^{\sigma^2/2}\Phi\left(\frac{B}{\sigma} - \sigma\right).$$

By replacing in the expression for $\overline{Q}$ we obtain

$$\overline{Q} = e^{m+\eta^2/2}\left[e^{B-\sigma^2/2}\left[1 - \Phi\left(\frac{B}{\sigma}\right)\right] + \Phi\left(\frac{B}{\sigma} - \sigma\right)\right],$$

$$P = \frac{\Phi\left(\dfrac{B}{\sigma} - \sigma\right)}{e^{B-\sigma^2/2}\left[1 - \Phi\left(\dfrac{B}{\sigma}\right)\right] + \Phi\left(\dfrac{B}{\sigma} - \sigma\right)}. \qquad (8)$$

The price will generally appear through the mean m and the bias B. The elasticity of the exchanged quantity with respect to the price p has a simple form which extends (4) (see Gourieroux and Peaucelle, 1989):

$$\frac{\partial \log \overline{Q}}{\partial \log p} = \frac{\partial \log \overline{D}}{\partial \log p} + \frac{\partial B}{\partial \log p}(1-P) \qquad (9).$$

It is equal to the elasticity of demand plus an additional term that takes into account the price effect on bias and the proportion $1-P$ of firms in excess demand. The introduction of the proportion of markets in a given regime, computed with appropriate weight, is linked with some results previously derived by Malinvaud (1982) for disequilibrium models with additive errors, and in Gourieroux, Laffont and Monfort (1984) for disequilibrium models with additive errors.

The value of the elasticity depends both on the derivative $\partial B/\partial \log p$ and on the bias B (through the proportion $1 - P$). However, this latter effect is bounded and, in any case, we have

$$\frac{\partial \log \overline{D}}{\partial \log p} \leq \frac{\partial \log \hat{Q}}{\partial \log p} \leq \frac{\partial \log \overline{\hat{D}}}{\partial \log p}. \tag{10}$$

When the bias is large $(B = +\infty)$, all the markets are demand constrained $(P = 1)$ and the elasticity of the exchanged quantity coincides with the elasticity of demand. When the bias is large in absolute value and negative $(B = -\infty)$, the markets are in excess demand $(P = 0)$ and the elasticity of the exchanged quantity coincides with the elasticity of expected demand. In the general case it is a convex combination of these two elasticities:

$$\frac{\partial \overline{Q}}{\partial \log p} = P\frac{\partial \log \overline{D}}{\partial \log p} + (1 - P)\frac{\partial \log \overline{\hat{D}}}{\partial \log p}.$$

The effect of the prediction error may be analyzed through the derivative $\partial \overline{D}/\partial \sigma$. This derivative is equal to

$$\frac{\partial \overline{Q}}{\partial \sigma} = \overline{D}\left[-\sigma e^{B-\sigma^2/2}\left[1 - \Phi\left(\frac{B}{\sigma}\right)\right] - \phi\left(\frac{B}{\sigma} - \sigma\right)\right],$$

and is always negative. The exchanged quantity diminishes when the predictions are less precise.

Finally, we may note that the asymptotic behavior of $\overline{Q}$ when σ is large depends heavily on the sign of the bias. Indeed, if the bias is nonnegative, we have $\lim_{\sigma \to \infty} \overline{Q}(\sigma) = \overline{D}$, but if the bias is negative, $\lim_{\sigma \to \infty} \overline{Q}(\sigma) = \overline{D}e^B$, and the disequilibrium remains asymptotically (see Figure 3).

Nonorthogonal Prediction Errors

The parametrization. Even if they are unbiased, predictions may not be optimal when the prediction error is correlated with the prediction, i.e., if $\text{cov}\,(\hat{d}, d-\hat{d}) \neq 0$. In such a case the available information has not been fully taken into account and the prediction might be improved by considering the linear regression of demand d on the prediction $\hat{d}$. This improved prediction is given by

$$\tilde{\tilde{d}} = m + \frac{\text{cov}\,(d, \hat{d})}{V(\hat{d})}(\hat{d} - m).$$

**Figure 3: The Exchanged Quantity
as a Function of σ**

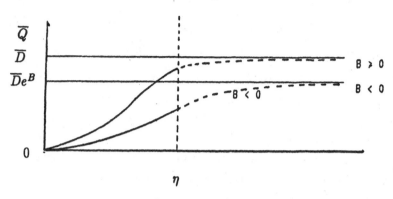

Precision σ

It is natural to introduce a parametrization of the variance-covariance matrix in which the correcting factor $\lambda = \text{cov}\,(d, \hat{d})/V(\hat{d})$ and the quality of the improved prediction, i.e., $\sigma^2 = V(d - \hat{d})$ appear simultaneously with the variance η^2 of demand. With this notation, the covariance matrix is given by

$$V\begin{bmatrix} d \\ \hat{d} \end{bmatrix} = \begin{bmatrix} \eta^2 & \dfrac{\eta^2 - \sigma^2}{\lambda} \\ \dfrac{\eta^2 - \sigma^2}{\lambda} & \dfrac{\eta^2 - \sigma^2}{\lambda^2} \end{bmatrix},$$

assuming that the correcting coefficient λ is positive (this latter condition is generally satisfied in practice).

The no-correlation case occurs when no correction is necessary, i.e., when the correction factor equals one. A measure of the information not used optimally for predicting d is $|\lambda - 1|$.

It will be useful to present this parametrization in another equivalent way. Indeed, if w denotes the centered, reduced, expected demand $w = \lambda(\hat{d} - m)/\sqrt{\eta^2 - \sigma^2}$, and v the reduced corrected prediction error, we obtain

$$\hat{d} - m = w\frac{\sqrt{\eta^2 - \sigma^2}}{\lambda},$$

$$d - m = w\sqrt{\eta^2 - \sigma^2} + \sigma v, \tag{11}$$

where

$$\begin{bmatrix} w \\ v \end{bmatrix} \sim N\left[\begin{pmatrix} 0 \\ 0 \end{pmatrix}, \begin{pmatrix} 1 & 0 \\ 0 & 1 \end{pmatrix} \right].$$

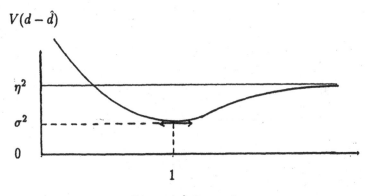

Figure 4: The Variance $V(d - \hat{d})$
as a Function of λ

Correction factor λ

The parameters have to satisfy the constraints $\eta^2 > \sigma^2$, $\lambda > 0$. Under model (11) the uncorrected prediction error is given by

$$V(d - \hat{d}) = V(d) + V(\hat{d}) - 2\text{cov}\,(d, \hat{d}) = \eta^2 + (\eta^2 - \sigma^2)\frac{1}{\lambda}\Big(\frac{1}{\lambda} - 2\Big).$$

The graph of this variance as a function of λ is given in Figure 4 and it attains its minimum value when orthogonality holds, i.e., when $\lambda = 1$.

Expression for the exchanged quantity. Due to the correlation between the prediction and the prediction error, the exchanged quantity has an expression in terms of integrals. It can be proved that this expression is

$$\overline{Q} = e^m E\left\{\exp\left[\frac{\sqrt{\eta^2 - \sigma^2}}{\lambda}w\right]\left[1 - \Phi\Big(\frac{1}{\sigma}\Big(\frac{1}{\lambda} - 1\Big)(\sqrt{\eta^2 - \sigma^2})w\Big)\right]\right\}$$

$$+ e^m e^{\sigma^2/2} E\left\{\exp[(\sqrt{\eta^2 - \sigma^2})w]\,\Phi\Big(\frac{1}{\sigma}\Big(\frac{1}{\lambda} - 1\Big)(\sqrt{\eta^2 - \sigma^2})w - \sigma\Big)\right\},$$

$$\tag{13}$$

where, as before, Φ is the cdf of the standard normal and w is a random variable with the standard normal distribution.

For the limit cases $\lambda = 0$ and $\lambda = +\infty$, it is easily seen that $\overline{Q} = \overline{D}$ and $\overline{Q} = E\{\min[D, e^m]\}$, respectively. In the case $\lambda = +\infty$, the variance of $\hat{d}$ is equal to zero or equivalently $\hat{d} = m$. This prediction coincides with the rational expectation in the absence of information. In particular, we know that the exchanged quantity associated with $\hat{d} = m$ is smaller than the ex-

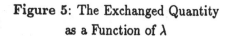

Figure 5: The Exchanged Quantity
as a Function of λ

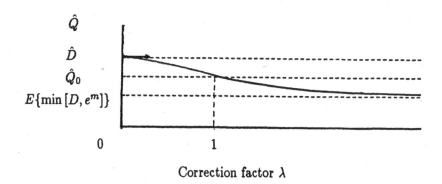

Correction factor λ

changed quantity corresponding to $\lambda = 1$, since for $\lambda = 1$ the prediction
is rational but does not coincide with $m = E\{d\}$. The evolution of the
exchanged quantity as a function of λ is described in Figure 5 above.

Some additional results might be obtained concerning the elasticity of
the exchanged quantity with respect to the correction factor λ (Gourieroux
and Peaucelle, 1989). Some bounds for the elasticity are given by the
following

Property 1. $\partial \log \overline{Q} / \partial \log \lambda$ *is less than or greater than* $-(\eta^2 - \sigma^2)(1 - P)$, *according to whether* $\lambda > 1$ *or* $\lambda < 1$.

5. Discussion of a Price-adjustment Equation

In the previous sections we have considered the case when the price
is fixed in the short run and we have studied the disequilibria created by
the expectations of demand by firms. However, in the medium term, the
aggregate disequilibria are likely to have some effects on the evolution of
the price. To analyze this effect, we introduce a price-adjustment equation,
taking into account the multiplicative form of the model and the possibility
of different speeds of adjustment, depending on the regime, i.e., whether
excess demand or excess supply is the case. The price-adjustment equation
is

$$\log p_t - \log p_{t-1} = \lambda_1 E\{(d_{t-1} - \hat{d}_{t-1})\Im_{d_{t-1}-\hat{d}_{t-1}>0}\}$$
$$+ \lambda_2 E\{(d_{t-1} - \hat{d}_{t-1})\Im_{d_{t-1}-\hat{d}_{t-1}<0}\}, \tag{14}$$

where $\lambda_1, \lambda_2 > 0$.

Since the two regimes exist simultaneously, the two effects, namely an increase in price when $d_{t-1} > \hat{d}_{t-1}$ and a decrease in price in the reverse case, are both introduced in the equation and may balance each other. If we denote $E\{d_{t-1} - \hat{d}_{t-1}\}$ by $-B(p_{t-1})$, the opposite of the prediction bias, and $V(d_{t-1} - \hat{d}_{t-1})$ by $\mu^2(p_{t-1})$, the mean prediction error, we obtain

$$\log p_t - \log p_{t-1} = \lambda_1\left[-B + B\Phi\left(\frac{B}{\mu}\right) + \mu\phi\left(\frac{B}{\mu}\right)\right]$$
$$+ \lambda_2\left[-B\Phi\left(\frac{B}{\mu}\right) - \mu\phi\left(\frac{B}{\mu}\right)\right],$$
$$\log p_t - \log p_{t-1} = \mu\left[\lambda_1(-\gamma + \Psi(\gamma)) - \lambda_2\Psi(\gamma)\right],$$

where $\gamma = B/\mu$ and $\Psi(\gamma) = \gamma\Phi(\gamma) + \phi(\gamma)$.

It is now interesting to study the asymptotic behavior of this difference equation, especially to see if it has a fixed point $\bar{p}$ and how this fixed point will depend on aggregate demand and aggregate expected demand.

It is easily seen that the function $\gamma \to \Psi(\gamma)/(-\gamma + \Psi(\gamma))$ is an increasing function which takes the values $0, 1, +\infty$ if γ equals $-\infty, 0, +\infty$ respectively. We deduce that there exists one and only one solution $\bar{\gamma}(\lambda_1/\lambda_2)$ to the equation

$$\frac{\Psi(\bar{\gamma})}{-\bar{\gamma} + \Psi(\bar{\gamma})} = \frac{\lambda_1}{\lambda_2}.$$

We deduce the following:

Property 2. *The price adjustment equation has a fixed point $\bar{p}$, if and only if the equation $B(\bar{p})/\mu(\overline{P}) = \bar{\gamma}(\lambda_1/\lambda_2)$ has a solution.*

This condition shows that an expectation scheme, i.e., knowledge of the two functions $B(p)$ and $\mu(p)$, is compatible with a stable price, if and only if the above equation has a solution. For example, unbiased expectations (in particular, rational expectations) satisfy this condition if and only if

$$\frac{B(p)}{\mu(p)} = 0 = \bar{\gamma}\left(\frac{\lambda_1}{\lambda_2}\right) \Longleftrightarrow \lambda_1 = \lambda_2.$$

In the opposite case, unbiased expectations would lead to a continuous increase (decrease) of the price if $\lambda_1 > (<)\lambda_2$. Moreover, it is seen that when the fixed point exists, it is determined only through λ_1, λ_2 and the quality of the expectations. It depends on the real part of the model, i.e., of the parameters m, η only through the bias and the precision of the predictions.

6. Econometric Perspectives

The previous analysis was undertaken with the idea of specific econometric applications. Indeed, firms are surveyed in France for obtaining short-run information. In these tendency surveys the questions are qualitative and concern the evolution of demand, expected demand and also the constraints experienced by firms. Of course, it is natural to study these variables jointly and the model outlined above may be used as a basis for such a study.

References

Demeter, K (1990) "The Form of Expected Demand in Hungary in a Mills Type Model," this volume.

Ginsburgh, V., Tishler, A. and Zang, I. (1980) "Alternative Estimation Methods for Two-Regime Models," *European Economic Review* **13**, 207-228.

Gourieroux, C., Laffont, J. J. and Monfort, A. (1984) "Econométrie des Modèles d'équilibre avec rationnement: une mise à jour," *Annales de l'INSEE* **55/56**, 5-37.

Gourieroux, C. and Laroque, G. (1985) "The Aggregation of Commodities in Quantity Rationing Models," *International Economic Review* **26**, 681-699.

Gourieroux, C. and Peaucelle, I. (1987) "Vérification empirique de la rationalité des anticipations de la demande par les entreprises," *Recherches Economiques de Louvain* **53**, 223-246.

_____ (1989) "L'effet sur le déséquilibre des anticipations de demande par les entreprises," CEPREMAP, mimeographed.

Hajivassiliou, V. A. (1983) "Estimating and Testing an Aggregative Disequilibrium Model of the US Labor Market," MIT, mimeographed.

Lambert, J. P. (1984) "Disequilibrium Macromodels Based on Business Survey Data," PhD Thesis, Louvain-la-Neuve.

Maddala, G. S. (1984) "Estimation of a Dynamic Disequilibrium Model with Rational Expectations," Working Paper, University of Florida.

Malinvaud, E. (1982) "An Econometric Model of Macrodisequilibrium Analysis," in M. Hazewinkel and A.H.J. Rinnooy Kan (eds), *Current Developments in the Interface of Economics, Econometrics and Mathematics*, Dordrecht-Boston: Reidel.

Muellbauer, J. (1978) "Macrotheory vs Macroeconometrics: The Treatment of Disequilibrium in Macromodels," Discussion Paper No. 59, Birkbeck College.

Quandt, R. E. (1988) *The Econometrics of Disequilibrium*, Oxford: Blackwell.

19

The Rationality of Adjustment Behavior in a Model of Monopolistic Competition ·

Gérard Duménil and *Dominique Lévy*

1. Introduction

Modeling behavior in terms of adjustment to disequilibria provides an alternative approach to decision-making models. By adjustment we mean the reaction to disequilibria observed in the past, as opposed to the maximization of an objective function on the basis of expected variables in the future.

The description of adjustment behavior is as old as economic theory (see Adam Smith (1776), Ch. 7; David Ricardo (1817), Ch. 4; Karl Marx (1894), Ch. 10). As they describe, capitalists seek the maximum return on their capital by moving fractions of this capital at each period, in response to profitability differentials. Our original adherence to adjustment is rooted in these classic analyses of competitive processes and the formation of natural prices.

The formal modeling of adjustment is, of course, more recent and can be traced to such works as Samuelson (1939) and Metzler (1941). Since then, adjustment has survived in a few heterodox contributions by Lovell (1961;1962), Kornai and Martos (1973;1981), Tobin (1975), Day and Groves

* We thank Mark Glick for his aid in the translation of this text into English.

(1975), Kornai (1980), Malinvaud (1982) and Simonovits (1985). We have made extensive use of adjustment in our work on the stability of capitalism (see also Duménil and Lévy (1989a) and (1989b)), in which the model is based on adjustment.

Adjustment has been criticized under the banner of *rationality*. Descriptions of behavior in these terms are rejected *ad hoc*. In our opinion, however, the exact nature of the relationship between maximization and adjustment has not been seriously addressed. The question of whether adjustment is or is not a rational behavior actually depends on the framework of the analysis. More precisely, we believe that it is possible to define adjustment equations and values of reaction coefficients to disequilibrium, which are rational within given contexts. Here we take rational in its full sense as the maximization of an objective function with rational expectations.

The purpose of this paper is to illustrate this general proposition in a model of *partial equilibrium*, in which we study the behavior of firms in their *price* and *output* decisions when confronted with a demand function that varies over time. Two different frameworks are considered in turn:

1) A monopoly facing a demand function subject to random shocks (see Holt and Simon (1954), Holt et al. (1960) and Blinder (1982));

2) Monopolistic competition without uncertainty, in which a number of firms compete within a given industry and the vagaries of the demand function are endogenous—they result from the variation of the average level of prices in the industry (i.e., they translate the changes in prices of competitors). To date, no result appears to have been demonstrated using this framework in the literature.

This study is divided into two sections, which correspond to the above frameworks. First, we study rational adjustment for the case of a monopoly. We then assume that demand is drifting slowly compared to the speed with which firms adjust supply to demand. Using this assumption, we obtain the exact form for modeling production decisions that is used in our work on stability.

The second section is devoted to monopolistic competition. There we study the individual behavior of firms whose individual demand varies as a result of price changes of competitors in the industry. We derive the aggregate "behavior" at the industry level.

This investigation requires the formation of price expectations. In conformity with our general line of argument, we assume rational expectations. Some conclusions about adjustment behavior in a model of monopolistic competition are offered in the last section.

2. Optimal Management: Monopoly

In the first two parts of this section we borrow from Blinder (1982) to construct the model and from Holt and Simon (1954) and Holt, Modigliani, Muth and Simon (1960) for its resolution. After presenting the model, we examine the behavior of firms with respect to price and output decisions and, lastly, investigate the comparatively quick adjustment of supply to demand by firms. With this assumption the form of the equations for adjustment is modified.

The Framework of Analysis

In this part we introduce the model in three steps: The general assumptions are briefly sketched; the modeling of demand is given; and production and inventory costs are discussed.

General assumptions. The challenge is to derive the optimal behavior of a firm in the following environment:

1) The firm is a monopoly or, at least, behaves as such.

2) The firm is confronted with a given demand function, which is known up to a stochastic additive disturbance.

3) The firm incurs two types of costs: production costs and disequilibrium costs, such as for inventory or for varying production. For simplicity, we abstract from the costs of varying production.

4) The firm must make its decisions concerning price and production levels while ignoring the value of the demand shock for the period. However, it forms rational expectations of the demand shock.

5) Markets are held after each production period:

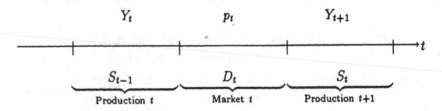

in which Y_t denotes the output of period t, D_t stands for demand or firm's sales, p_t for the price set by the firm on market t, S_t for inventories at the end of market t (held during production $t+1$). For accounting reasons, one obtains:

$$S_t = S_{t-1} + Y_t - D_t. \tag{1}$$

6) To take advantage of certainty equivalence, i.e., the fact that only the average value of random variables actually matters, the demand function is linear and cost functions are quadratic.

We consider the decision of the firm at the end of market 0. At this date S_0 is known and the firm must decide on Y_1 and p_1.

The demand function. The demand function is

$$D_t = d_0 - d_1 p_t + \eta_t, \tag{2}$$

in which η_t is a random shock and d_0 and d_1 are two constant parameters. With this model of demand the revenue function is quadratic.

We assume that the stochastic variable η_t follows an $AR(1)$ process:

$$\eta_t = \rho\eta_{t-1} + \nu_t \quad \text{with} \quad 0 \leq \rho \leq 1, \tag{3}$$

in which ν_t is an independently and identically distributed disturbance. For $\rho = 0$ equation (3) corresponds to the case in which η_t is itself such a disturbance term. The opposite case of $\rho = 1$ models a random walk. The assumption of an $AR(1)$ process is not required in the following computation. It is only necessary in the subsection below on rational adjustment behavior in order to derive the value of coefficients φ and φ' in equations (19) and (20).

Production and inventory costs. These are assumed to be quadratic:

$$\text{Production costs}: \quad \frac{c}{2}Y_t^2, \tag{4}$$

$$\text{Inventory costs}: \quad \frac{c_s}{2}(S_t - \overline{S})^2 + c_s'. \tag{5}$$

Quadratic production costs correspond to the case of diminishing returns. The inventory *cost function* can be analyzed as the sum of two distinct costs:

1) The cost of storing and maintaining inventories, which is an increasing quadratic function of the level of inventories.

2) The cost of losing sales, which is a decreasing function of the level of inventories (see Blinder (1982), footnote 4, p. 337).

In equation (5) $\overline{S}$ is the value of S, for which the sum of these two costs is minimum. Since c_s' does not play any role in the determination of the optimal behavior, it can be set to zero.

The Derivation of Price and Output Decisions

In this part we present the firm's profit-maximizing behavior, define the targets around which the firm will gravitate and discuss rational adjustment behavior.

Profit maximizing. The firm *maximizes its expected profits*

$$\Pi = E_0 \sum_{t=1}^{\infty} \delta^t \left(p_t(d_0 - d_1 p_t + \eta_t) - \frac{c}{2}Y_t^2 - \frac{c_s}{2}(S_t - \overline{S})^2 \right), \tag{6}$$

where δ is a discount factor and the expectation is taken as of time zero.

This maximization is constrained by the accounting identity (1). With Lagrange multipliers λ_t the problem becomes that of the determination of a critical point of the Lagrangian:

$$\Pi + E_0 \sum_{t=1}^{\infty} \delta^t \lambda_t (-S_t + S_{t-1} + Y_t - d_0 + d_1 p_t - \eta_t).$$

The first-order conditions in addition to equation (1) are:

$$cY_t = \lambda_t, \tag{7}$$

$$p_t = \frac{1}{2}\left(\lambda_t + \frac{d_0 + \eta_t}{d_1}\right), \tag{8}$$

or

$$D_t = \frac{d_0 + \eta_t - \lambda_t d_1}{2}, \tag{8'}$$

$$c_s(S_t - \overline{S}) = \delta \lambda_{t+1} - \lambda_t. \tag{9}$$

The second-order conditions obviously hold.

We use the same notation for variables S_t and η_t and for their expected values at time zero. (The firm decides on p_t and Y_t and, consequently, knows these values with certainty.)

Targets. The equilibrium values can be obtained from equations (7), (8) and (9) for $\eta_t = 0$:

$$\tilde{Y} = \frac{d_0}{2 + d_1 c}, \tag{10}$$

$$\tilde{p} = \frac{d_0}{d_1} \frac{1 + c d_1}{2 + c d_1}, \tag{11}$$

$$\tilde{S} = \overline{S} - (1 - \delta) \frac{d_0 c}{c_s (2 + d_1 c)}. \tag{12}$$

The two first equations correspond to the straightforward atemporal treatment of a monopoly. Only d_0, d_1 and c are considered in these equations. Conversely, inventory costs c_s and the discount rate δ are involved in the third equation, which defines the target value for the stock of inventories.

If ρ is strictly smaller than 1, the equilibrium values determined above can be interpreted as the target around which the variables gravitate.

Rational adjustment behavior. We now turn to the study of the dynamics of the above system. After substituting (7) in (9), using (8), we obtain a second-order inhomogenous difference equation in Y:

$$\delta Y_{t+1} - \alpha Y_t + Y_{t-1} = \beta_t \quad \text{for} \quad t = 2, 3, \ldots, \tag{13}$$

with

$$\alpha = 1 + \delta + \frac{c_s}{c}\left(1 + \frac{d_1 c}{2}\right) \quad \text{and} \quad \beta_t = -\frac{c_s}{2c}(d_0 + \eta_t).$$

Let μ be a real number. We first define

$$Z = \sum_{t=1}^{\infty} \mu^{t-1} Y_t \quad \text{and} \quad B(\mu) = \sum_{t=2}^{\infty} \mu^{t-1} \beta_{t-1},$$

then multiply equation (13) by μ^{t-1}, and sum from $t = 2$ to $t = \infty$:

$$\frac{\delta}{\mu}(Z - Y_1 - \mu Y_2) - \alpha(Z - Y_1) + \mu Z = B(\mu). \tag{14}$$

We choose μ with a modulus smaller than 1, such that the coefficient of Z is equal to zero. Thus, μ is a zero of:

$$\mu^2 - \alpha\mu + \delta = 0. \tag{15}$$

It is easy to show that only one positive value of μ, namely μ_1, with a modulus smaller than 1, exists. Thus, equation (14) becomes:

$$\mu_1 Y_1 - \delta Y_2 = B(\mu_1). \tag{16}$$

A second equation is required in order to determine Y_1. We use equations (9) for $t = 1$, and (1), (7) and (8):

$$\delta Y_2 - (\alpha - \delta)Y_1 = \frac{c_s}{c}\left(S_0 - \overline{S} - \frac{d_0 + \eta_1}{2}\right). \tag{17}$$

Equations (16) and (17) allow for the determination of Y_1:

$$Y_1 = \tilde{Y} - \varepsilon(S_0 - \tilde{S} - \Delta), \tag{18}$$

with

$$\varepsilon = \frac{c_s}{c(\alpha - \delta - \mu_1)} > 0 \quad \text{and} \quad \Delta = \frac{1}{2}\sum_{t=1}^{\infty}\mu_1^{t-1}\eta_t.$$

If η_t satisfies equation (3), then the rational expectation of η_t after market 0, is $\eta_t = \rho^t \eta_0$, and $\Delta = \frac{1}{2}\frac{\rho\eta_0}{1-\mu_1\rho}$, where η_0 measures the demand shock, i.e., the difference between the actual demand D_0 and its model: $\eta_0 = D_0 - (d_0 - d_1 p_0)$.

Thus, equation (18) can be written as:

$$Y_1 = \tilde{Y} - \varepsilon(S_0 - \tilde{S}) + \varphi\eta_0, \tag{19}$$

with

$$\varphi = \frac{\varepsilon}{2}\frac{\rho}{1-\mu_1\rho}.$$

The price decision can be derived from equations (7), (8) and (19):

$$p_1 = \tilde{p} - \varepsilon'(S_0 - \tilde{S}) + \varphi'\eta_0, \tag{20}$$

with

$$\varepsilon' = \frac{c}{2}\varepsilon \quad \text{and} \quad \varphi' = \frac{c}{2}\varphi + \frac{\rho}{2d_1}.$$

Both equations (19) and (20) describe typical adjustment behavior, and this concludes the demonstration that adjustment can be a rational behavior. The following economic comments can now be made:

1) A large value of inventories S_0 results in small values of Y_1 and p_1.

2) A large inventory cost c_s results in large values for the coefficients ε, φ, ε' and φ', which measure the reactions of firms to disequilibrium.

3) A large value of ρ, which means that demand is more sticky, has no effect on ε and ε', but increases φ and φ'.

The last two remarks correspond to Blinder's "main theorem" (see Blinder (1982), Theorem 1, p. 337), for φ and φ', and to Blinder's Proposition 4 (p. 341) for ε and ε'.

A Quick Response of Supply to Demand

In this part we derive the specific forms of rational adjustment under the assumption that firms respond quickly in the short run to the disequilibrium between supply and demand, in comparison to the rather sticky drift of the demand function. After introducing the problem, we then analyze successively the quick and slow components of the process.

The problem. In the previous two parts we defined a recursion relation with five variables: Y, p, S, D and η (see (19), (20), (1), (2) and (3)). These equations account for the transition from period 0 to period 1, but the same process can be repeated, and the same system accounts for any transition from $t - 1$ to t.

In the overall process two different speeds of adjustment must be distinguished:

1) The exogenous speed of variation of demand shocks η. This speed is modeled by parameter ρ in equation (3). A large value of ρ is equivalent to a slow variation of the demand function.

2) The endogenous speed of adjustment of supply to demand, which concerns the decision to produce, the price decision and the level of inventory.

We believe that in real economies the first process is slow compared to the second. Firms react quickly to the disequilibrium between supply and demand, whereas the return of demand to its equilibrium value is slower. Output can be adjusted to demand far before the return of demand to equilibrium is realized. In extreme cases, such as, for example, in the steel industry during the recent years of hardship, the return to a normal capacity utilization rate can be very long, whereas inventories can be rescaled in a rather short span of time, as a result of reduced production.

We study the limit case, distinguishing two different dynamics:

1) For a given demand function after a shock we analyze the dynamics of outputs, prices and inventories.

2) Assuming that the above adjustment of outputs, prices and inventories is constantly realized, we study the dynamics associated with the return of demand to equilibrium.

The quick component of dynamics. Three variables are involved in this first component of the dynamical process, since the shock has been "frozen" at its initial value η, and D can be eliminated:

$$Y_t = \tilde{Y} - \varepsilon(S_{t-1} - \tilde{S}) + \varphi\eta,$$
$$p_t = \tilde{p} - \varepsilon'(S_{t-1} - \tilde{S}) + \varphi'\eta,$$
$$S_t = S_{t-1} + Y_t - (d_0 - d_1 p_t + \eta).$$

Since η is given, the fixed point in this recursion is not $(\tilde{Y}, \tilde{p}, \tilde{S})$ as in equations (10), (11) and (12), but is shifted. For example, one has:

$$Y^* = \tilde{Y} + \frac{2 - \rho}{2 + d_1 c}\eta. \tag{21}$$

The study of the stability of this recursion is straightforward—stability is always insured.

The sticky component of dynamics. We now assume that η varies with time, and that equation (21) must be written as:

$$Y_t = \tilde{Y} + \frac{2 - \rho}{2 + d_1 c}\eta_t. \tag{22}$$

Variable η_t measures the difference between the actual demand observed, which is obviously known, and the model used by the firm for demand. The determination of this model is difficult, especially at a distance from equilibrium. We will derive another form of the decision to produce, from which the demand shock has been eliminated.

Beginning with equation (19), at time t,

$$Y_t = \tilde{Y} - \varepsilon(S_{t-1} - \tilde{S}) + \varphi \eta_{t-1},$$

we substitute the value of η_{t-1} from equation (22) in the above equation:

$$Y_t = \tilde{Y} - \varepsilon(S_{t-1} - \tilde{S}) + \sigma(Y_{t-1} - \tilde{Y}), \tag{23}$$

with

$$\sigma = \frac{2 + d_1 c}{2 - \rho} \varphi. \tag{24}$$

In a similar manner for prices, we have:

$$p_t = \tilde{p} - \varepsilon'(S_{t-1} - \tilde{S}) + \sigma'(Y_{t-1} - \tilde{Y}), \tag{25}$$

with

$$\sigma' = \frac{2 + d_1 c}{2 - \rho} \varphi'. \tag{26}$$

The strong point in equations (23) and (25) is that only observed values of the variables are involved, and no *computed* values (in which a model of the economy is implied, as in the case of η). The problem the firm faces is only to determine the reaction coefficients as closely as possible from their optimal values. Parenthetically, one can notice that the same forms are obtained for equations (23) and (25) from the consideration of costs of varying production (see Holt et al. (1960)).

3. Optimal Management: Monopolistic Competition

In Section 2 the parameters d_0 and d_1, which define the demand function (see (2)), are constant and the firm is a monopolist. Here we focus on the case of monopolistic competition within an industry, and d_0 and d_1 depend on the prices of competitors or, rather, on the average price prevailing in the industry. Thus, the individual demand schedule with which a firm i is confronted is a function of p^i, its own price, and p, the average price.

The Framework of Analysis

In this part we present the general framework of analysis and make some assumptions about the construction of the model. In studying the industry, we assume that all firms remain in a vicinity of equilibrium. As a result, it is possible to resort to linear developments of the equations. If X_t and Y_t are two variables whose equilibrium values are X^* and Y^*, we substitute $X^*Y^* + X^*(Y_t - Y^*) + Y^*(X_t - X^*)$ for X_tY_t, neglecting terms such as $(X_t - X^*)(Y_t - Y^*)$.

The perspective is that of *partial equilibrium*. We consider an industry composed of n identical firms. It is, therefore, necessary to make an assumption about the total demand addressed to the industry. We assume that the total purchasing power M, destined for the purchase of the output of the industry, is given (and independent from the prices in the industry).

Total purchasing power is shared among firms according to the *individual demand function*:

$$D^i = A\left(1 - \psi\left(\frac{p^i}{p} - 1\right)\right), \tag{27}$$

in which the average level of prices is defined by $p = \frac{1}{n}\sum_{i=1}^{n}p^i$, and A is a constant defined by $\sum_{i=1}^{n}D^ip^i = M$. If firms remain in a vicinity of equilibrium, then $A = M/np$. In equation (27) ψ is a parameter which accounts for the intensity of price competition among firms. If all prices are equal, each firm receives an equal share of total demand: M/np. Then (27) can be written in a more traditional form as $D^i = d_0 - d_1 p^i$, with

$$d_0 = \frac{1}{n}\frac{M}{p}(1 + \psi) \quad \text{and} \quad d_1 = \frac{1}{n}\frac{M}{p^2}\psi. \tag{28}$$

In addition to the sharing of total demand as expressed in equation (27), we could add a random variable η^i, with the condition that the sum of all shock at the industry level be equal to zero: $\sum_{i=1}^{n}\eta^i = 0$. For simplicity, we will abstract from this component, which is not essential to the demonstration.

The firms must carry production costs and inventory costs. We assume that these costs do not depend on the average price p of the industry. This is equivalent to stating that inputs are purchased outside the industry. These costs are considered given and constant.

When the firm maximizes its profits, it assumes that p, the average price in the industry, does not depend on its own price (the firm is small).

In this computation the firm must make price expectations about p for the future. In conformity with the general purpose of this study—the derivation of rational adjustment behavior—we assume that the firm forms *rational expectations*.

Individual Behavior in Monopolistic Competition

We now discuss equilibrium, introduce an assumption concerning ψ and determine rational behavior in order to derive individual behavior in monopolistic competition.

Equilibrium. The average price p in the industry can have a priori any value. For a given p the individual demand functions are determined (see equation (28)). On the basis of these demand functions, and using equations (10) and (11), we can define the price and output targets, $\tilde{p}(p)$ and $\tilde{Y}(p)$, respectively. Since d_0 and d_1 are independent of i, the same is true for the targets.

For a given p the individual price targets, $\tilde{p}(p)$, can differ from p. We define the *equilibrium price* p^* as the price for which firms choose the average price for individual targets, i.e., $\tilde{p}(p^*) = p^*$. We then obtain:

$$\tilde{p}(p^*) = p^* = \left(\frac{\psi}{\psi-1}\frac{cM}{n}\right)^{1/2}, \tag{29}$$

$$\tilde{Y}(p^*) = Y^* = \frac{\psi-1}{\psi c}p^*. \tag{30}$$

It is possible to verify that, when equilibrium prevails, the sum of the output targets of the n firms is equal to total demand for p^*, i.e., M/p^*.

When the industry is not at equilibrium in the sense that $p \neq p^*$, we say that disequilibrium prevails. This obvious property must be stated unambiguously, since in sharp contrast to most models used in economics, our model still has a meaning out of equilibrium:

1) The behavior of agents in a Walrasian model is only rational in an equilibrium.

2) The behavior of agents in our model is rational in and out of equilibrium.

The ambiguity about equilibrium and disequilibrium is due to the two different meanings that can be given to the term equilibrium itself:

1) An equilibrium is a fixed point in a dynamic model; the term is used

in this sense in our study.

2) At each period in the dynamic process described in this part, disequilibrium prevails in the above sense. However, each step can be characterized as a *Nash equilibrium*. Each behavior is optimal, when we consider the behavior of other producers as given.

The assumption $\psi > 3$. The output target $\tilde{Y}(p)$ can be a *priori* an increasing or decreasing function of p, depending on the value of ψ. One can expect, under ordinary circumstances, that $\tilde{Y}(p)$ will be an increasing function of its argument: If the prices p of all the competitors of firm i increase, while p^i remains constant, then buyers will demand more from i, and the target $\tilde{Y}(p)$ should be raised. One can show that this is the case, in a vicinity of equilibrium, if $\psi > 3$. In the remainder of this study we will assume that $\psi > 3$.

Rational behavior. In order to derive the behavioral equations we resort to the same method as in Section 2 (construction of the Lagrangian, derivation of the first-order conditions). First, we linearize the equations. For example, the substitution of (7) in (8'), yields:

$$D_t^i = Y^* - \frac{\psi - 1}{2}(Y_t^i - Y^*) + \frac{\psi - 3}{2}Y^* x_t \quad \text{with} \quad x_t = \frac{p_t - p^*}{p^*}.$$

The derivation is identical to that in Section 2 up to equation (13), which becomes:

$$\delta Y_{t+1}^i - \alpha_t Y_t^i + Y_{t-1}^i = \beta_t. \tag{31}$$

The important transformation is that α varies with time. We linearize $\alpha_t Y_t^i$, i.e., substitute $\alpha^* Y_t^i + (\alpha_t - \alpha^*)Y^*$ for this term in equation (31). Using the notation

$$\alpha^* = 1 + \delta + \frac{c_s}{c}\frac{1 + \psi}{2} \quad \text{and} \quad \beta_t' = \frac{c_s}{2c}Y^*(1 + \psi + (3 - \psi)x_t), \tag{32}$$

we obtain:

$$\delta Y_{t+1}^i - \alpha^* Y_t^i + Y_{t-1}^i = \beta_t'.$$

Still following the demonstration in Section 2, we get the new form of equation (16):

$$\mu_1(Y_1^i - Y^*) - \delta(Y_2^i - Y^*) = B, \tag{33}$$

with

$$B = \frac{c_s}{c}\frac{3-\psi}{2}Y^*\mu_1\Sigma_2 \quad \text{and} \quad \Sigma_T = \sum_{t=T}^{\infty}\mu_1^{t-T}x_t;$$

here μ_1 satisfies equation (15) with $\alpha = \alpha^*$. In a similar manner equation (17) can now be written as:

$$\delta(Y_2^i - Y^*) - \left(1 + \frac{c_s}{c}\frac{1+\psi}{2}\right)(Y_1^i - Y^*) = \frac{c_s}{c}\left(\frac{3-\psi}{2}x_1 + S_0^i - S^*\right). \tag{34}$$

The equation for the decision to produce follows from equations (33) and (34):

$$Y_1^i = Y^* - \varepsilon(S_0^i - S^*) + \varepsilon\frac{\psi-3}{2}Y^*\Sigma_1, \tag{35}$$

in which

$$\varepsilon = \frac{c_s}{c}\frac{1}{\alpha - \delta - \mu_1} = \frac{\delta - \mu_1}{\delta}\frac{2}{\psi + 1}. \tag{36}$$

For the price decision we have:

$$p_1^i = p^* - \varepsilon'(S_0^i - S^*) + \varepsilon'\frac{\psi-3}{2}Y^*\Sigma_1 + \frac{1+\psi}{2\psi}p^*x_1. \tag{37}$$

With $\varepsilon' = \frac{c}{2}\varepsilon$ the above forms for the output and price decisions are similar to those derived in Section 2 (see equations (19) and (20)), with two differences:

1) By construction no random shock appears in the equations.

2) A new term is present, the sum over time of $x_t = \frac{p_t - p^*}{p^*}$. This term corresponds to the specific effect of monopolistic competition. It measures the impact on individual behavior of the variation of the expected average price in the future at the industry level. Equations (35) and (37) do not define real adjustment behavior, since expectations are still considered. This behavior will be derived below.

The behavior of firms is summarized in equations (35) and (37). In determining this behavior, we must, however, make a complete plan for the future and also compute Y_t^i and p_t^i over time. The following equation for prices will be used in what follows:

$$p_t^i = p^* - \varepsilon'(S_{t-1}^i - S^*) + \varepsilon'\frac{\psi - 3}{2}Y^*\Sigma_t + \frac{1+\psi}{2\psi}(p_t - p^*). \quad (38)$$

Adjustment Behavior

In this part we analyze the overall dynamics and derive the equations modeling rational adjustment, first at the level of the industry, then at the level of one individual firm.

Industrial rational adjustment behavior. Expectations are implied in the two behavior equations (35) and (37). We assume rational expectations by summing equation (38) over i for all firms and identify $\frac{1}{n}\sum_{i=1}^n p_t^i$, the average price level derived from the price decisions of individual firms, and p_t, the average price expected by firms. We then obtain:

$$\left(\frac{1}{\varepsilon} + \frac{3-\psi}{2}\right)x_t + s_{t-1} - \frac{\psi-3}{2}\mu_1\Sigma_{t+1} = 0, \quad (39)$$

with

$$s_t = \frac{S_t - S^*}{Y^*} \quad \text{and} \quad S_t = \frac{1}{n}\sum_{i=1}^n S_t^i.$$

In this notation S_t is the average level of inventory in each industry.

In order to determine x_t it is necessary to follow the dynamics of inventories. We define Y_t as the average individual production level $Y_t = \frac{1}{n}\sum_{i=1}^n Y_t^i$. We know from:

1) the total value of inventories for the whole industry, $S_t = S_{t-1} + Y_t - \frac{1}{n}D_t$,
2) total demand for the industry, $D_t = \frac{M}{p_t} = \frac{np^*Y^*}{p_t}$, and
3) the result of the aggregation of the first-order condition, as in equation (8),

that

$$s_t = s_{t-1} + 2x_t. \quad (40)$$

The system formed by equations (39) and (40) allows for the determination of the unknowns. We seek a solution of the form $x_t = x_1\rho^{t-1}$ and

$s_t = s_0 \rho^t$. Such a solution exists, if $x_1 = -\varepsilon_\alpha s_0$ with $\varepsilon_\alpha = \frac{1-\rho^*}{2}$, and if ρ^* satisfies:

$$\left(\rho^* - \frac{\mu_1}{\delta}\right)(1 - \mu_1\rho^*) - \varepsilon\frac{\psi - 3}{2}(1 - \mu_1)\rho^* = 0. \qquad (41)$$

It is easy to show that, for $\psi > 3$, equation (41) has one and only one zero ρ^*, which verifies $\mu_1/\delta < \rho^* < 1$ (the other zero is real and larger than $1/\mu_1$). Thus, the two equations, which reflect the aggregate effects of individual behavior (equations (35) and (37)) at the industry level can be written as follows:

$$Y_1 = Y^* - \varepsilon_\alpha(S_0 - S^*), \qquad (42)$$

$$p_1 = p^*\left(1 - \varepsilon_\alpha\frac{S_0 - S^*}{Y^*}\right). \qquad (43)$$

A comparison with equations (35) and (37) leads to the following observations:

1) The terms corresponding to future prices are absent in the above equations, and only past disequilibrium $(S_0 - S^*)$ is considered.

2) It can be shown that ε_α is larger than ε. This is due to the firms' consideration of the reactions of other producers, as will be shown below.

Conversely, equations (42) and (43) are very similar to those obtained in Section 2 of this study (equations (19) and (20)) for the monopoly (without the effect of shocks, from which we abstracted in Section 3).

The aggregate behavior described above is definitely distinct from that of a monopoly facing the aggregate demand function. With the assumptions made above this monopoly would choose $Y = 0$ and $p = \infty$.

Individual rational adjustment behavior. We can now rewrite the equations defining individual behavior and compute the sum over the expectations for the industry prices. From equations (35) and (37) we derive:

$$Y_1^i = Y^* - \varepsilon(S_0^i - S^*) - \varepsilon_s(S_0 - S^*), \qquad (44)$$

$$p_1^i = p^* - \varepsilon'(S_0^i - S^*) - \varepsilon'_s(S_0 - S^*), \qquad (45)$$

in which:

$$\varepsilon_s = \frac{1-\rho^*}{2} - \varepsilon > 0, \quad \varepsilon' = \frac{c}{2}\varepsilon,$$

and

$$\varepsilon'_s = \frac{c}{2}\left(\varepsilon_s + \frac{\psi+1}{\psi-1}\frac{1-\rho^*}{2}\right) = \frac{c}{2}\left((1-\rho^*)\frac{\psi}{\psi-1} - \varepsilon\right).$$

The aggregation of equation (44) for the whole industry yields equation (42), since $\varepsilon_\alpha = \varepsilon + \varepsilon_s$.

Equations (44) and (45) above describe rational behavior expressed in terms of adjustment. Enterprises change their production levels and prices in response to the past differences between supply and demand:

1) Coefficients ε and ε' express the impact of the difference between supply and demand as it is felt at the level of individual firms, by the observation of their own inventories, on firms' output and price decisions, respectively.

2) Coefficients ε_s and ε'_s express the impact of the difference between supply and demand at the industry level, on firms' price and output decisions, respectively. Present excess supply in the industry leads to the expectation that competitors will diminish their prices and that individual demand will be reduced. This expectation induces firms to diminish both their outputs and prices, even more than they would do on the basis of their individual observations (their own inventories).

4. Conclusions

Two main conclusions about adjustment behavior can be drawn:

1) For appropriate forms of the equations and values of the reaction coefficients, adjustment behavior is rational in frameworks in which demand is subject to variations.

2) This result does not necessarily follow from the existence of uncertainty, as in the case of the monopoly, but also from the mere variation of demand in a fully deterministic model, as in the case of monopolistic competition, from which we exclude uncertainty (which obviously could be added).

References

Blinder, A. S. (1982) "Inventories and Sticky Prices: More on the Micro-foundations of Macroeconomics," *American Economic Review* 72, 334-348.

Day, R. and Groves, T., Eds. (1975) *Adaptive Economic Models*, New York: Academic Press.

Duménil, G. and Lévy, D. (1989a) "Individual Adjustment to Disequilibrium and the Stability of Long-term Equilibrium," Paper presented at *Micromodels 1989*, Liblice, Czechoslovakia.

Duménil, G. and Lévy, D. (1989b) "Micro Adjustment Behavior and Macro Stability," *Seoul Journal of Economics* 2, 1-37.

Holt, C. C., Modigliani, F., Muth, J. F. and Simon, H. A. (1960) *Planning Production, Inventories and Work Force*, Englewood Cliffs, NJ: Prentice Hall.

Holt, C. C. and Simon, H. A. (1954) "Optimal Decision Rules for Production and Inventory Control," *Proceedings of the Conference on Operations Research in Production and Inventory Control*, in: Simon (1982), 137-180.

Kornai, J. (1980) *The Economics of Shortages*, Amsterdam: North Holland.

Kornai, J. and Martos, B. (1973) "Autonomous Control of the Economic System," *Econometrica* 41, 509-528.

——— , (1981) *Non-Price Control*, Amsterdam: North Holland.

Lovell, M. (1961) "Manufacturers' Inventories, Sales Expectations, and the Acceleration Principle," *Econometrica* 29, 293-314.

——— , (1962) "Buffer Stocks, Sales Expectations, and Stability: A Multisector Analysis of the Inventory Cycle," *Econometrica* 30, 267-296.

Malinvaud, E. (1982) "Théorie Macro-économique," in *Evolutions Conjoncturelles*, Tome 2, Paris: Dunod.

Marx, K. (1894) *Capital*, Vol. III, New York: First Vintage Book Edition, 1981.

Metzler, L. A. (1941) "The Nature and Stability of Inventory Cycles," *Review of Economic Statistics* 3, 113-129.

Ricardo, D. (1817) *The Principles of Political Economy and Taxation*, London: Dent and Son, 1960.

Samuelson, P. A. (1939) "Interactions between the Multiplier Analysis and the Principle of Acceleration," *Review of Economic Statistics* **21**, 75-78.

Simon, H. A., Ed. (1982) "Models of Bounded Rationality," in *Economic Analysis and Public Policy*, Vol. 1, Cambridge, MA: MIT Press.

Simonovits, A. (1985) "Dynamic Adjustment of Supply under Buyer's Forced Substitution," *Zeitschrift für Nationalökonomie, J. of Economics* **45**, 357-372.

Smith, A. (1776) *The Wealth of Nations*, London: Dent and Son, 1964.

Tobin, J. (1975) "Keynesian Models of Recession and Depression," *American Economic Review, Papers and Proceedings*, **65**, 195-202.

PART SIX

Strategies and General Equilibrium

20

Maximin vs. Nash Equilibrium: Theoretical Results and Empirical Evidence ·

Manfred J. Holler and *Viggo Høst*

1. Introduction

Von Neumann and Morgenstern (1944) introduced the maximin solution into the theory of games where "solution is plausibly a set of rules for each participant which tell him how to behave in every social situation which may conceivably arise" (p. 31). It is understood that "the rules of rational behavior must provide definitely for the possibility of irrational behavior on the part of the others" (p. 32). Accordingly, a solution contains "the statement of how much the participant under consideration can get if he behaves 'rationally.' This 'can get' is, of course, presumed to be minimum; he may get more if the others make mistakes" (p. 33). This contrasts with the widely-held view of contemporary game theory that "the solution of a noncooperative game has to be a Nash equilibrium" (van Damme, 1987, p. 3).

Needless to say, the two positions assume different qualities for the decision-makers: Nash equilibrium presupposes that all agents act rationally and are expected to act rationally while maximin allows for irrational behavior by fellow agents. As a consequence, the question of which of the

---

* The authors gratefully acknowledge the comments of Peter Skott on an earlier version of this paper

two concepts is the "right one" cannot be decided on theoretical grounds alone. In this paper, we present the results of an empirical study which, however, builds strongly on the theoretical properties of the two concepts and their relations to one another. More specifically, the empirical study makes use of the fact that for all 2×2 matrix games the payoff values of the mixed-strategy Nash equilibrium are equal to the maximin payoffs if the maximin solution implies mixed strategies. This is demonstrated in Section 2 of the paper. Section 3 presents empirical evidence that decision makers prefer the maximin solution in the case of mixed strategies. In order to test which of the two solutions gives an appropriate description of decision-making in corresponding strategic situations, a variable-sum market entry game has been presented to business and economics students at Aarhus University. The sample, which has been tested for homogeneity, provides significant evidence in favor of maximin. The concluding Section 4 hints at a theoretical justification for the use of the maximin criterion when there are mixed solutions.

2. A Class of Unprofitable Equilibria

In this section[1] we shall show that for all 2×2 matrix games, the payoff values of the mixed-strategy (Nash) equilibrium are equal to maximin payoffs if maximin implies completely mixed strategies. First, we define a 2×2 game, Γ, by the matrix in Table 1. In order to make sure that there

Table 1. Game Γ.

| | | Player 2 | |
		s_{21}	s_{22}
	s_{11}	(a, α)	(b, β)
Player 1			
	s_{12}	(c, γ)	(d, δ)

---

[1] See Holler (1987), (1988) and also related results in Wittman (1985).

exists an equilibrium in mixed strategies and that maximin implies mixed strategies, we assume

$$a > d > c > b \quad \text{and} \quad \beta > \gamma > \delta > \alpha. \tag{1}$$

As we will see from (4), (8), (10), and (11) below, the ordinal ranking in (1) is a sufficient, but not a necessary, condition for guaranteeing that both the Nash equilibrium and the maximin solution imply mixed strategies. Players 1 and 2 choose strategies s_{11} and s_{21} with probabilities p and q, respectively, Of course, $1 - p$ and $1 - q$ apply to s_{12} and s_{22}, respectively.

The (expected) payoff of Player 1 is

$$\begin{aligned} U_1(p,q) &= pqa + p(1-q)b + (1-p)qc + (1-p)(1-q)d \\ &= p[q(a-b-c+d) + b - d] + qc + (1-q)d. \end{aligned} \tag{2}$$

The standard first order condition for maximizing $U_1(p,q)$ is straightforward:

$$\frac{\partial U_1}{\partial p} = U_1' = q(a - b - c + d) + b - d = 0 \tag{3}$$

However, since U_1 is linear in p, U_1' does not depend on p and thus Player 1 cannot choose a mized strategy so that (3) is satisfied. There is, however, a value q^* so that (3) applies,

$$q^* = \frac{d-b}{a-b-c+d} \tag{4}$$

and the expected payoff of Player 1 is fixed at the level

$$U_1^* = q^*c + (1 - q^*)d = \frac{ad - bc}{a - b - c + d} \tag{5}$$

The following result is immediate:

Result A. *If Player 2 chooses strategy q^*, then any strategy p is a best reply.*

Analogously, we can derive from $U_2(p,q)$ and its partial derivative $\partial U_2/\partial q = U_2'$ a strategy p^* for Player 1 so that $U_2' = 0$ and $U_2(p^*) = U_2^*$ is independent of q, i.e., the strategy of the second player. Thus we have

Result B. *If Player 1 chooses strategy* p^*, *then any* q *is a best reply.*

Results A and B imply that (p^*, q^*) is a Nash equilibrium: p^* is a specific best reply to q^* and q^* is a specific best reply to p^*. Next, we shall show that the equilibrium values, U_1^* and U_2^* are identical to the corresponding maximin values, $\hat{U}_1$ and $\hat{U}_2$, if both imply mixed strategies. We demonstrate this for $U_1^* = \hat{U}_1$, but it also applies to $U_2^* = \hat{U}_2$. We rearrange (2) so that

$$U_1(p,q) = q\left[pa - pb + (1-p)c - (1-p)d\right] + pb + (1-p)d. \qquad (6)$$

If Player 1 chooses p so that

$$pa - pb + (1-p)c - (1-p)d = 0, \qquad (7)$$

that is to say, so that

$$\hat{p} = \frac{d-c}{a-b-c+d} \qquad (8)$$

then $U_1(p,q)$ is independent of q and thus of the decision of Player 2 and thus satisfies maximin.

From (6), (7) and (8), the maximin value of Player 1 can be derived as

$$\hat{U}_1 = \hat{p}b + (1-\hat{p})d = \frac{ad-bc}{a-b-c+d} \qquad (9)$$

Comparing (5) and (9) (and the analogous equations for Player 2), we obtain

Result C. *The values of mixed strategy equilibrium are identical with the values of the maximin solution if the strategies of the latter are mixed strategies as well.*

Result C implies that the equilibrium is (*uniformly*) *unprofitable*, since equilibrium payoffs are equal to maximin payoffs for both players.[2]

Corresponding results can be obtained for U_2. We obtain

(a) the equilibrium strategy given by

$$p^* = \frac{\delta-\gamma}{\alpha-\beta-\gamma+\delta} \qquad (10)$$

---

[2] For the definition, see Harsanyi (1977), p. 106.

(b) the maximin strategy

$$\hat{q} = \frac{\delta - \beta}{\alpha - \beta - \gamma + \delta} \tag{11}$$

(c) and the identity of the equilibrium value, U_2^*, and of the maximin value, $\hat{U}_2$, so that

$$U_2^* = \hat{U}_2 = \frac{\alpha\delta - \beta\gamma}{\alpha - \beta - \gamma + \delta} \tag{12}$$

From a comparison of (8) and (10) or (4) and (11) we obtain

Result D. *Equilibrium strategies generally prescribe different behavior from maximin strategies if both are mixed.*

While the equilibrium strategy of Player i, p_i^*, is calculated with respect to the payoffs of Player j, the maximin strategy, $\hat{p}_i$, is derived from i's payoff values, and only accidentally will p_i^* be equal to $\hat{p}_i$ results. In general, the maximin strategy of Player i does not imply a best reply to the maximin strategy of Player j. Player i may achieve a higher payoff than $\hat{U}_i$ if he chooses a best reply to the maximin strategy of Player j. However, by doing this, Player i generally risks receiving a lower payoff than $\hat{U}_i$ if Player j does not play his maximin strategy $\hat{p}_j$. By definition, Player i has to select his maximin strategy if he wants to guarantee himself $\hat{U}_i$. If he plays his equilibrium strategy p_i^*, a value $U_i < U_i^* = \hat{U}_i$ may result if Player j does not choose the corresponding p_j^* equilibrium strategy.

3. The Case Study

Result D makes it possible to test whether decision-makers follow maximin strategies or whether they choose equilibrium strategies. More specifically, we have tested the following hypothesis for the hypothetical strategic decision problem described above:

The Maximin Hypothesis (MH). *In 2 × 2 games players choose maximin strategies instead of equilibrium strategies if maximin and equilibrium strategies are both mixed.*

The Equilibrium Hypothesis (EH). *In 2×2 games players choose equilibrium strategies instead of maximin strategies if maximin and equilibrium strategies are both mixed.*

Due to the theoretical results of Section 2, we know that the decisions of the agents will not be biased by different payoff expectations implied in

MH and **EH**. However, the unprofitability property described in Result C requires mixed strategies, and mixed strategies cause problems for the testing of the two hypotheses. An important assumption of the following test is that, given a homogeneous sample of respondents, each response can be interpreted as a draw from repeated choices of a single respondent within a stationary decision setting. Note in particular that this stationarity assumption excludes learning or hedging against uncertainty.

In other words, it is assumed that if m respondents out of n choose the (pure) stragey s_k instead of s_h, then the ratio m/n is an estimator of the probability that an individual respondent will choose s_k when facing the decision problem. This "equivalence property" is applied in the following, but its application presupposes a homogeneous sample of respondents. Consequently, the test of homogeneity is a major concern of our analysis.

Given the game Γ in Table 1, and a homogeneous sample of respondents acting as Player 1, the statistical hypotheses are as follows:

$$
\begin{aligned}
H_0 &= (\textbf{EH}): \quad p = p^* = \frac{\delta - \gamma}{\alpha - \beta - \gamma + \delta} \\
H_1 &= (\textbf{MH}): \quad p = \hat{p} = \frac{d - c}{a - b - c + d}
\end{aligned}
\tag{13}
$$

The test is a simple binomial test, and the test statistic is the number of respondents choosing strategy s_{11}. If the respondents are not homogeneous, then the sample has to be divided into homogeneous subsamples and it is then possible to test the two hypotheses for each subsample.

We submitted the questionnaire (see Appendix) to 202 students of Economics and Business Administration at the University of Aarhus and asked them to indicate a choice between the two pure strategies s_{11} (not to enter the market) and s_{12} (to enter the market). The total sample consists of two subsamples; 129 first-year students of Economics and Business Administration and 73 third or fourth-year students of Business Administration.

According to the figures of the payoff matrix in the Appendix, the hypotheses (13) are the following:

$$
\begin{aligned}
H_0 &= (\textbf{EH}): \quad p = 5/12 \\
H_1 &= (\textbf{MH}): \quad p = 1/5.
\end{aligned}
\tag{14}
$$

In order to control for homogeneity, we asked the students to answer eight questions on demographic and socio-economic issues. These eight questions listed in the Appendix represent in our view the most likely factors influencing strategic behavior. The sample will be assumed to be homogeneous if the respondents' choices of pure strategies are independent of the answers to these questions. As we expected, variable 1 (year of entrance to the University) and variable 2 (age) were strongly negatively correlated and variable 6 (work) and variable 7 (income) were stronly positively correlated. Consequently, only one variable from each correlated pair was allowed to enter the model. Thus, the data include one response variable and seven possible predictor variables. We define the response variable Y as

$$Y = \begin{cases} 1 & \text{if respondent chooses } s_{11}, \\ 0 & \text{if respondent chooses } s_{12}. \end{cases}$$

We have chosen to describe the possible relation between the response variable Y and all (or a subset of the) seven predictor variables by means of the logit model.[3] We then have

$$P_i = \Pr\{Y_i = 1\} = \frac{1}{1 + \exp(-\beta_0 - \beta_1 x_{i1} - \cdots - \beta_7 x_{i7})} \qquad i = 1, \ldots, 202$$

$$(15)$$

where P_i is the probability that the ith respondent chooses strategy s_{11}, β_0 is the constant term, β_j is the jth regression parameter, and x_{ij} is the jth predictor variable for the ith respondent.

Separate models using a maximum of six predictor variables for each of the two subgroups of students were also analyzed. The procedure PROC LOGIST in the computer package SAS was used to estimate the models and test the significance of the predictor variables. The results are extremely clear: none of the variables, whether analyzed in isolation or combined with others, was found to have any statistical influence on the response variables. The lowest prob-value of any regression coefficient among all the estimated models was 0.15. This number was found for variable 3 (sex) in the subgroup of first-year students. All other prob-values in models with either one or more predictor variables were larger.

The prob-values of the likelihood ratio tests for testing that all regression parameters are equal to zero (except for the constant term) in the two subsamples and the total sample are 0.78, 0.86, and 0.65, respectively,

---

[3] Since the logistic regression model has far fewer assumptions than the linear discriminant model (for example, no assumption of multivariate normality for the covariates), logistic regression is preferred to discriminant analysis (Press and Wilson, 1978).

Table 2. Response Frequencies.

Pure Strategy	First Year Students	Third/Fourth Year Students	Total Sample
s_{11}	22	18	40
s_{12}	107	55	162
Total	129	73	202

and the predictor variables then have no statistical influence on the response variable. In order to examine whether the two subsamples can be combined, we consider the 2 × 2 frequency table in Table 2.

Testing for the homogeneity of the two subsamples gives a prob-value of $P \simeq 0.20$. These tests clearly indicate that the respondents behave as if they were a homogeneous group with reespect to the decision problem. Thus it is possible to test the hypothesis (14) using a binomial test.

Assuming that the total sample represents 202 drawings from a Bernoulli population, the estimate $\bar{p} = 0.198$ of the probability p suggests that the respondents behave like an individual player who applies the mixed maximin strategy $\hat{p} = 1/5 = 0.20$, and not the equilibrium strategy $p^* = 5/12 = 0.412$. Indeed, further calculations are unnecessary. But as an illustration of the strength of the conclusion, the prob-value of testing $H_0 : p^* = 5/12$ against $H_1 : p = 1/5$ is found to be less than 10^{-9} and the prob-value of testing H_1 against H_0 is equal to 0.56.

Table 3. Probabilities of Type I and Type II Errors.

α	β
0.01	< 0.000001
0.001	$\simeq$ 0.00005
0.0001	$\simeq$ 0.0007

Risks of type I and type II errors (α and β values belonging together) are given in Table 3 and the probabilities of both types of errors are clearly negligible.

4. Conclusion

The theoretical and empirical results of our analysis challenge the view that the Nash equilibrium is the one and only adequate solution of a non-cooperative game. In the case of a mixed-strategy equilibrium, deviation does not hurt the deviating player and thus there is no incentive for a player to follow the Nash strategy. This applies to all mixed-strategy equilibria: they are weak and, in general, unstable (Harsanyi, 1977, pp. 124-127), and thus, as stated by Shubik (1985, p. 251) they "may be only of peripheral interest." The fact that they are nonprofitable in 2×2 matrix games, if maximin is mixed, may add to the lack of incentive implied by weakness and render equilibrium behavior even more unlikely than does the missing penalty for unilateral deviation.

Given the lack of incentives in unprofitable equilibria, it seems plausible to assume that "players will exercise prudence when it is costless to do so" (Pearce, 1984, p. 1031) and choose maximin strategies. Thus, the concept of cautiously rationalizable strategies, introduced in Pearce (1984), supports our empirical findings.

Appendix: Questionnaire

There are two potential suppliers 1 and 2 and a new market for water beds. The suppliers have two alternatives:
1. To enter the market for water beds.
2. To continue traditional business and *not enter* the market for water beds.

Assume that the traditional market as well as the profits of the two suppliers will change if one or both of the suppliers enter the new market.

Both the strategic alternatives of suppliers and the economic consequences are summarized in the following matrix. The profits are measured in units of 10,000 Danish kroner.

The combination (4,1) tells us, for example, that Supplier 1 gets 40,000 kroner and Supplier 2 10,000 kroner if both suppliers enter the new market.

Table A-1. The Profit Matrix

		Supplier 2	
		not enter	enter
Supplier 1	not enter	(8,0)	(0,7)
	enter	(2,6)	(4,1)

Assume that you are Supplier 1. What alternative will you choose?

Enter the market   ○   Not enter the market   ○

Note that there is no *logical* correct answer to the decision problem. We just want to know which alternative you prefer. In order to analyze the material, we also need the following information from you.

1. In which year did you start at University?
2. How old are you (years)?
3. Sex (M/F)?
4. Social status of parents:
   a) Academics, higher-ranking employees, managers;
   b) Self-employed in urban industry;
   c) Self-employed farmers;
   d) Skilled workers and lower-ranking employees;
   e) Unskilled workers and non-employed.
5. Where did you spend the longest period of your life?
   a) In a city with more than 1,000,000 inhabitants;
   b) In a city with 100,000–1,000,000 inhabitants;
   c) In a town with 10,000–100,000 inhabitants;
   d) In a town with less than 10,000 inhabitants?
6. How many hours of paid work do you have per month?
7. What is your disposable income (including loans) per month?
8. Did you ever sleep in a water bed ? (Yes/No)

References

van Damme, E. (1987) *Stability and Perfection of Nash Equilibria*, Berlin: Springer.

Harsanyi, J. C. (1977) *Rational Behavior and Bargaining Equilibrium in Games and Social Situations*, Cambridge: Cambridge University Press.

Holler, M. J. (1987) "The Maximin of Mixed Strategies in Two-Person Games," Memo No. 1987-36, Institute of Economics, University of Aarhus.

Holler, M. J. (1988) "Strategic Social Choice and Mixed-Strategy Equilibria," Memo No. 1988-9, Institute of Economics, University of Aarhus.

von Neumann, J. and Morgenstern, O. (1944) *Theory of Games and Economic Behavior*, Princeton: Princeton University Press.

Pearce, D. G. (1984) "Rationalizable Strategic Behavior and the Problem of Perfection," *Econometrica* 52, 1029-1050.

Press, S. J. and Wilson, S. (1978) "Choosing Between Logistic Regression and Discriminant Analysis," *Journal of the American Statistical Association* 73, 699-705.

SAS Institute Inc. (1986) *SUGI Supplemental Library User's Guide*, Version 5, Cary NC: SAS Institute Inc., 269-293.

Shubik, M. (1985) *Game Theory in the Social Sciences: Concepts and Solutions*, Cambridge, MIT Press.

Wittman, D. (1985) "Counter-Intuitive Results in Game Theory," *European Journal of Political Economy* 1, 77-89.

21

The Valuation of Economic
Information ·

Nicholas M. Kiefer

1. Introduction

Information collecting and processing are ongoing activities in a modern economy. Firms estimate demand and costs when planning production, marketing managers estimate the effectiveness of marketing strategies, consumers estimate the quality of a potential purchase (or even estimate their preferences), farmers estimate prices in allocating acreage. In a planned distribution network, planners must forecast local needs, available supplies and availability of distribution channels. Information is typically costly; some sacrifice of current reward is required to obtain information. The information obtained may turn out to be useful, in that it is relevant for future decisions, or it may not. Thus, investment in information is much like investment in a risky asset. How much information should an economic agent accumulate?

Particular realizations of this decision problem have been studied in the extensive statistical literature on the bandit problem (see Berry and Fristedt, 1985) and in the economics literature on control of stochastic processes with unknown parameters (see Kiefer, 1989). In the bandit problem agents choose among discretely many actions, each of which yields infor-

---

* I am grateful to the National Science Foundation and IREX for support, and thank Ken Burdett, Bent Jesper Christensen and Richard Quandt for useful comments.

mation on a specific project. The problem gets its name from the physical realization in the form of a slot machine with many levers ("arms"), each having unknown payoff probabilities. Playing an arm generates information about that arm; that information may be useful in deciding which arm to play next. Recent work in economics has considered continuous action spaces, rather than a discrete set of arms. Consider, for example, the case of a monopolist producing to meet stochastic demand with unknown mean function. By varying output the monopolist can accumulate observations, which will help to estimate the mean demand function. The monopolist's problem has been studied by Aghion, Bolton and Julien (1987), Kiefer (1989) and McLennan (1984). The case of oligopoly introduces strategic considerations in information collection and revelation—see Mirman and Urbano (1988) for a simple model. Strategic considerations also arise in a planning setting, as in Stefanski and Pilarska (1990).

Results on asymptotic learning of unknown parameters are available in both literatures. In many models a martingale convergence argument can be used to establish that beliefs about unknown parameters converge to a limit. Thus, information is accumulated and uncertainty reduced until there is no reason to collect additional information. A key question addressed in these models is whether beliefs converge to certainty. Results on this question in the general case are given by Easley and Kiefer (1988). The controlled linear model is studied by Kiefer and Nyarko (1989); these papers cite many additional references to the literature.

Most of the available literature focuses on the asymptotic behavior of the sequences of beliefs about unknown aspects of the economy. Particular features of the demand for information are not studied, in part because the models set up are too general for specific results on these demand functions to be obtained, and in part because of the emphasis on the important question of "convergence to rational expectations"—do optimizing agents learn all that can be learned? A notable exception to this tendency is the literature on testing in a labor market, for example, Burdett and Mortensen (1983). In this literature tests are available at some cost. These tests measure a worker's ability on some task, providing information to the worker as well as to potential employers. The worker's willingness to pay for a test depends on his prior assessment of his abilities. Another exception is Grossman, Kihlstrom and Mirman (1977), who establish that consumption of a good increases when quality information is proportional to quantity and repeat purchases are possible.

In this paper the demand for information is studied in a simple, two-period parametric model. Information collected in the first period may lead to improved allocations and, hence, higher utility in the second period.

However, information is costly, and period one consumption must be reduced to finance the investment in information. Thus, we abstract for the present from long-run considerations and dynamics, but we are able to analyze the investment decision closely. Since we study a particular parametrization, and even here there remain open questions, our results at this point are merely suggestive. However, we have shown that it is feasible to set up a model in which investment in information is an ongoing activity, governed by the same economic rules as investment in any other risky asset.

2. The Stochastic Utility Model

We consider a model in which nature chooses the state of the world and then allows an agent to purchase information correlated with the state before making his allocations.

The Final-Period Problem

The single-period, state-dependent objective function for the agent is given by $r(x, y, \theta)$, where x and y are quantities of goods and θ indexes the "state of the economy". We will suppose that there are two possible states of the economy, one in which reward is solely obtained from x and the other in which reward is solely obtained from y. The state of the economy is realized anew, independently, each period with equal probabilities (1/2) attached to each state. The marginal probability 1/2 is common knowledge—agents may use different probabilities because they obtain stochastic "inside" information about θ after nature makes the draw. With this assumption we can write the reward function as

$$r(x, y, \theta) = \theta u(x) + (1 - \theta)v(y), \qquad \theta \in \{0, 1\}.$$

The functions $u(.)$ and $v(.)$ have interpretations as utility or profit functions. We will say more about their properties later. The agent does not know θ, but he has beliefs $\mu = \text{Prob}(\theta = 1)$, which may be different from 1/2 based perhaps on information purchased directly, or on an economic model. With these beliefs, the agent can calculate expected reward

$$Er(x,y,\theta) = R(x,y,\mu) = \mu u(x) + (1-\mu)v(y), \qquad \mu \in [0,1],$$

a nonstochastic function which can be maximized with respect to x and y.

Suppose that the agent has available an endowment of m dollars to allocate between x and y. Later we will consider the possibility of investment in another good: information. For the present we concentrate on the second-period allocation decision given beliefs μ. Since the second period is the last and current investment in information has no current payoff, there will be no investment in information in the second period. Suppose that the price of x is p and the price of y is 1. The relevant budget constraint is $m = px + y$.

To simplify the problem, suppose that $u(\ )$ and $v(\ )$ are the same functions, so that the agent does not have preferences about the state of the world—except those induced by the price differential between x and y. Further, suppose that these functions are

$$u(x) = \log x, \qquad v(y) = \log y.$$

A routine constrained maximization gives the demand functions

$$x = \mu m/p, \qquad y = (1-\mu)m.$$

Substitution yields maximized expected utility as a function of beliefs

$$V(\mu) = \mu\log(\mu m/p) + (1-\mu)\log((1-\mu)m).$$

With this function in hand we can turn to the two-period problem and consider the question of information.

Information

For the present we can be reasonably general about our notion of information, keeping in mind, however, that the term is used in the standard economic sense of "evidence" or "data", not in a precise engineering sense. The important thing is the updating of beliefs in period one, about the state in period two —these beliefs are given by the marginal probability that $\mu = 1/2$ before any information is processed—to beliefs in period two, μ^*, a conditional probability. Note that beliefs about next period's state do not depend on beliefs about the current state. Let i be the amount of information purchased. One way to think about i is that an investment in information yields a draw from a probability distribution, which depends on the unknown state of the world θ. Larger values of i yield more draws, or perhaps a draw from a more tightly concentrated distribution. The transition equation for beliefs is

$$\mu^* = b(i, \epsilon),$$

where ϵ is the stochastic observation whose distribution depends on i and the state of the economy and $b(\quad)$ is Bayes' Rule. Letting $f_1(\epsilon|i)$ be the density of ϵ when $\theta = 1$ and investment in information is i, and $f_2(\epsilon|i)$ be the density when $\theta = 0$, we can give more detail about the function $b(\quad)$:

$$\mu^* = b(i, \epsilon) = 0.5 \, f_1/(0.5 \, f_1 + 0.5 \, f_2) = f_1/(f_1 + f_2),$$

where the arguments of f_1 and f_2 have been dropped to reduce clutter. The denominator is the predictive distribution of ϵ, which immediately implies that $E\mu^* = 0.5$; the agent expects to have the same beliefs next period as he does this period. The marginal effect of information, $\partial b/\partial i = b_i$ will be important below. Clearly, $Eb_i = 0$.

The Two-Period Problem

The optimization problem facing our agent in the first period is

$$\max \{\mu \log x + (1 - \mu)\log y + EV(\mu^*)\},$$

with respect to x, y and i, subject to

$$m = px + y + ci, \qquad \mu^* = b(i, \epsilon),$$

and $x, y, i > 0$.

This budget constraint does not allow saving for or borrowing from the future in the first period. Thus, the only connection between periods is that investment in information in period one yields returns in period two. Without this possibility the problem would be only a sequence of two independent one-period problems. This setup is chosen so that it is possible to focus on the role of information. Let λ be the multiplier associated with the budget constraint, substitute in the transition equation for beliefs, and assume an interior solution, so that the inequality constraints do not have to be imposed formally. Then the first-order conditions are

$$\mu/x - \lambda p = 0,$$
$$(1 - \mu)/y - \lambda = 0,$$
$$EV'b_i - \lambda c = 0,$$
$$px + y + ci = m.$$

Since c, the price of a unit of information, is positive and λ is the marginal utility of wealth, also positive, $EV'b_i > 0$ at the optimum. Note that the third equation depends only on i and not on the allocations x and y. Since $Eb_i = 0$, the condition implies that the correlation between the marginal effect of information on beliefs and the marginal effect of beliefs on expected utility is positive.

Upon some manipulation—exploiting the separability of utility in x, y and i—we obtain an expression characterizing the optimal value of i:

$$EV'b_i = c/(m - ci).$$

Note that this expression implies that the demand for information about next period's state does not depend on how confident one is about the current period state. This is a result of our utility specification, which implies that the income elasticities are unity. In general, confidence in current period assessments of the state could be expected to shift consumption toward the present. The only way to do that in this model is to reduce the investment in information.

Upon differentiating the expression for $V(\mu)$ given above and simplifying, we obtain

$$V'(\mu) = V' = \log(m\mu/p) - \log(m(1 - \mu)).$$

Collecting terms, we get

$$V'(\mu) = \log(\mu/(1 - \mu)) - \log p.$$

Since $Eb_i = 0$,

$$EV'b_i = E\log(\mu/(1 - \mu))b_i,$$

making the correlation between next period's log odds and the effect of new information on next period's probability positive. The sign of the effect of information on the log odds is the same as that of the effect on the probability, so the correlation between next period's probability and the effect of information on that probability is also positive.

In order to derive the demand curve for information we need to study the function

$$\Psi(i) = E \log \left(\mu/(1-\mu) \right) b_i.$$

Note that this is a purely technical relationship which needs to be analyzed; $\Psi(i)$ involves no economic considerations and no assumptions on behavior. This function is exogenous, rather like the usual idea of a production relationship, not endogenous like a demand relationship. To make some headway in understanding $\Psi(i)$ we will need to be more specific about the way in which information is generated and processed.

Information (Again)

The specific shape of the technical relationship $\Psi(i)$ will depend on the assumptions about the densities f_1 and f_2 and their dependence on information i. We assume that the density f_1 is normal with mean 1 and the density f_2 is normal with mean 0. Both densities have precision i. A purchase of i units of "information" is a purchase of a draw from a normal distribution with a mean θ and precision i (variance $1/i$). After purchasing the draw, we calculate the posterior probabilities of the state, and the allocation between x and y is made. The posterior probability that $\theta = 1$, conditional on z being observed, comes from

$$\mu^* = f_1/(f_1 + f_2).$$

With our normal distributions the log odds take a simple form,

$$\log \left(\mu^*/(1-\mu^*) \right) = i(z - 0.5).$$

Clearly, the expectation of μ^* taken against the predictive distribution $(f_1 + f_2)/2$ is equal to 0.5. The derivative is

$$\partial \mu^*/\partial i = (f_1' f_2 - f_1 f_2')/D^2,$$

where

$$f_1' = -(0.5)(z-1)^2 f_1,$$
$$f_2' = -(0.5)z^2 f_2,$$
$$f_1 = \exp\{-(0.5)(z-1)^2 i\},$$
$$f_2 = \exp\{-(0.5)z^2 i\},$$

and $D = f_1 + f_2$. The terms $i^{1/2}/(2\pi)^{1/2}$ have been cancelled.

The function $\Psi(i) = E\log(\mu^*/(1-\mu^*))\,\partial\mu^*/\partial i$ is not analytically tractable, but it is relatively simple to evaluate numerically. For each i in a grid of 50 values from .2 to 10 the expectation is evaluated by 16-point Gaussian quadrature. In each case the integration is performed over the range $-3i^{-1/2}$ to $1+3i^{-1/2}$. The resulting function is plotted in Figure 1. This figure shows a graph that resembles a negative exponential. With this in mind we consider approximating $\Psi(i)$ by a negative exponential. A regression of $\log\Psi(i)$ on a constant and i yields

$$\log\Psi(i) = -0.931 - 0.254i + e$$
$$(0.019)\quad(0.003)$$

with $R^2 = 0.991$, MSE $= 0.004$.

Figure 1: $E\log(\mu/(1-\mu))\,d\mu/di$

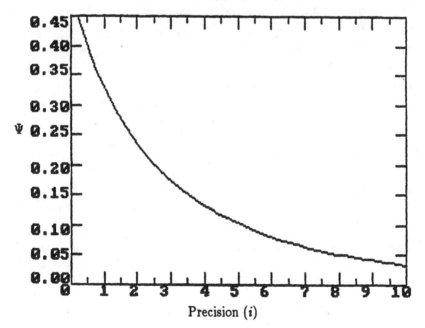

Precision (i)

with 50 "observations". Standard errors are in parentheses. While it would be inappropriate to assume normality of the errors and read much into the standard errors, it is nevertheless true that the regression explains all but about 0.9% of the variance in $\log \Psi$.

A Demand Function for Information

Recall the first-order condition determining the demand for i,

$$c/(m - ci) = EV'b_i = \Psi(i).$$

On substituting $\Psi(i) = \beta_0 \exp\{-\beta_1 i\}$, taking logarithms and rearranging, we have

$$\log(c/\beta_0) + \beta_1 i = \log(m - ci)$$
$$= \log(1 - ci/m) + \log m$$
$$\approx -ci/m + \log m,$$

using a first-order approximation to the log. This is a good approximation if ci/m is near 0—note that this is the budget share allocated to information collection. Solving, we get the messy expression

$$i(m, p, c) = (\log(m/c) + \log \beta_0)/(\beta_1 + c/m).$$

This function is increasing in m and decreasing in c, as expected.

It is useful to plot the demand function for information as an aid to intuition. The approximation is most appropriate when ci/m is near zero. We take $m = 1.0$ and $p = 1.5$. Note that when c is very small, i is likely to be large, so controling ci/m will take some care. We begin with $c = 1/2$ and vary c around that value to calculate the demand function. For the values we choose, the error in the linear approximation to the logarithm varies around the value .0045 – a little over 10%.

Figure 2 plots the demand for precision, i, of information about the next period's state as a function of the price of precision, c. The demand function is downward sloping and appears to be convex. The fitting of a negative exponential (regressing $\log(i)$ on c) yields an R^2 of .992. That simple functional form is, thus, a good approximation to the demand function for fixed income. The budget share allocated to information does vary with income. It is decreasing. Thus, although the allocation of $m - ci$ between

Figure 2: Demand for Precision

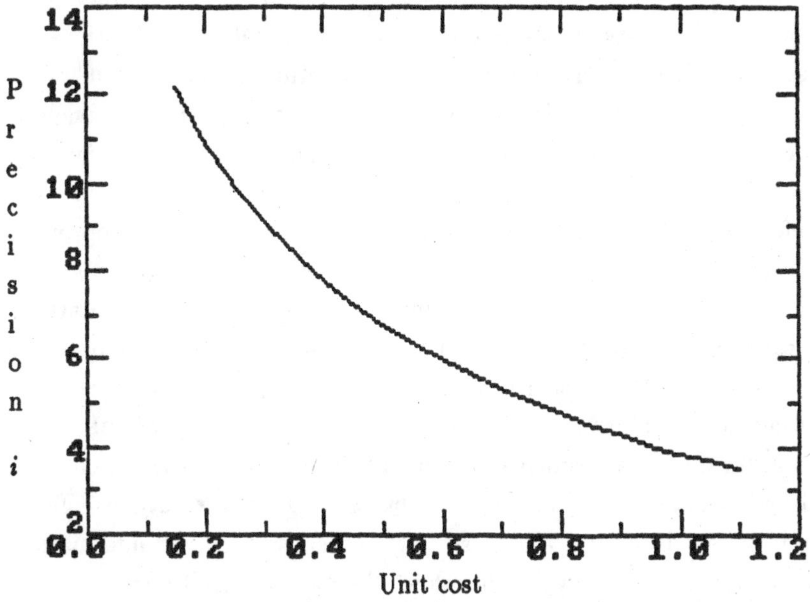

x and y is done according to constant budget shares, the "first-stage" allocation of m between i and commodities is not. The Engel curve for information, a plot of information versus income, appears very slightly concave (this plot is not shown).

3. Conclusion

The model of Section 2 exhibits a "demand for costly information" function determined jointly with demands for current consumption goods. Information is separable from other goods in determining first-period allocations; thus, a two-stage budgeting procedure is optimal. First, allocate resources between current consumption and information; then, allocate among current consumption goods. This feature of the model follows from intertemporal separability and not from other simplifying assumptions. On the other hand, the complicated transition equation for processing information, Bayes' Rule, leads to a complicated calculation for the demand for information, even when the reward functions are extremely simple. We found that the demand function was downward sloping, as expected, and the Engel curve was upward sloping. The budget share allocated to information was decreasing in income (this probably depends on the particular specification chosen). It would be a useful exercise for developing insight to extend the model of Section 2 to accommodate alternative utility specifications, and to extend the time horizon so as to obtain implications for the stochastic process of consumption and investment over time. It would also be worthwhile to consider distributions other than normals, though in that case, the problem of quantifying the concept of information is more difficult.

Information is a remarkable good, which yields utility by improving allocations. Agents with higher expenditures purchase more of all goods, including information, and therefore, make better future-period allocations than other agents. Agents with fewer resources will make worse allocations (in an expected value sense) than those with more, simply as a result of investing in less information. Unlike consumption goods, information is not consumed by use; two agents, each having bought an observation with precision i, can each obtain precision $2i$ by exchanging observations . Thus, there is a clear incentive, absent strategic considerations, for information to be disseminated widely. Although at the partial equilibrium level the demand for information can be analyzed like the demand for other goods, the market for information is likely to exhibit unusual characteristics and the role of information in determining equilibrium is substantial. Results on equilibrium are given by Allen (1984), who emphasizes the role of prices in conveying information, and by Feldman (1987), who explicitly incorporates the dynamics of learning.

References

Aghion, P., Bolton, P. and Julien, B. (1987) "Learning Through Price Experimentation by a Monopolist Facing Unknown Demand," Working Paper, Univ. of California, Berkeley.

Allen, B. (1984) "Equilibria in Which Prices Convey Information: The Finite Case," in M. Boyer and R. Kihlstrom (Eds.) *Bayesian Models in Economic Theory*, Amsterdam: Elsevier Science Publishers.

Berry, D. A. and Fristedt, B. (1985) *Bandit Problems: Sequential Allocation of Experiments*, London: Chapman and Hall.

Burdett, K. and Mortensen, D. T. (1981) "Testing for Ability in a Competitive Labor Market," *Journal of Economic Theory* **25**, 42-66.

Easley, D. and Kiefer, N. M. (1988) "Controlling a Stochastic Process with Unknown Parameters," *Econometrica* **56**, 1045-1064.

Feldman, M. (1987) "An Example of Convergence to Rational Expectations with Heterogeneous Beliefs," *International Economic Review* **28**, 635-650.

Grossman, S. J., Kihlstrom, R. E. and Mirman, L. J. (1977) "A Bayesian Approach to the Production of Information and Learning by Doing," *Review of Economic Studies* **44**, 533-547.

Kiefer, N. M. (1989) "Optimal Collection of Information by Partially Informed Agents," *Econometric Reviews* **7**, 113-148.

Kiefer, N. M and Nyarko, Y. (1989) "Optimal Control of an Unknown Linear Process with Learning," to appear in *International Economic Review*.

McLennan, A. (1984) "Price Dispersion and Incomplete Learning in the Long Run," *Journal of Economic Dynamics and Control* **7**, 331-347.

Mirman, L. J. and Urbano, A. (1988) "Asymmetric Information and Endogenous Signalling: The Case of Unknown Intercept and Random Output," *Journal of Economic Theory* **25**, 42-66.

Stefanski, J. and Pilarska, M. (1990) "The Enterprise and the Economic Center: Control and Cooperation," in this volume.

22

Equilibrium with Nonstandard Prices in Exchange Economies

Valeri Marakulin

1. Introduction

In this paper we study some models of economic equilibrium. We propose an approach based on the application of the techniques and methods of nonstandard analysis to economic equilibrium models. The main idea is the introduction and study of the properties of equilibria with "nonstandard prices," but standard consumption plans for economic agents. For this purpose, a method for estimating the cost of an agent's consumption plan is introduced into the model, which is finer than the traditional one and allows a more exact evaluation of economic states. This makes it possible to prove the existence of equilibria without Slater's condition or any of its analogues that are necessary for proving the existence of the usual equilibria. Detailed considerations of these results and other problems that appear in economic models with nonstandard prices are discussed in Marakulin (1988).

Nonstandard methods were applied for the first time in mathematical economics by Brown and Robinson (1975). In that paper, the set of economic agents is identified with the initial segment $\{1, 2, \ldots, n\}$ of nonstandard natural numbers, where n is an infinite integer. They proved Edgeworth's conjecture about the coincidence of the core of the economy and the set of Walrasian equilibria in the limit. These ideas have subsequently been developed by others (see Rashid, 1987). However, the technique of nonstandard analysis does not appear to have been applied to the investigation of economic equilibrium.

At present, there are three conceptions of nonstandard analysis: classical, nonclassical and radical. We follow the classical notation of Robinson found in Davis (1977). Methods of nonstandard analysis are based on including the "standard universum of mathematical reasoning" $\mathcal{U}$ in the "nonstandard universum" $^*\mathcal{U}$ which contains both infinitesimals and infinite objects.

The transfer principle is a meaningful concept of nonstandard analysis and establishes the connection between standard and nonstandard mathematics. This principle is as follows: any sentence (formula) will be true in standard mathematics if and only if it is true in nonstandard mathematics. The mapping, which adjoins standard objects to nonstandard ones, could be understood as a replenishment or expansion of standard sets. In this fashion, the mappings of standard sets would be interpreted as expansion mappings of nonstandard sets. In particular, $\Re$ is included in its own expansion $^*\Re$, which contain nonzero infinitesimals and infinite numbers, while retaining all the formal properties of $\Re$. For example, the number $\alpha \in {}^*\Re$ is said to be infinitesimal if $|\alpha| < |r|$ for all $r \in \Re$, $r \neq 0$. The relationship $p \approx q$ is equal to the infinitesimal $p - q$. The set of all numbers that are infinitesimally equal to p is known as a monad and denoted by $\mu(p)$. A nonstandard vector $p = (p_1, p_2, \ldots, p_\ell)$ is a vector with nonstandard components.

2. The Models

The following formal model of an exchange economy is studied:

$$\mathcal{E}_0 = \langle N, \{X_i, \mathcal{P}_i\}_{i \in N}, w \rangle.$$

Here $N = \{1, 2, \ldots, n\}$ is a set of economic agents, $X_i \subset \Re^\ell$ is the ith agent's consumption set, $w \in \sum_N X_i$ is the initial endowment of the economy and ℓ is the number of products. Agent i's preferences are described by a point–to–set mapping

$$\mathcal{P}_i \colon \prod_N X_i \to 2^{X_i},$$

where the set $\mathcal{P}_i(x) \subset X_i$ is the collection of all product bundles strictly preferred to the bundle x_i by the ith agent in the state $x = (x_1, x_2, \ldots, x_n)$. The symbol $\mathcal{P}_i(x|x_i)$ denotes the set $\mathcal{P}_i(x)$ where the ith component of vector x is equal to the ith agent's consumption plan x_i.

The dual description of Pareto's states will be based on nonstandard prices. States of the economy that allow such a description are called equilibria by Pareto. From this point of view, the following theorem may be called the theorem on the coincidence of Pareto-optimal states and nonstandard Pareto-equilibria. Let $X = \prod_N X_i$ and

$$E(M, w) = \left\{ x \in (\Re^\ell)^M \mid \sum_M x_i = w \right\}, \tag{1}$$

where $M \subset N$, $M \neq \emptyset$ and $w \in \Re^\ell$.

Definition 1. *A state $x \in X$ is said to be Pareto-optimal if $x \in E(N, w)$ and*

$$\prod_M \mathcal{P}_i(x) \cap E(M, x_M) = \emptyset \tag{2}$$

for all $M \subseteq N$, $M \neq \emptyset$, where $x_M = \sum_M x_i$.

The set of states that satisfy Definition 1 is called the Pareto-boundary. Note that this unusual definition of the Pareto-optimality of states is employed in order to allow for the possibility of satiation in agents' preferences, that is, to allow for the possibility that $\mathcal{P}_i(x) = \emptyset$ for some agents.

Theorem 1. *Let the following conditions hold for all $i \in N$: $\mathcal{P}_i$ are convex, $x_i \notin \mathcal{P}_i(x|x_i)$, and for all $\lambda \in (0,1)$ if $y \in \mathcal{P}_i(x|x_i)$, then*

$$\lambda y + (1 - \lambda)x_i \in \mathcal{P}_i(x|x_i). \tag{3}$$

Then, $x \in E(N, w)$ is Pareto-optimal if and only if there exists a price vector $p \in \Re^\ell$, such that

$$\langle p, \mathcal{P}_i(x) \rangle > \langle p, x_i \rangle, \quad \forall i \in N. \tag{4}$$

Proof. We shall only sketch the main idea of the proof. A detailed proof follows standard arguments. We now prove (4) from the conditions of the theorem. It may be asserted that $x_i = 0$ for all $i \in N$, that is to say, $x = 0$. Define

$$M = \{ i \in N \mid \mathcal{P}_i(0) \neq \emptyset \}, \quad \mathcal{P}^M = \prod_M \mathcal{P}_i(0).$$

The result is established by induction on the dimension of space T which includes X_i for all $i \in N$. When $\dim T = 1$, the result follows by applying the separation theorem to sets $E(M,0)$ and $\mathcal{P}^M$. Let $\dim T > 1$. By Definition 1,

$$\mathcal{P}^M \cap E(M,0) = \emptyset.$$

Using the separation theorem, we can find a functional f which separates these sets:

$$f(\mathcal{P}^M) \geqq f\big(E(M,0)\big).$$

Since $E(M,0)$ is a subspace of $(\Re^\ell)^M$, f must be zero on $E(M,0)$. Hence, the vector $\tilde{f} \in (\Re^\ell)^M$, which represents the functional, has the form

$$\tilde{f} = (\tilde{p}, \tilde{p}, \ldots, \tilde{p}), \quad \tilde{p} \in \Re^\ell,$$

since we have $\langle \tilde{p}, \mathcal{P}_i(0) \rangle \geqq 0$ for all $i \in N$, by the construction of f. Let $T' = \{ y \in \Re^\ell \mid \langle \tilde{p}, y \rangle = 0 \}$. According to the induction hypothesis, there exists nonstandard p', such that

$$\langle p', \mathcal{P}_i(0) \cap T' \rangle > 0, \quad i \in N.$$

Let

$$p = \tilde{p} + \epsilon \cdot p',$$

where $\epsilon > 0$ is a nonstandard number satisfying $\epsilon \cdot |p'| \approx 0$. Now we show that the vector p is the desired one. If $y \in \mathcal{P}_i(0)$ and $y \in T'$, then

$$\langle p, y \rangle = \langle \tilde{p}, y \rangle + \epsilon \cdot \langle p', y \rangle = \epsilon \cdot \langle p', y \rangle > 0.$$

For $y \notin T'$ we have

$$\langle p, y \rangle = \langle \tilde{p}, y \rangle + \epsilon \cdot \langle p', y \rangle \geqq \delta - \epsilon |p'| d > 0,$$

since $\epsilon |p'| d \approx 0$ when $d = \|y\|$ and $\delta = \langle \tilde{p}, y \rangle > 0$ is a standard number. ∎

It can be seen from the proof of Theorem 1 that in the finite-dimensional case standard convex sets with an empty intersection can be strictly separated by a nonstandard hyperplane. In fact, this result is not connected with either the dimensional or the topological properties of the space (see Marakulin, 1988). We now extend model $\mathcal{E}_0$ by adding a formal cost mechanism, which is necessary for the definition of economic equilibrium, i.e., for defining ownership relations. This can be accomplished in the traditional way. Let Q be the set of all permissible prices and let $\alpha_i : Q \to \Re$ be the profit functions of the agents, where $\alpha_i(p)$ is the income of the ith participant when the price is $p \in Q$. Thus, we have the following model:

$$\mathcal{E}_1 = \langle N, \{X_i, \mathcal{P}_i, \alpha_i\}_{i \in N}, Q, w \rangle.$$

The definition of a standard budget set with nonstandard prices is of vital importance for the introduction of an equilibrium with nonstandard prices but standard consumption plans for the agents. Let $^*Q$ be the set of all permissible nonstandard prices and let the agents' profit functions be replaced by their images

$$^*\alpha_i : {}^*Q \to {}^*\Re, \quad i \in N.$$

It stands to reason that $Q \subset {}^*Q$ and that the functions α_i are "extended" from Q to the functions $^*\alpha_i$ defined on $^*Q$. This permits us later to use the symbol α_i (with the domain $^*Q$) instead of $^*\alpha_i$.

We now introduce nonstandard budget sets

$$\text{Bud}_i(p) = \{x \in {}^*X_i \mid \langle x, p \rangle \leqq \alpha_i(p)\}, \quad p \in {}^*Q$$

by analogy with the standard case. Here $\text{Bud}_i(p) \subset {}^*X_i$, that is, the budget set consists of nonstandard consumption plans. To return to the standard case, instead of $\text{Bud}_i(p)$, we take its standard part, $\text{st}\,\text{Bud}_i(p)$, defined as

$$\text{st}\,\text{Bud}_i(p) = \{x \in X_i \mid \exists y \in \text{Bud}_i(p) : y \approx x\}. \tag{5}$$

By definition, this is a standard set, but note that it can be empty for nonempty $\text{Bud}_i(p)$.

There is another way of defining a standard budget set with nonstandard prices. Let us consider a usual budget mapping $B_i : Q \to 2^{X_i}$ that is treated as a point-to-point mapping and take its $*$-image

$$^*B_i : {}^*Q \to {}^*(2^{X_i}).$$

Here $^*(2^{X_i})$ is the set of all internal subsets of $^*X_i$ (see Davis, 1977). Now the set $^*B_i(p)$ can be taken as a nonstandard budget set. However, the sets $^*B_i(p)$ have the same "structure" as those defined above by the transfer principle:

$$^*B_i(p) = \{y \in {}^*X_i \mid \langle p, y \rangle \leqq {}^*\alpha_i(p)\} = \text{Bud}_i(p).$$

Thus, the two definitions are equivalent, but instead of $\text{Bud}_i(p)$ we now have the convenient notation ${}^*B_i(p)$, (which is not the $*$-image of $B_i(p)$ with $p \in Q$). Thus, a budget set with nonstandard prices means that

$$\text{st } {}^*B_i(p) = \text{st Bud}_i(p).$$

Now we are ready to introduce the notion of a nonstandard equilibrium. This notion will be analogous to the usual idea of equilibrium in the standard case, with the condition that the budget sets of agents are replaced by sets of the form of (5).

Definition 2. *A pair $(\bar{x}, \bar{p}) \in X \times {}^*Q$ is called an equilibrium with nonstandard prices if it satisfies the following conditions:*

1. *Attainability:*
$$\bar{x}_i \in \text{st } {}^*B_i(\bar{p}), \quad i \in N, \tag{6}$$

2. *Individual rationality:*
$$\mathcal{P}_i(\bar{x}) \cap \text{st } {}^*B_i(\bar{p}) = \emptyset, \quad i \in N, \tag{7}$$

3. *Balance:*
$$\sum_N \bar{x}_i = w. \tag{8}$$

If condition (8) is replaced by the requirement

$$\sum_N \bar{x}_i \leq w, \tag{9}$$

we refer to the case as one of semiequilibrium.

The theorems about the existence of nonstandard equilibria will be stated with the following assumptions:

Assumption 1: The sets X_i are convex and closed in $\Re^\ell$, $i \in N$.

Assumption 2: (Continuity of preferences). Mappings $\mathcal{P}_i$ have open graphs in $X \times X_i$, $i \in N$.

Assumption 3: (Convexity and irreflexivity). For all $x = (x_1, \ldots, x_n) \in X$ and $p \in Q$, $x_i \notin \text{conv } \mathcal{P}_i(x \mid x_i)$ for all $i \in N$.

Assumption 4: (Continuity of profits). The functions $\alpha_i : Q \to \Re$ are continuous for all $i \in N$.

Assumption 5: For every $p \in Q$ there exist $x_1 \in X_1$, $x_2 \in X_2, \ldots, x_n \in X_n$, such that $\langle p, x_i \rangle \leqq \alpha_i(p)$, $i \in N$, (that is, $B_i(p) \neq \emptyset$ for all $p \in Q$, $i \in N$).

Assumption 6: (Walras' law). For every $p \in Q$, $\sum_N \alpha_i(p) = \langle p, w \rangle$.

We first state an auxiliary proposition. Let $\mathcal{X}, \mathcal{Y}$ be metric spaces and $A \subset {}^*\mathcal{X}$ and $\mathcal{L} \subset {}^*\mathcal{Y} \times {}^*\mathcal{X}$ be internal subsets. Let

$$B = \mathrm{si}\, \mathcal{L} = \{ z \in \mathcal{Y} \times \mathcal{X} \mid \mu(z) \subset \mathcal{L} \},$$

where $\mu(z)$ is the monad of the point z. The set B can be treated as the graph of some correspondence $\tilde{B} : \mathcal{Y} \to \mathcal{X}$ (here $\tilde{B}(y)$ is a section of B along $\mathcal{X}$). The same is also true for $\mathcal{L}$, where $\tilde{\mathcal{L}} : {}^*\mathcal{Y} \to {}^*\mathcal{X}$ and $\mathrm{Gr}\, \tilde{\mathcal{L}} = \mathcal{L}$.

Proposition 1.

$$D = \{ y \in \mathcal{Y} \mid \tilde{B}(y) \cap \mathrm{st}\, A = \emptyset \} \supset \mathrm{st}\, \{ y' \in {}^*\mathcal{Y} \mid \tilde{\mathcal{L}}(y') \cap A = \emptyset \} = C$$

Proof. Let $y \in \mathcal{Y} \backslash D$. We can find $x \in \mathcal{X}$ such that $\mu(y, x) \subset \mathcal{L}$ and $x \in \mathrm{st}\, A$. Since $\mu(y, x) = \mu(y) \times \mu(x)$ and $\mu(x) \cap A \neq \emptyset$, there is a $z \in A$, $z \approx x$. From this it follows that $\mu(y) \times \{ z \} \subset \mathcal{L}$, i.e., $z \in \tilde{\mathcal{L}}(y') \cap A$, $y' \approx y$. Thus, the condition

$$\tilde{B}(y) \cap \mathrm{st}\, A \neq \emptyset$$

implies

$$\cap_{y' \approx y} \tilde{\mathcal{L}}(y') \cap A \neq \emptyset$$

By construction, if $y \in C$, there is a $y' \in {}^*\mathcal{Y}$ such that $y' \approx y$ and $\tilde{\mathcal{L}}(y') \cap A = \emptyset$. Hence,

$$\cap_{y' \approx y} \tilde{\mathcal{L}}(y') \cap A = \emptyset$$

and

$$\tilde{B}(y) \cap \mathrm{st}\, A = \emptyset,$$

that is $y \in D$. ∎

Theorem 2. *If $\mathcal{E}_1$ satisfies Assumptions 2–6, $X_i = \mathfrak{R}_+^\ell$, $i \in N$, and $Q = \mathfrak{R}_+^\ell \backslash \{0\}$, then a semiequilibrium with nonstandard prices exists.*

Proof. Consider the economy $\mathcal{E}_1$ in the case of the price set

$$Q(\epsilon) = \{p \in \Re^{\ell} \mid \sum_{j=1}^{\ell} p_j = 1,\ p_j \geqq \epsilon,\ j = 1, \ldots, \ell\}, \quad \epsilon > 0$$

and compact consumption sets

$$X_i = \Re_+^{\ell} \cap \{(x_1, \ldots, x_{\ell}) \mid x_j \leqq c,\ j = 1, \ldots, \ell\},$$

where c is a sufficiently large number. Furthermore, as is usual, we shall reduce the model to a noncoalition game with $n + 1$ players. In this game, the $(n+1)^{\text{th}}$ player plays the role of a price-setting body. Other players correspond to the economic agents of $\mathcal{E}_1$, their objective being to "maximize their own utilities on their budget sets."[1] Now we search for the Nash equilibria of this game. Since the budget sets depend continuously on $p \in Q(\epsilon)$ (since $p \gg 0$ and Assumption 4 is true), and the other conditions for the existence of Nash equilibria are satisfied by Assumptions 1–3, we conclude (see Makarov, 1981 and Shafer and Sonnenschein, 1975) that there exists a Nash equilibrium $(x^{\epsilon}, p^{\epsilon})$, $x^{\epsilon} = (x_1^{\epsilon}, \ldots, x_n^{\epsilon}) \in \prod_N X_i$, $p \in Q(\epsilon)$, such that

$$x_i^{\epsilon} \in B_i(p^{\epsilon}), \qquad i \in N; \tag{10}$$

$$P_i(x^{\epsilon}) \cap B_i(p^{\epsilon}) = \emptyset, \qquad i \in N; \tag{11}$$

$$\langle p^{\epsilon}, \sum_N x_i^{\epsilon} - w \rangle = \max_{p \in Q(\epsilon)} \langle p, \sum_N x_i^{\epsilon} - w \rangle. \tag{12}$$

This conclusion holds for all $\epsilon \in \Re$, $\epsilon > 0$. Since the transfer principle is applicable to these conditions, we obtain the following true statement: for every $\epsilon \in {}^*\!\Re$, $\epsilon > 0$, there exists a pair $(x^{\epsilon}, p^{\epsilon}) \in {}^*\!X \times {}^*\!Q(\epsilon)$ such that conditions (10)–(12) are satisfied if all "standard constants" are replaced by their *-images (i.e., *-s are added to the B_i, P_i, $Q(\epsilon)$). We consider $\epsilon > 0$, $\epsilon \approx 0$, and the corresponding pair $(x^{\epsilon}, p^{\epsilon})$ satisfying (10)–(12) (in a nonstandard sense). The set X is compact; hence (see Davis, 1977, Theorem I.6) every point of ${}^*\!X$ is situated near a standard point, i.e., there exists $\overline{x} \in X$ such that $\overline{x} \approx x^{\epsilon}$. Now we shall show that a pair $(\overline{x}, p^{\epsilon})$ is a nonstandard semiequilibrium.

From the construction of the budget sets and (10) it follows that

$$\overline{x}_i \in \operatorname{st} {}^*\!B_i(p^{\epsilon}),$$

---

[1] This approach is considered in detail in Makarov (1981).

which proves (6). We apply Proposition 1 to establish (7). Let $\mathcal{P}_i = \tilde{\mathcal{L}}$, $\mathcal{Y} = \prod_N X_j$, $\mathcal{X} = X_i$, $A = {}^*B_i(p^\epsilon)$. From (11) and the above proposition we obtain

$$[\text{si}\,{}^*\mathcal{P}_i](\overline{x}) \cap \text{st}\,{}^*B_i(p^\epsilon) = \emptyset, \quad i \in N.$$

Now we use Assumption 2 which, together with the construction of si ${}^*\mathcal{P}_i$, yields $\mathcal{P}_i \subset \text{si}\,{}^*\mathcal{P}_i$ (in fact, $\mathcal{P}_i = \text{si}\,{}^*\mathcal{P}_i$). This proves (7).

Finally, we have to prove that (9) holds. Suppose that $\sum_N \overline{x}_i - w \nleq 0$. Then, according to (12) and $\overline{x} \approx x^\epsilon$,

$$\left\langle p^\epsilon, \sum_N \overline{x}_i - w \right\rangle > \delta > 0, \tag{13}$$

where δ is a standard number. On the other hand, from (10) we have

$$\langle p^\epsilon, x_i^\epsilon \rangle \leqq \alpha_i(p^\epsilon), \quad i \in N.$$

Adding these inequalities and using Assumption 6, we obtain

$$\left\langle p^\epsilon, \sum_N x_i^\epsilon \right\rangle \leqq \langle p^\epsilon, w \rangle.$$

Finally, after transition from x^ϵ to $\overline{x}$, we have

$$\left\langle p^\epsilon, \sum_N \overline{x}_i - w \right\rangle \leqq \beta$$

for some $\beta \approx 0$, which contradicts (13). ∎

In the analysis of Theorem 2, attention should be paid to Assumption 5, which guarantees nonempty budget sets. This assumption is weaker than traditional assumptions similar to Slater's condition and others. Assumption 5 is the main reason for the introduction and investigation of nonstandard equilibria, a new type of economic equilibrium. However, Assumptions 1–6 are not sufficient for the existence of equilibria with a balance requirement such as (8). The reason for this situation is a particular type of satiation arising in the nonstandard case. Makarov (1981) suggests a notion of equilibrium with transfer costs for the investigation of situations with satiated preferences. This notion may be treated as an extension of the usual Walrasian equilibrium. Still, the notion of equilibrium with transfer costs is a convenient instrument for examining the problems of existence of Walrasian equilibria. Since satiation is typical of the situations considered by us (but not strictly in the same sense as in the standard case), it is natural to use the idea of transfer costs in the nonstandard case. We turn to this task now.

Definition 3. *A triple* (x, p, δ), *where* $x \in X$, $p \in {}^*Q$, $\delta = (\delta_1, \ldots, \delta_n)$ $\in {}^*\Re^N$, $\delta \geq 0$, *is called a nonstandard equilibrium with transfer costs if it satisfies the following conditions:*

1. *Attainability:*

$$x_i \in \mathrm{st}\, {}^*B_i(p, \alpha_i(p) + \delta_i), \qquad i \in N; \tag{14}$$

2. *Individual rationality:*

$$P_i(x) \cap \mathrm{st}\, {}^*B_i(p, \alpha_i(p) + \delta_i) = \emptyset, \qquad i \in N; \tag{15}$$

3. *Balance:*

$$\sum_N x_i = w. \tag{8'}$$

The transfer costs $\delta_i \geq 0$, $\delta_i \in \Re$ consist essentially of a modification of the cost mechanism in the standard case. Those agents who consume their optimal bundle of goods, (i.e., agents who are satiated in their budget sets), can pass the remainig costs to other agents in the economy. These costs, which are equal to the difference between the agent's profits and the costs of his consumption plans, can be a number of the standard type or an infinitesimal. It is possible that the agent does not get satiated in the common sense that $P_i(x) \neq \emptyset$, but for any increase of his utility, the incremental cost (possibly infinitesimal) is infinitely large with respect to the rest of the cost. This is the main innovation brought about by nonstandard methods with respect to the notions of prices and transfer costs. As a possible scheme for redistributing the remaining costs among agents, one can imagine that there exists a bank and that the agents give their surplus costs to this bank. The bank must return these costs to the owners, if they desire it, and credits the participants in the economy. This is the conventional view.

Theorem 3. *If the model $\mathcal{E}_1$ satisfies Assumptions 1–6, the sets X_i are bounded and $0 \in \operatorname{int} Q$, then there exist nonstandard equilibria with transfer costs.*

Proof. Let (1) the economy $\mathcal{E}_1$ be augmented by an agent with index 0; (2) $X_0 = X_0^\epsilon = \{x \in \Re^\ell \mid \|x\| \leqq \epsilon\}$, $\epsilon > 0$ be his consumption set; (3) $\alpha_0^\epsilon(p) = -(\epsilon/2)\|p\|$, $p \in Q$ be his profit function; (4) $\mathcal{P}_0(x) = \emptyset$, $x \in X^\epsilon$ be the preference of this agent, where $X^\epsilon = X_0^\epsilon \times \prod_N X_i$; and (5) $N_0 = N \cup \{0\}$.

We now define new profit functions for the agents in $\mathcal{E}_1$. Let

$$\alpha_i^\epsilon(p) = \alpha_i(p) + \frac{\epsilon}{2n}\|p\|, \qquad i \in N.$$

We can assume without loss of generality that Q is the ball with unit radius centered on 0. As a result, we obtain the following economy:

$$\mathcal{E}(\epsilon) = \left\langle N_0, \{X_i, \mathcal{P}_i, \alpha_i^\epsilon\}_{i \in N_0}, Q, w \right\rangle.$$

It follows from the construction that the functions α_i^ϵ are continuous,

$$\sum_{N_0} \alpha_i^\epsilon(p) = \sum_N \alpha_i(p) + n\frac{\epsilon}{2n}\|p\| - \frac{\epsilon}{2}\|p\| = \sum_N \alpha_i(p) = \langle p, w \rangle, \qquad (16)$$

and if $p \neq 0$, then

$$\alpha_i^\epsilon(p) - \inf_{x \in X_i} \langle p, x \rangle = \alpha_i(p) - \inf_{x \in X_i} \langle p, x \rangle + \frac{\epsilon}{2n}\|p\| \geqq \frac{\epsilon}{2n}\|p\| > 0, \quad i \in N,$$

$$\alpha_0^\epsilon(p) - \inf_{x \in X_0} \langle p, x \rangle = -\frac{\epsilon}{2}\|p\| - (-\|p\|\epsilon) = \frac{\epsilon}{2}\|p\| > 0.$$

$$(17)$$

From (16), (17) and the assumptions of Theorem 3, it follows that model $\mathcal{E}(\epsilon)$ constructed here satisfies all the conditions of Makarov's (1981) theorem on the existence of equilibria with transfer costs in the standard case. Note that Makarov's theorem can be proved by the method noted in the proof of Theorem 2. This technique reduces the original problem to the problem of existence of Nash equilibria in a game with $(n + 1) + 1$ players. Here, the continuity of the budget mappings at zero is ensured by replacing the profit functions of agents by the functions $\alpha_i^\epsilon(\cdot) + d(\cdot)$, where $d(\cdot)$ is a nonnegative, continuous function, which equals zero on the boundary of Q and $d(0) > 0$. Finally, we have the following statement: for all $\epsilon > 0$, $\epsilon \in \Re$, there exists $\delta_i(\epsilon) \in \Re$, $\delta_i(\epsilon) \geqq 0$, $i \in N$, a pair $(x_o^\epsilon, x^\epsilon) \in X_0^\epsilon \times X$ and a price vector p such that

$$\|x_o^\epsilon\| \leqq \epsilon, \quad x_i^\epsilon \in B_i(p^\epsilon, \alpha_i^\epsilon + \delta_i), \quad i \in N; \qquad (18)$$

$$\mathcal{P}_i(x^\epsilon) \cap B_i(p^\epsilon, \alpha_i^\epsilon + \delta_i) = \emptyset, \quad i \in N; \tag{19}$$

$$\sum_N x_i^\epsilon + x_0^\epsilon = w, \tag{20}$$

where

$$B_i(p^\epsilon, \alpha_i^\epsilon + \delta_i) = \left\{ x \in X_i \mid \langle p, x \rangle \leqq \alpha_i^\epsilon(p) + \delta_i(\epsilon) \right\}.$$

In this case, we can apply the transfer principle and add asterisks to all standard constants, which is a substitution of standard constants by their *-images. Now consider $\epsilon \approx 0$, and examine the pair (x^ϵ, p^ϵ) that satisfies (18)–(20). Since $x^\epsilon \in {}^*X$ and X is compact, x^ϵ is situated near a standard point. Let $\bar{x} = \operatorname{st} x^\epsilon$. Now we shall show that $(\bar{x}, p^\epsilon)$ is a nonstandard equilibrium of the model $\mathcal{E}_1$ with transfer costs $\delta_i' = \delta_i(\epsilon) + (\epsilon/2n)\|p\| \geqq 0$, $i \in N$. After passing st into (18) we have

$$\bar{x}_i \in \operatorname{st} {}^*B_i(p^\epsilon, \alpha_i(\cdot) + \delta_i'), \quad i \in N.$$

A standardization of (20), with $x_0^\epsilon \approx 0$, gives

$$\sum_N \bar{x}_i = w.$$

Finally, using Proposition 1 in the case ${}^*\mathcal{P}_i = \tilde{\mathcal{L}}$, $\mathcal{Y} = \prod_N X_j$, $\mathcal{X} = X_i$, $A = {}^*B_i(p^\epsilon, \alpha_i + \delta_i')$ and relation (19), we have

$$[\operatorname{si} {}^*\mathcal{P}_i](\bar{x}) \cap \operatorname{st} {}^*B_i(p^\epsilon, \alpha_i + \delta_i') = \emptyset, \quad i \in N.$$

Finally, recalling that $\mathcal{P}_i \subset \operatorname{si} {}^*\mathcal{P}_i$ from Assumption 2, we get the relation (15) after replacing si ${}^*\mathcal{P}_i$ by $\mathcal{P}_i$ in the last formula. ∎

3. Conclusion

In conclusion, we summarize the results that characterize the structure of the budget sets and the nonstandard properties of the budget mapping. More detailed results and proofs can be found in Marakulin (1988). Here we use the following notation. Let $\alpha: Q \to \Re$ be some function and let $X \subset \Re^\ell$. The budget set of the traditional type is

$$B(\alpha, p) = \left\{ x \in X \mid \langle p, x \rangle \leqq \alpha(p) \right\}, \quad p \in Q$$

and its nonstandard analogue is

$$^*B(\alpha,p) = \{x \in {^*X} \mid \langle p,x \rangle \leq {^*\alpha(p)}\}, \quad p \in {^*Q},$$

where

$$\mathrm{st}\,^*B(\alpha,p) = \{x \in X \mid x \approx y, \; y \in {^*B(\alpha,p)}\}$$

is the budget set with nonstandard prices. Usual budget sets correspond to the budget mapping $B(\alpha): Q \to 2^X$, where $[B(\alpha)](p) = B(\alpha,p)$.

Proposition 2. *The set* $\mathrm{st}\,^*B(\alpha,p)$ *is closed in* X *and, if* X *is convex, then* $\mathrm{st}\,^*B(\alpha,p)$ *is convex.*

Proposition 3. *Let* 2^X *have the topology of closed limits. Then the point-to-set mapping* $B(\alpha)$ *will be continuous at a point* $p \in Q$ *if and only if for all* $p' \in {^*Q}$, $p' \approx p$ *implies*

$$B(\alpha,p) = \mathrm{st}\,^*B(\alpha,p').$$

If the function $\alpha(\cdot)$ *is continuous at* $p \in Q$, *then*

$$\mathrm{st}\,^*B(\alpha,p') = \{x \in X \mid \langle \mathrm{st}\,p', x \rangle \leq \mathrm{st}\,\alpha(p') = \alpha(p)\}, \quad p' \approx p.$$

Thus, the approach suggested in this paper for constructing the budget sets of the agents differs from the traditional way only at the points of discontinuity of the budget mapping $B(\alpha)$, i.e., at points where Slater's condition does not hold.

Proposition 4. *Every* $p \in {\mathfrak{R}^\ell}$ *unambiguously determines the collection* $\pi(p) = \{e_1, \dots, e_k\}$ *of orthonormal standard vectors such that*

$$p = \lambda_1 e_1 + \cdots + \lambda_K e_K, \quad \lambda_j \in {\mathfrak{R}}, \quad j = 1, \dots, K$$

and the coefficients $\lambda_j > 0$ *satisfy the conditions*

$$\frac{\lambda_{j+1}}{\lambda_j} \approx 0, \quad j = 1, \dots, K-1.$$

We examine the case where the profit function of the agent takes the form $\alpha(p) = \langle p, w \rangle$, where $w \in \Re^\ell$ is the vector of initial endowments. Here we write $B(w,p)$ instead of $B(\alpha,p)$. Let

$$B(m, w, p) = \left\{ x \in X \mid x \cdot e_j = w \cdot e_j, \ j = 1, \ldots, m-1, \ x \cdot e_m \leqq w \cdot e_m \right\}$$

for $m \leqq K$, and let

$$B(m, w, p) = \left\{ x \in X \mid x \cdot e_j = w \cdot e_j, \ j = 1, \ldots, m \right\}$$

for $m = K+1$. Here a natural K is defined by the vector p from Proposition 4.

Proposition 5. *If X is a convex polyhedron and $w \in \Re^\ell$ is a standard vector, then*

$$\mathrm{st}\, {}^*B(w,p) = B(m, w, p)$$

for some $m \leqq K + 1$ and, if $m \leqq K$, there exists $x \in B(m, w, p)$ such that

$$\langle x, e_m \rangle < \langle e_m, w \rangle.$$

This result actually demonstrates a lexicographic organization of the set $\mathrm{st}\, {}^*B(w,p)$. Note the possibility of characterizing the sets taking the form $\mathrm{st}\, {}^*B(\delta,p)$, where $\delta \in {}^*\!\Re$ and

$$^*B(\delta,p) = \left\{ x \in {}^*X \mid \langle p, x \rangle \leqq \delta \right\}.$$

We do it with the help of the following simple method. Let us replace the set X by $X_1 = X \times \{1\}$ and the vector p by $p_1 = (p, -\delta)$ (where the dimension is $\ell + 1$). Now the condition $\langle p_1, x_1 \rangle \leqq 0$, $x_1 \in {}^*X_1$ will be equivalent to $\langle p, x \rangle \leqq \delta$, $x \in {}^*X$ and the set

$$\mathrm{st}\, {}^*B(0, p_1) = \left\{ x \in X_1 \mid \exists y \in {}^*X_1 \colon p_1 y \leqq 0, x \approx y \right\}$$

is characterized by Proposition 5. Thus it is sufficient for us to take a projection of this set on the first ℓ components.

We present one more result.

Proposition 6. *Let X be a convex polyhedron and $\delta \in {}^*\!\Re$. Then, for every $y \in \mathrm{st}\, {}^*B(\delta,p)$,*

$$\mathrm{st}\, {}^*B(y, p) \subset \mathrm{st}\, {}^*B(\delta, p).$$

Then two consequences follow. (1) If X is a convex polyhedron and $\delta \in {}^*\Re$, then

$$\text{st}\,{}^*B(\delta,p) = \bigcup_{y\in\text{st}\,{}^*B(\delta,p)} \text{st}\,{}^*B(y,p).$$

(2) If X is a convex polyhedron and $x \in {}^*X$ is placed near a standard point, then

$$\text{st}\,{}^*B(\text{st}\,x,p) \subset \text{st}\,{}^*B(x,p)$$

and the reverse inclusion is false.

References

Brown, D. J. and Robinson, A. (1975) "Nonstandard Exchange Economies," *Econometrica* **43**, 41-56.

Davis, M. (1977) *Applied Nonstandard Analysis*, New York: Wiley.

Makarov, V. L. (1981) "Some Results on General Assumptions about the Existence of Economic Equilibrium," *Journal of Mathematical Economics* **8**, 87-100.

Marakulin, V. M. (1988) "Equilibrium with Nonstandard Prices and Its Properties in Mathematical Economic Models," Discussion Paper No. 18, Institute of Mathematics, Siberian Branch of the Academy of Sciences of the USSR, Novosibirsk.

Rashid, S. (1987) "Economies with Many Agents: An Approach Using Nonstandard Analysis," Baltimore: Johns Hopkins University Press.

Shafer, W. and Sonnenschein, H. (1975) "Equilibrium in Abstract Economies without Ordered Preferences," *Journal of Mathematical Economics* **2**, 345-348.

23

Rationing Schemes and Markets

Valeri A. Vasiliev

1. Introduction

This paper deals with models of coordinated states in mixed economies introduced in Makarov and Vasiliev (1982, 1986). The distinctive feature of these models is the presence of dual markets for each commodity. The first market is characterized by fixed prices and quantity rationing; the second market is one with flexible prices. In this paper we present the conditions for existence, Pareto-optimality and coalitional stability of the coordinated states.

2. The Model

We consider a model of the interaction between the fix-price and the flexible-price markets. This model is described by the following:

$$\mathcal{E} = \langle N, \{X_i', X_i'', Y_i, Z_i, u_i, \beta_i, d_i, w^i\}_N, q, Q \rangle, \qquad (1)$$

where $N = \{1, \ldots, n\}$ is a set of economic agents, $q \in \Re_+^\ell$ is a fixed price vector (rigid prices); $Q \subseteq \Re^\ell$ is the set of all feasible flexible prices; $X_i' \subseteq \Re^\ell$ is the consumption set of agent $i \in N$, available to him under the fixed prices q; $X_i'' \subseteq \Re^\ell$ is the consumption set of agent $i \in N$, available to him under the flexible prices from the set Q; $Y_i \subseteq \Re^\ell$ is the production set of $i \in N$; $Z_i \subseteq X_i' \times X_i'' \times Y_i$ is the set of feasible states for $i \in N$.

As usual, we denote by $u_i \colon Z_i \longrightarrow \Re$ and $w^i \in \Re^\ell$ the utility function and the endowment, respectively, of agent $i \in N$ and by $d_i \colon Y_i \times Q \longrightarrow \Re$

his basic-income function. Finally, we denote by $\beta_i : Y_i \longrightarrow X_i'$ the rationing scheme of agent $i \in N$, which determines his maximum feasible consumption at the fixed prices q. Subsequently, we shall also use the notation $y^{(i)} = y^i + w^i$, and also denote by $p \cdot a$ the inner product of the vectors p and a:

$$p \cdot a = \sum_{k=1}^{\ell} p_k a_k, \qquad p, a \in \Re^\ell.$$

As is seen from the description of model $\mathcal{E}$, we assume the existence of two markets for every commodity. In the first market, prices are fixed at q and the allocation of goods brought to the second market is determined by a rationing scheme which is a function of the agent's production. On the second market, the prices p are determined by the mechanism of equating demand and supply within the range of possibilities permitted by the set Q.

Before defining the budget sets of the participants, let us recall that the functions d_i characterize only basic income. Total income is obtained from $d_i(y^i, p)$ and additional income from $(p-q)^+ \cdot (\beta_i(y^i) - x''^i)$, where a^+ is the positive variation of the vector a ($a_k^+ = \max\{a_k, 0\}$, $k = 1, \ldots, \ell$). In other words, it is assumed that when $p_k > q_k$, each participant buys from the first market the full amount $\beta_{ik}(y^i)$ of the commodity k at the fixed price q_k, and the excess amount $\beta_{ik}(y^i) - x''^i$ is bought (if this amount is negative) or sold (if this amount is positive) at price p_k on the second market.

Accordingly, the budget sets $B_i^q(p)$ of economic agents $i \in N$ at prices $p \in Q$ are defined as follows:

$$B_i^q(p) = \left\{ z^i \in Z_i(\beta) \mid q \cdot x''^i + p \cdot x'''^i \leq \overline{d}_i(x''^i, y^i, p) \right\}, \qquad (2)$$

where

$$Z_i(\beta) = \left\{ z^i = (x''^i, x'''^i, y^i) \in Z_i \mid x''^i \leq \beta_i(y^i) \right\},$$
$$\overline{d}_i(x''^i, y^i, p) = d_i(y^i, p) + (p-q)^+ \cdot (\beta_i(y^i) - x''^i).$$

We now introduce demand sets and excess demand sets at prices $p \in Q$:

$$\mathcal{D}_i^q(p) = \left\{ z^i \in B_i^q(p) \mid \mathcal{P}_i(z^i) \cap B_i^q(p) = \emptyset \right\},$$
$$E_i^q(p) = \left\{ x^i \in \Re^\ell \mid \exists (x''^i, x'''^i, y^i) \in \mathcal{D}_i^q(p), [x^i = x''^i + x'''^i - y^{(i)}] \right\},$$

where

$$\mathcal{P}_i(z^i) = \left\{ \tilde{z}^i \in Z_i(\beta) \mid u_i(\tilde{z}^i) > u_i(z^i) \right\}.$$

Denote by $Z_{\mathcal{E}}(N) = Z(N)$ the set of all states $(x'^i, x'''^i, y^i)_N \in \prod_N Z_i(\beta)$ which are balanced: $\sum_N(x'^i + x'''^i) = \sum_N y^{(i)}$.

Definition 1. *The state $\bar{z} \in Z(N)$ is called coordinated if there exists a price vector $\bar{p} \in Q$ such that $\bar{z}^i \in \mathcal{D}_i^q(\bar{p})$, $i \in N$.*

The set of all coordinated states of the model $\mathcal{E}$ will be denoted by $W^q(\mathcal{E})$.

We shall now formulate one of the main conditions providing for the existence and efficiency of coordinated states.

Assumption 1. For all $p \in Q$ and $(y^i)_N \in \prod_N Y_i$, the inequalities

$$\sum_N d_i(y^i, p) \geq q \cdot \sum_N \beta_i(y^i) + p \cdot \left[\sum_N y^{(i)} - \sum_N \beta_i(y^i)\right] \qquad (3)$$

are valid.

According to condition (3), at prices $p \in Q$ and production activity level $(y^i)_N$, economic agents have sufficient aggregate basic income to acquire the maximum possible aggregate volume of rationed goods $\sum_N \beta_i(y^i)$ at the fixed prices q and to buy the rest of the produced goods $\sum_N y^{(i)} - \sum_N \beta_i(y^i)$ at the flexible prices p.

We shall show that Assumption 1 guarantees the Pareto-optimality of coordinated allocations. Since the model under consideration is not traditional, we give the corresponding formal definition:

Definition 2. *Allocation $(z^i)_N \in Z(N)$ will be called Pareto optimal (efficient) if there does not exist another allocation $(\tilde{z}^i)_N \in Z(N)$ such that $\tilde{z}^i \in \mathcal{P}_i(z^i)$ for all $i \in N$.*

Proposition 1. *If $\mathcal{E}$ satisfies Assumption 1, then every allocation $z \in W^q(\mathcal{E})$ is Pareto-optimal.*

Proof. Let $\bar{z} = (\bar{x}'^i, \bar{x}'''^i, \bar{y}^i)_N \in W^q(\mathcal{E})$. If some $z = (x'^i, x'''^i, y^i) \in Z(N)$ satisfies the condition $z^i \in \mathcal{P}_i(\bar{z}^i)$, $i \in N$, then we have for coordinated prices $\bar{p}$, corresponding to $\bar{z}$,

$$q \cdot x'^i + \bar{p} \cdot x'''^i > d_i(y^i, \bar{p}) + (\bar{p} - q)^+ \cdot (\beta_i(y^i) - x'^i), \quad i \in N.$$

Summing up these inequalities, we obtain

$$\bar{p} \cdot \sum_N (x'^i + x''^i) > [(\bar{p} - q) - (p - q)^+] \sum_N x'^i$$

$$+ (\bar{p} - q)^+ \cdot \sum_N \beta_i(y^i) + \sum_N d_i(y^i, \bar{p})$$

$$= (\bar{p} - q)^+ \cdot \sum_N \beta_i(y^i) - (\bar{p} - q)^- \cdot \sum_N x'^i + \sum_N d_i(y^i, \bar{p}),$$

where $(a^-)_k = \max\{-a_k, 0\}$, $k = 1, \ldots, \ell$. Hence, using the inclusion $z \in Z(N)$ and inequality $(\bar{p} - q)^- \geqq 0$, we have

$$\sum_N d_i(y^i, \bar{p}) < \bar{p} \cdot \sum_N y^{(i)} - (\bar{p} - q) \cdot \sum_N \beta_i(y^i).$$

But the last inequality contradicts Assumption 1. Thus $\bar{z}$ is Pareto-optimal. ∎

Before determining the conditions for the non-emptiness of $W^q(\mathcal{E})$, we introduce some auxiliary notation. For each $p \in Q$, write

$$B_N^q(p) = \prod_N B_i^q(p),$$

$$B_N(p) = \left\{ (x'^i, x''^i, y^i)_N \in \prod_N Z_i(\beta) \,\Big|\, p \cdot \sum_N (x'^i + x''^i - y^{(i)}) \leqq 0 \right\}.$$

Then, for definiteness let

$$Q = \left\{ p \in \Re_+^\ell \,\Big|\, \sum_{k=1}^\ell p_k \leqq 1 \right\}, \quad S = \left\{ p \in Q \,\Big|\, \sum_{k=1}^\ell p_k = 1 \right\}.$$

Among the conditions that ensure that we can apply the lemma of Gale, Nikaido and Debreu (Nikaido, 1968) to the correspondence $E^q(p) = \sum_N E_i^q(p)$ is the following assumption.

Assumption 2. For any $p \in S$ and $(z^i)_N \in B_N^q(p)$ there exists $(\bar{z}^i)_N \in B_N(p) \cap B_N^q(p)$ such that $u_i(\bar{z}^i) \geqq u_i(z^i)$ for all $i \in N$.

It is not difficult to see that from the formal point of view this assumption is equivalent to one of the conditions of the above-mentioned lemma:

$$\forall p \in S, \exists \Delta \in E^q(p) \text{ such that } p \cdot \Delta \leqq 0.$$

Now let[1]

$$d_{(i)}(y^i, p) = d_i(y^i, p) + (p - q)^+ \cdot \beta_i(y^i),$$
$$\delta_i(y^i, p) = \inf \left\{ p \vee q \cdot x'^i + p \cdot x'''^i \mid (x'^i, x'''^i, y^i) \in Z_i(\beta) \right\}.$$

Assumption 3. For any $i \in N$ and $p \in Q$ there exists $y^i \in Y_i$ such that

$$d_{(i)}(y^i, p) \geqq \delta_i(y^i, p), \tag{4}$$

where, for $p \in S$, the inequality is strict.

A more limited but simpler variant of (4) is as follows:

$$\forall p \in Q, \exists y^i \in Y_i \quad \text{such that} \quad p \cdot \beta_i(y^i) \leqq p \cdot y^{(i)}.$$

Taking into account that the budget sets $B_i^q(p)$ can be represented as

$$B_i^q(p) = \left\{ (x'^i, x'''^i, y^i) \in Z_i(\beta) \mid p \vee q \cdot x'^i + p \cdot x'''^i \leqq d_{(i)}(y^i, p) \right\},$$

we have

Proposition 2. *If Assumption 3 is valid for a model of type (1), then $B_i^q(p) \neq \emptyset$ for all $i \in N$ and $p \in Q$.*

Passing to some conditions that are mainly of a technical character, we introduce some necessary notation:

$$\tilde{Z}(N) = \left\{ (x'^i, x'''^i, y^i)_N \in \prod_N Z_i(\beta) \, \Big| \, \sum_N (x'^i + x'''^i - y^{(i)}) \leqq 0 \right\},$$
$$\tilde{Z}_i = \Pr_{Z_i} \tilde{Z}(N).$$

Assumption 4. (a) For all $i \in N$ the sets X_i' are convex, closed and bounded from below, and the sets X_i'' and Y_i are convex and compact; (b) Functions u_i, β_i, and d_i are continuous; (c) For all $i \in N$ and $k = 1, \ldots, \ell$, the functions $d_{(i)}$ and β_{ik} are concave with respect to y^i, and the functions u_i are concave by combination of variables; (d) There exists $i_0 \in N$, such that Z_{i_0} is locally saturated upwards as x''^{i_0};[2] (e) For all $i \in N$ and $z \in \tilde{Z}(N)$, the sets $\mathcal{P}_i(z^i)$ are not empty.

---

[1] Here $(p \vee q)_k = \max\{p_k, q_k\}$, $k = 1, \ldots, \ell$.

[2] This means that $z^{i_0} = (x'^{i_0}, x'''^{i_0}, y^{i_0}) \in \tilde{Z}_{i_0} \implies (x'^{i_0}, x'''^{i_0} + u, y^{i_0}) \in \tilde{Z}_{i_0}$ for all $u \in \mathcal{R}_+^\ell$ such that $\|u\| < \delta(z^{i_0})$.

Condition (d) means that an economic agent with a sufficiently "large" consumption set exists in the second market. All goods are desirable for this agent.

The rest of the requirements of Assumption 4 have standard interpretations.

Theorem 1. *If model $\mathcal{E}$ satisfies the conditions of Assumptions 1–4, then $W^q(\mathcal{E}) \neq \emptyset$.*

Proof. Let us introduce the modified budget and quasi-demand correspondences:

$$\tilde{B}_i^q(p) = \left\{ z^i \in Z_i(\beta) \,\middle|\, q \cdot x'^i + p \cdot x'''^i \leq \bar{d}_i(x'^i, y^i, p) + \frac{1 - \|p\|}{n} \right\},$$

$$\tilde{D}_i^q(p) = \left\{ z^i \in \tilde{B}_i^q(p) \,\middle|\, P_i(z^i) \cap \tilde{B}_i'^q(p) = \emptyset \right\},$$

where $\tilde{B}_i'^q(p)$ is that part of $\tilde{B}_i^q(p)$ for which the budget constraint is a strict inequality

$$q \cdot x'^i + p \cdot x'''^i < \bar{d}_i(x'^i, y^i, p) + \frac{1 - \|p\|}{n}.$$

Further, denote by $\tilde{E}^q(p)$ the aggregated excess quasi-demand at prices p:

$$\tilde{E}^q(p) = \left\{ \sum_N (x'^i + x'''^i - y^{(i)}) \,\middle|\, (x'^i, x'''^i, y^i) \in \tilde{D}_i^q(p), i \in N \right\}$$

and observe that the correspondence $p \longrightarrow \tilde{E}^q(p)$, $p \in Q$, satisfies all the requirements of the Gale-Nikaido-Debreu lemma (Nikaido, 1968). Indeed, Assumption 3 implies nonemptiness of $\tilde{B}_i^q(p)$ for all $p \in Q$, and condition (a) of Assumption 4, together with the concavity and continuity of β_i, $\bar{d}_i$ and u_i, guarantee convexity and compactness of $\tilde{D}_i^q(p)$. Thus, all the sets $\tilde{E}^q(p)$, $p \in Q$, are non-empty, convex and compact. Since all X_i'' and Y_i are compact sets, X_i' are bounded from below and β_i are continuous, we conclude that $\cup_{p \in Q} \tilde{E}^q(p)$ is bounded. Thus, to verify upper-semicontinuity of $\tilde{E}^q$ it is sufficient to prove that the graph of $\tilde{E}^q$ is closed. However, under the assumptions of the continuity of β_i, d_i and u_i, it is not difficult to prove that all correspondences $p \longrightarrow \tilde{D}_i^q(p)$, $i \in N$ are closed. Hence, by the definition of $\tilde{E}^q$, it is closed too.

According to the above argument, the correspondence $\tilde{E}^q$ satisfies all the requirements of the Gale-Nikaido-Debreu Lemma. Applying this Lemma, we obtain the following: There exists $\bar{p} \in Q$, $\bar{x}^{\prime i}$, $\bar{x}^{\prime\prime i}$, $\bar{y}^i$ and $\Delta \in -\Re^\ell_+$ such that

$$(\bar{x}^{\prime i}, \bar{x}^{\prime\prime i}, \bar{y}^i) \in \tilde{D}^q_i(\bar{p}), \qquad i \in N \tag{5}$$

$$\sum_N (x^{\prime i} + x^{\prime\prime i} - y^{(i)}) = \Delta, \tag{6}$$

$$\bar{p} \cdot \Delta \leq 0. \tag{7}$$

It is clear that under condition (e) of Assumption 4 we have

$$q \cdot \bar{x}^{\prime i} + \bar{p} \cdot \bar{x}^{\prime\prime i} = d_i(\bar{y}^i, \bar{p}) + (\bar{p} - q)^+ \cdot (\beta_i(\bar{y}^i) - \bar{x}^{\prime i}) + \frac{1 - \|\bar{p}\|}{n}, \quad i \in N.$$

Adding $(\bar{p} - q) \cdot \bar{x}^{\prime i}$ to each side, we may rewrite these equalities as follows:

$$\bar{p} \cdot (\bar{x}^{\prime i} + \bar{x}^{\prime\prime i}) = [d_{(i)}(\bar{y}^i, \bar{p}) - (\bar{p} - q)^- \cdot \bar{x}^{\prime i}] + \frac{1 - \|\bar{p}\|}{n}, \quad i \in N.$$

Summing and using (6) and Assumption 1, we have

$$\bar{p} \cdot \sum_N \bar{y}^i + \bar{p} \cdot \Delta \geq \bar{p} \cdot \sum_N \bar{y}^{(i)} + \left[(q - \bar{p}) \cdot \sum_N \beta_i(\bar{y}^i) \right.$$

$$+ (\bar{p} - q)^+ \cdot \sum_N \beta_i(\bar{y}^i) - (\bar{p} - q)^- \cdot \sum_N \bar{x}^{\prime i} \bigg] + (1 - \|\bar{p}\|)$$

$$= \left[\bar{p} \cdot \sum_N \bar{y}^{(i)} + (\bar{p} - q)^- \cdot \left(\sum_N \beta_i(\bar{y}^i) - \sum_N \bar{x}^{\prime i} \right) \right]$$

$$+ (1 - \|\bar{p}\|).$$

Consequently,

$$(\bar{p} - q)^- \cdot \left[\sum_N (\beta_i(\bar{y}^i) - \bar{x}^{\prime i}) \right] + (1 - \|\bar{p}\|) \leq \bar{p} \cdot \Delta. \tag{8}$$

Using (7) and the nonnegativity of all the items on the left hand side of (8), we obtain

$$\|\bar{p}\| = 1,$$

$$\bar{p} \cdot \Delta = 0,$$

$$(\bar{p} - q)^- \cdot \left[\sum_N (\beta_i(\bar{y}^i) - \bar{x}^{\prime i}) \right] = 0. \tag{9}$$

Since $\|\bar{p}\| = 1$, it follows from the definition of $\tilde{B}_i^q(\bar{p})$ that $\bar{z}^i \in B_i^q(\bar{p})$ for all $i \in N$. Using the inclusion $\bar{p} \in S$ and Assumption 3, it is not difficult to prove that $\mathcal{P}_i(\bar{z}^i) \cap B_i^q(\bar{p}) = \emptyset$ for all $i \in N$. Thus, $\bar{z}^i$ are maximal elements of $B_i^q(\bar{p})$ for all $i \in N$. To finish the proof of Theorem 1, it is sufficient to verify that $\bar{z} \in Z(N)$. From conditions (b) and (d) of Assumption 4 it follows that $\bar{p}_k > 0$ for all $k = 1, \ldots, \ell$. Since $\Delta \leqq \vec{0}$ and $\bar{p} \cdot \Delta = 0$, we obtain $\Delta = \vec{0}$. ∎

Finally, let us consider some conditions which not only provide for efficiency, but also for the coalitional stability of the coordinated allocations. First, we introduce the notion of the core of $\mathcal{E}$.

Definition 3. *The coalition $T \subseteq N$ improves upon allocation $(z^i)_N \in Z(N)$ if there exists $(\tilde{z}^i)_N \in Z(N)$ such that*

$$u_i(\tilde{z}^i) > u_i(z^i), \qquad i \in T,$$
$$\sum_T (\tilde{x}'^i + \tilde{x}''^i - \tilde{y}^{(i)}) = \vec{0}.$$

Denote by $C^\beta(\mathcal{E})$ the collection of all states from $Z(N)$ that cannot be improved upon by any coalition T; we call $C^\beta(\mathcal{E})$ the core of $\mathcal{E}$.

Furthermore, in order to obtain stronger conditions of coalitional stability, we propose the notion of the fuzzy core of the mixed economy $\mathcal{E}$. For this purpose, we consider the usual fuzzy coalitions, which are understood to be elements of the set

$$\sigma_0^F = (0, 1]^N \backslash \{\vec{0}\}.$$

The value of the kth component of a fuzzy coalition $t = (t_1, \ldots, t_n)$ is interpreted as the degree of participation of k in the coalition

$$\operatorname{supp} t = \{i \in N \mid t_i > 0\}.$$

Definition 4. *A fuzzy coalition $t = (t_1, \ldots, t_n) \in \sigma_0^F$ improves upon allocation $z \in Z(N)$ if there exists $\tilde{z} \in \prod_N Z_i(\beta)$ such that*

$$u_i(\tilde{z}^i) > u_i(z^i), \qquad i \in \operatorname{supp} t;$$
$$\sum_N t_i(\tilde{x}'^i + \tilde{x}''^i) = \sum_N t_i \tilde{y}^{(i)}.$$

Denote by $C_F^\beta(\mathcal{E})$ the collection of all states from $Z(N)$ that cannot be improved upon by any coalition $t \in \sigma_0^F$. We call $C_F^\beta(\mathcal{E})$ the fuzzy core of $\mathcal{E}$. We now describe a class of models of type (1) whose coordinated states are stable in the sense of Definition 4.

Assumption 5. For all $i \in N$, $p \in Q$ and $y^i \in Y_i$, the inequalities

$$d_i(y^i, p) \geqq q \cdot \beta_i(y^i) + p \cdot \left(y^{(i)} - \beta_i(y^i) \right) \tag{12}$$

are valid.

It is clear that condition (12) is a "personalized" form of Assumption 1: not only the grand coalition N as a whole, but each participant $i \in N$ has basic income, which guarantees the acquisition of a maximum possible amount of the rationed goods, $\beta_i(y^i)$, at the fixed prices q and the purchase of the rest, $y^{(i)} - \beta_i(y^i)$, at the flexible prices p.

Theorem 2. *If $\mathcal{E}$ satisfies Assumption 5, then each coordinated allocation of $\mathcal{E}$ belongs to $C_F^\beta(\mathcal{E})$.*

Proof. To prove the inclusion

$$W^q(\mathcal{E}) \subseteq C_F^\beta(\mathcal{E}) \tag{13}$$

we assume, on the contrary, that some $z \in W^q(\mathcal{E})$ can be improved upon by a fuzzy coalition $t = (t_1, \ldots, t_n) \in \sigma_0^F$. According to Definition 4, in this case there exists a state $\tilde{z} = (\tilde{x}'^i, \tilde{x}'''^i, \tilde{y}^i) \in \prod_N Z_i(\beta)$, for which conditions (10) and (11) are valid. Since $z \in W^q(\mathcal{E})$, from (10) we have

$$q \cdot \tilde{x}'^i + p \cdot \tilde{x}'''^i > d_i(\tilde{y}^i, p) + (p - q)^+ \cdot \left(\beta_i(\tilde{y}^i) - \tilde{x}'^i \right), \quad i \in \text{supp}\, t,$$

where the components of p are the coordinated prices associated with z. Multiplying these inequalities by the corresponding components of the vector t and summing up, we obtain by Assumption 5

$$q \cdot \sum_N t_i \tilde{x}'^i + p \cdot \sum_N t_i \tilde{x}'''^i > q \cdot \sum_N t_i \beta_i(\tilde{y}^i)$$
$$+ p \cdot \sum_N t_i \left(\tilde{y}^{(i)} - \beta_i(\tilde{y}^i) \right) + (p - q)^+ \cdot \sum_N t_i \left(\beta_i(\tilde{y}^i) - \tilde{x}'^i \right).$$

If we add $(p - q) \cdot \sum_N t_i \tilde{x}'^i$ to each part of this inequality, we can rewrite it in the following form:

$$p \cdot \sum_N t_i (\tilde{x}'^i + \tilde{x}'''^i) > p \cdot \sum_N t_i \tilde{y}^{(i)} + (p - q)^- \cdot \sum_N t_i \left(\beta_i(\tilde{y}^i) - \tilde{x}'^i \right).$$

The application of (11) yields

$$(p-q)^- \cdot \sum_N t_i\big(\beta_i(\tilde{y}^i) - \tilde{x}'^i\big) < 0.$$

This contradicts the nonnegativity of $(p-q)^-$ and inequalities $\tilde{x}'^i \leqq \beta_i(\tilde{y}^i)$, which follows from the condition $\tilde{z}^i \in Z_i(\beta)$, $i \in N$. This contradiction proves the inclusion (13). ∎

Corollary. Under Assumption 5 each coordinated allocation is coalitionally stable in the sense of Definition 3.

In order to establish a more precise bound for $W^q(\mathcal{E})$, let us consider the "standard part" $\mathcal{E}_0$ associated with $\mathcal{E}$:

$$\mathcal{E}_0 = \big\langle N, \{Z_i(\beta), w^i, u_i\}_N, Q\big\rangle.$$

Model $\mathcal{E}_0$ differs from $\mathcal{E}$ in two respects:

(1) Prices are flexible in both markets in $\mathcal{E}_0$;

(2) total income of each agent in $\mathcal{E}_0$ has the standard form

$$\bar{d}_i(x'^i, y^i, p) = p \cdot y^{(i)}.$$

The set of balanced allocations $\mathcal{E}_0$ is equal to the corresponding set of $\mathcal{E}$ and the budget set $B_i(p)$ of agent i in $\mathcal{E}_0$ has the form given by

$$B_i(p) = \big\{z^i \in Z_i(\beta) \mid p \cdot (x'^i + x'''^i) \leqq p \cdot y^{(i)}\big\}.$$

Definition 5. A state $\bar{z} \in Z(N)$ is an equilibrium allocation of $\mathcal{E}_0$, if there exists $\bar{p} \in Q$ such that

$$\bar{z}^i \in B_i(\bar{p}), \qquad i \in N,$$
$$\mathcal{P}_i(\bar{z}^i) \cap B_i(\bar{p}) = \emptyset, \qquad i \in N.$$

The set of equilibrium allocations of $\mathcal{E}_0$ is denoted by $W(\mathcal{E}_0)$

As usual, we say that preferences u_i are nonsatiated if $\mathcal{P}_i(z^i) \neq \emptyset$ for all $i \in N$, $z \in Z(N)$.

Theorem 3. Let $\mathcal{E}$ satisfy Assumption 5. If the Z_i are convex, the $d_{(i)}$ are continuous, the β_{ik} are concave and the u_i are concave and nonsatiated, then every coordinated allocation of $\mathcal{E}$ is an equilibrium state of $\mathcal{E}_l$.

Proof. Suppose that $\bar{z} \in W^q(\mathcal{E})$ and let $\bar{p}$ be the corresponding coordinated prices. We shall show that under the conditions of Theorem 3

$$\bar{z}^i \in B_i(\bar{p}), \qquad i \in N, \qquad\qquad (14)$$
$$B_i(\bar{p}) \subseteq B_i^q(\bar{p}), \qquad i \in N. \qquad\qquad (15)$$

Indeed, it is not difficult to verify that

$$q \cdot \bar{x}^{\prime i} + \bar{p} \cdot \bar{x}^{\prime\prime i} = d_{(i)}(\bar{y}^i, \bar{p}) - (\bar{p} - q)^+ \cdot \bar{x}^{\prime i} \qquad (16)$$

for all $i \in N$. For this purpose, suppose

$$q \cdot \bar{x}^{\prime i} + \bar{p} \cdot \bar{x}^{\prime\prime i} < d_{(i)}(\bar{y}^i, \bar{p}) - (\bar{p} - q)^+ \cdot \bar{x}^{\prime i}$$

for some $i \in N$. Using the nonsatiation of u_i, we can find $\tilde{z}^i \in Z_i(\beta)$ such that $u_i(\tilde{z}^i) > u_i(\bar{z}^i)$. From this inequality and the concavity of u_i and β_{ik} we obtain

$$z^i_t = \bar{z}^i + t(\tilde{z}^i - \bar{z}^i) \in Z_i(\beta),$$

and

$$u_i(z^i_t) > u_i(\bar{z}^i)$$

for all $t \in (0,1]$. Hence, from the continuity of $d_{(i)}$ we have that $z^i_t \in \mathcal{P}_i(\bar{z}^i) \cap B^q_i(\bar{p})$ for t small enough. But this contradicts $\bar{z} \in W^q(\mathcal{E})$.

If we add $(\bar{p} - q) \cdot \bar{x}^{\prime i}$ to both parts of (16) and apply Assumption 5, we may rewrite these expressions as follows:

$$\bar{p} \cdot (\bar{x}^{\prime i} + \bar{x}^{\prime\prime i}) \geqq \bar{p} \cdot \bar{y}^{(i)} + (\bar{p} - q)^- \cdot (\beta_i(\bar{y}^i) - \bar{x}^{\prime i}), \qquad i \in N \qquad (17)$$

Adding these inequalities and taking into account

$$\sum_N (\bar{x}^{\prime i} + \bar{x}^{\prime\prime i}) = \sum_N \bar{y}^{(i)},$$

we obtain

$$(\bar{p} - q)^- \cdot \sum_N (\beta_i(\bar{y}^i) - \bar{x}^{\prime i}) \leqq 0.$$

From this inequality and from the nonnegativity of $(\bar{p}-q)^-$ and $\beta_i(\bar{y}^i) - \bar{x}^{\prime i}$ we obtain

$$(\bar{p} - q)^- \cdot (\beta_i(\bar{y}^i) - \bar{x}^{\prime i}) = 0 \qquad (18)$$

for all $i \in N$. From (17), (18) and the balancedness of allocation it follows that

$$\bar{p} \cdot (\bar{x}^{\prime i} + \bar{x}^{\prime\prime i}) = \bar{p} \cdot \bar{y}^{(i)}, \qquad i \in N.$$

These last equalities prove the inclusion (14).

As for (15), it is clear that under Assumption 5, for $z^i = (x^{\prime i}, x^{\prime\prime i}, y^i) \in B_i(\bar{p})$, we have

$$\bar{p} \cdot y^{(i)} \leqq d_i(y^i, \bar{p}) + (\bar{p} - q) \cdot \beta_i(y^i). \qquad (19)$$

If we use the inequalities $(\bar{p} - q) \cdot \beta_i(y^i) \leqq (\bar{p} - q)^+ \cdot \beta_i(y^i) - (\bar{p} - q)^- \cdot x'^i$, which follows from the condition $x'^i \leqq \beta_i(y^i)$, $i \in N$, we may rewrite (19) as:

$$\bar{p} \cdot y^{(i)} \leqq d_{(i)}(y^i, \bar{p}) + (\bar{p} - q)^+ \cdot \left(\beta_i(y^i) - x'^i\right) + (\bar{p} - q) \cdot x'^i. \qquad (20)$$

Hence, under the assumption that $\bar{p} \cdot (x'^i + x'''^i) \leqq \bar{p} \cdot y^{(i)}$, it follows from (20) that

$$q \cdot x'^i + \bar{p} \cdot x'''^i \leqq d_i(y^i, \bar{p}) + (\bar{p} - q)^+ \cdot \left(\beta_i(y^i) - x'^i\right).$$

This inequality proves the validity of the inclusion

$$B_i(\bar{p}) \subseteq B_i^q(\bar{p}).$$

Thus, $\bar{z}^i \in B_i(\bar{p})$, $\mathcal{P}(\bar{z}^i) \cap B_i(\bar{p}) = \emptyset$, for all $i \in N$, and $\bar{z} \in W^q(\mathcal{E})$, which proves Theorem 3. ∎

Remark. If we repeat (with some simplifications) the proof of Theorem 2, we can establish that $W(\mathcal{E}_0) \subseteq C_F^\beta(\mathcal{E})$ for each model $\mathcal{E}$ of type (1). Consequently, the inclusion $W^q(\mathcal{E}) \subseteq W(\mathcal{E}_0)$ gives a more precise estimate of $W^q(\mathcal{E})$ than does (13). However, it should be noted that, under quite general assumptions, $W(\mathcal{E}_0)$ coincides with $C_F^\beta(\mathcal{E})$ (Vasiliev, 1988). Hence, under Assumption 5, the role of the fixed prices q is the concretization of the choice from $W(\mathcal{E}_0)$. Note that the interconnection between coordinated and equilibrium states takes place in the general case as well. If we take an arbitrary model of type (1) and consider the process

$$q_{n+1} = p_n, \qquad n = 1, 2, \ldots \qquad (21)$$

where p_n are coordinated prices under fixed prices q_n, and $q_1 = q$—the initial fixed prices—then, under slight restrictions, $p_* = \lim p_n$ is an equilibrium price vector for $\mathcal{E}_0$ if the limit exists. An analogous statement is valid for the sequence of coordinated allocations $x_n \in W^{q_n}(\mathcal{E})$ corresponding to the fixed prices q_n from (21): $\lim x_n \in W(\mathcal{E}_0)$.

References

Makarov, V. L., Vasiliev, V. A., et al. (1982) "On Some Problems and Results of Modern Mathematical Economics," (in Russian) *Optimization* 30, 5-87.

———— (1986) "Equilibrium, Rationing and Stability," (in Russian) *Optimization* **38**, 5-120.

Nikaido, H. (1968) *Convex Structures and Economic Theory*, New York: Academic Press.

Vasiliev, V. A. (1988) "On Coordinated States in Economies with Two Types of Prices," (in Russian) *Optimization* **42**, 23-41.

24

The Edgeworth Conjecture
for a Production Economy
Without Ordered Preferences

Monique Florenzano

1. Introduction

In the last twenty years two decisive improvements have extended general equilibrium analysis. The first one is a gain in economic realism. Mas-Colell (1974) proved a remarkable existence theorem dispensing with completeness as well as transitivity of preferences. Up until then, both requirements were considered as characteristic of the "rational consumer": but many counter-examples show that few real decision-making agents would pass this rationality test, either at the collective or the individual level. Just as older utility functions had been replaced by preference orderings, the pioneering work of Mas-Colell and its continuation proved that the exposition of the general equilibrium analysis can omit these orderings and work only with preference mappings.

The second improvement is that more interpretations of the general equilibrium model are now possible. In the Arrow-Debreu model a commodity is defined by its physical properties, location and date of availability and the states of the world in which it is available. Intertemporal equilibrium (when the number of periods is not finite), uncertainty (when the number of the states of the nature is not finite) and commodity differentiation (when a good or a service is defined by some characteristics which can vary continuously) all require that the original assumption of a finite number of commodities be dropped and the economy be defined in an infinite-dimensional commodity space. As a matter of fact, since a seminal paper by Bewley (1972), a lot of research in general equilibrium theory has been devoted to getting equilibrium existence theorems in larger and larger classes of commodity spaces.

The aim of the present paper is to extend, in both these lines, an old but significant result of normative economics: the Debreu-Scarf theorem. We consider the meaning of this theorem using the problem of an efficiently organized economy with a specified distribution of resources. The core of the economy is the set of all attainable allocations, which no coalition can "block" by reallocating its resources among its members in a way that improves its welfare. Under the usual assumptions a Walrasian equilibrium allocation belongs to the core; the *Edgeworth conjecture* is a converse statement, which holds that, under certain conditions, the core of a private ownership economy "shrinks" with increasing numbers of agents and converges on the set of Walrasian equilibrium allocations. If we define an Edgeworth equilibrium more precisely as an attainable allocation whose r-fold repetition belongs to the core of the r-fold replica of the original economy for any positive integer r, then a reasonable statement of the Edgeworth conjecture is that for any Edgeworth equilibrium, under certain conditions, there exists a price system to which consumers and producers are adapted in such a way that the pair, allocation-price, is a Walrasian equilibrium.

This statement is proved by Debreu-Scarf (1963) for an exchange economy with ordered preferences defined in a finite-dimensional commodity space. The main thrust of our paper is to prove an analogue for production economies, without ordered preferences, defined in a Hausdorff linear topological space.

Before presenting this, we set the main definitions and notations and prove that Edgeworth equilibria exist under very mild conditions, which are the same in both the finite- and infinite-dimensional case.

In the finite-dimensional case Edgeworth equilibria are Walrasian quasi-equilibrium allocations of a convex economy under the classical assumptions of continuity, convexity and local nonsatiation of preferences. Added to the first one, this result confirms the existence results for quasi-equilibria of a production economy without ordered preferences (developed in the literature around 1975).

In the infinite-dimensional case it is well known that Walrasian equilibria may not exist under the standard assumptions. Here we use an additional assumption that unifies the interiority assumptions as well as the uniform properness assumptions used since 1983 to get the existence of Walrasian equilibria. We define a hypothetical economy, whose Edgeworth equilibria can be embedded in the set of the Edgeworth equilibria of the original economy, and we prove that the Edgeworth equilibria of this economy are Walrasian quasi-equilibrium allocations of the original one.

As a by-result of this general equivalence theorem, we present in the final section a general existence theorem for quasi-equilibria in the infinite-dimensional case, which extends most of the recent results. A more detailed description with complete proofs can be found in Florenzano (1988).

2. Core, Edgeworth Equilibria and Fuzzy Core of a Private Ownership Economy

In a Hausdorff linear topological space (L, σ) as commodity space, let us consider a private ownership economy with a finite set M of consumers and a finite set N of producers, standardly defined:

$$\mathcal{E} = \left((X^i, P^i, \omega^i)_{i \in M}, \ (Y^j)_{j \in N} \ (\Theta^{ij})_{i \in M, \, j \in N} \right).$$

To each consumer i we associate: a *consumption set* $X^i \subset L$; an *initial endowment* $\omega^i \in L$; and a *preference correspondence* $P^i : \Pi_{k \in M} X^k \to X^i$. If $x = (x^k) \in \Pi_{k \in M} X^k$, then $P^i(x)$ is interpreted as the set of the elements of X^i, which are (strictly) preferred by agent i to x^i when the consumption of each agent $k \neq i$ is equal to x^k. For each producer j, there is a *production set* $Y^j \subset L$. For all $i \in M$ and for all $j \in N$, $\Theta^{ij} \geq 0$ is a *contractual claim* of the consumer i on the profit of the producer j; the Θ^{ij} are assumed to verify, for every $j \in N$, that $\sum_{i \in M} \Theta^{ij} = 1$.

Let $X = \Pi_{i \in M} X^i$, $\omega = \sum_{i \in M} \omega^i$ and $Y = \sum_{j \in N} Y^j$. An allocation $x = (x^i) \in X$ is said to be *attainable* for economy $\mathcal{E}$, if $\sum_{i \in M} x^i \in \sum_{i \in M} \omega^i + Y$. Here $\hat{X}$ denotes the set of all attainable allocations of the economy.

Now let $\mathcal{M}$ be the family of all nonempty subsets of M, i.e., the family of all *coalitions* of consumers. In order to define the productive power of each coalition, we assume that a coalition $B \in \mathcal{M}$ has the technology set $\sum_{i \in B} \Theta^{ij} Y^j$ at its disposal in producer j. This kind of assumption, which can be found in Rader (1964), Nikaido (1968), Hildenbrand (1970) and Aliprantis et al. (1987), lies on the idea that the relative shares Θ^{ij} reflect consumers' stockholdings, which represent proprietorships of production possibilities.

If $X^B = \Pi_{i \in B} X^i$, then $x^B \in X^B$ is an *attainable assignment* for the coalition B, if $\sum_{i \in B} x^{iB} = \sum_{i \in B} \omega^i + \sum_{i \in B} \sum_{j \in N} \Theta^{ij} Y^j$. Here $\hat{X}^B$ denotes the set of all attainable assignments for the coalition B.

For each $B \in \mathcal{M}$ a preference correspondence $P^B : X \to X^B$ can also be defined by:

$$P^B(x) = \left\{ z^B = (z^{iB}) \in X^B \mid z^{iB} \in P^i(x) \quad \forall i \in B \right\}.$$

We interpret $P^B(x)$ as the set of the elements of X^B, which is unanimously preferred to x by the members of the coalition B. A coalition B is said to *block* an attainable allocation $x \in \hat{X}$, if there exists $z^B \in \hat{X}^B \cap P^B(x)$.

The *core* of $\mathcal{E}$ is classically defined as the set $\mathcal{C}(\mathcal{E})$ of all attainable allocations, which is not blocked by any coalition.

Now let r be any positive integer. We consider the r-fold *replica* of the economy $\mathcal{E}$, composed of r subeconomies identical to the original $\mathcal{E}$. The economy

$$\mathcal{E}^r = \left((X^{iq}, P^{iq}, \omega^{iq})_{\substack{i \in M \\ q=1,\dots,r}}, (Y^{iq'})_{\substack{j \in N \\ q'=1,\dots,r}}, (\Theta^{iqjq'})_{\substack{i \in M, j \in N \\ q,q'=1,\dots,r}} \right)$$

is defined as follows: for each $j \in N$, r producers of type j have the same production set $Y^{jq'} = Y^j$; for each $i \in M$, r consumers of type i have the same consumption set $X^{iq} = X^i$ and the same initial endowment $\omega^{iq} = \omega^i$. For preferences and ownership of initial holdings and production possibilities, each consumer (i, q) is restricted within his subeconomy; that is, $P^{iq} : \Pi_{k \in M} X^{kq} \to X^{iq}$ is defined by $P^{iq}(x) = P^i(x)$, and

$$\Theta^{iqjq'} = \begin{cases} \Theta^{ij}, & \text{if } q = q'; \\ 0, & \text{if } q \neq q'. \end{cases}$$

If $\bar{x} \in \hat{X}$, an allocation (which assigns the same consumption bundle $\bar{x}^i$ to each consumer (i, q), $q = 1, \dots, r$) belongs to the core of $\mathcal{E}^r$, if and only if there exist no $S \subset M \times \{1, \dots, r\}$, $S \neq \emptyset$, and no x' in $\Pi_{(i,q) \in S} X^i$, such that:

(1) $\sum_{(i,q)\in S} x^{iqS} \in \sum_i (\operatorname{card} S(i))\, \omega^i + \sum_i (\operatorname{card} S(i)) \sum_j \Theta^{ij} Y^j$, where $S(i) \overset{\text{def}}{=} \{q \in \{1, \ldots, r\} \mid (i,q) \in S\}$ and card $S(i)$ denotes the number of elements of $S(i)$;

(2) $x^{iqS} \in P^i(\bar{x})$ for all $(i,q) \in S$.

Let $C^r(\mathcal{E})$ denote the set of all such $\bar{x} \in \hat{X}$. Aliprantis et al. (1987) define an Edgeworth equilibrium as an element of $C^e(\mathcal{E}) = \cap_{r \geq 1} C^r(\mathcal{E})$.

Setting $t^i = [\operatorname{card} S(i)]/r$, $t = (t^i)_{i \in M}$ and denoting for each i, such that $t^i > 0$, $x^{it} = \sum_{q \in S(i)} x^{iqs}/[\operatorname{card} S(i)]$ (provided that each X^i and $P^i(\bar{x})$ are convex), we can replace (1) and (2) by the following:

(3) $\sum_{t^i > 0} t^i x^{it} \in \sum_{i \in M} t^i \omega^i + \sum_{i \in M} t^i \sum_{j \in N} \Theta^{ij} Y^j$;

(4) $x^{it} \in P^i(\bar{x})$ for all $i : t^i > 0$.

Here t^i is a rational number in $[0,1]$; this can be understood as the *rate of participation* of i to the coalition S, while x^{it} is the mean consumption that i achieves by participating in the coalition.

If we allow, as does Aubin (1979), that the rates of participation take all values in the real interval $[0,1]$, then $\bar{x} \in \hat{X}$ belongs to $C^f(\mathcal{E})$, the *fuzzy core* of $\mathcal{E}$, if there exist no $t = (t^i) \in [0,1]^M \setminus \{0\}$ and no $x^t \in \Pi_{t^i > 0} X^i$ satisfying (3) and (4).

It is worth noticing that, under the usual convexity assumptions, which will be made later, the core concepts defined in this section satisfy the following obvious relations:

$$C^f(\mathcal{E}) \subset C^e(\mathcal{E}) = \cap_{r \geq 1} C^r(\mathcal{E}) \subset C(\mathcal{E}).$$

3. Nonemptiness Theorems

Let us assume the following about economy $\mathcal{E}$ (provided that X is endowed with the topology induced by the product topology on L^M):

Assumption A_1. For all $i \in M$, X^i is convex and $\omega^i \in X^i$; for all $x \in$, $x^i \notin P^i(x)$; P^i has σ^M-open lower sections (i.e., for every $z^i \in X^i$, the set $(P^i)^{-1}(z^i) = \{x \in X \mid z^i \in P^i(x)\}$ is σ^M-open in X).

Assumption A_2. For all $j \in N$, $0 \in Y^j$.

Assumption A_3. Y is convex and $\hat{X}$ is σ^M-compact.

Moreover, if τ is a vector space topology on L, not necessarily identical to the initial topology of L, let us consider the following additional assumption:

Assumption A$_4$. For all $i \in M$, for all $x \in X$, $P^i(x)$ is τ-open in X^i.

Proposition 1. *Assume A$_1$–A$_3$. Then $C^e(\mathcal{E}) \neq \emptyset$.*

Proposition 2. *Assume A$_1$–A$_4$. Then $C^f(\mathcal{E}) \neq \emptyset$.*

Proof. In order to give an idea of the proof of these two nonemptiness theorems, let us define: $T = [0,1]^M \setminus \{0\}$, $T_Q = T \cap Q^M$ (where Q is the set of the rational numbers); if r is any positive integer, we set

$$T_r = \{t = (t^i)_{i \in M} \in T \mid rt^i \in \{0, 1, \ldots, r\} \quad \forall i \in M\}.$$

For any $t \in T$, we set :

$$Y^t = \sum_{i \in M} t^i \sum_{j \in N} \Theta^{ij} Y^j,$$

$$X^t = \Pi_{t^i > 0} X^i,$$

$$\hat{X}^t = \left\{ x^t \in X^t \mid \sum_{t^i > 0} t^i x^{it} \in \sum_{i \in M} t^i \omega^i + Y^t \right\},$$

$$P^t(x) = \{z^t \in X^t \mid z^{it} \in P^i(x) \quad \forall i : t^i > 0\}.$$

Here, Y^t, $\hat{X}^t$, $P^t : X \to X^t$ may be respectively interpreted as the *production set*, the *attainable set* and the *preference correspondence* of the *fuzzy coalition* t. Moreover, under the convexity criteria in Assumption A$_1$, we have

$$C^r(\mathcal{E}) = \{x \in \hat{X} \mid \hat{X}^t \cap P^t(x) = \emptyset, \quad \forall t \in T_r\},$$

$$C^e(\mathcal{E}) = \{x \in \hat{X} \mid \hat{X}^t \cap P^t(x) = \emptyset, \quad \forall t \in T_Q\},$$

$$C^f(\mathcal{E}) = \{x \in \hat{X} \mid \hat{X}^t \cap P^t(x) = \emptyset, \quad \forall t \in T\}.$$

If

$$\Delta^T = \Big\{ \lambda = (\lambda_t) \in \mathcal{R}^T \mid \lambda_t \geqq 0 \quad \forall t \in T, \lambda_t = 0 \text{ for almost all } t,$$

$$\sum_{t \in T} \lambda_t t^i = 1 \quad \forall i = 1, \ldots, m \Big\},$$

and if Y is convex, then economy $\mathcal{E}$ satisfies the following *balance condition*:

$$\lambda \in \Delta^T \implies \sum_{t \in T} \lambda_t Y^t \subset Y.$$

The nonemptiness of $C^r(\mathcal{E})$ for any $r \geq 1$ is first proved under the assumption that L is $\mathbf{R}^\ell$, the ℓ-dimensional Euclidian space. In view of the balance property of $\mathcal{E}$, the argument is strongly related to the fixed-point argument used in Florenzano (1987a) to prove that, under similar assumptions, the core of a balanced coalitional production economy is nonempty. It depends on a fixed-point theorem borrowed from Gale and Mas-Colell (1975).

By considering traces of economy $\mathcal{E}$ on finite-dimensional subspaces of the commodity space, we extend the result to the infinite-dimensional case. Then it is easily seen that for every $r \geq 1$, $C^r(\mathcal{E})$ is a σ^M-closed subset of $\hat{X}$. On the other hand, if $r' > r$, then $C^{r'}(\mathcal{E}) \subset C^r(\mathcal{E})$. In view of the σ^M-compactness of $\hat{X}$, the nonemptiness of $C^e(\mathcal{E})$ (from Proposition 1) is straightforward. After making the individual production sets convex, we find that $C^J(\mathcal{E})$ coinciding with $C^e(\mathcal{E})$ follows from Assumption A_4, so that the nonemptiness of $C^J(\mathcal{E})$ (from Proposition 2) is quite obvious.

4. Equivalence Theorems

We now denote by τ the vector space topology considered on L. Let L' be the conjugate space of (L, τ). For each p of L' we consider the functions:

$$\forall j \in N, \ \pi^j(p) = \sup p \cdot Y^j,$$

and the correspondences:

$$\forall i \in M, \ \gamma^i(p) = \{x^i \in X^i \mid p \cdot x^i \leq p \cdot \omega^i + \sum_j \Theta^{ij} \pi^j(p)\},$$

$$\delta^i(p) = \{x^i \in X^i \mid p \cdot x^i < p \cdot \omega^i + \sum_j \Theta^{ij} \pi^j(p)\}.$$

Here $p \rightarrow p.\omega^i + \sum_j \Theta^{ij} \pi^j(p)$ is the *income function* of consumer i, according to his endowment and stock-holding system; $p \rightarrow \gamma^i(p)$ is his budget correspondence.

A *quasi-equilibrium* of $\mathcal{E}$ is a point $(\bar{x}, \bar{y}, \bar{p}) \in \Pi_{i \in M} \ X^i \times \Pi_{j \in N} \ Y^j \times L' \setminus \{0\}$, such that:

(1) $\forall i \in M, \bar{x}^i \in \gamma^i(\bar{p})$ and $P^i(\bar{x}) \cap \delta^i(\bar{p}) = \emptyset$, (i.e., preference condition);

(2) $\forall j \in N, \bar{p} \cdot \bar{y}^j = \pi^j(\bar{p})$, (i.e., profit maximization);

(3) $\sum_{i \in M} \bar{x}^i = \sum_{j \in N} \bar{y}^j + \sum_{i \in M} \omega^i$, (i.e., balance of supply and demand).

In this case, $\bar{x}$ is said to be a Walrasian quasi-equilibrium allocation.

An *equilibrium* of $\mathcal{E}$ is a quasi-equilibrium $(\bar{x}, \bar{y}, \bar{p})$, such that for all $i \in M$, $P^i(\bar{x}) \cap \gamma^i(\bar{p}) = \emptyset$. In this case $\bar{x}$ is said to be a Walrasian equilibrium allocation. $W(\mathcal{E})$ (resp. $QW(\mathcal{E})$) denotes the set of Walrasian equilibrium (resp. quasi-equilibrium) allocations of $\mathcal{E}$.

It is easily seen that $W(\mathcal{E}) \subset \mathcal{C}^f(\mathcal{E})$. The purpose of this section is to prove some converse statements under the following assumptions:

Assumption B_1. For all $i \in M$, X^i is convex; for all $x \in X$, $P^i(x)$ is τ-open in X^i, convex and $x^i \notin P^i(x)$;

Assumption B_2. For all $j \in N$, Y^j is convex and $0 \in Y^j$;

Assumption B_3. If $x \in \hat{X}$, then $x^i \in \overline{P^i(x)}$ (the τ-closure of $P^i(x)$) for every i;

and an additional assumption, to be specified later, in the infinite-dimensional case.

In the finite-dimensional case we have the following result:

Proposition 3. *Assume* B_1–B_3 *and* $L = \mathcal{R}^\ell$. *Then* $\mathcal{C}^f(\mathcal{E}) \subset QW(\mathcal{E})$.

Proof. The proof of Proposition 3 does not differ from the proof given in the ordered case; it is based on a separation argument applied to $\{0\}$ and $G = co\big(\cup_{i \in M}(P^i(\bar{x}) - \sum_j \Theta^{ij} Y^j - \omega^i)\big)$, the convex hull of (.).

If (L, τ) is any Hausdorff linear topological space, we need an interiority assumption in order to apply a similar separation argument. Let us first define the correspondences $P : X \to X$ and $R : X \to X$ by

$$P(x) = \{x' \in X \mid x'^i \in P^i(x) \quad \forall i \in M\},$$
$$R(x) = \{x' \in X \mid P^i(x') \subset P^i(x) \quad \forall i \in M\}.$$

The definition of R does not imply by itself any transitivity property on the preference correspondences. In the *transitive case*, i.e., if for each i, P^i can be identified as the asymmetric part of a complete preorder $\overset{i}{\succsim}$ on X^i, then $R(x) = \{x' \in X \mid x'^i \overset{i}{\succsim} x^i$ for all $i \in M\}$.

We posit the following assumption:

Assumption C. There exists a convex cone Z (with vertex 0), nonequal to L, with a *nonempty* τ-interior $i(Z)$, such that either:

Assumption C_1. $x \in \Pi_{i \in M} X^i$ and $\sum_{i \in M} x^i \in \omega + Y + Z \Longrightarrow R(x) \cap \hat{X} \neq \emptyset$; or

Assumption C_2. $x \in \Pi_{i \in M} X^i$ and $\sum_{i \in M} x^i \in \omega + Y + Z \Longrightarrow (P(x) \cup \{x\}) \cap \hat{X} \neq \emptyset$.

Now let us consider the economy $\mathcal{E}_Z$ deduced from $\mathcal{E}$ by the addition of a fictitious producer, which has Z as a production set. We also assume that $\Theta^{iz} = 1/\mathrm{card}\, M$ for all $i \in M$, and set

$$\mathcal{E}_Z = ((X^i, P^i, \omega^i)_{i \in M}, (Y^j)_{j \in N}, Z, (\Theta^{ij})_{i \in M, j \in N}, (\Theta^{iz})_{i \in M}).$$

Note that the core (resp. the fuzzy core) of $\mathcal{E}_Z$ can be embedded in the core (resp. the fuzzy core) of $\mathcal{E}$ in the following sense: If $\bar{x} \in \mathcal{C}(\mathcal{E}_Z)$ (resp. $\mathcal{C}^f(\mathcal{E}_Z)$), then, under Assumption C_1, $\bar{\bar{x}} \in R(\bar{x}) \cap \hat{X}$ belongs to $\mathcal{C}(\mathcal{E})$ (resp. $\mathcal{C}^f(\mathcal{E})$); under Assumption C_2, $\mathcal{C}(\mathcal{E}_Z) \subset \mathcal{C}(\mathcal{E})$ and $\mathcal{C}^f(\mathcal{E}_Z) \subset \mathcal{C}^f(\mathcal{E})$.

The next proposition gives an infinite-dimensional analogue of Proposition 3. Its proof is based on a separation argument applied to 0 and $G = co(\cup_{i \in M} (P^i(\bar{x}) - \sum_j \Theta^{ij} Y^j - Z - \omega^i))$.

Proposition 4. *Assume B_1–B_3. Then, under Assumption C_1, if $\bar{x} \in \mathcal{C}^f(\mathcal{E}_Z)$, $R(\bar{x}) \cap \hat{X} \subset QW(\mathcal{E})$. Under Assumption C_2, $\mathcal{C}^f(\mathcal{E}_Z) \subset QW(\mathcal{E})$.*

To end this section, let us remark that Proposition 4 proves only that *some* allocations in $\mathcal{C}^f(\mathcal{E})$, but not necessarily all of them, can be decentralized by a price system as quasi-equilibria of $\mathcal{E}$. However, it will be seen later that, in some applications, $\mathcal{C}^f(\mathcal{E}_Z)$ coincides with $\mathcal{C}^f(\mathcal{E})$.

5. Applications

Proposition 4 can be applied to economies that satisfy some interiority assumption à la Duffie (1986) as well as to economies satisfying some uniform properness assumption à la Mas-Colell (1986).

More precisely, let AY and, for every j, let AY^j denote the asymptotic cones of Y and Y^j; in the transitive case let $\mathcal{D}$ be the *preference-generated set* defined by Debreu (1962):

$$\mathcal{D} = \left\{ \sum_{i \in M} x^i - \sum_{i \in M} \omega^i \mid x^i \in P^i(\hat{X}) \quad \forall\, i \in M \right\},$$

with D the cone (having vertex 0) generated by $\mathcal{D}$.

Proposition 5. *If AY has a nonempty τ-interior, Assumption C_1 of Proposition 4 can be satisfied with $Z = AY$ (or any convex cone with a* nonempty τ-interior contained in AY). In the transitive case, if $(AY - D)$ has a nonempty τ-interior, then Assumption C_1 of Proposition 4 can be satisfied with $Z = AY - D$ (or any convex cone with a nonempty τ-interior contained in $AY - D$). Moreover, in this last case, if $Z = \sum_{j \in N} AY^j - D$ has a nonempty τ-interior, then $C^j(\mathcal{E}_Z)$ coincides with $C^j(\mathcal{E})$.

The uniform properness assumptions are formulated in the case of a locally convex-solid topological vector lattice (L, τ) as commodity space. We use the terminology of Aliprantis and Burkinshaw (1978) and refer to their book for a statement of the main properties of these spaces. Let us use $\leq$ as the order relation on L, $<$ as the associated strict relation, and $\wedge$ and $\vee$ as the classical lattice notations for infimum and supremum. As usual, for an element x of L, let x^+, x^- and $|x|$ denote, respectively, the *positive part*, the *negative part* and the *absolute value* of x; L^+ is the *positive cone* of L.

Let $\mathcal{V}_\tau(0)$ be a basis of convex and solid o-neighborhoods. We now give two slightly different formulations for uniform properness of preferences in the transitive case and the general case.

In the transitive case we say that preferences are *uniformly proper*, if the following assumption is satisfied:

Assumption D_1. For all $i \in M$, there exists $v^i > 0$ and $V^i \in \mathcal{V}_\tau(0)$, such that, for all $x^i \in X^i$, $\lambda \geq 0$ and $u \in V^i$,

$$x^i + \lambda v^i + \lambda u \in X^i \Longleftarrow x^i + \lambda v^i + \lambda u \overset{i}{\succsim} x^i.$$

In the general case we follow Zame (1987) and say that preferences are *uniformly proper*, if the following assumption is satisfied:

Assumption D_2. For all $i \in M$, there exist $v^i > 0$ and $V^i \in \mathcal{V}_\tau(0)$, such that, for all $x \in \Pi_{i \in M} X^i$, $\lambda > 0$ and $u \in V^i$,

$$x^i + \lambda v^i + \lambda u \in X^i \Longrightarrow x^i + \lambda v^i + \lambda u \in P^i(x).$$

Then v^i is interpreted as a direction of *strict desirability* for i.

For production we follow Richard (1986) and say that each production set is *uniformly proper*, if the following assumption is satisfied:

Assumption D_3. For all $j \in N$, there exist $v^j > 0$ and $V^j \in \mathcal{V}_\tau(0)$, such that, for all y^j in Y^j, $\lambda \geq 0$ and $u \in V^j$,

$$(y^j - \lambda v^j + \lambda u)^+ \leq y^{j+} \Longrightarrow y^j - \lambda v^j + \lambda u \in Y^j;$$

or, equivalently, $\lambda u^+ \leqq y^{j-} + \lambda v^j \implies y^j - \lambda v^j + \lambda u \in Y^j$.

But uniform properness of the total production set can also be stated in the following way:

Assumption D_4. There exists $v^Y > 0$ and $V^Y \in \mathcal{V}_\tau(0)$, such that, for all $y \in Y$, $\lambda \geqq 0$ and $u \in V^Y$,

$$(y - \lambda v + \lambda u)^+ \leqq y^+ \implies y - \lambda v^Y + \lambda u \in Y;$$

or, equivalently, $\lambda u^+ \leqq y^- + \lambda v^Y \implies y - \lambda v^Y + \lambda u \in Y$.

Assumption D_3 (resp. D_4) means that each Y^j (resp. Y) has an "almost asymptotic cone" with a nonempty τ-interior: every point of Y^j (resp. Y) is the vertex of a τ-open cone, the points of which can be produced as far as they correspond to an output less than the initial point.

Obviously, Assumption D_3 implies Assumption D_4, with $v^Y = \sum_{j \in N} v^j$ and $V^Y = \cap_{j \in N} V^j$.

The following proposition is the analogue of Proposition 5. Its proof extensively uses the decomposition property of vector lattices.

Proposition 6. *Assume for all* $i \in M$ *that* $\omega^i \in X^i = L^+$. *Then, under Assumptions* D_1 *and* D_4 *in the transitive case (resp.* D_2 *and* D_4 *in the general case), Assumption* C_1 *in the transitive case (resp.* C_2 *in the general case) of Proposition 4 can be satisfied with:*

$$Z = \{\lambda(-v + u) \mid \lambda \geqq 0, \ u \in V\},$$
$$v = v^Y + \sum_{i \in M} v^i, \ V \subset V^Y \cap (\cap_{i \in M} V^i),$$

with $V \in \mathcal{V}_\tau(0)$, *such that* $v \notin V$. *Moreover, under Assumptions* D_1 *and* D_3 *in the transitive case, if*

$$Z = \{\lambda(-v + u) \mid \lambda \geqq 0, \ u \in V\},$$

with $v = \sum_{i \in M} v^j + \sum_{i \in M} v^i$, $V \subset (\cap_{j \in N} V^j) \cap (\cap_{i \in M} V^i)$ *and* $V \in \mathcal{V}_\tau(0)$ *such that* $v \notin V$, *we can then prove that* $C^j(\mathcal{E})$ *coincides with* $C^j(\mathcal{E}_Z)$.

6. Existence of Quasi-Equilibria Revisited

Now let us simultaneously consider the two vector space topologies σ and τ on the commodity space L.

If $C^j(\mathcal{E}_Z)$ coincides with $C^j(\mathcal{E})$, then the addition of Assumptions A_1–A_3 (written for L endowed with σ) to Assumptions B_1–B_3 (written for L endowed with τ) guarantees for economy $\mathcal{E}$ the existence of quasi-equilibria with prices in $(L,\tau)'$. We saw in the previous section that this condition is satisfied in the *transitive case*, if $Z = \sum_{j \in N} AY^j - D$ has a nonempty τ-interior, or when (L,τ) is a locally convex topological vector lattice, under uniform properness conditions of Assumption D_1 on preferences and uniform properness conditions of Assumption D_3 on *each* production set. This last case is addressed by Aliprantis et al. (1987), who obtain in Theorem 5.10 the same existence theorem as does Richard (1986).

In all other cases let us assume the following about economy $\mathcal{E}$:

Assumption A_1'. For all $i \in M$, X^i is convex σ-closed and $\omega^i \in X^i$; for all $x \in X$, $x^i \notin P^i(x)$; P^i has σ^M-open lower sections and τ-open upper sections.

Assumption A_2'. For all $j \in N$, Y^j is convex, σ-closed and $0 \in Y^j$.

Assumption A_3'. $\hat{X}$ is σ^M-compact.

Assumption A_3''. For all $j \in N$, $\hat{Y}^j$ is σ-compact.

Assumption B'. If $x \in \hat{X}$, then $x^i \in \overline{P^i(x)}$ (the τ-closure of $P^i(x)$) for every $i \in M$.

Assumption C'. There exists a σ-closed convex cone Z (with vertex 0) with a nonempty τ-interior $i(Z)$, such that either:

Assumption C_1'. $x \in X$ and $\sum_{i \in M} x^i \in \omega + Y + Z \Longrightarrow R(x) \cap \hat{X} \neq \emptyset$;

or

Assumption C_2'. $x \in X$ and $\sum_{i \in M} x^i \in \omega + Y + Z \Longrightarrow (P(x) \cup \{x\}) \cap \hat{X} \neq \emptyset$.

We first state a nonemptiness theorem, which has as corollaries several existence theorems for quasi-equilibria of $\mathcal{E}$.

Proposition 7. *If Assumptions A_1'–A_3' and Assumptions C_1' or (C_2' and A_3'') hold, then $C^j(\mathcal{E}_Z)$ is nonempty.*

Corollary 1. *If Y is σ-closed and if AY has a nonempty τ-interior, then $\mathcal{E}$ has a quasi-equilibrium under Assumptions A_1', A_2, A_3' and B'.*

To go further we need to make an assumption about the commodity space L, which relies on the topologies τ and σ considered on L:

Assumption E_1. (L, τ) is a Hausdorff locally convex topological vector space and τ has a basis $\mathcal{V}_\tau(0)$ of convex circled and σ-*closed* o-neighborhoods V, whose gauge p_v is a norm.

Assumption E_2. (L, τ) is a Hausdorff locally convex-solid topological vector lattice and τ has a basis $\mathcal{V}_\tau(0)$ of convex solid and σ-*closed* o-neighborhoods V, whose gauge p_v is a norm.

Under these two assumptions, if $V \in \mathcal{V}_\tau(0)$ and if $v \notin V$, then the convex cone generated by $\{v\} + V$ is σ-closed. In view of Propositions 5 and 6, Proposition 7 has the following corollaries:

Corollary 2. *Under Assumptions* E_1, A_1'–A_3' *and* B', *if* $(AY - D)$ *has a nonempty* τ-*interior, then* $\mathcal{E}$ *has a quasi-equilibrium.*

Corollary 3. *Under Assumptions* E_2, A_1'–A_3' *and* B' *it follows that, under Assumptions* D_1 *and* D_4 *in the transitive case and under Assumptions* D_2, D_4 *and* A_3'' *in the general case,* $\mathcal{E}$ *has a quasi-equilibrium.*

It should be noticed that in the three corollaries the quasi-equilibrium price belongs to $(L, \tau)'$. As is well known, standard additional assumptions on ω and irreducibility of economy $\mathcal{E}$ guarantee that the quasi-equilibrium is an equilibrium of $\mathcal{E}$ (see Jones (1987), Zame (1987) and Florenzano (1987b)).

Assumption E_1 is satisfied if (L, τ) is a normed space, the conjugate normed space of some other normed space M, with $\sigma = \sigma(L, M)$. If (L, τ) is any normed Riesz space with the Fatou property, let $L_n^\sim$ be the order-continuous dual of L, and $L_n' = L' \cap L_n^\sim$. If L_n' separates the points of L, then Assumption E_2 is satisfied with $\sigma = \sigma(L, L_n')$.

These cases cover commodity spaces of economic interest as L_∞, $ca(K)$, and L_p, $p \geq 1$.

References

Aliprantis, C. D., Brown, D. J. and Burkinshaw, O. (1987) "Edgeworth Equilibria in Production Economies," *J. of Economic Theory* 43, 252-291.

Aliprantis, C. D. and Burkinshaw, O. (1978) *Locally Solid Riesz Spaces,* New York: Academic Press.

Aubin, J. P. (1979) *Mathematical Methods of Game and Economic Theory,* Amsterdam: North-Holland.

Bewley, T. F. (1972) "Existence of Equilibria in Economies with Infinitely Many Commodities," *J. of Economic Theory* 4, 514-540.

Debreu, G. (1962) "New Concepts and Techniques for Equilibrium Analysis," *International Economic Review* 3, 257-273.

Debreu, G. and Scarf, H. (1963) "A Limit Theorem on the Core of an Economy," *International Economic Review* 4, 235-246.

Duffie, D. (1986) "Competitive Equilibria in General Choice Spaces," *J. of Mathematical Economics* 14, 1-23.

Florenzano, M. (1987a) "On the Nonemptiness of the Core of a Coalitional Production Economy without Ordered Preferences," to appear in *J. of Mathematical Analysis and Applications.*

––––––– (1987b) "Equilibrium in a Production Economy on an Infinite-Dimensional Commodity Space: A Unifying Approach," Working Paper #8740, CEPREMAP.

––––––– (1988) "Edgeworth Equilibria, Fuzzy Core and Equilibria of a Production Economy without Ordered Preferences," Working Paper #8822, CEPREMAP, to appear in *Journal of Mathematical Analysis and Applications.*

Gale, D. and Mas-Colell, A. (1975) "An Equilibrium Existence Theorem for a General Model without Ordered Preferences," *J. of Mathematical Economics* 2, 9-15.

Hildenbrand, W. (1970) "Existence of Equilibria for Economies with Production and a Measure Space of Consumers," *Econometrica* 38, 608-623.

Jones, L. E. (1987) "Existence of Equilibria with Infinitely Many Commodities—Banach Lattices Reconsidered," *J. of Mathematical Economics* 16, 89-104.

Mas-Colell, A. (1974) "An Equilibrium Existence Theorem without Complete or Transitive Preferences," *J. of Mathematical Economics* 1, 237-246.

———— (1986) "The Price Equilibrium Existence Problem in Topological Vector Lattices," *Econometrica* **54**, 1039-1055.

Nikaido, H. (1968) *Convex Structures and Economic Theory*, New York: Academic Press.

Rader, J. T. (1964) "Edgeworth Exchange and General Economic Equilibrium," *Yale Economic Essays* **4**, 133-180.

Richard, S. F. (1986) "Competitive Equilibria in Riesz Spaces," Mimeograph, GSIA, Carnegie-Mellon Univ.

Zame, W. R. (1987) "Equilibria in Production Economies with an Infinite-Dimensional Commodity Space," *Econometrica* **55**, 1075-1108.

25

Pareto-Optima in an Infinite Horizon Economy with Recursive Preferences

Rose-Anne Dana and *Cuong Le Van*

1. Introduction

The purpose of this paper is to provide a framework to discuss the
stability and instability of a stationary intertemporal economy. To avoid
multiplicity problems, we study the dynamic properties of Pareto-optima,
which we describe as the function of a trajectory of a well-defined dynamic
system related to the characteristics of the model.

We consider an economy with an infinite horizon, i.e., where a finite
number of agents live for an infinite number of discrete periods. The set
of goods producible at each date is invariant in time and depends only
on capital stocks available in a previous period. Agents have stationary
utilities, usually called "recursive utilities" in the literature, rather than
additively separable utilities.

In the last few years a lot of attention has been focused on recursive utilities. Roughly speaking, papers can be classified in two categories. The first, which follows Koopmans' early work (1960, 1964) and
also Streufert (1986a), is concerned with the axiomatics of preferences leading to a recursive representation of utilities. The second tries to describe
the dynamic properties of models where one or several agents have recursive preferences—see Beals and Koopmans (1969), Iwai (1972), Lucas and
Stokey (1984), Benhabib et al. (1985a, 1985b), Epstein (1987a, 1987b) and
Boyd (1986).

We carry this work one step further: we use many consumption goods in a more general setting. In particular, a Pareto-optimal allocation can be viewed as a function of the trajectory of a dynamic system on the product of the capital space by the simplex, as has been shown by Lucas and Stokey (1984), Dana and Le Van (1988) and Epstein (1987a). This approach characterizes a Pareto-optimum as the maximizer of a weighted sum of the utilities of the different agents. Unless agents have separable utilities, this approach does not seem to be very tractable because the dynamic system involved is not characterized simply.

The methods that have been used in the one-agent separable case do not carry over trivially. A dynamic system has been concurrently defined by Benhabib et al. (1985b) and Epstein (1987b) on the set of couples of capital stock and utilities that can be reached by $n - 1$ agents from that capital stock. They use the fact that a Pareto-optimum maximizes the utility of one agent given that his/her utility and the others' utilities are attainable. This paper deals with the second approach.

In order to construct and characterize the dynamic system we eliminate consumption variables; show that the search for Pareto-optima of a stationary intertemporal economy, where agents have recursive utilities, can be transformed into a generalized McKenzie problem with a recursive criterion (and for which Bellman's and Euler's equations still hold); and provide a framework to draw general conclusions from the dynamic results that have been obtained for the one-agent additively separable case.

Accordingly, the paper is organized as follows: in Section 2 we recall the axiomatics of recursive utilities and generalize the findings of Koopmans et al (1964) and Lucas and Stokey (1984). In Section 3 we introduce a generalized version of McKenzie's model. In Section 4 we show that every Pareto-optimum is a solution of a generalized McKenzie model. An "abstract" state space is introduced as the space of couples of capital stock and utilities that can be reached by $n - 1$ agents from that capital stock; generalized "technological conditions" are then defined on that abstract space, and a recursive criterion defined on sequences of its elements.

2. Recursive Representation

Following Beals and Koopmans (1969) and Lucas and Stokey (1984), we introduce an *aggregator* function, defined as follows:

Definition 2.1. *Let q be an integer. Let C be a closed convex set of $\Re_+^q$. A function W from $C \times \Re_+$ into $\Re_+$ is an aggregator function, if it satisfies the following properties:*

$W1$: continuous; $\exists\, M > 0$, such that $W(x,0) \le M$, for all $x \in C$;

$W2$: concave;

$W3$: $\exists\, \beta \in [0,1)$ such that $|W(x,z) - W(x,z')| \le \beta|z - z'|$, for all $x \in C$, for all z, for all $z' \in \Re_+$;

$W4$: $z < z' \implies W(x,z) \le W(x,z')$, for all $x \in C$.

Let X be the space $(\Re_+^m)^\infty$ endowed with the product topology. An element in X is denoted by $\tilde{x} = (x_0,\ x_1,\ ...)$. Let L denote the shift operator on X, i.e., $L\tilde{x} = (x_1,\ x_2,\ ...)$.

Let Q be a closed, convex, L-invariant subset of X; S will denote the space of bounded continuous functions from Q into $\Re_+$ endowed with the sup-norm, $\|u\| = \sup_{x \in Q} u(\tilde{x})$. Let $f_r : X \to (\Re_+^m)^{r+1}$ be the map $\tilde{x} \to (x_0, x_1, ..., x_r)$ and let $C = f_r(Q)$. Then we have the following theorem:

Theorem 2.1. *With every aggregator W defined on $C \times \Re_+$, one can associate an operator on S as follows:*

$$T_W u(\tilde{x}) = W\big(f_r(\tilde{x}),\ u(L\tilde{x})\big). \tag{1}$$

T_W is a contraction. Hence, there exists a unique u, which is concave, such that, for all $\tilde{x} \in Q$,

$$u(\tilde{x}) = W\big(f_r(\tilde{x}),\ u(L\tilde{x})\big). \tag{2}$$

Proof. Let T_W be defined by (1). Then $T_W u$ belongs to S, since it is continuous and bounded on Q; indeed, by $W1$ and $W3$ we get, for all $\tilde{x} \in Q$,

$$|T_W u(\tilde{x})| \le \beta|u(L\tilde{x})| + W\big(f_r(\tilde{x}),0\big) \le \beta\|u\| + M. \tag{3}$$

By $W3$, it is clear that T_W is a β-contraction on S. The unique fixed point u is concave, since T_W maps concave functions, under $W2$ and $W4$, into themselves.

Let us introduce the following axioms:

$W2' : W$ is concave and for every $z, W(., z)$ is strictly concave;

$W4' : (x, z) \neq (x', z')$ and $(x, z) \leq (x', z')$ implies $W(x, z) < W(x', z')$;

$W5 : 0 \in C$ and $W(0, 0) = 0$.

The following proposition is proved in Dana and Le Van (1988):

Proposition 2.1. a) *If W satisfies $W1$, $W2'$, $W3$, $W4'$, then u is strictly concave.* b) *If W satisfies $W1$, $W2$, $W3$, $W4'$, then u is increasing.* c) *If W satisfies $W1 - W5$, then $u(0) = 0$.*

3. A Generalized McKenzie Model

Consider a quadruple (A, T, C, W), which satisfies this hypothesis:

$A1 : A$ is a closed convex subset of $\Re_+^p$ with non-empty interior;

$A2 : T$ is a set valued continuous correspondence from A into A with non-empty compact convex values; its graph $C = \{(x_0, x_1),\ x_0 \in A,\ x_1 \in T(x_0)\}$ is closed and convex;

$A3 : W$ is an aggregator defined on $C \times \Re_+$ and, for every fixed (x_0, z), the map $W(x_0, ., z)$ is strictly concave.

Let $X = (\Re_+^p)^\infty$ be endowed with the product topology.

Let $Q = \{\tilde{x} \in X,\ x_0 \in A,\ x_{t+1} \in T(x_t),$ for all $t \geq 0\}$. Then Q is a closed convex L-invariant subset of X and $C = f_1(Q)$. It follows from Theorem 2.1 that there exists a unique continuous concave function u from Q into $\Re_+$ which satisfies the following condition: for all $\tilde{x} \in Q$,

$$u(\tilde{x}) = W\big(x_0, x_1, u(L\,\tilde{x})\big). \tag{4}$$

As, for all $\bar{x}_0 \in A$, the set $X(\bar{x}_0) = \{(\tilde{x}) \in X,\ x_{t+1} \in T(x_t),$ for all $t \geq 0,\ x_0 = \bar{x}_0\}$ is compact, the following problem $P_{x_0,u}$ has a solution: maximize $u(\tilde{x})$, with $\tilde{x} \in Q$, and x_0 fixed in A.

Under $A3$, the solution is unique and forms the trajectory of a dynamic path obtained by letting $V : A \to \Re_+$ denote the value of $P_{x_0,u}$, which gives:

Theorem 3.1. a) *V is the unique solution to Bellman's equation*

$$V(x_0) = \max \Big\{ W\big(x_0, x_1, V(x_1)\big),\ x_1 \in T(x_0) \Big\} \tag{5}$$

and *is concave and continuous;* b) $\tilde{x}$ *solves* $P_{x_0,u}$, *if and only if* $x_t = \varphi^t(x_0)$
with

$$\varphi(x_0) = \arg\max\Big\{W\big(x_0, x_1, V(x_1)\big), \ x_1 \in T(x_0)\Big\}. \tag{6}$$

The proof of this theorem follows from standard dynamic programming.

Let us now assume that $A2' : T$ satisfies $A2$, and that C has a non-empty interior. Recalling the following property, we then have:

Lemma 3.1. *Let G be a continuous, convex, compact-valued correspondence from $\Re^m$ into $\Re^m$. Assume $x^0 \in \text{int } G(k^0)$, and there then exists a neighbourhood $V(k^0)$ of k^0, such that for every k in $V(k^0)$, x^0 belongs to $G(k)$.*

The proof of Lemma 3.1 may be found in Dana and Le Van (1988).

We then have:

Proposition 3.1. *Assume that $\big(x_0, \ \varphi(x_0)\big)$ is in the interior of C and that $W(\,.\,, x_1, z)$ is differentiable for every fixed (x_1, z). Then V is differentiable at x_0 and one has:*

$$V'(x_0) = \frac{\partial W}{\partial x_0}\Big(x, \ \varphi(x_0), \ V\big(\varphi(x_0)\big)\Big). \tag{7}$$

Proof. As $\big(x_0, \ \varphi(x_0)\big) \in \text{int } C$, by Lemma 3.1 there exists a neighbourhood $N(x_0)$ of x_0, such that $\varphi(x_0) \in T(x)$, for all $x \in N(x_0)$. Then one has:

$$W\Big(x, \ \varphi(x_0), \ V\big(\varphi(x_0)\big)\Big) \le W\Big(x, \ \varphi(x), \ V\big(\varphi(x)\big)\Big),$$

for all $x \in N(x_0)$. Apply Benveniste and Scheinkman's (1979) Lemma 1 to get the result.

The following proposition is also straightforward:

Proposition 3.2. *Let $\{\tilde{x}_t\}$ be an optimal solution. Assume that W is differentiable and that $\big(\tilde{x}_t, \ \tilde{x}_{t+1}, \ V(\tilde{x}_{t+1})\big)$ is in the interior of $C \times \Re_+$, for every $t \ge 0$. Then $\{\tilde{x}_t\}$ satisfies Euler's equation:*

$$\frac{\partial W}{\partial x_1}(\tilde{x}_t, \tilde{x}_{t+1}, \tilde{z}_{t+1}) + \frac{\partial W}{\partial z}(\tilde{x}_t, \tilde{x}_{t+1}, \tilde{z}_{t+1})\frac{\partial W}{\partial x_0}(\tilde{x}_t, \tilde{x}_{t+2}, \tilde{z}_{t+2}) = 0 \tag{8}$$

with

$$\bar{z}_t = V(\bar{x}_t), \quad \text{for all } t \geq 0. \tag{9}$$

Let us introduce this hypothesis:

$W6 : W$ is continuously differentiable.

4. A Model of Pareto-Optimality

Notations

Throughout this section, we shall use the following notations:

i) In $\Re^h$, where h is an integer,

$$z' \geq z \Longleftrightarrow \text{for all } j = 1, \ldots, h, \qquad z_j' \geq z_j,$$
$$z' > z \Longleftrightarrow z' \geq z \quad \text{and} \quad z' \neq z,$$
$$z' \gg z \Longleftrightarrow z_j' > z_j, \text{ for all } j;$$

ii) X_h to denote the space $(\Re_+^h)^\infty$ endowed with the product topology;
iii) $x^i \in \Re^h$, for all $i = 1, \ldots, n$, to denote $(x^1, \ldots, x^n)$ and $\hat{x} = \sum_{i=1}^n x^i$.

The Economy

We consider an economy with n consumers, each of them living for an infinite number of periods $t = 1, 2, \ldots$. The economy is described by the following list:

$$\mathcal{E} = (X_m; \ W^i, \ i = 1, \ldots, n; \ X_p; \ B; \ k_0).$$

Here X_m is the consumption space of each agent. Agent i has utility function $u^i : X_m \to \Re_+$ defined by an aggregator W^i. Now X_p is the space of sequences of capital, and B is the "technology correspondence." It associates with a capital stock k a set of pairs (x, y) of current consumption goods x and next period capital stock y, which are jointly producible. The initial capital stock is denoted by k_0. We shall explicate the assumptions made on the preferences of the agents and the technology.

Preferences

For every i, W^i is an aggregator function defined on $\Re_+^m \times \Re_+$, which satisfies $W1, W2', W3, W4', W5, W6$. By Theorem 2.1 and example (2), agent i's preferences can be represented by a utility function $u^i : X_m \to \Re_+$, which verifies, for all $\tilde{x}^i \in X_m$, that

$$u^i(\tilde{x}^i) = W^i\left(x_0^i, u^i(L\,\tilde{x}^i)\right). \tag{10}$$

It follows from Proposition 2.1 that u^i is strictly concave increasing and that $u^i(0) = 0$.

Technology

The technology is characterized by a correspondence $B : \Re_+^p \to \Re_+^m \times \Re_+^p$ with the following properties:

$B0 : B$ is continuous;
$B1 :$ for each k, $B(k)$ is convex, compact, non-empty;
$B2 : (x,y) \in B(k)$, and $0 \le (x',y') \le (x,y)$ implies $(x',y') \in B(k)$;
$B3 : 0 \le k' \le k$ implies $B(k') \subseteq B(k)$;
$B4 :$ if $(x,y) \in B(k)$ and $(x',y') \in B(k')$, then for all $\lambda \in [0,1]$, $\left((\lambda x + (1-\lambda)x'),\ (\lambda y + (1-\lambda)y')\right) \in B(\lambda k + (1-\lambda)k')$;
$B5 :$ there exists $x > 0$, such that $(x,y) \in B(0)$;
$B6 : k > 0$ implies that there exist $x > 0$, $y > 0$, $(x,y) \in B(k)$;
$B7 :$ if $(x,y) \in B(k)$ and $(x',y') \in B(k')$ and $(x,y,k) \ne (x',y',k')$, then for all $\lambda \in (0,1)$, there exists $x'' > \lambda x + (1-\lambda)x'$, such that $\left(x'',\ \lambda y + (1-\lambda)y'\right) \in B(\lambda k + (1-\lambda)k')$;
$B8 :$ the map $(k,y) \to \{x|(x,y) \in B(k)\}$ is lower semi-continuous.

Feasible Consumption Paths and Utility Sets

A consumption path $(\tilde{x}^i) \in (X_m)^n$ is *feasible* from k_0, if it belongs to

$$X(k_0) = \left\{(\tilde{x}^i) \in (X_m)^n,\ \exists\,\tilde{k} \in X_p,\ (\hat{x}_t, k_{t+1}) \in B(k_t)\right\}, \tag{11}$$

for all $t \ge 0$; k_0 given.

The *utility attainable set* from k_0 is defined by

$$U(k_0) = \left\{(z_i) \in \Re_+^n;\ z^i = u^i(\tilde{x}^i);\ (\tilde{x}^i) \in X(k_0)\right\}. \tag{12}$$

We then have the following theorem:

Theorem 4.1. *Assume $W1$, $W2'$, $W3$, $W4$, $W5'$, $B0$-$B6$.*

a) *For every k, $U(k)$ is compact, strictly convex and satisfies free disposal: for all $u \in U(k)$, $0 \le u' \le u$ implies $u' \in U(k)$;*
b) *for every $\lambda \in [0,1]$, $\lambda U(k) + (1-\lambda)U(k') \subset U(\lambda k + (1-\lambda)k')$;*
c) *for all $k \ge 0$, $U(k)$ has non-empty interior;*
d) *the correspondence, denoted by U, from $\Re_+^p$ into $\Re_+^n : k \to U(k)$ is continuous.*

The proof is contained in Dana and Le Van (1988).

Description of Pareto-Optimality

Recall that a consumption path $(\tilde{x}^i) \in X(k_0)$ is *Pareto-optimal*, if there exists no $(\tilde{x}^i{}') \in X(k_0)$, such that $(u^i(\tilde{x}^i{}')) > (u^i(\tilde{x}^i))$. Let $\pi^{-1} : \Re^n \to \Re^{n-1}$, $(z_1, z_2, \ldots, z_n) \to (z_2, \ldots, z_n)$ and $A = \text{graph } \pi^{-1} U$.

From Theorem 4.1 we know that A is closed convex and has a nonempty interior. Let $\zeta_0 = (k_0, (z_0^i)_{i \ge 2}) \in A$ be given. Now $(z_0^i)_{i \ge 1}$ is a Pareto-optimal utility vector, if and only if z_0^1 solves the following:

$$\max\{z^1;\ z^i \ge z_0^i,\ i \ge 2,\ (z^i)_{i \ge 1} \in U(k_0)\}. \tag{13}$$

Since $U(k_0)$ is compact, (13) has a solution. Let $V(\zeta_0)$ denote the value of this problem. Then (13) can be rewritten as:

$$\max\{W^1(x_0^1, z_1^1);\ W^i(x_0^i, z_1^i) \ge z_0^i,\ i \ge 2;\ \exists k_1, \\ (\hat{x}_0, k_1) \in B(k_0) \text{ and } (z_1^i) \in U(k_1)\}. \tag{14}$$

Let $\zeta_1 = (k_1, (z_1^i)_{i \ge 2}) \in A$. Then one has:

$$V(\zeta_0) = \max\{W^1(x_0^1, V(\zeta_1));\ W^i(x_0^i, z_1^i) \ge z_0^i,\ i \ge 2; \\ (\hat{x}_0, k_1) \in B(k_0),\ \zeta_1 \in A\}. \tag{15}$$

The main purpose of this section is to show that problem (13) *is equivalent to a generalized McKenzie model* with state space A and characteristics we shall define next.

Consider the following correspondence $T : A \to A$

$$\zeta_0 \to \{\zeta_1;\ \exists(x^i), i \ge 1, (\hat{x}, k_1) \in B(k_0), \\ W^i(x^i, z_1^i) \ge z_0^i,\ \text{for all } i \ge 2;\ \zeta_1 \in A\}. \tag{16}$$

Let $C = $ graph T as in Section 2. Clearly, C is closed and convex. Define $\psi : C \to \Re_+^m$ by

$$\psi(\zeta_0, \zeta_1) = \{x^1 \in \Re_+^m; \; \exists \, x^i, i \geq 2, (\hat{x}, k_1) \in B(k_0);$$
$$W^i(x^i, z_1^i) \geq z_0^i, \text{ for all } i \geq 2\}. \tag{17}$$

Now ψ has a closed convex graph as well, and (15) can then be rewritten as

$$V(\zeta_0) = \max \left\{ W^1(x_0^1, V(\zeta_1)), \; x^1 \in \psi(\zeta_0, \zeta_1), \; \zeta_1 \in T(\zeta_0) \right\}. \tag{18}$$

Let us first prove that T and ψ have the following fundamental properties.

Proposition 4.1. *Assume W1, W2', W3, W4', W5, W6 and B0-B8. Then T and ψ are continuous, compact, convex-valued correspondences.*

Proof. The proof, which is the most difficult of the paper, is given in Dana and Le Van (1987).

Let us next define $\bar{W} : C \times \Re \to \Re$ and $\bar{x} : C \times \Re \to \Re_+^m$ by

$$\bar{W}(\zeta_0, \zeta_1, z) = \max \left\{ W^1(x, z), x \in \psi(\zeta_0, \zeta_1) \right\} \tag{19}$$

and

$$\bar{x}(\zeta_0, \zeta_1, z) = \arg \max \left\{ W^1(x, z), x \in \psi(\zeta_0, \zeta_1) \right\}. \tag{20}$$

Then (18) can be rewritten as

$$V(\zeta_0) = \max \left\{ \bar{W}(\zeta_0, \zeta_1, V(\zeta_1)), \; \zeta_1 \in T(\zeta_0) \right\}. \tag{21}$$

Let us show that $\bar{W}$ is an aggregator.

Proposition 4.2. *$\bar{W}$ satisfies W1, W2, W3, W4.*

We next construct an abstract McKenzie problem with value function $V(\zeta)$. Consider the quadruple $(A, T, C, \bar{W})$ with T defined by (16), and $C = $ graph T and $\bar{W}$ defined by (19). Let

$$Q = \{\tilde{\zeta}, \zeta_0 \in A, \; \zeta_{t+1} \in T(\zeta_t), \text{ for all } t \geq 1\}.$$

As in Section 2, by Theorem 2.1, one can associate with $\bar{W}$ a unique continuous function $\bar{U} : Q \to \Re$, such that

$$\bar{U}(\tilde{\zeta}) = \bar{W}\left(\zeta_0, \zeta_1, \bar{U}(L\tilde{\zeta})\right).$$

Consider the following problem:

$$\max \bar{U}(\tilde{\zeta}) = \bar{W}\left(\zeta_0, \zeta_1, \bar{U}(L\tilde{\zeta})\right),$$

subject to $\zeta_t \in T(\zeta_{t-1})$, and ζ_0 given.

This problem has a solution. As in Section 2, its value function $\bar{V}$ is the unique solution to Bellman's equation:

$$\bar{V}(\zeta_0) = \max\left\{\bar{W}\left(\zeta_0, \zeta_1, \bar{V}(\zeta_1)\right), \; \zeta_1 \in T(\zeta_0)\right\}. \tag{22}$$

As V satisfies (22), $\bar{V}(\zeta_0) = V(\zeta_0)$. Let

$$\varphi(\zeta_0) = \arg\max\left\{\bar{W}\left(\zeta_0, \zeta, \bar{V}(\zeta)\right), \; \zeta \in T(\zeta_0)\right\}. \tag{23}$$

We next show that the optimal solution to (14) can be characterized using φ. For $(\zeta_0, \zeta_1) \in C$, let $\left(x^i(\zeta_0, \zeta_1)\right)$ denote the optimal solution to the problem:

$$\max\left\{W^1\left(x^1, V(\zeta_1)\right), \; (\hat{x}, k_1) \in B(k_0), \atop W^i(x^i, z_1^i) \geq z_0^1, \text{ for all } i \geq 2\right\}. \tag{24}$$

From Dana and Le Van (1987) we have the following:

Lemma 4.1. $\left(x^i(.\,,.\,)\right)$ is continuous.

Theorem 4.2. Assume W1, W2', W3, W4', W5, W6 and B0-B8. Then $(\bar{\tilde{x}}^i)$ is a Pareto-optimal consumption path from k_0 if and only if there exists ζ_0, such that $\bar{x}_t^i = x^i\left(\varphi^t(\zeta_0), \varphi^{t+1}(\zeta_0)\right)$ for every t and i.

Proof. Let $(\bar{\tilde{x}}^i)$ be a Pareto-optimal consumption path from k_0. Let $z_0^i = u^i(\bar{\tilde{x}}^i)$ for $i \geq 1$ and $\zeta_0 = \left(k_0, (z_0^i)_{i \geq 2}\right)$.

From the previous discussion we know that $(\bar{z}_0^1, \ldots, \bar{z}_0^m)$ is a Pareto-optimal utility if and only if $(\bar{z}_1^i)$, $(\bar{z}_0^i)$, $\bar{k}_1$ are such that, $W^1(\bar{x}_0^1, \bar{z}_1^1)$ solves

$$\max\left\{W^1(x_0^1, z_1^1), \; x_0^1 \in \psi(\zeta_0, \zeta_1), \; \zeta_1 \in T(\zeta_0)\right\}.$$

We also know, from (14) and (15), that $\bar{z}_1^1 = V(\bar{\zeta}_1)$; from (24) that $(\bar{x}_0^i) = x^i(\zeta_0, \bar{\zeta}_1)$; and from (23) that $\bar{\zeta}_1 = \varphi(\zeta_0)$. Thus, $(\bar{x}_0^i) = x^i(\zeta_0, \varphi(\zeta_0))$.

It follows from $B7$ that there exists a unique $(\tilde{\bar{k}})$ associated with $(\tilde{\bar{x}}^i)$. It can easily be shown that $(\tilde{\bar{x}}^i)$ is a Pareto-optimal from k_0 if and only if $(L^t \tilde{\bar{x}}^i)$ is Pareto-optimal from $\bar{k}_t$ for every t.

Let $z_t^i = u^i(L^t \tilde{\bar{x}}^i)$ and $\bar{\zeta}_t = (\bar{k}_t, (\bar{z}_t^i)_{i\geq 2})$. If $(L^t \tilde{\bar{x}}^i)$ is Pareto-optimal from $\bar{k}_t$, as (13) is stationary, then the previous argument implies that $\bar{x}_t^i = x^i(\bar{\zeta}_t, \varphi(\bar{\zeta}_t))$ and $\bar{\zeta}_{t+1} = \varphi(\bar{\zeta}_t)$. Assuming, by induction, that $\bar{\zeta}_t = \varphi^t(\zeta_0)$, we then have $\bar{\zeta}_{t+1} = \varphi(\varphi^t(\zeta_0)) = \varphi^{t+1}(\zeta_0)$.

Conversely, assume that $\bar{x}_t^i = x^i(\varphi^t(\zeta_0), \varphi^{t+1}(\zeta_0))$ for all i and for all t. From (24) we know the constraints are saturated. Thus, $W^i(\bar{x}_t^i, \bar{z}_{t+1}^i) = \bar{z}_t^i$ for all $i \geq 2$ and for all $t \geq 0$. (If not, one could decrease $\bar{x}_t^i$ by ϵ and increase $\bar{x}_t'$ by ϵ, so that constraints would still be fulfilled, contradicting the optimality of $\bar{x}_t^1$.) We claim that this implies that $\bar{z}_t^i = u^i(L^t \tilde{\bar{x}}^i)$ for all t. Indeed, $u^i(\tilde{\bar{x}}^i) = W^i(\bar{x}_0^i, u^i(L \tilde{\bar{x}}^i))$ by definition. Thus,

$$\left| u^i(\tilde{\bar{x}}^i) - \bar{z}_0^i \right| \leq \beta \left| u^i(L \tilde{\bar{x}}^i) - z_1^i \right| \leq \beta^t \left| u^i(L^t \tilde{\bar{x}}^i) - z_t^i \right| \cdots .$$

As u^i is bounded, this implies that $u^i(\tilde{\bar{x}}^i) = \bar{z}_0^i$ and, by induction, that $u^i(L^t \tilde{\bar{x}}^i) = \bar{z}_t^i$. Thus, $\zeta_0 = \left(k_0, (u^i(\tilde{\bar{x}}^i))_{i\geq 2}\right)$. Given ζ_0, the direct proof above implies that the sequence $\left(x^i(\varphi^t(\zeta_0), \varphi^{t+1}(\zeta_0))\right)$ is Pareto-optimal from k_0.

References

Beals, R. and Koopmans, T. (1969) "Maximizing Stationary Utility in a Constant Technology," *S.I.A.M. J. of Applied Math.* 17, 1001-1015.

Benhabib, J., Majumdar, M. and Nishimura, K. (1985a) "Global Equilibrium Dynamics with Stationary Recursive Preferences," Working Paper.

Benhabib, J., Jafarey, S. and Nishimura, K. , (1985b) "The Dynamics of Efficient Intertemporal Allocations with Many Agents Recursive Preferences and Production," Working Paper.

Benveniste, L. M. and Scheinkman, J. A. (1979) "On the Differentiability of the Value Function in Dynamic Model of Economics," *Econometrica* 47, 727-732.

Boyd, J. H. (1986) "Recursive Utility and the Ramsey Problem," Working Paper 60, Rochester Center for Economic Research.

Dana, R.-A. and Le Van, C. (1987) "Optimal Growth and Pareto-Optimality," Working Paper 8723, CEPREMAP.

————, (1988) "On the Structure of Pareto-Optima in an Infinite Horizon Economy where Agents Have Recursive Preferences," to appear in *J. of Optimization Theory and Applications.*

Epstein, L. G. (1987a) "The Global Stability of Efficient Intertemporal Allocations," *Econometrica* **55**, 329-355.

————, (1987b) "A Simple Dynamic General Equilibrium Model," *J. of Economic Theory* **41**, 68-95.

Iwai, K. (1972) "Optimal Economic Growth and Stationary Ordinal Utility: A Fisherian Approach," *J. of Economic Theory* **4**, 88-93.

Koopmans, T. (1960) "Stationary Ordinal Utility and Impatience," *Econometrica* **28**, 287-309.

Koopmans, T., Diamond, P. and Williamson, R. (1964) "Stationary Utility and Time Perspective," *Econometrica* **32**, 82-100.

Lucas, R. and Stokey, N. (1984) "Optimal Growth with Many Consumers," *J. of Economic Theory* **32**, 139-171.

McKenzie, L. W. (1985) "Optimal Economic Growth and Turnpike Theorems," in *Handbook of Mathematical Economics* **III**, North Holland: Amsterdam, New York.

Scheinkman, J. A. (1976) "On Optimal Steady States of *n*-Sector Growth Models when Utility Is Discounted," *J. of Economic Theory* **12**, 11-20.

Streufert, P. A. (1986a) "The Recursive Expression of Consistent Intergenerational Utility Functions," Working Paper 8609, Univ. of Wisconsin–Madison.

Author Index

Subject Index